Applied Linguistic

C000181620

Modern primary teachers must adapt literacy programmes and ensure efficient learning for all. They must also support children with language and literacy difficulties, children learning English as an additional language and possibly teach a modern foreign language. To do this effectively, they need to understand the applied linguistics research that underpins so many different areas of the language and literacy curriculum. This book illustrates the impact of applied linguistics on curriculum frameworks and pedagogy. It captures the range of applied linguistics knowledge that teachers need, and illustrates how this is framed and is used by policy makers, researchers, teacher educators and the other professions who work with teachers in schools. It considers how to effect professional development that works. It is essential reading for primary teachers but also for speech and language therapists, educational psychologists, learning support teachers and all those doing language or literacy research in the primary classroom.

SUE ELLIS studied for her first degree, in Theoretical Linguistics and Language Pathology, at the University of Essex and is currently a Reader in Literacy and Language Education at the University of Strathclyde. Her research, teaching and consultancy interests are in literacy development, teacher education and in how to make literacy policy work in practice. Her current research projects are on children's understanding and use of characterisation in writing, and on literacy policy development in Scotland and Malawi. With Kathy Hall, Usha Goswami, Colin Harrison and Janet Soler, she has co-edited *Interdisciplinary Perspectives on Learning to Read* (2010).

ELSPETH MCCARTNEY is a Reader in Speech and Language Therapy at the University of Strathclyde. She has qualifications as a teacher and as a speech and language therapist, and teaches and researches in the field of childhood speech and language impairment and therapy, particularly for children of primary-school age. Her major publications concern interventions for children with specific language impairment, following funded research projects, and teacher–therapist co-professional working practices. She is a Fellow of the Royal College of Speech and Language Therapists.

Applied Linguistics and Primary School Teaching

Edited by

Sue Ellis
and
Elspeth McCartney

CAMBRIDGE
UNIVERSITY PRESS

CAMBRIDGE
UNIVERSITY PRESS

University Printing House, Cambridge CB2 8BS, United Kingdom

Published in the United States of America by Cambridge University Press, New York

Cambridge University Press is part of the University of Cambridge.

It furthers the University's mission by disseminating knowledge in the pursuit of education, learning and research at the highest international levels of excellence.

www.cambridge.org
Information on this title: www.cambridge.org/9781107696877

First published 2011
First paperback edition 2014

A catalogue record for this publication is available from the British Library

Library of Congress Cataloguing in Publication data
Applied Linguistics and Primary School Teaching / [edited by] Sue Ellis, Elspeth McCartney.
    p.   cm
Includes bibliographical references and index.
ISBN 978-0-521-19354-2
1. Language arts (Elementary)–Curricula.   2. English language–Study and teaching (Elementary)–Foreign speakers.   3. Applied linguistics.
I. Ellis, Sue.   II. McCartney, Elspeth.
LB1576.A67 2010
372.6–dc22
2010049738

ISBN 978-0-521-19354-2 Hardback
ISBN 978-1-107-69687-7 Paperback

Contents

Part II   The range and focus of applied linguistics research

Part III   Empowering teachers and teachers' use of knowledge

Figures

Tables

Contributors

KENN APEL is Professor of Communication Science and Disorders at the Florida State University, Tallahassee. He has over twenty years of experience conducting research and teaching classes on language learning and working with children, adolescents, and adults with language problems and language-based learning deficits. His current research focuses on the underlying linguistic components that support the development of reading and spelling, including morphological awareness and orthographic knowledge and processing. He is the former Editor-in-Chief for *Language, Speech, and Hearing Services in the Schools* (2007–2009), and is a fellow and certified member of American Speech-Language-Hearing Association (ASHA).

JANE BRIGGS is a senior lecturer in English in Education at the University of Brighton, leading the English team. Her teaching predominantly focuses on English in primary ITE and her research focuses on how teachers and children can explore texts and writing for thinking together to enhance the quality of the children's experience. Jane is particularly interested in the teacher's role as authentic meaning maker, working in partnership with the children.

GREG BROOKS retired at the end of 2007 having completed thirty years' virtually full-time educational research, much of it in the area of language and literacy. He worked for nineteen years at the National Foundation for Educational Research in Slough, before being awarded a personal Chair in the School of Education at the University of Sheffield. An abiding interest has been the link between spoken and written language, in particular the family of teaching approaches known as phonics. He wrote the review of the phonics element of England's *National Literacy Strategy*, co-authored a systematic review of the use of phonics in initial literacy teaching, and was a member of England's Rose committee, which reviewed the early years reading curriculum.

PETER BRYANT is Professor Emeritus of Wolfson College, University of Oxford and Senior Research Fellow in the Department of Education, University of Oxford. His interests are in the fields of developmental psychology, cognitive, linguistic and perceptual development, and the learning of reading, spelling and mathematics.

JOANNE COCKSEY completed her undergraduate psychology degree in Bristol and her Postgraduate Certificate in Education in Exeter and then joined the Language and Cognitive Development research group at the University of Oxford. In Oxford, she worked as a graduate research assistant to Professor Kate Nation on a prospective longitudinal project exploring the precursors to reading development and reading difficulties in young children. Joanne is currently completing her doctorate in Clinical Psychology at the University of Hertfordshire and maintains an active interest in language and literacy research.

ANGELA CREESE is Professor of Educational Linguistics at the University of Birmingham. She is author of a number of books and articles on multilingualism and linguistically diverse classrooms. Her books include *Multilingualism: A Critical Perspective* (2010); *English as an Additional Language: Approaches to Teaching Linguistic Minority Students* (2010); *Volume 9: Ecology of Language, Encyclopedia of Language and Education* (2009); *Teacher collaboration and talk in multilingual classrooms* (2005); and *Multilingual Classroom Ecologies* (2003). Angela's research interests are situated in educational linguistics, linguistic ethnography, teacher collaboration and multilingual pedagogies in community learning contexts. She has held a number of ESRC funded grants researching multilingualism in complementary schools.

HENRIETTA DOMBEY is Professor Emeritus of Literacy in Primary Education at the University of Brighton. Since the start of her teaching career, when she was confronted with a class of 7-year-olds with very little purchase on written language, she has been passionately interested in the teaching of reading. A central focus of this interest has been the interactions between teachers, children and texts. A past chair of the National Association for the Teaching of English and past president of the United Kingdom Literacy Association, she has worked extensively with teachers and teacher educators to develop professional thinking and action.

SUE ELLIS studied for her first degree, in theoretical linguistics and language pathology at the University of Essex and is currently a reader in Literacy and Language at the University of Strathclyde. Her research, teaching and consultancy interests are in literacy development, teacher education and in how to make literacy policy work in practice. Her current research projects are on children's understanding and use of characterisation in writing, and on literacy policy development in Scotland and Malawi.

VIV ELLIS is University Lecturer and Tutor for English Education at the University of Oxford where he convenes the centre for Sociocultural and

Activity Theory Research. He completed his Ph.D. at the University of London Institute of Education and worked as an English teacher in secondary schools before moving into higher education. In his research, he maintains a focus on learning, subject English and the education of teachers. With Anne Edwards and Peter Smagorinsky, he has edited *Cultural-Historical Perspectives on Teacher Education and Development: Learning Teaching* (2010).

JENNIFER HAMMOND is an Associate Professor and Honorary Associate in the Faculty of Arts and Social Sciences (Education), University of Technology, Sydney. She has taught for many years in the fields of language and literacy education, ESL education and research design. Her research interests are in literacy development; classroom interaction, and the implications of socio-cultural and systemic theories of language and learning in ESL education. She has published widely in these areas. She is currently involved in research that addresses the needs of refugee students in Australian schools.

MARY HARTSHORNE is Head of Quality and Outcomes at I CAN, a UK children's communication charity. She has responsibility for ensuring high quality, evidenced programmes of work and manages a team of specialist professionals from education and speech and language therapy. She is a specialist speech and language therapist with a master's qualification in special educational needs and many years' experience of working in education – both as a practitioner and manager. She is a trainer and lecturer in speech, language and communication needs and has authored many of I CAN's discussion papers, including *The Cost to the Nation of Children's Poor Communication*. Her focus has been developing the classroom as an environment for language development, and looking at the ways that teachers and therapists can work together in schools. A specific interest is the link between speech, language and communication needs and emotional, social and behavioural difficulties.

AFRA AHMED HERSI is an assistant professor and the Director of the Literacy Program in the Teacher Education Department of Loyola University Maryland. Her scholarly interests include the literacy and language development of adolescent English language learners, immigration and social identity development, social context education and critical multicultural education. She has worked previously as a secondary history teacher and is currently a teacher educator for undergraduate and graduate students pursuing a secondary education certification, and for K-12 reading specialist and reading teachers.

DEBORAH A. HORAN is an assistant professor in Language and Literacy Studies at the University of Texas at Austin. Her scholarly interests include the sociolinguistic study of language, literacy and culture within the contexts of both elementary and teacher education. Her background includes work as an elementary Spanish-English bilingual teacher, composition instructor and teacher educator for early childhood and elementary teachers, bilingual teachers and K-12 reading specialists.

ELSPETH JAJDELSKA is a lecturer in English Studies at the University of Strathclyde. She studied English at the Universities of Glasgow and Leeds, and has taught at the Jagiellonian University in Krakow, Poland. In her research she is interested in applying findings in psychology, linguistics and education to historical literary problems. She is the author of two articles on the history of reading in the eighteenth century, as well as a monograph, *Silent Reading and the Birth of the Narrator* (2007). She is currently working on changing cultures of verbal performance, including oratory and oral reading, in the same period. In 2006–2007 she collaborated with Sue Ellis on an Arts and Humanities Research Council Knowledge-Transfer grant.

ADAM LEFSTEIN is Senior Lecturer at the Department of Education, Ben Gurion University of the Negev, Israel. His research and teaching focus on the intersections of policy, pedagogy and classroom interaction, and in how linguistic ethnography can be used to support educational practice. He is also affiliated with the Institute of Education, University of London, where he directs an ESRC-funded study of continuity and change in classroom interactional patterns. Recent and forthcoming publications include articles in the *American Educational Research Journal*, *Reading Research Quarterly* and the *Teachers College Record*.

CAROLYN LETTS qualified as a speech and language therapist in 1977, having previously completed a degree in French and Linguistics. In her first job she worked with a variety of bilingual (Welsh/English) clients. She studied for a Ph.D. at the University of Reading, looking at clinical interaction. She has been lecturing on speech and language therapy courses for many years, and has worked at Newcastle University since January 2000. Her research interests include the early identification and subsequent progression of children with language difficulties, and speech and language impairment in bilingual children. She is currently working on a new version of *The Reynell Developmental Language Scales*.

JULIE J. MASTERSON is Professor of Communication Sciences and Disorders at Missouri State University, where she teaches courses in phonology, language-learning disabilities and research design. She received her master's degree from Baylor and her Ph.D. from the University of Memphis. She is a fellow of the American Speech-Language-Hearing Association and was ASHA Vice President for Research and Technology from 2001 to 2003. She served as President of the Council of Academic Programs in Communication

Sciences and Disorders from 2006 to 2007. She has been an associate editor for the *American Journal of Speech-Language Pathology* and has served as a guest associate editor for the *Journal of Speech and Hearing Research, Language, Speech, and Hearing Services in Schools.*

ELSPETH MCCARTNEY is a Reader in Speech and Language Therapy in the School of Psychological Sciences and Health, University of Strathclyde. She has qualifications as a teacher and as a speech and language therapist, and teaches and researches in the field of childhood speech and language impairment and therapy, particularly for children of primary-school age. Her major publications concern interventions for children with specific language impairment, following funded research projects, and teacher–therapist co-professional working practices. She is a Fellow of the Royal College of Speech and Language Therapists.

GEMMA MOSS is Professor of Education at the Institute of Education, University of London. She specialises in the study of literacy policy; gender and literacy; and children's informal literacy practices and their relationship to the school curriculum. She has held a succession of research grants from the ESRC on these topics. She has also recently co-directed an evaluation of the use of interactive whiteboards in London's secondary schools on behalf of the Department for Education and Science. Her most recent book is *Literacy and Gender: Researching Texts, Contexts and Readers* (2008).

DEBRA MYHILL is Professor of Education at the University of Exeter, and is Dean of the College of Social Sciences and International Studies. Her research interests focus principally on aspects of language and literacy teaching, particularly writing and grammar, and talk in the classroom. She is the author of *Better Writers*; *Talking, Listening, Learning: Effective Talk in the Primary Classroom*; and co-editor of the *Sage Handbook of Writing Development.*

KATE NATION is a professor in Experimental Psychology at the University of Oxford and a Fellow of St John's College, Oxford. Following her D.Phil. in Psychology at the University of York in 1994, she remained a member of the York department before moving to Oxford in 2002. Her research interests include the development of language and literacy, both in typical and atypical development. She has particular interests in children's language comprehension difficulties, and in the development of visual word recognition. Further information about her research can be found at www.psy.ox.ac.uk/lcd.

TEREZINHA NUNES is Professor of Educational Studies and Fellow of Harris-Manchester College, Oxford University. She started her career as a clinical psychologist in Brazil and moved to a research career by obtaining a doctorate in psychology at City University of New York, where she was supported by a Fulbright Scholarship. Her work spans the domains of children's literacy and numeracy, including both hearing and deaf children's learning, and her focus of analysis covers cognitive and cultural issues, with a special interest in educational applications. Her literacy research focuses on the connections between moprhological awareness, spelling and vocabulary growth.

JESSIE RICKETTS completed her doctoral research at the University of Oxford in 2008. For her thesis, she employed experimental and longitudinal designs to explore the relationship between oral language and reading skills in typically developing children, children with impaired reading comprehension and children with dyslexia. Subsequently, Jessie continued her literacy research at the Institute of Education, University of London, before becoming Senior Research Fellow at the Centre for Educational Development, Appraisal and Research at the University of Warwick in 2009. Her research is concerned with language and literacy development in typically developing children and children with language and literacy difficulties.

ALISON SEALEY is Senior Lecturer in Modern English Language at the University of Birmingham. She has published widely on the policy and practice of teaching English in primary schools, having previously worked as a teacher and teacher educator. She was the principal investigator on the ESRC–funded research project to investigate corpus-based learning about language in the primary school. She has written extensively on a range of areas of linguistic and social research, including journal articles on corpus linguistics, sociolinguistics, applied linguistics and social theory. She is the author, with Bob Carter, of *Applied Linguistics as Social Science* (2004), and of *Researching English Language* (2010).

VIVIENNE SMITH teaches in the School of Education at the University of Strathclyde. She researches into children's development as readers, critical literacy and children's literature. Recent publications include: 'Learning to be a reader: promoting good textual health' in P. Goodwin (2008) *Understanding Children's Books*; 'Making and breaking frames: crossing the borders of expectation' in J. Evans (2009) *Talking Beyond the Page: Reading and Responding to Picturebooks*; and 'Comprehension: a social act: Texts, contexts and readers' in K. Hall *et al.* (2010) *Interdisciplinary Perspectives on Learning to Read*.

JULIA SNELL is a research officer at the Institute of Education, University of London. She is currently working on two projects: (1) an ethnographic study of continuity and change in classroom interactional patterns; (2) a study of the use of video in teacher professional development and the resulting social dynamics of teacher learning. Her other research interests include making use of linguistic ethnographic methodologies to study language variation and processes of social identification, especially in relation to the use of 'non-standard' linguistic varieties, and the relationship between language, education and social class.

DANIEL TIERNEY is Reader in Language Education at the University of Strathclyde in Glasgow. He was National Development Officer for Modern Languages in Primary Schools in Scotland, with responsibility for training and evaluation of the national programme to introduce languages into primary schools. He has written three books in the Young Pathfinder series for the Centre for Information on Language Teaching. He is the Scottish representative on the Early Language Learning Advisory Forum and served on QCA's working group on primary languages. His recent research has explored early language learning, pupil attitudes and teachers' views of pedagogy and implementation. He has spoken widely on this theme across the UK and in a number of European countries.

ELIZABETH B. WILSON-FOWLER is a doctoral student in Communication Science and Disorders at the Florida State University, Tallahassee. She has eight years of clinical experience working with students with language-learning disability in public school and private practice settings. Her research interests include identifying college students' metalinguistic skills that contribute to reading and spelling ability. She is a certified member of the American Speech-Language-Hearing Association.

MAGGIE VANCE is a lecturer in Language and Education at the University of Sheffield. She is a speech and language therapist who has worked with children with speech language communication needs in a range of educational settings. She is currently Programme Director of a postgraduate distance learning course for qualified teachers and speech and langauge therapists who have an interest in children with special educational needs/additonal learning needs, and of an undergraduate certificate programme for teaching and learning support assistants. Maggie is co-editor of the journal *Child Language Teaching and Therapy*.

DOMINIC WYSE is a senior lecturer in Primary and Early Years Education at the University of Cambridge, and Fellow of Churchill College, Cambridge, and a member of the Centre for Commonwealth Education. He was a primary teacher for eight years, which included posts in London, Bradford and Huddersfield, and then lectured in Primary Education at Liverpool John Moores University for eight years, latterly as a Reader. His research focuses on curriculum, pedagogy and policy with a major strand on the teaching of English, language and literacy. His research on curriculum innovation includes a three-year project funded by the National Gallery in London. He is a lead co-editor of *The Routledge International Handbook of English, Language and Literacy Teaching* and he is working on the 3rd edition of *Teaching English, Language and Literacy*. He is associate editor of the *Cambridge Journal of Education*.

Preface

Sue Ellis and Elspeth McCartney

Many of the chapters in this edited collection began as papers given at an invited seminar series sponsored by the University of Strathclyde, the British Association of Applied Linguistics and Cambridge University Press. The seminars, *Applied linguistics: what should primary teachers know, and how?*, explored the relationship between applied linguistics, primary education and teacher knowledge. They sought to review some of the ways that applied linguistics impacts on the modern primary school curriculum and our understanding of it, and to explore the type of understandings of applied linguistics that could empower primary school teachers to create an effective and appropriate curriculum for all children in their charge.

In proposing the seminar series, four important themes were considered. One was the direct contribution that applied linguistics researchers have made to the content of the language and literacy curriculum in primary schools and to how it is framed and taught. A second explored the role of applied linguistics in understanding how language is used in schools and communities, and the wider implications of this for teachers and education policy makers. The third theme concerned the implications of legislation for inclusive education: as primary school classes increasingly include children with speech, language and communication difficulties, class teachers must work effectively with professionals such as educational psychologists, learning-support teachers and speech and language therapists to adapt curriculum content and delivery in order to support and develop the speech, language and communication of such educationally vulnerable children. The fourth theme concerned the variety of languages spoken in the modern primary school and the new knowledge demands this makes of teachers.

Discussion of the papers ranged across both *what* modern primary teachers might be expected to know and *how* such knowledge might most usefully be contextualised and developed effectively. Seminar participants explored the changing context of primary education, the range of demands on primary teachers to engage with applied linguistics ideas and frameworks, and the explicit and implicit assumptions and beliefs about the knowledge that class teachers might be expected to have. The debates reflected different views of the core knowledge that is needed, the form that such knowledge might take if it is effectively to enhance teaching capacity, and the most efficient and helpful ways to develop applied linguistics knowledge in initial and continuing teacher education, as well as the role of educational policy in driving, shaping and institutionalising this new knowledge.

Seminar speakers and participants were cross-disciplinary researchers from the fields of linguistics and ethnographic-, discourse- and corpus-linguistics; psycho-linguistics; literature; psychology; English language learning; foreign language learning and speech and language therapy, as well as education policy makers, and those involved in initial primary teacher education and continuing professional development. We have sought to maintain this broad range of perspectives in the selection and content of chapters for this book.

We should like to thank the University of Strathclyde, the British Association of Applied Linguistics and Cambridge University Press for sponsoring the seminar series, which led to the commissioning of this book, and to David Alcock, former Education Librarian, University of Strathclyde, for bibliographic expertise. Our thanks go also to the seminar participants and speakers for stimulating papers and thought-provoking discussion.

Editors' notes and conventions

In adopting editorial conventions for this volume, we have been concerned with accessibility, and therefore with keeping technical language to a minimum. Where authors have wished to highlight specific letters, letter combinations or words, we have either underlined them, or used brackets, single quotation marks or italics. Words in foreign and ancient languages are also italicised.

Where the context is non-specific, we have used the term 'child' throughout, rather than 'pupil' or 'student', to avoid international confusion or confusion with student teachers, and to avoid privileging educational terms over those used outside school. We have in general used UK professional titles, but have asked all authors to be highly specific about the countries and jurisdictions to which they are referring, as policies and practices are often limited to designated geographical and political areas. Please note that the Former Department for Children, Schools and Families (DCSF) in England changed to the Department for Education on 12th May 2010. The current web address is: www.education.gov.uk.

We have used Scottish English modern spelling throughout, which happily is identical to that of British English.

Introduction

Sue Ellis and Elspeth McCartney

Rationale for this book: the linguistically aware teacher

Primary school teachers across the world are responsible for developing children's talking and listening, reading and writing skills. They are responsible for assessing development in these areas and for creating learning environments in which language and literacy learning can thrive.

Knowledge from research in linguistics and applied linguistics now underpins much of the primary school language and literacy curriculum. Obvious examples include the teaching of phonics and phonological awareness, genre-based approaches to writing and to reading comprehension, and of course the teaching of modern foreign languages. Primary teachers draw on frameworks derived from applied linguistics when they seek to understand these aspects of the curriculum, and to analyse children's phoneme awareness, spelling, reading strategies or writing attainment. Evidence from applied linguistics research prompts teachers to bridge the language and literacy gaps between home and school or to use the relationship between oral language, reading and writing to make learning in the classroom more efficient. It helps primary teachers consider how to adapt the curriculum to meet the needs of individuals with defined language and literacy difficulties, or the needs of bilingual and multilingual children who are learning English as an additional language at school.

Finally, applied linguistics research contributes to our understanding of classroom pedagogy and curriculum organisation. For example, it offers insights into group interaction and classroom discourse and, as such, has the capacity to inform how teachers teach and how they manage their classes to ensure more efficient learning. It offers a framework to help us understand the gendered way that pupils network around books, and offers the potential of a research-based approach to organising the curriculum and resources in ways that help to address gender gaps in literacy attainment.

Why this, why now?

In the current educational climate it is particularly important that teachers have an understanding of applied linguistics. First, there is increasing international focus on raising academic attainment, and many countries have policy developments focused around 'excellence agendas'. To raise attainment, teachers are required to teach efficiently, to tailor the curriculum for particular schools and classes, and to support individual children to achieve success at school. This means that teachers need in-depth understanding of curriculum knowledge but also wider knowledge, for example, of linguistic ethnography to understand how beliefs about literacy are shaped, how a range of resources – cultural, social, linguistic and material – affect children's mastery of reading, language and writing conventions, how they affect the ways that children take advantage of the language and literacy opportunities offered in school, and what schools and teachers can do about this. Teachers are often making decisions about curriculum content, organisation and delivery in a 'high-stakes' environment, with regular scrutiny of classroom practice. This makes it even more important that curriculum decisions are based on clear analysis and evidence from research. Understanding the basis of the language and literacy curriculum and of language and literacy development allows teachers and education policy makers to make reliable decisions and to explain their decisions to others.

The second reason for an enhanced knowledge of applied linguistics amongst primary teachers is that school populations are changing. The global economy has increased international mobility. In any metropolitan area it is now the norm to find bilingual and multilingual children. Primary teachers are responsible for adapting the curriculum to meet the needs of this diverse range of children. They need to understand the linguistic issues such children face and how to adapt the curriculum to promote rapid language learning.

Diversity is not just a question of the number of languages children speak. Inclusion policies within the legislative frameworks of many countries mean that children with individual language and literacy difficulties or with speech, language and communication impairments are also present in many classrooms (for an international review of this, see Ainscow and Sandill 2010). Legislation often puts education staff in the driving seat and it is the role of the primary teacher to ensure partnership working, effective support, and development opportunities for all children.

Partnership working is the third reason that modern primary teachers need an understanding of applied linguistics if they are to meet the demands of the current educational climate. Successful primary teaching in modern schools requires primary teachers to work with a number of other professionals, including English as an additional language teachers, and mother-tongue support teachers; learning support teachers; educational psychologists, and speech and language therapists. Teachers will often be involved in consultancy approaches, where language teaching or interventions are planned amongst several professionals, but delivered in the classroom by education staff under the immediate direction of the primary teacher. In such co-professional situations, it is useful for primary teachers to understand the ways that linguistics frameworks are used by other professionals.

However, few primary teachers currently study linguistics in pre-service courses, few teacher educators have expertise in the area, and linguistics can seem a 'difficult' subject, with little relevance to the crowded teacher education programme. As a result primary teaching graduates may lack sufficient linguistic knowledge to recognise where their literacy-teaching frameworks come from, or understand how to adapt and apply them appropriately. They may also lack a knowledge base to analyse children's talk and literacy development, and lack a linguistic metalanguage to help them think about progression or to communicate with other professionals. A lack of such knowledge runs the risk of unreliable decision-making, based on habit rather than evidence, and may result in inefficient teaching and discriminatory practices, however unintentional.

This book seeks to advance the concept of a linguistically aware primary school teacher and suggests how an applied linguistics knowledge base might be constructed: a knowledge base centred on the mainstream school curriculum, that acknowledges diversity and equips teachers to understand the support needs of children with additional speech, language and communication needs, and of bilingual and multilingual children who do not have a language learning difficulty, but for whom the English of the mainstream classroom is an additional language to be mastered.

The development of the book

In developing this book, we took an intentionally broad view of applied linguistics. We made no distinction between topics that might be considered 'pure' as opposed to 'applied', as long as they were relevant to teaching in primary schools. In this we reflected the breadth of interest of the sponsors of the seminar series on which this volume is based, the British Association of Applied Linguistics (BAAL), which aims as an organisation to be 'a forum for people interested in language and the applications of linguistics'. This breadth allowed an eclectic selection of speakers to be invited to the seminars. Presenters were asked to contribute chapters to this volume, and their topics were augmented by chapters from invited authors based in Australia, the UK and the USA. BAAL members, education policy makers, teacher educators, psychologists and speech and language therapists also attended the seminars.

Seminar presenters were based in the UK and were mostly language researchers aligned with three professional groups – educationalists, speech and language therapists (SLTs) and psychologists. Many taught on pre-service qualifying courses whose graduates would collaborate as professionals in primary schools. However, despite their common interests, presenters from different professional groups did not all know each other, and had not accessed each other's work. In one rather striking case, two presenters from the same university but aligned to different professional groups met at the seminar for the first time. They found many interests in common.

As well as a range of professional disciplines relevant to primary schools, we sought contributions reflecting a range of linguistic methodologies (including ethnographic-, discourse-, corpus- and psycho-linguistics) and of professional concerns (literature; language development; teacher education; foreign language teaching; psychology; English as an additional language, and speech and language therapy). In particular, we were interested in what we felt could be a changing set of demands on primary teachers across the globe. We sought scholars who had considered the diversity of present-century primary classrooms and the challenges presented by current research into the language and literacy curriculum.

The consideration of such a wide range of topics risks incoherence and fragmentation. However, we would submit that presenting this range of ideas was in itself useful in furthering academic knowledge. It also promoted the type of co-professional interchanges needed to deal with diverse and mobile classroom populations. And importantly, it reflected the complexities of knowledge, opinion, policy, professional requirements and classroom practices facing primary teachers as they consider children's language and literacy learning.

To ameliorate a potential over-abundance of models and methodologies, we asked contributors to focus on two questions related to their field of expertise: 'what do primary teachers need to understand so that applied linguistics is relevant to their professional work?' and 'how is such understanding built?' We hoped in this way to uncover some practical approaches to the issues facing the classroom teacher. The different shapes of professional discourse, policy structures and the variety of contexts in which they operate, inevitably mean that both these questions need to be problematised and Part I focuses on this.

The diverse knowledge frames that primary teachers need

In introducing a text such as this, there is a temptation to concentrate on convergent opinion, rather than stressing the range of views expressed. Yet diversity is one clear message from both the chapters in this book and the seminar papers and discussion which preceded them. Rather than ignoring diversity, we sought to embrace it. Part II broadly addresses 'what' do primary teachers need to understand and illustrates the breadth of applied linguistics approaches to the study of language and literacy, although the influence of applied linguistics is so wide that this section can only illustrate this. However, Part II suggests that no single perspective has a monopoly on 'truth' but that each appropriates different ideas and methodologies from linguistics, and uses them to different ends. Each perspective generates insights into learning, and has implications for what should happen in classrooms and this book illustrates that important pedagogical insights for primary teachers come from the full range of research.

One participant wrote, after the original seminars: 'It is both stimulating and a bit horrifying, to hear and then try to integrate, the range of perspectives in other disciplines.' However, the important issue may not be the range of perspectives, but how this range is handled. Diversity is only a problem if one seeks agreement in the form of a single, convergent or integrated approach. Perhaps an effective and efficient primary teacher can, and should, develop a deep familiarity and facility with a wide range of knowledge-frames, each providing different pedagogical insights. If difficult choices must be made about what is most desirable, it is important that such choices are informed by a broad view of what is possible and that consideration is given to the roles and affordances of both initial and continuing professional development.

The costs of attaining such fluency are undoubtedly great – in time, effort and, of course, money and ultimately, decisions about what primary teachers need to know must be made after considering the domains in which such knowledge is likely to impact. Part III of this book tracks some possible ways forward, illustrating approaches specifically designed for teachers and offering tools that may be immediately useful.

What matters? Fundamental principles

Decisions about the applied linguistics knowledge that primary teachers need to understand should be informed by the fundamental principles that apply to all education – issues such as children's rights and the nature of knowledge. They should also recognise and acknowledge the changing realities that impact on what teachers do and that shape how they think about teaching and learning.

Children's rights

Pedagogies that arise from linguistic methodologies and knowledge frames are interwoven with other realities of working in a modern primary school. One important reality, as stated, is the need to foreground the rights of children who have speech, language and communication difficulties, and of children who are learning English as an additional language. An absolute requirement is that all those involved in education are mindful of the arguments about the increasing diversity of school populations.

There is evidence that teachers at present lack sufficient understanding to meet the diverse needs of such children. In this book, Maggie Vance reviews this evidence in relation to the inclusion of children with speech, language and communication needs, and Jessie Ricketts and her colleagues present research indicating that teachers may not notice the comprehension problems of children who do not have diagnosed needs. Both Angela Creese and Carolyn Letts in their chapters outline the evidence related to teaching children who are learning English as an additional language, whilst Deborah Horan and Afra Ahmed Hersi suggest that current teacher education provision does not equip teachers to meet these diverse needs. Clearly, where educational policies extend a welcome to all children into the primary classroom, teachers need to be empowered with appropriate linguistic knowledge to ensure all children's educational wellbeing.

Another aspect of children's rights is the right of all children to have analytical and 'noticing' teachers, who recognise progress in a variety of dimensions, can celebrate achievement and can take a diagnostic view of attainment. An understanding that allows teachers to bring a variety of applied linguistics lenses to children's work allows them to spot patterns in 'errors' and promote new ways of understanding. Many chapters illustrate this, for example: Debra Myhill does so in the context of children's writing; Terezinha Nunes and Peter Bryant and also Kenn Apel and his colleagues do so in the context of children's spelling, and Vivienne Smith in the context of reading children's picture books.

The language used to talk about achievement, progress and attainment shapes professional understandings. Applied linguistics provides a metalanguage with which teachers can discuss children's engagement, development and attainment in language and literacy. As Debra Myhill points out, teachers will not necessarily share this metalanguage with children, but need it none the less if they are to recognise child progress.

Emerging knowledge

Another reality is that knowledge, including knowledge about language and about literacy teaching and learning, is not fixed but evolving. One reaction to this may be to suggest that knowledge is unimportant, since it will soon be superseded. In our view, the evolving nature of knowledge makes it even more important that teachers' professional understandings are complex and are constructed from a wide range of perspectives. It is not just that emerging research knowledge can inform how teachers interpret curriculum content, assessment and pedagogical guidance, although Alison Sealey's description of work on linguistic corpora (described in Part II) suggests that it has the potential to completely revolutionise the pedagogy of grammar and vocabulary teaching.

Fundamentally, it is that the understanding of emergent knowledge thrives when teachers have a solid grounding in current frameworks and a clear grasp of the enquiry-driven nature of such frameworks. By building and exploring knowledge from a variety of theoretical perspectives, professionals anchor and deepen what they know. Thus, also in Part II, Elspeth Jajdelska gives insights on narrative comprehension from a historical research paradigm, which complement those from the psychology paradigm offered by Jessie Ricketts, Joanne Cocksey and Kate Nation.

Other realities of emerging knowledge concern the organisation and implementation of the curriculum. Gemma Moss uses linguistic ethnography to explain how, often fleeting and unacknowledged, participation in language and literacy practices taking place at the 'edge' of school life, can shape children's identities, interests and understandings of what it means to be a reader. Adam Lefstein and Julia Snell use sociolinguistics to analyse patterns of classroom discourse between teachers and their pupils, challenging current practice by showing how some ingrained patterns serve to actually undermine, rather than promote, learning.

Inter-professional and co-professional working

On a purely pragmatic level, the work of a primary teacher does not take place in isolation. Classroom teachers will need, at some time, to communicate with SLTs, learning support teachers, specialists in English as an additional language, foreign language teachers and educational psychologists. Without a shared metalanguage for talking about language use and development, confusions can arise.

Any discussion of a metalanguage automatically raises issues about 'what counts' and 'who decides'; decisions about linguistic terminology obviously reflect views about what is important and about models of child learning. Some professions, such as SLTs, have already made decisions about relevant models. These professionals, and the models they use, are part of the wider landscape of primary teachers' work, and have to be recognised. Shared descriptive terms are important for understanding what matters to other professionals and what they count as evidence. Such shared understandings underpin effective collaboration.

Curriculum policy

New policy initiatives place demands upon teachers and schools. These may focus on specific schemes, such as the introduction of foreign language teaching in the primary school, discussed by Dan Tierney, or general policy concerns such as social and linguistic inclusion. But policy has a more widespread and subtle influence than this: policy frameworks shape what matters, what teachers are expected to know, and how they are expected to use this knowledge. Dominic Wyse, using policy development in England as a case study, begins the book by illustrating how decisions about national curriculum policies in England have shaped the primary classroom and primary teachers' knowledge and understanding of literacy and literacy teaching in that country. He argues that policy development can be rather arbitrary and, may lack robust systems of 'checks and balances'. In such circumstances, teachers need access to knowledge frameworks that will keep their work grounded and evidence based to ensure balance.

Who decides? The selection of topics for this book

An important conclusion from the seminars and from this book is that, if researchers, policy makers and practitioners are to embrace the wide range of knowledge-frames required for primary teaching, the thorny issue about how the different perspectives 'play out' in policy and practice needs wider acknowledgment and discussion. Kathy Hall (Hall 2010; 2002) highlights the problems that arise when the different lenses for viewing reading and readers compete for policy leverage: 'different lines of reading research have emphasised different practices with consequences for learners and representations of competence. Depending on the viewing frame, certain features of literacy are deemed to be relevant, to merit attention and so are carefully detailed, while other features are glossed over, consigned as background and so rendered less relevant' (Hall 2010: 15).

How policy choices emerge is not the concern of this book. But by choosing authors and topics in the first place, the editors have in effect presented their view of the knowledge that matters, and it is incumbent on us to explain where this view came from. The choices we made were not driven purely by our own interests, by a narrow research agenda or by current policy emphases. They were driven by an awareness of the ways that primary classes are changing in terms of the diverse language skills and knowledge that children bring to school, and the changing demands of the primary curriculum. We would argue that decisions about the nature of 'what should matter' in primary teachers' knowledge of applied linguistics, must reflect such changing landscapes rather than personal enthusiasms, strength of rhetoric or disciplinary muscle.

The range of contexts in which primary teachers work means that no one is in a position to construct a definitive list of 'important things to know', even were such a list desirable. Different contexts will require a different depth and scope of knowledge, and we would suggest that teachers are best positioned to select sensibly, according to their own circumstances.

Useful and less useful knowledge: how teachers need to understand

There is wide agreement in the book that applied linguistics knowledge that does not impact upon children's experiences is not the type of knowledge that is required. Authors are clear that applying knowledge for primary teaching should focus on applications of relevant aspects of research, not on learning linguistics and then trying to apply it. Teachers do not need knowledge that is so abstract it requires them to 'translate' it into the classroom and work out its potential usefulness. Nor do they need knowledge that is completely bounded by programmes or activities. Agreement on three types of applied knowledge can be extracted from this book: knowledge that is *tailored* to the curriculum, knowledge that allows language to be *analysed*, and knowledge that fosters *pedagogical creativity*.

Knowledge that is tailored to the curriculum: The authors in this book recognise that teachers need highly specific and relevant knowledge, directly arising from, and applicable to, curriculum and classroom realities. This is more useful than providing extensive information of the sort used by applied linguistics researchers that requires teachers to work out what is and is not useful in the context of the classroom. Other professions, notably speech and language therapists (SLTs), have taken a similar view of the need to tailor linguistic knowledge, in their case to support clinical application. SLTs have made confident, professional decisions about the ideas, techniques and applications that are most helpful. For example, frameworks for syntactic and phonological analyses are routinely taught in pre-service speech and language therapy courses, and used in practice, in the context of helping SLTs make decisions about how to proceed with a particular client.

In arguing for tailored knowledge, the intention is to recognise the complexity and variety of tasks that primary teachers face, and the different ways knowledge can be introduced and understood. Several authors (including Myhill; Ellis and McCartney; Smith; Jajdelska; Hammond; Hartshorne; Horan and Hersi; and Ellis and Briggs) argue that the process of tailoring research knowledge must be dynamic and that knowledge tailored in this way results in productive and evidence-based applications, and new insights. Such knowledge provides a cornerstone for understanding that frees teachers from simply 'delivering' pre-packaged programmes and policies handed down from on high. Tailored knowledge should empower teachers to ensure that conversations with the policy makers and professional regulators who currently control much of a primary teacher's practice are evidence-based and measured.

Knowledge that develops an analytical 'eye': There is also a focus on the knowledge teachers need to analyse talk, reading and writing and to make appropriate changes at an individual, class, stage or whole-school level. To deliver a 'noticing teacher', who ensures children's rights, teachers need to know how to use their knowledge to respond analytically to needs, whether presented by individuals or by whole communities. Identifying what children currently understand (as evidenced by their spoken and written texts and by their reading) should prompt teaching that is more focused, and is delivered at the point when it is most meaningful and helpful for the child. Of course, not all analytic techniques need to be applied to teaching; some help develop content knowledge, and Greg Brooks makes an impassioned plea for knowledge of the international phonetic alphabet in this context. Nor can the knowledge of analytical techniques be totally divorced from the tailored curriculum, a point emphasised throughout this book: Jennifer Hammond stresses the need for ongoing diagnostic assessment of children's language and literacy strengths to identify and target needs; Terezinha Nunes and Peter Bryant highlight the need to assess children's understanding of morphology, Elspeth Jajdelska illustrates how analysing the linguistic features of modern texts can help teachers avoid potential comprehension difficulties and Angela Creese discusses how an analysis of children's bilingual knowledge may be used productively. How the teaching profession can build such analytical knowledge is a strong feature of Part III, where procedures and targeted approaches are offered by Henrietta Dombey and Jane Briggs; Greg Brooks; Kenn Apel and his colleagues; Sue Ellis and Elspeth McCartney; and Carolyn Letts. Mary Hartshorne discusses an approach that allows teachers to analyse their own competencies.

Knowledge that fosters pedagogical creativity: Another common theme is that teachers need to link their linguistic knowledge to the activities and behaviours that help learners build capacity in talking, listening, reading and writing. Combined with knowledge that is tailored and analytical this allows teachers to link different linguistic knowledge domains in ways that are purposeful and enabling and that promote curiosity and inquiry-driven learning processes. Teachers then acknowledge the importance of child-to-child as well as child-to-adult interactions around texts and language activities. These points are evidenced by many researchers, such as Debra Myhill, Terezinha Nunes and Peter Bryant, Alison Sealey, Vivienne Smith, Adam Lefstein and Julia Snell, Gemma Moss and Angela Creese, amongst others. The powerful pedagogies that these researchers capture and promote have the potential to re-define curriculum frameworks, to re-focus them and make them less atomistic in delivery. Knowledge framed in this way ensures that teachers' understandings are applicable to classroom learning and to the realities of teaching.

Developing teacher understanding

Even given appropriate knowledge, framed in a way that is suitable for primary teachers' main concerns, the question of how teachers construct and use their knowledge remains problematic. It is worth acknowledging that adapting professional practices and understandings in the light of new and evolving knowledge presents challenges to all professions: neurosurgeons must learn to use new techniques and instruments; lawyers must update their knowledge in the light of case law and new legislation. Primary teachers are no different from these professionals. However, what may be different is the systems environment in which they work. Everyone has a 'lay opinion' on schools and literacy and primary teachers are subject to a level of public comment and scrutiny to which few other professions are exposed.

The question of *how* teachers might understand is addressed by authors in terms of how (and when) teachers might best be inducted into knowledge. In the final chapter of the book, Ellis and Briggs are concerned lest the editors seek to generate an 'essential list' of applied linguistics items that 'teacher educators input and their students output'. Such models undoubtedly exist, whether as a first step for debate or as dictats for action. However, this book does not adopt such a naive model of learning.

In the past, linguistics appears to have had something of a mixed record in contributing to the education of teachers. Several authors comment on how they do *not* want teachers to be taught, and approaches that would *not*, in their view, be useful. Some of these concerns are founded, at least in part, in earlier experiences of attempts to increase teachers' linguistic understandings. Greg Brooks gives a personal account of over-complex attempts to introduce linguistic content into teacher education over several decades in the UK which have 'sunk without trace'. Dominic Wyse denies the utility of 'pages and pages of subject knowledge requirements' prescribed by policy agendas, despite the lack of evidence for such policy enjoinders. Policy makers need to be sure that topics are covered which lead to a model of appropriate content, that is fairly static and does not lead to creative teaching.

The concerns of many authors are that teachers exposed to such impoverished learning models could in turn divorce their language teaching from meaningful interactions around talk and print. Jennifer Hammond raises this issue. She fears that a commonsense assumption that teaching should focus on 'the basics' of literacy (including phonological awareness, spelling, punctuation and grammar) could lead to these aspects being taught to children without meaningful engagement with text. Deborah Horan and Afra Ahmed Hersi are also concerned that the seemingly obvious 'solution' to teachers' need for language knowledge – requiring them to complete linguistic coursework – may provide only decontextualised knowledge. These authors argue for deep engagement and practical learning experiences to transform knowledge, so that teachers learn when and how to use it in classroom practice.

Several authors point out that knowledge is not constructed in a neat and comprehensive way; it needs to be actively built by the teacher and linked to the task(s) in hand. Primary teachers need not just declarative knowledge (knowing *that*) but procedural and conditional knowledge (knowing *how* and *when* to apply it). This book contains many examples of how this is being accomplished in different contexts and settings.

When knowledge is offered might also be important. Henrietta Dombey and Jane Briggs outline a carefully designed set of learning experiences to support teaching and learning which is fitted into busy initial teacher education courses. Pre-service courses tend to offer a platform to develop shared frameworks, with smaller and more cohesive communities of practitioners, strong imperatives to focus on application, and education faculty staff who tend to be comparatively well networked with each other and with the wider world. However, the short duration of initial teacher education courses and their crowded curricula mean that it is difficult to find the time to devote to learning the linguistics required. Time problems also affect in-service learning: Dan Tierney mentions a telling example of a twenty-seven day programme of training for practising primary teachers in which they must acquire sufficient linguistic competence in a foreign language to teach their pupils.

There are also matters of learner focus to consider. Ellis and McCartney suggest that pre-service teaching students who are working for a limited period in a school, who are often less secure in their teaching skills and curricular knowledge, and who benefit from focused advice from class teachers on an 'as and when it is needed' basis, may not welcome a detailed focus on the linguistic knowledge to design interventions for children with language or communication needs. Practising teachers who are more secure in their core pedagogical knowledge, have few opportunities to get advice from others but bear full responsibility for such children in their class, and who are in a position to notice long-term improvements, on the other hand, welcome the information.

These examples provide evidence that continued study of linguistics as an aspect of continuing professional developmental will be required. However, continuing professional development presents the challenge of addressing wider, less-coherent, less-stable and less-connected groups of practising professionals. Research shows that schools can often conceive of continuing professional development as 'inputs' or 'provision', rather than as outputs in terms of the development and learning of their workforce (Bubb and Earley 2008). This has led to a change of focus on networks of knowledge and towards technologically based, individualised approaches based on self-analysis and reflection on competencies, such as the framework described in this book by Mary Hartshorne. Perhaps the next step for those interested in promoting applied linguistics is to consider how researchers and practitioners can be more effectively connected, the types of knowledge exchange initiatives that can promote such connections, and the type of evaluations that focus on outputs rather than inputs (Borko 2004; Bubb and Earley 2007).

Organisation of this book

The range of perspectives outlined above has been organised into three parts. Part I, *Policy and diversity in the twenty-first-century primary school*, outlines the changing landscape of primary schools and teacher education, how this shapes what teachers know and what they need to know, about applied linguistics, with illustrations from the UK, Australia and the USA. It describes important policy developments and changes in the nature of pupil cohorts that are creating new landscapes for teaching as a result of discrete policy initiatives, such as the drive for modern foreign languages to be taught in primary schools, and inclusion policies that make classroom teachers responsible for children with diagnosed literacy and language needs. It also reflects changes which are less within the control of politicians and policy makers; for example, globalisation and technological developments have created a more mobile population that has hugely increased the numbers of children in primary schools who speak English as an additional language.

Part II, *The range and focus of linguistics research*, illustrates how research that uses applied linguistics knowledge and methodologies is providing new insights that are informing our understandings of teaching, learning and the curriculum. Drawing on multidisciplinary research perspectives, it illustrates the diversity of research on language and literacy and different ways in which applied linguistics perspectives are being used to understand what teachers and children can do, and how they can do it more effectively.

Part III, *Empowering teachers and teachers' use of knowledge*, considers issues that arise from notions of 'useful knowledge'. Knowledge can be framed and developed in powerful and less powerful ways. It is not enough simply to consider what needs to be 'known', one also needs to consider the ways of gaining and using knowledge. The most powerful ways of framing and developing knowledge are those that actually impact on what teachers notice about the language and literacy practices of the children they teach, and which lead to actions. Part III offers a range of approaches that are intended to affect how teachers respond to what children bring, and how they can be supported in changing their classroom practices, curriculum policies, teaching content and pedagogical frameworks to better challenge their pupils and meet their needs.

Conclusion

This book therefore argues for linguistic understanding as part of the proper professional knowledge of the primary teacher. It suggests that ideas of systematic linguistic learning and applied linguistic content may be re-framed so that they draw their coherence from the professional demands of the classroom, rather than the disparate, and sometimes conflicting and frequently contested frameworks of researchers and policy makers.

We hope that the BAAL seminar series, and this book, offer a positive contribution to the conversations that need to take place about what teachers need to know, and how. There is an exciting amount of knowledge and research that is important and applicable.

This book emphasises the need to commit time and resources to primary teachers' understanding of linguistics in a thoughtful way. This means that it is important to recognise the variety of realities teachers face and the changing contexts in which they work. Researchers, teacher educators and policy makers clearly need to focus on effective and efficient models of knowledge, and to frame this knowledge in terms of how it is realised in the classroom. Discussion needs to focus on knowledge that is tailored, analytical and pedagogically useful, and links both to research evidence and the realities of the classroom.

However, evidence from past approaches suggests that restricting decisions to these groups may not offer the type of knowledge that is needed, in the form that is needed, and when it is needed. The voices of primary teachers themselves need to be heard. They are largely missing from this book, and from the literature in general, in a way that few other professions would tolerate.

What this book shows clearly is that there are imperatives that mean the need to develop primary teachers' professional knowledge of linguistics is pressing. In moving beyond the present situation, the gaps in support for teachers acquiring linguistic understanding remain striking and deserve serious consideration. This is not just an issue of curriculum development but of children's rights.

Part I

Policy and diversity in the twenty-first-century primary school

Introduction to Part I

Sue Ellis and Elspeth McCartney

Part I identifies some key aspects of the changing landscape in primary education and how these are impacting on the everyday knowledge about applied linguistics that modern primary teachers develop. Its authors reflect on the need for this knowledge, the form that such knowledge can most usefully take, and the wider political and social questions of who decides what matters, why and how.

Some aspects of the changing landscape in primary education are outwith the control of teachers and educational policy makers, although they impact on their work. Jennifer Hammond notes a global concern with language and literacy achievement, but also that the biggest influences on achievement are located far away from the domain of the school or classroom. She focuses on one factor affecting language and literacy attainment, the number of children who speak a different language in school from the language(s) they speak at home. Jennifer Hammond writes from an Australian perspective about children with English as an additional language, but the issue is one that affects teachers, teacher educators, researchers and education policy makers across the western world. For example, in England, figures from the Department for Children, Schools and Families have shown that one in twenty schools now have native English speakers as a minority of their school population, and 600 of these schools have fewer than a third of native English speakers. The picture is further complicated because the pattern is unevenly distributed, and London can now claim to be the most linguistically diverse city in the world, with 54.1 per cent of children in inner London speaking English as an additional language (Baker and Eversley 2000) and more than 300 languages spoken by children in the city's schools (DCSF 2008d; NLT 2010).

At the start of this new millennium, children speaking a language other than English at home also represented 20 per cent of the school-age population in the USA (Hoffman and Sable 2006). Deborah Horan and Afra Ahmed Hersi examine the implications of the linguistic changes that have occurred in North American classrooms over the past decade and discuss the dilemmas they create for those involved in designing and implementing pre-service

17

education courses for student teachers. If student teachers are to learn to apply their linguistic knowledge sensitively, they need highly contextualised learning, in which they not only develop pedagogical and content knowledge that is informed by applied linguistics, but learn to operationalise this knowledge appropriately and effectively to teach English language learners. This may require teacher education courses in which student teachers practise and reflect on their language teaching under the guidance of specialists, rather than simply as part of a more generalised placement learning experience. Horan and Hersi give examples of why this type of knowledge matters, and of how the shifting needs of children and of teachers must feed upwards to impact on the thinking of those who are involved in teacher education policy and course design.

Other changes are those introduced by educational policy makers whose aim is to make educational interventions more effective or the school curriculum more in tune with the economic needs of the country. The moves towards inclusion, particularly for children with specific language, communication and literacy impairments in mainstream classrooms and the drive to teach modern foreign languages in primary schools are both examples of this type of innovation. Each policy initiative demands a new and different knowledge of applied linguistics, and increases the need to focus on the knowledge and frameworks that effective primary teachers need. Maggie Vance considers the clinical linguistic knowledge needed to support speech-, language- and communication-disordered children in mainstream classrooms and shows how this knowledge, if it underpins teaching, can also benefit all children in the class. Dan Tierney deals with an issue that is new and generating much discussion in countries such as England, but has existed for longer in Europe, Canada and Scotland: modern language teaching in the primary school. His chapter argues that different models of teaching and the nature of the languages being taught make different demands on the type of applied linguistics knowledge that primary teachers require, but that all teaching methodologies need to promote the transfer of knowledge across contexts, so that children know how to use their new facility in language outwith the classroom.

However, all knowledge is framed by the context in which it is developed and used. Dominic Wyse reminds us that national policy frameworks, which in many countries are centralised, shape teacher knowledge and how it is used at every level, namely the classroom, the school, the local authority or district, and at the levels of initial teacher education and continuing professional development. Both Wyse and Hammond call for stronger, more coherent and more multilayered links between the frameworks and knowledge generated by researchers and theorists and the development and use of teacher knowledge. Wyse outlines six principles that, he suggests, could form a basis for discussing primary teachers' knowledge of applied linguistics, and he reminds us that the development of such knowledge extends over a professional lifetime, and is not restricted to initial teacher education courses. His principles foreground many of the research studies described in Part II, and the discussion issues that are raised in the introduction. For this reason, it is fitting that his is the first chapter of this Part, and the final thought of this introduction.

1   The control of language or the language of control? Primary teachers' knowledge in the context of policy

Dominic Wyse

Introduction

In this chapter it is argued that decisions about teacher knowledge are inextricably linked with decisions about national curriculum policies and that these increasingly have been affected by political control. The chapter concentrates on the example of England, showing how national curriculum reform, in most phases of the education system, has had an impact on requirements for teachers' knowledge. As a consequence of the wide range of potential linguistic topics that could inform teaching, it is recommended that the selection of appropriate topics should be informed by principles that limit and focus the range of knowledge. Successful implementation of such principles needs to take account of the tension between political control and evidence-informed practice if new knowledge is to inform teaching and learning.

The concern of this book, namely the linguistic knowledge that it is important for primary teachers to understand, is affected by a wider concern: who decides what primary teachers need to understand? The question is important because even the most logical and persuasive case for a particular kind of linguistic knowledge is unlikely to achieve the impact and influence it deserves if some of the answers to this question are not considered. In this chapter I explore the influence that political processes have had on decisions about subject knowledge, which, I reveal, are inextricably linked with curriculum and pedagogical reform. My argument in this chapter is that understanding the political context for reform of teaching is necessary if recommendations for specific content, linguistic or other, are to be realised in primary teachers' practice.

Globally, reform of education systems has increasingly focused on teachers as a major factor in enhancing learning and educational quality (Tatto 2007). However, Tatto's thesis is that in many cases top-down political operationalisation of this focus has resulted in control of education being taken away from teachers and teacher educators. This change in the locus of control, Tatto argues, is often at the expense of teacher-owned deep levels of knowledge and critical thinking, the kind of knowledge that may be likely to result in increases in learning and teaching quality. Issues around control can be seen as basic tensions between a commitment to the pursuit of a particular form of efficiency, and a commitment to social justice (Ball 1997: 257). Ball (2008) has suggested that globalisation is a key idea in relation to policy development. In particular, it forms a spatial frame within which policy discourses and policy formulation are set. For example, education has been implicated in the discourse and processes of globalisation through the idea of the *knowledge economy*. Ball (2008) notes that globalisation has to be treated with care and is subject to extensive debate, and that globalisation can, if the term is used too casually, be used to 'explain' almost anything. Wyse and Opfer (2010) argue, in their examination of the context for the current national curriculum and national literacy strategy in England, that one feature of political generalisation about globalisation is that processes of globalisation are *perceived* by politicians as a risk, a perception that is implicated in a decline in trust of professionals and increased regulation of their work.

In view of increasing appeals to globalisation, Tikly's (2004: 194) cautions are important. The hegemonic role of economics in the development of educational programmes, with associated targets and quantifiable indicators, often ignores processes at the heart of education, namely those of the curriculum and pedagogy, that have a direct bearing on the kinds of knowledge teachers are required to understand. Tikly describes such global economics-driven policy as a new imperialism that can be challenged by grass roots social movements, representing 'globalisation from below' (2004: 193), linked to specific forms of critical pedagogy.

Paradoxically, in view of the top-down approach adopted over a sustained period of time by politicians in England, Coffield *et al.* (2007) noted a new model of public service reform was being proposed in England that included the idea of 'users shaping the service from below'. However, this still did not appear to acknowledge that professionals may be at least as informed and effective as governments at taking decisions. Rather than a positive and decisive move based on principle, the new model can be seen as a politically expedient response to growing tensions resulting from top-down control. Coffield *et al.* (2007) complained that the evidence base for the new model of public service reform was weak and that the different elements are likely to be in conflict with each other because 'A simple model has been arrived at by the expedient of understating all the difficulties and complexities inherent in each of its four main elements' (Coffield *et al.* 2007: 66).

This brief overview suggests that models of educational implementation can be understood as part of an international and global context. The main themes of this theoretical framework have influenced the following analysis of curriculum reform in England. England is a useful case to examine because aspects of its curriculum reform processes have been adopted in other countries, and because the reform effort was located by politicians explicitly in a global context. The case reveals the ways that primary teachers' knowledge is linked to curriculum and pedagogy in a range of contexts, particularly in the school curriculum and the curriculum for teacher training.

Reform of the school curriculum in England

An ambition to create a 'world class education system' through a standards agenda was at the heart of the *New Labour* project when the Labour party entered government in 1997, coupled with a unique top-down reform mechanism (Earl *et al.* 2003). Teacher knowledge became a significant issue as part of the development of highly specified national strategies for literacy and numeracy. This mechanism for curriculum reform was applied to all phases of education over a twelve-year period and extended a process that had begun with the first national curriculum for schools. As the development of a national curriculum was so significant, and because it directly and indirectly influenced later curriculum reform in England, including in teacher training, it is helpful to examine some of the historical context.

Prior to 1988 the state in England had little formal control over the curriculum; hence the well-known description of the primary classroom as 'a secret garden'. However, it would be an exaggeration to suggest that teachers had total control of the curriculum, and hence there was a complete lack of systematic whole-school planning. While it is true that primary teachers and schools had a great deal of autonomy over the curriculum and its teaching, this was not completely without external influences. Local authorities were influential in shaping curricula through their contact with schools and through in-service training. Her Majesty's Inspectorate had influence through the inspection process and through publication, and initial teacher educators had influence during teacher training and as part of in-service training of teachers. However, following a speech by UK Prime Minister James Callaghan at Ruskin College in 1976, pressure was intensified for government to increase control through the establishment of a national curriculum. In due course the Education Reform Act 1988 (ERA) (HMSO 1988) gave statutory power over the curriculum to the English Secretary of State for Education. The proposals for a national curriculum and associated testing system were controversial, as an analysis of consultation responses showed (Haviland 1988).

The year 1997 marked another shift in the nature of state control. Whereas the ERA had limited its control of the curriculum to programmes of study, attainment targets and statutory testing, the introduction of national literacy and numeracy strategies specified in great detail the content of the curriculum and its sequence in a series of 'objectives'. Teaching methods were specified to the extent that a lesson was prescribed as lasting one hour, and that hour should be divided into timed segments, which broadly represented introduction, main activities and 'plenary'. Technically the national strategies were non-statutory; however, words such as 'compliance' and 'fidelity' were used in relation to the strategies. Also, the role of the inspectorate had changed, with the result that the inspection process became more punitive. Strong expectations were expressed that schools, and teacher education departments, should be following the prescriptions of the national strategies. Local authorities who previously had 'advisory teachers' now had 'consultants' whose main role was to ensure that teachers adhered closely to the strategies.

In 2006 Sir Jim Rose produced a report which recommended that synthetic phonics should be the teaching method for reading in the early years. This resulted in another first for government: control over the method of teaching. The recommendations of the Rose Report were acted upon very quickly and with considerable force. One aspect was to ensure that the curriculum for the youngest children, as represented in all documentation, followed the recommendations. So in September 2008 the early years guidance was replaced by the Early Years Foundation Stage, hence the early years were covered by a statutory curriculum for the first time, a move which secured government control of the curriculum from birth to 18 years, and, as we see below with regard to teacher training, even beyond 18.

Reform of the teacher training curriculum in England

The model for changes to the school curriculum were reflected in the first centralised curriculum for teacher training. As with the school curriculum, government acquired greater control of the teacher training curriculum post-1988. However, it was not until government Circular 10/97 (DfEE 1997) that the first national curriculum for teacher education was introduced. This was quickly followed by Circular 4/98 which specified, for the first time, pages and pages of subject knowledge requirements in the core subjects of English, mathematics and science, and information and communications technology (ICT). 'Circular 10/97 introduced the first ever national curriculum for initial teacher training ... The requirements in this Circular will equip all new teachers with the knowledge, understanding and skills needed to play their part in raising pupil performance across the education system' (DfEE 1998e: 3).

In addition to the new requirements for delivery of a particular kind of subject knowledge, teacher training institutions were required to formally 'audit' their student teachers' subject knowledge (in addition to any university assessments that were already being carried out) and national skills tests in English, mathematics and ICT were imposed, including a spelling test for trainee teachers, despite the fact that many were postgraduates and some were even enrolled on master's-level qualifications.

These circulars were followed by the introduction of 'professional standards' in 2002, revised in 2008 (TDA 2008b), including the addition of requirements to cover teachers' advancement through the profession. However, the previous detailed specific requirements for subject knowledge were relegated to further guidance, as knowledge was now summarised in standards for trainee teachers who should:

Q 14 Have a secure knowledge and understanding of their subjects/curriculum areas and related pedagogy to enable them to teach effectively across the age and ability range for which they are trained.

Q 15 Know and understand the relevant statutory and non-statutory curricula and frameworks, including those provided through the National Strategies, for their subjects/curriculum areas, and other relevant initiatives applicable to the age and ability range for which they are trained. (TDA 2009b)

The requirement to have a secure knowledge and understanding of the statutory and non-statutory curricula means that the specific knowledge required is dependent on the nature of those curricula. For example, from 1997 onwards significant emphasis was placed on phonological knowledge and traditional grammar knowledge, on the basis that these topics received strong emphasis in the National Literacy Strategy Framework for Teaching (noted above), which teachers had to deliver. The links made between the curriculum that teachers had to deliver and the subject knowledge required as part of teacher training raises the following question: to what extent are curricula informed by an authoritative evidence base?

This question has bedevilled policy implementation. Excessive Government prescription is, on principle, open to criticism but the problem is exacerbated if recommendations are not seen to be informed by the strongest possible evidence base. Such strong evidence is needed to ensure the appropriateness of structures, the coherence and the relevance of policies, and to act as a check on unnecessary bureaucracy. This question of evidence, and the principle of evidence-based policy development, is raised later, after consideration of the linguistic knowledge that teachers need to acquire.

What linguistic knowledge do teachers need?

In view of the duration of teacher training courses any consideration of the linguistic knowledge required for trainee teachers must be established on the basis that there will be a limit to the amount of knowledge that can be covered. Therefore the expectation should be that teachers will continue to acquire knowledge throughout their careers. The vast range of potential linguistic knowledge means that coherent principles are required to focus the priorities for knowledge. Building on Wyse and Jones (2008) the following principles are offered as an example of what might be appropriate and to explore further the way such principles link with teacher knowledge. The principles were created by reflecting on some of the linguistic features that appeared to be common to much of the research and theory synthesised in Wyse and Jones (2008). I have also taken the opportunity to extend these reflections in preparation for this chapter. The principles cannot be definitive because such principles would require collaborative agreement by interested parties, but they are intended as a starting point for consideration.

- Communication of understandable meaning is the driving force of language.
- The context for English/language teaching is linked to the quality of teaching and learning.
- Analysis of language in use should form the basis for appropriate knowledge for pupils and teachers.
- Language is constantly changing hence descriptive accounts of language are more appropriate than prescriptive accounts.
- Experiencing and reflecting on the processes of reading and writing are an important resource to enhance teaching and learning.
- Language and social status (or power) are inextricably linked.

Space precludes detailed accounts of the implications of each of these principles so I restrict myself to one or two examples for each.

Communicating meaning and the context for teaching

Since communication of understandable meaning is a driving force of language, the aims and objectives of teaching will ensure that meaning is a constant point of reference and a purpose for language activities and interaction. Exercises that narrowly focus on small components of language and literacy, at the expense of whole 'texts' (in the very broadest sense) and at the expense of understanding of meaning, are inappropriate. This principle is related to the second principle about context. For example the teaching of writing is most effective when the emphasis is on the process of writing coupled with structured teaching such as strategy instruction (Wyse, Andrews and Hoffman 2010). This contrasts with more decontextualised teaching such as formal grammar teaching, which has not been shown to have a positive impact on children's writing (Wyse 2001).

Language in use and language change

The importance of the analysis of language in use, the third principle, can also be seen in relation to grammar. Teachers' knowledge about English grammar should be informed by work such as that of Crystal (cf. Crystal 2004), which explicitly recognises the historical changes to English including the influences of English as a world language and influences from new technology. A knowledge of language in use is also built on recognition of the importance of grammars created on the basis of corpus data (e.g. Carter and McCarthy 2006 and see Sealey this volume) as opposed to those based on Latinate rule-based assumptions. A rather more simple example is teaching of punctuation. Custom and practice has often resulted in schools requiring pupils to use double speech marks to demarcate direct speech. But a cursory analysis of, for example, modern children's literature reveals that direct speech is usually punctuated using single speech marks. Analysis of language in use enhances teacher knowledge and leads to more accurate teaching. These examples also serve the next principle well as they remind us that although some conventions of language are relatively stable (spelling for example) others are subject to much more change. Vocabulary is a particularly noticeable example of language change but new ways of combining words and phrases are also part of the changing linguistic landscape. Perhaps one of the most dramatic features of this language change is the way that English progresses as a world language, and what the linguistic consequences of this are for teachers around the world (see Wyse, Andrews and Hoffman 2010).

Experiencing language

Teachers are experienced readers and writers relative to their pupils and have a personal linguistic expertise and resource to draw upon. Their experience needs to be enhanced by the opportunity to reflect upon their own processes of reading and writing, as a means to better understand the processes that their pupils might experience. Greater knowledge of the processes of writing can come from psychological accounts (e.g. Hayes 2006), but knowledge of the craft of writing acquired by professional writers, which is increasingly accessible in published forms (e.g. Gourevitch 2007), is also relevant, notwithstanding the differences between expert and novice writers.

Language and power

The final principle reflects the idea that linguistic knowledge needs to include understandings about the language backgrounds of people in school communities that teachers are likely to encounter. The central concern here is not only the way in which standard English(es) is(are) established but also the implications that conceptions of standard English, and its deployment, have on citizens. A particularly unfortunate example of (mis-)conception of standard English is the way in which trainee teachers who use non-standard oral varieties of English are sometimes criticised by tutors on the basis that their language does not represent a good model of English – in spite of the fact that their meaning is entirely clear to their pupils. This brings us back to the first principle: if communication of understandable meaning is the driving force of language, then the question is not whether a teacher uses standard English or not, but rather whether they can be understood, and whether their communication helps their pupils learn. Empirical evidence on this specific point is scarce.

From principles to practice: the teaching of reading

In order to explore the possible influence of the principles I have outlined above I now turn to consideration of a specific topic that is addressed as part of teacher training. The teaching of reading is to many people one of the most, if not the most, important topic about which teachers need a strong knowledge base. However, before considering the detail of teaching reading it is important to recognise that the teaching of English/language is delivered by primary teachers as part of the whole primary curriculum. To take a straightforward example, the fact that all subjects require that pupils can read and write necessitates clear understanding of the way that teaching different subjects might be informed by the teaching of reading and writing, and vice versa. Knowledge and understanding in this broader sense is also reflected in the way that the teaching of reading is part of the context of the teaching of language/English as a subject. Teaching the modes of reading, writing and language requires understanding of the distinctive processes that comprise each, and where these processes are interlinked.

With regard to the teaching of reading, the first principle about the communication of meaning is reflected in the knowledge that texts are created by authors who aim to engage readers with their unique message. This necessitates teacher knowledge about the range of texts, knowledge about the quality of texts for pupils, and about the ways that texts support, or hinder, learning and the teaching of reading. The principle also informs the idea that the teaching of beginning readers locates comprehension of meaning as the primary focus of teaching and learning, to which other aspects such as decoding are important but subservient.

The importance of the context for English/language teaching has been revealed most sharply in the debates about top-down versus bottom-up reading teaching. There is considerable evidence that contextualised phonics teaching (that combines top-down and bottom-up emphases) is more likely to be effective than discreet teaching of the alphabetic code in isolation (a bottom-up approach: for reviews of the research see Wyse and Goswami 2008; Wyse 2010). The phonics debate, including what is relevant evidence, should form part of the knowledge base for teachers. This will also necessitate understanding a modest range of technical terms. But the main emphasis should be on knowledge of the larger trends in research, such as the fact that although there is powerful evidence that phonics teaching is a small but important part of early reading, this must be balanced in the mind of the teacher with many other aspects of reading teaching, such as pupil motivation, text selection, teaching for comprehension, strategies for accessing meaning of words, and so on. This knowledge includes the idea that contextualised phonics teaching is effective because new understandings can be applied in real contexts in order to consolidate what are often complex areas of learning for pupils. The use of whole texts also enables systematic comprehension teaching to be very closely linked with phonics teaching.

The importance of language in use, the third principle, is reflected in the texts chosen to support the teaching of reading. Trade books reflect language in use more than reading scheme/basal readers (see Levy 2009 for an analysis of the impact of different kinds of books on young readers). The language of trade books is of course still a literary construct – a comparison with a transcribed conversation reveals this all too well – but they have an authenticity that is not a feature of reading scheme books constructed with a controlled vocabulary necessary to support word decoding. Language in use may also be a feature of the interaction that teachers have with pupils about books. For example, teachers can focus on the ways in which features of professionally authored texts might inform their pupils' writing.

One way that language change is evident is through texts. Comparisons between classic children's literature and newer books can be a productive way to investigate this phenomenon. Addition of new words as revealed in texts is a key part of language change. For dictionary compilers the search for established new words is a recurrent process that aids the creation of new printed editions and more regular additions to web-based formats. Some knowledge about such processes is of value to teachers because it should encourage them to be open minded in relation to questions about words. For example, the assumption by some children that the letter q is always followed by the letter u in English could be quickly investigated by examining a good dictionary.

One possible way to think about the process of reading is to reflect on one's own reading. However, although this can be valuable, it is important to recognise that the processes of the experienced reader have important differences from the beginning reader. For that reason close analysis of individual children's reading is an important part of teachers' knowledge. Part of this requires structured opportunities to work with children on a one-to-one basis to support their reading. But this needs to be combined with reading research and theory on processes of reading to provoke further reflection. There is a tremendous publication resource to draw on but Clay's (1979) seminal work remains significant because of its pedagogy, its focus on the child, its focus on interaction and strategies, and the evidence base for its effectiveness (e.g. D'Agostino and Murphy 2004).

The final principle, about langauge and power, relates most directly to teachers' professionalism. For example, it implies a critical approach to texts, particularly policy texts, as their purpose and language often position teachers in particular ways, not least through obligation to comply. But the principle also entails understanding issues such as sociocultural factors and their links with language (a compelling example of this was Labov's (1972) work on Black English Vernacular). It also requires sensitivity to the way that the status of teachers affects their relationships with pupils and their parents/guardians.

I have shown how the principles outlined above can appropriately be applied to the teaching of reading. However, the current approach to the teaching of reading in England reveals a tension between evidence-informed practice and political control of the curriculum. It is dominated by the requirement to use the approach known as *synthetic phonics* as a result of government's decision to adopt the recommendations of the aforementioned Rose Report (Rose 2006) in full. As a consequence pressure has been brought to bear on teacher-training courses to ensure that synthetic phonics is being taught to trainees. Training events have been held through the Primary National Strategy structure of consultants, and materials produced, to put forward a particular view of subject knowledge in relation to the teaching of reading. The emphasis of this training was based on the version of the *simple view of reading* outlined in the appendix to the Rose Report.

The evidence base for the Rose Report has attracted much controversy (see Gouch and Lambirth 2008; Kershner and Howard 2006; Lewis and Ellis 2006; Wyse and Styles 2007; Ellis 2007; Wyse and Goswami 2008). To summarise this debate, the compulsion to use one approach to the teaching of reading is not sufficiently supported by evidence (Wyse and Goswami 2008). One of the dangers of the strong emphasis on synthetic phonics is that it comes at the expense of a more balanced view of the teaching of reading. For example under the pressure to comply with synthetic phonics there is a risk that other important areas, such as comprehension and the centrality of meaning, will not be given due attention in practice, both in schools and in teacher training. A more thorough consideration of the evidence would have revealed that the following features are also significant aspects of effective teaching of reading:

- the important place of complete texts including children's literature to motivate children and to provide a realistic and meaningful context for teaching
- careful consideration of how word recognition and comprehension are combined as part of teaching
- the combination of word analysis skills and prediction when encountering unknown texts
- the importance of writing as a way to develop reading. (Wyse 2010)

The case of reading shows that government prescription has not been sufficiently informed by the evidence base, and reveals the challenges of ensuring
that appropriate linguistic knowledge is at the core of teachers' work.

Conclusion

An important consideration in relation to thinking about the linguistic knowledge that teachers need is how requirements for subject knowledge are established. In this chapter I have shown how the model of curriculum reform in
England that began with a national curriculum in 1988 has been used as the
basis for curriculum development resulting in increased political control and
more detailed specification of requirements over time. This model of curriculum development that has ultimately affected all phases of education from
the early years to teacher training has had a direct influence on the kinds
of linguistic knowledge that teachers are expected to have. The imperatives
for knowledge created by political processes have led to a tension between
evidence-informed knowledge and government prescription, seen particularly
in the policy on early reading that adopted a 'one-size-fits-all' approach. In
view of the problems of political control associated with the twelve years of the
National Literacy Strategy, this was a worrying development.

Things however may be changing in England. It was hoped that a vision-
ary report based on a two-year enquiry into the English national curriculum
from the House of Commons Children, Schools and Families Committee
(2009) that recommended greater autonomy over the curriculum would have
a decisive influence. Unfortunately the rationale for changes to the national
curriculum put forward by the conservative-liberal democrat government
elected in 2010 suggests that many of the problems of the past are to be
repeated. In view of the myriad competing possibilities for linguistic knowledge it is important to establish principles which themselves are an appropriate feature of knowledge for teachers, but which also enable the selection of
the most relevant topics for training, and implementation in the classroom.

2 Working with children who speak English as an additional language: an Australian perspective on what primary teachers need to know

Jennifer Hammond

Introduction

In this chapter I address questions of what primary school teachers need to know primarily from the perspective of the needs of children for whom English is an additional language (EAL children). In addition, as I am located in Australia, the chapter is very much located within the Australian educational context and in relation to debates that are current in that context.

Australia, like the UK and other developed English-speaking countries, has significant numbers of established and more recently arrived immigrants within its population. General estimates are that around 20 to 25 per cent of children attending school in Australia are from non-English-speaking backgrounds, and significant numbers of these children need support with their development of spoken and written English. Such children tend to be clustered in large urban schools where factors such as poverty and social disruptions also frequently impact on the student populations. As the Organisation for Economic Cooperation and Development International Student Assessment (OECD PISA) results consistently show, there is a correlation between low educational achievement and factors such as socio-background, ethnicity and status as a second language learner (Lokan, Greenwood and Creswell 2000; Thompson and de Bortoli 2006). This is true in Australia, as elsewhere, and the result is that many children from linguistically and culturally diverse backgrounds in Australia do less well in school than their more socially and economically advantaged peers.

Although EAL children themselves are diverse in terms of their socio-economic, linguistic and cultural backgrounds, they all face the dual task of learning English, whilst also learning through English. As numerous researchers have acknowledged, this dual task places considerable demands on children (Cummins 2000; Gibbons 2002). It also places demands on their teachers who need to recognise the linguistic resources, both in English and in their mother tongue, that children bring to school, as well as the demands that such young people face as they engage with academic concepts in different curriculum subjects. The additional challenge for teachers working with EAL children is to provide equitable access to education.

In Australia, the education of EAL children has frequently been seen as a minority issue and as the responsibility of specialist EAL teachers. However, in this chapter, I challenge that assumption, and argue that the education of EAL children is in fact a mainstream issue. There are two major strands in my argument. The first is a simple numerical one. As indicated, significant proportions of children in the Australian school system are from non-English-speaking backgrounds. It is thus highly likely that, at some point in their careers, the majority of primary teachers in Australia will work with EAL children. An understanding of the rich sources of opportunity, as well as the challenges of working with EAL children, is thus part of the essential knowledge that equips teachers for work in Australian schools. The second strand is a theoretical one. I suggest there are theoretical reasons for arguing that responsibility for the language and literacy development of EAL children cannot be segregated from children's engagement with curriculum knowledge. Further, the kind of knowledge that equips teachers to work with EAL children overlaps to a considerable extent with the knowledge that will enable teachers to design and implement programmes that address the needs of other children. Thus my overall argument in the chapter is that EAL education is not just a minority issue, and, in addition, that the knowledge that enables teachers to understand and address needs of EAL children is likely to result in pedagogical practices that also benefit other children.

I begin the chapter by addressing the role of theories in understanding the kind of knowledge about language and literacy required of teachers.

The importance of theories of language and literacy

For children who are learning English while at the same time learning through English, language and literacy learning are obviously of central importance, and thus teachers' knowledge about the nature and development of language and literacy is also of central importance. In the many years I have been working with teachers of EAL children, I have found extensive recognition of the importance of language and literacy teaching, but considerable confusion about how best to support their language and literacy development. In recent research, for example, my colleagues and I asked teachers about what they saw as their EAL children's greatest needs. There was unanimous agreement that support with language and literacy development was the greatest need, but there was also considerable confusion about how to address that need (Hammond 2008). As one of the teachers we later interviewed said: 'Most teachers don't have the skills to do that [teach more complex aspects of language and literacy] and I don't. I look at it [children's written work], I say, "You haven't expressed this very clearly." To pinpoint what they need to do is sometimes quite difficult and it's very time consuming.'

It might be expected that in the twenty-first century, educators and applied linguists would by now have reached definitive conclusions regarding the knowledge of language and literacy required by teachers, and the ways in which they should use that knowledge to teach all the children for whom they are responsible. After all, teaching of language, including reading and writing, in one form or another has been a core component of school curricula for centuries. However the highly complex nature of language and literacy mean that such issues are still hotly contested. In Australia, questions about the nature of language and literacy and the kind of knowledge needed by teachers are very topical as we are enmeshed in debates around the development of a national curriculum. National guidelines that will shape the teaching of English, history, science and mathematics in all Australian states are currently being developed (National Curriculum Board 2009). While the development of guidelines for history, science and mathematics has proceeded relatively smoothly, the English curriculum has generated extensive and intense debates.

Specifically, the debates address questions about the relationship between language and literacy and about the relationship between digital literacy and language. Some of the most vocal participants in the debates argue for the place of the 'basics', including phonological awareness, spelling, punctuation and grammar in language and literacy education. Ensuing debates have generally not questioned the importance of these components, but their relative priority in relation to a broader emphasis on text-level organisation and cohesion; on overall fluency in reading and writing; and on the place of multimodal and critical literacy in language and literacy education. There is broad agreement that grammar should be part of the curriculum, but intense disagreement over which grammar, and to what end grammar should be taught. There is agreement that oral language needs to be included in the English curriculum but disagreement over what this means. There is agreement that young people should be able to engage critically with information that is available to them aurally, digitally or in written texts, but disagreement about the place and priority of critical literacy within a curriculum.

These debates raise questions that are relevant to this chapter. At one level the debates can be seen as different lobby groups ensuring their turf is protected. However, at another level they reflect very different theoretical understandings about the nature of language and literacy, and thus they raise serious questions about a highly contested curriculum area. These theoretical understandings, I suggest, can be characterised very broadly as 'language to convey information', versus 'language to construct meanings'. In the former, language is regarded essentially as a system for encoding and decoding messages. Here the system itself is seen as a neutral technology, and the educator's task is seen primarily as teaching the technology of the system so that ideas and information can be conveyed efficiently and accurately. As Reddy (1979) pointed out many years ago, this 'conduit' view of language sits comfortably with widely held assumptions about the nature of language, and thus, either implicitly or explicitly, it is prevalent in our society. Evidence of this view of language can be seen, for example, in current debates not in the requirement to teach the 'basics' of language and literacy, but in the expectation that aspects of the basics (such as phonemic awareness, spelling or grammar) can usefully be taught in isolation from meaningful spoken or written texts.

In Australia, many applied linguists and educators (myself included) have been influenced by the work of Halliday and others in systemic functional linguistics (e.g. Christie and Martin 1997; 2007; Halliday 1978; 1994), and also by the work of those involved with multi-modal and critical literacy (e.g. Freebody and Luke 2003; Luke 1993; Unsworth 2001). As a result we work with different understandings of language and of literacy: that language is a social semiotic system; that, as speakers or writers, we make choices within this system; and that these choices construct meaningful texts. Rather than simply transmitting meanings, language choices are seen as centrally involved in constructing meanings, and thus the language system is seen as far from neutral. From this perspective, the role of teachers is to draw children's attention to the system itself, including features of text organisation, cohesion, paragraph construction, grammar and vocabulary. Their role is also to support children's developing abilities to take, and make, meanings across different registers and genres of language, and to draw their attention to the ways in which choices in their own and others' use of language construct specific meanings.

The point I would want to emphasise here is that theories of language and literacy matter. Our responses to questions about the relationship between language and literacy: the relative importance of oral and written English; the place of multi-modal literacy; the relative priorities of different levels of texts: including phonemic awareness, spelling, sentence structure, paragraphs, text organisation and cohesion; our views on the importance of grammar (and which grammar); our recognition of genres; and the importance we attach to critical literacy are all shaped by our theoretical understanding of the nature of language and literacy, whether articulated or implicit.

Implications of theories are far reaching. In the introduction to the chapter I suggested that teaching of language and literacy cannot be segregated from the teaching of curriculum knowledge. Yet, a 'conduit' view of language implies that it can (and is evident in requests such as 'Can you teach them English so that I can get on with teaching science'). A functional, semiotic perspective emphasises a very strong relationship between language and content. From this perspective, language and literacy learning are seen as central to learning in all key curriculum subjects. As Lemke (1990) has argued in relation to science, learning science is learning the language of science. Coffin (2005) has made similar arguments in relation to the language of history. Such perspectives are reflected in the general emphasis on 'language across the curriculum' in Australia and elsewhere in recent years. They are also reflected in programmes where language and literacy support for EAL children is interwoven with teaching of curriculum content.

If we accept the interrelationship between language and curriculum content, there are further implications for the kind of knowledge needed by teachers. Teachers need to understand the nature of academic language and literacy. They need to recognise the increasing demands of academic language that children face as they engage at deeper levels with curriculum knowledge across the years of primary school and into secondary school; they need to understand the relationship between spoken and written language, and they need to understand the increasingly 'written-like' nature of both spoken and written texts in educational knowledge (Macken-Horarik 1996). With regard to science, for example, engagement with academic language and literacy will include initiation into the registers of scientific language. In turn this will involve at least scientific (technical) vocabulary, grammatical structures that enable young people to explain, describe, summarise, question and argue and the ability to understand and produce extended oral and written texts with an awareness of generic structure and cohesion.

Thus far in this chapter, I have highlighted the importance of theories of language and literacy, and I have addressed, at a fairly general level, the kind of knowledge that is relevant for primary school teachers. It could be argued, however, that the various domains of knowledge I have referred to are relevant for all teachers, and that there is little in what I have suggested that is specific to the knowledge required by teachers of EAL children. The question then arises, what, if anything, is special about the knowledge required of teachers working with EAL children? In what follows, I address this question and I also attempt to tease out in more detail, the kind of knowledge about language and literacy that is required of primary teachers working with EAL children.

What is distinctive about knowledge for EAL education?

Some years ago, at a time of intense debate about literacy policy in Australia, my colleague Beverley Derewianka and I wrote an article in which we argued there *is* such a thing as specialist EAL knowledge (Hammond and Derewianka 1999). I revisit that paper here in some detail as it is relevant to my overall argument in this chapter. At that time, following outcomes from national assessments, EAL children had been identified as one group that was not achieving required literacy standards. As a result, many EAL children were placed in remedial literacy programmes. It was our view that such programmes failed to acknowledge both the legitimate achievements of young people who were learning and studying in their second (or third) language, and also failed to address their genuine areas of educational need – in oral language development as well as in literacy development, and in the cultural adjustment that children were required to make as they participated in mainstream Australian schools. If teachers were to recognise and meet the needs of their EAL children, we argued, they needed to know at least the following:

- knowledge of the nature of English;
- knowledge of first and second language development (including understanding of cross cultural relationships);
- knowledge of relevant language teaching methodologies (both of EAL and of literacy teaching methodologies).

We recognised that much of what was included in these categories also constituted important knowledge for all teachers, especially for those whose prime responsibility was supporting children's literacy development, but we argued that EAL teachers required a level of linguistic and cultural knowledge and sensitivity that went beyond that required of other teachers. Thus our view was that the difference lay in the level and depth of required knowledge, as well as in the nature of that knowledge. We suggested that while related theories and models of curricula were likely to inform both EAL and literacy education, the distinctive needs of EAL children meant that EAL teachers were required to draw on these theories and models in ways that differed from those deployed by other teachers. Thus, the organisation of EAL programmes, we suggested, differed from programmes designed for other children, as did the selection and sequencing of teaching activities and specific tasks.

Of particular significance in that paper, and more generally to questions of the kind of knowledge required of primary teachers, was a more detailed account of knowledge of the nature of language. In our earlier paper, Derewianka and I argued that EAL teachers require an extensive theoretical knowledge of language at the levels of discourse, lexico-grammar and phonology. More specifically, we suggested, they required:

- a knowledge of spoken and written genres of their culture;
- an awareness of the linguistic demands of various curriculum areas;
- an extensive and explicit understanding of English grammar and an understanding of how systems of grammar differ between languages;
- an understanding of how the systems of lexico-grammar in English are drawn upon in making meanings appropriate to the various formal and informal contexts in which children function;
- an understanding of the phonological and alphabetic systems of their own and other languages.

We went on to address the nature of good EAL programmes. Effective EAL programmes, we suggested, address the needs of children at a whole-school level, and hence involve more than planning and teaching in individual classrooms. They include at least the following features:

- strategies at the level of the school's language and literacy policy for addressing the needs of EAL children, from the newly arrived to the 'hidden' third phase learners;
- a range of organisational models (new arrival, team-teaching, parallel teaching, integrated or withdrawal as appropriate) which recognise the diversity of EAL children and the need for intensive English study particularly with older children;
- effective procedures to develop comprehensive learner profiles and to place children into appropriate programmes;
- on-going diagnostic assessment of language and literacy strengths and weaknesses so that individual learning programmes can be developed to target identified needs and facilitate accelerated rates of learning which are appropriate for age, academic needs and interests of children;
- use of teaching/learning strategies which provide intensive, explicit, targeted and timely intervention in areas such as:
  - concentrated oral language development, including interaction strategies;
  - English pronunciation, stress and intonation;
  - listening comprehension;
  - Roman alphabetic script and mechanics of handwriting, where necessary;
  - English phonic relationships and spelling;
  - English syntax and grammatical features;
  - text-level features such as cohesion and the structuring of texts;
  - extensive vocabulary development;
  - explicit teaching of reading comprehension strategies, especially for older children and for those not already literate in their mother tongue (reading for different purposes, skimming, scanning, drawing on background knowledge, inferring, predicting, critical reading);
  - induction into technical knowledge and language of particular curriculum areas;
  - familiarisation with relevant cultural and social knowledge (values, traditions, history, literature, behaviours);
- selection and/or design of texts and materials that are appropriate to EAL children's level of English language proficiency, and that acknowledge and exploit EAL students' prior knowledge and cultural experiences.

We acknowledged that good literacy programmes also require many of these features. However, in our view, the distinction lay in the extent of systematic teaching of, and about, both spoken and written language; and the degree of structured support that is required to assist EAL children to develop the control of linguistic and cultural resources that are necessary for successful study across the curriculum (Gibbons 2002). This is not to suggest that literacy programmes do not need to provide systematic support for children. They do, but because the needs of EAL and English speaking children are different, the nature of that support will be different.

As I revisit that paper, I find I agree with much of what we wrote at that time. Since writing that paper, however, my colleagues and I have been involved with research that has specifically addressed questions of quality of teaching (Hammond and Gibbons 2005; Hammond 2008; Gibbons 2008). As a result of that research, I would now add to the above list a stronger emphasis on understanding of discipline and curriculum knowledge, and I would also add more emphasis on understanding the ways of designing and implementing programmes that *challenge* as well as *support* children in their engagement with mainstream curricula. In what follows, I briefly describe that research to explain these additions.

Knowledge of high-challenge, high-support programmes

In our research, my colleagues and I worked with teachers in schools characterised by high proportions of EAL children in their mainstream classes. A number of these schools were regarded as difficult to work in, and in some the general expectations of academic outcomes were low. The prevailing views were that certain entrenched educations practices were 'all that could be hoped for in the particular situation of this classroom, in this school and with these students' (Johnston and Hayes 2008). The purpose of our research was to challenge such views by working with invited teachers to plan and implement high-challenge, high-support programmes, and to document and analyse the impact of these programmes. While, not surprisingly, there was broad agreement amongst the research team teachers that learning environments characterised by high challenge and high support were most likely to promote effective learning, the task as we all saw it, was to articulate more specifically what such learning environments actually looked like in practice: which factors teachers needed to take into account in planning their programme; how they went about designing and implementing such programmes; and what knowledge underpinned their decisions. Our aim was to be able to draw on this research to provide examples of what was possible for other teachers and educators who were working (or intending to work) in similar contexts.

Our initial research addressed the *high support* dimension. Here, we worked with an apprenticeship model of learning that was based on Vygotskian theories of learning (Vygotsky 1978). Thus we worked with the assumption that learning occurs primarily in social interaction when learners interact collab-oratively with more knowledgeable others. Such assumptions drew in particu-lar on Vygotsky's notion of the zone of proximal development – that is, the argument that most effective learning occurs in the zone between what learn-er's are currently able to understand and do, and what becomes possible when they are supported and guided by more knowledgeable others. We also worked with the metaphor of 'scaffolding' (Gibbons 2002; 2003; Hammond 2001; Hammond and Gibbons 2005; Mercer 1994; Wells 1999) to tease out ways in which knowledgeable others (in our case, the teachers) were able to provide strong guidance and support when needed, but were also able to withdraw that support and hand over responsibility as learners became increasingly able to work independently.

Our initial analysis of classroom data indicated that when working with high support, teachers needed both to 'design-in' that support and to be open to the 'contingent' teachable moments that arise during classroom interactions with their children. With regard to designed-in support, teachers needed to know how to analyse children's abilities and needs; analyse curriculum demands; identify realistic but challenging goals based on children's needs and curricu-lum demands. They also needed to know how to plan different levels of sup-port for diverse learners through selecting and sequencing combinations of whole-class, group and independent tasks that gradually increased the level of challenge, but also provided target support as needed. In addition, teachers needed to be able to recognise the teachable moment, and to draw, as appropri-ate, on a range of strategies to provide targeted support at the moment of need (Hammond and Gibbons 2005).

As well as addressing high support in classrooms, our research addressed *high challenge* (Hammond 2008; Gibbons 2008). Our aim was to challenge the young people to engage at a deep level with curriculum knowledge and understanding. To address this aim we drew on some of the 'tools' available from educational initiatives promoting high-quality teaching in Australia and elsewhere (Queensland Productive Pedagogies 2002; NSW Quality Teaching Initiative 2003, 2004; Newmann and Associates 1996). These tools included 'Rich Tasks', 'Essential Questions', and 'Substantive Conversations'. The research outcomes provided evidence that these tools were effective in assist-ing teachers to clarify the 'big ideas' and knowledge structures of relevant curriculum content, and to develop tasks that had intellectual rigour and rele-vance beyond the classroom. The tools also assisted teachers in moving from a focus on what aspects of the curriculum content needed to be included in their programmes, to a focus on why this curriculum content constituted significant knowledge. Thus the classroom emphasis shifted from *what* children were doing to *why* they were doing it. The research outcomes further suggest that if teachers are to engage children in intellectually challenging curricula they, themselves, need to have a deep level of understanding of that curriculum knowledge.

A further dimension emerged as important in our research – that of affect. The importance of affect in learning environments has long been acknowledged (e.g. Dufficy 2005). However, in Australia at least, this seems primarily to have been conceived in terms of supportive and warm classroom environment, where for example, children are understood as individuals, where they experience friendly and respectful teacher–student and school–community relationships. Our research confirmed the major importance of these elements in classrooms with high numbers of EAL children, but highlighted a further element in relation to affect – that of respect for children as learners. Of central importance here was teachers' expectation of their children's abilities. As indicated earlier, overall expectations of children's academic achievements were often low in our research schools. Yet when programmes that deliberately raised the level of intellectual challenge were implemented, teachers reported that their expectations of what many of their EAL children could achieve also rose. In turn, teachers' beliefs that their children were capable of intellectual engagement enabled the children to begin to conceive of themselves as successful learners, to be more confident in their abilities, to engage more seriously with curriculum knowledge, and to enjoy learning. Recognition of the power of high expectations is not new (Mehan 1992), but our research highlighted the interrelationship between respect for children as learners and what van Lier (2004) refers to as prolepsis – the ability for children to imagine themselves in a future where they are successful learners. It also highlighted ways in which such respect was realised in teacher–student interactions: where there was genuine space for children's voices; where children were regarded as 'worthy conversational partners' (Gibbons 2009); where what children had to say was listened to seriously; and where there was a reciprocity in the interactions between teacher and children (Dufficy 2005).

What can we conclude from this research that is relevant to the knowledge required of primary teachers who are working with EAL children?

First, the research confirms that what teachers do in their classrooms matter. It suggests that learning is not simply developmental, but rather the learning environment plays a major role in children's educational achievement. The teacher plays a central role in shaping the learning environment and in shaping the kinds of interactions that occur within classrooms, and, as a result, also plays a central role in children's educational achievement. The research confirms the importance of teachers' knowledge of theories of language and literacy, but also highlights the importance of theories of learning. It suggests the importance of teachers' deep engagement with curriculum knowledge and the importance of teachers' awareness of the role of affect, where account is taken both of children as people and as potentially successful learners. Thus outcomes from the research enable me to add to the list identified in the earlier Hammond and Derewianka (1999) paper. My list of what primary teachers need to know in order to work effectively with EAL children incorporates the list from the earlier paper, but can now be summarised as follows:

- theories of language and literacy, including knowledge of the nature of language, extensive knowledge of language systems at the levels of text, paragraph, grammar, vocabulary, spelling and punctuation; and an understanding of first and second language development;
- theories of learning, and an understanding of implications for planning, designing and implementing programmes designed to address specific needs of children in relation to demands of curriculum
- in-depth knowledge of relevant curriculum content
- knowledge about children as individuals and as learners: knowledge of the significance of affect in constructing supportive learning environments and knowledge of the impact of expectations on children's educational achievement; knowledge of intercultural understandings.

Conclusion

In this chapter, I have addressed questions of what it is that primary teachers need to know primarily from an Australian perspective and from the perspective of teachers who are working with EAL children. I have argued in the chapter that although there is a distinction between what EAL teachers need to know and what other teachers need to know, there are also substantial areas of overlap. The distinction, I have suggested, lies in the depth of knowledge required of EAL teachers, and in their abilities to recognise the specific needs of EAL children and to respond to those needs by developing programmes that both challenge and support. Thus I have argued that the knowledge that will enable teachers to work effectively with EAL students is knowledge that has a broader relevance to teachers' work with other students.

This knowledge, I have suggested, must include theoretically informed understandings of language and literacy, and of language development. While focusing primarily on knowledge about language and literacy, I have drawn on recent research into high-challenge, high-support pedagogies to argue that teachers need also to know about theories of learning, about relevant curriculum content, and about their students – as people and as learners. And finally, teachers need to know how to draw on all of the above to design and implement programmes that meet the specific needs of diverse learners.

Overall, my list of what teachers need to know is extensive. For applied linguists and educators involved with teacher undergraduate programmes, the task is to prioritise what knowledge is most important and most useful, and to be realistic about what is possible to achieve within an undergraduate programme. My own view here is that the highest priority is the development of an orientation to thinking theoretically about language, language development and learning. It is impossible for students to learn everything that is necessary, desirable and useful in their teaching of diverse students within the one undergraduate degree. However, it is possible for them to begin to develop theoretical understandings that will provide a framework for ongoing and cumulative learning over the lifetime of their professional work. Some years ago, Lo Bianco and Freebody (1997: 35) described this as developing a 'strong pedagogical framework'. I find this notion of a 'strong pedagogical framework' particularly useful as it highlights the importance of developing a strong theoretically informed basis from which decisions about planning and teaching can be made in a principled manner.

Preparing for diversity: the alternatives to 'linguistic coursework' for student teachers in the USA

Deborah A. Horan and Afra Ahmed Hersi

Introduction

During a one-on-one tutoring session, a pre-service teacher, Sharon, reads aloud a non-fiction children's book about water. The kindergarten child, Elaina, experiences this English text in her second language. On the last page, the book's illustration depicts a body of water, referred to in the text as a 'lake'. As Elaina reads the pictures, she reacts with certainty to Sharon's misreading of the printed words:

ELAINA: No. That's a pond.
SHARON: Well, it looks like a pond, but that's a lake. Do you know what a lake is?
ELAINA: No, but I have been to a pond.

Sharon and Elaina's interaction represents the challenge facing all educators, whether they are student teachers, qualified teachers or those working in initial and continuing teacher education contexts: No two children bring identical linguistic resources to their learning and increased linguistic and cultural diversity has become a common reality across all contexts. All educators must learn to build upon the diverse knowledge and experiences that pupils bring to the classroom. This includes the social, cultural and linguistic resources from both in-school and out-of-school literacy practices. The question facing policy makers concerned to find the most efficient way to develop teacher knowledge and the teacher educators who design pre-service courses is: how might student teachers, such as Sharon, best learn to develop the language and literacy resources of children, such as Elaina?

In this chapter we consider the challenges of preparing pre-service teachers for the range of linguistic diversity and literacy development existing within twenty-first-century classroom contexts. Such diversity transcends continents to encompass not only the USA (Gerald and Hussar 2003) but other places with similar demographic trends (Portes and Rumabaut 2001; Suárez-Orozco 2004).

Contextualised practice: a model for learning to teach reading in the USA

Today's classrooms are changing and in the face of such change it is important to ask how to effectively and efficiently prepare pre-service student teachers to meet the needs of the increasingly diverse pupil cohorts to be found in the twenty-first century classrooms. Between 1979 and 2007, the number of school-age children (children aged 5–17 years) in the USA who spoke a language other than English at home increased from 3.8 to 10.8 million (Planty *et al.* 2009). Statistics for large urban schools, such as New York City, reveal that 48 per cent of students represent more than 100 languages from immigrant-headed households. This growing wave of linguistic diversity is not limited to large cities. It includes rural areas and small cities, such as Dodge City, Kansas, where more than 30 per cent of the children enrolled in public schools are the children of immigrants (Suarez-Orozco and Suarez-Orozco 2001). These trends towards diversity are evident not only in the USA (Gerald and Hussar 2003), but in countries around the globe (see Hammond, Chapter 2 of this volume).

Yet despite these trends, the overwhelming majority of teachers in the USA do not have licensure, and have been given no relevant training, in working with language minority pupils or in teaching linguistically diverse pupils (Beykont 2002). The disparity between pre-service teacher preparation and current pupil needs has led US teacher educators to focus increasing attention on how pre-service courses for student teachers can better prepare them to be linguistically responsive (Grant and Wong 2003; Lucas *et al.* 2008). Some conversations about this emphasise the importance of pre-service student teachers 'knowing' more about language (Fillmore and Snow 2002; Kucer 2001) whilst others focus on pre-service teachers 'doing and applying' in the sense of developing practical knowledge through field-based experiences in contexts with linguistically diverse children (Homza, Ngo and Mitchell 2008). Equally important dialogues emphasise the need to problematise pre-service student teachers' cultural identities (Au 2002) and their attitudes and beliefs about cultural and linguistic diversity (Garmon 2004; Okawa 2000; Rogers, Marshall and Tyson 2006) to ensure equity and address unintended discrimination.

Common recommendations from those who advocate pre-service student teachers 'knowing' more about language have included adding a linguistics strand (such as an introductory course in linguistics) to pre-service teacher education courses or embedding language awareness into a required education course (Fillmore and Snow 2002; Gebhard *et al.* 2008). Supplementing required literacy methods with a linguistics course in this way seems a commonsense approach to expanding pre-service student teachers' knowledge and understanding of language and creating teachers who are more linguistically aware. However, questions remain about whether such linguistic knowledge may become decontextualised and whether it will automatically lead to linguistically responsive teachers unless there are opportunities to apply it by working closely with children in school-based or out-of-school settings (referred to here as *field-based experiences*). An alternative model, therefore, is one based on an authentic teaching apprenticeship. This model allows pre-service teachers to develop personal practical knowledge under the mentorship of instructors and supervisors (Golombek 1998; Harmon, Hedrick, Strecker and Martinez 2001). It provides time and a context that prompts student teachers to develop, apply and tease out the significance of their developing linguistic and instructional knowledge. It also has added potential of providing early and positive opportunities to recognise and address any misconceptions that pre-service teachers may hold about children from linguistically diverse backgrounds.

Knowledge and skills are essential in teaching, whether it is knowledge of the subject matter, of how to lead discussions, of how to organise and manage instructional groupings, or of how children learn. However, knowledge and skills about pedagogy and content are not enough for effective teaching (Darling-Hammond and Brandford 2005). Teachers' attitudes, their expectations and their knowledge of how to incorporate the cultures and linguistic experiences of pupils into their teaching also affect the quality and nature of the learning opportunities they offer. Thus teachers' wider sociolinguistic knowledge has a significant influence on what pupils learn.

Field-based experience within diverse contexts, allows pre-service teachers to develop this important sociolinguistic knowledge at the same time as developing their ability to apply it. The approach has the potential to target not only their knowledge base, but their understanding of how and why such knowledge matters. In Chapter 16 of this volume, Greg Brooks gives a personal illustration of the futility of providing useful information without a clear explanation of why it might matter. Field-based work helps student teachers to situate their developing knowledge and skills about teaching, particularly the teaching of reading, as a contexualised practice that should be influenced by the diverse cultural and sociolinguistic backgrounds of their pupils (Darling-Hammond and Brandford 2005; Lucas, Villegas and Freedson-Gonzalez 2008). Likewise, such authentic experiences situate learning to teach reading as a similarly contextualised sociolinguistic practice in the diverse population of teachers who work in US schools.

Many researchers have observed rich traditions of literacy and knowledge across different families, cultures and contexts which, if understood, acknowledged and appropriately built-upon by teachers, can lead to children who are linguistically and culturally diverse becoming more successful in school (Gandra 2002; Moll and Gonzalez 2004). In an influential study on the use of students' 'funds of knowledge' in classroom instruction, Moll and his colleagues (Moll and Gonzalez 2004; Moll and Arnot-Hopffer 2005) found that Latino/a students' academic performance is strengthened when students' community knowledge is tapped as a resource. Au (1980) found that when teachers' incorporate into their lessons, participation structures that are similar to 'talk stories' in Hawaiian culture, the reading achievement of Hawaiian second-grade students significantly increased. Similarly, in a four-year longitudinal evaluation of the *High School Puente Project* in California, Gandra (2002) found that those Latino/a students who participated in a rigorous academic preparation programme that incorporated community-based research and writing, academic counseling and opportunities to interact with community leaders, attended college at twice the rate of those who did not participate in the programme.

Heath (1983; 2000; 2004; Heath and Wolf 2005) has long argued that it is important for schools, policy makers and researchers to widen the lens and look beyond mainstream language and literacy practices in the design and delivery of the language curriculum. A deep understanding of teaching and learning as a contexualised practice, influenced by culture, is one mechanism that would enable pre-service teachers to draw on the language and literacy traditions that their pupils bring into the classroom (Gee 2002; Heath 1983; Au and Jordan 1981).

Developing applied sociolinguistic knowledge through field-based experiences

There are a number of models for building field-based experiences into pre-service teacher-education courses in the USA. Field-based experiences might occur within the primary school placements (such as student teaching placements) that, in the USA, are associated with teacher certification. Alternatively, field-based experiences might take the form of supplemental tutoring opportunities embedded within courses focusing solely on literacy methods and which are led by tutors with specific expertise in literacy.

Tutoring that is embedded within such literacy methods courses provides support and impetus for pre-service student teachers to engage in an iterative and reflective cycle, developing core knowledge of sociolinguistics, language and literacy development, teaching content and appropriate pedagogies alongside their understanding of the interrelationships between these elements. On a procedural and evaluative level, they can explore how to apply this knowledge to meet the needs of bilingual students, and then reflect on their experiences with the guided support of a literacy instructor. As a precursor to the experience of independent teaching, these supplemental field-based experiences can allow pre-service student teachers to construct more finely tuned understandings of children's individual language and literacy resources. With guided reflection, they learn to apply and tease out the significance of their linguistic and literacy knowledge and how this relates to their pedagogical methods, with the added potential of opportunities to recognise and challenge misconceptions about children and consider how to build creatively upon the language and literacy experiences that children bring into classrooms.

In the remaining part of this chapter, we share scenarios that focus on supplemental one-on-one tutoring of reading, as well as on other field-based experiences that occur before a full student teaching placement. These scenarios take place within a literacy course that focuses on reading instruction, both small group and whole class. They illustrate the potential of this social constructivist approach to develop useful learning, by which we mean learning that is embedded in practice and is therefore efficient and effective. We will address three important knowledge domains to illustrate this: how pre-service student teachers can learn to develop pupils' *academic language* using informational texts; how, with guidance from teacher educators, pre-service student teachers develop practical knowledge about *written language* development and finally how they learn about *morphology* and its connection to comprehension (and see Nunes and Bryant, this volume, who also discuss this issue). Common across these illustrations is the attention paid to linguistically diverse pupils within learning communities as pupils engage in language and literacy activities.

Academic language: meaningful interactions with informational texts

All children enter elementary school with the language resources they have developed in their communities and homes (Heath 1983; Pellegrini 2002). School learning requires that children confront new ways of using language; they must learn new and different language structures, learn to construct meaning from both oral and written language, learn to connect complex ideas and to recognise new genre features and text types. They will develop new linguistic and literacy strategies that will help them use different types of literacy and use literacy for different purposes (Diaz-Rico and Weed 2002; Duke 2000; Hall and Sabey 2007). Well-planned exposure to informational texts is particularly crucial for language learners that require the school context to develop academic English.

For pre-service student teachers, learning to plan effectively and to respond to the academic language needs of diverse children is one way to situate core language knowledge within reading instruction. Field-based experiences show pre-service student teachers such as Sharon, how to respond to the 'teachable moments' that arise when children like Elaina encounter new constructs, such as 'lake'. Sharon needed to instantly offer contrasting examples of the types of activities that could occur in ponds (rowing in a small boat) and lakes (water skiing with a speed boat) to convey the relative size of these bodies of water. In terms of developing this student teacher's core knowledge, the event illustrates how children acquire some word knowledge incidentally during reading. Her course work and reflective discussion with her teacher-educator, will enable Sharon to explore why *incidental vocabulary acquisition* alone is insufficient to meet the demands of academic language. From this, Sharon will understand why *intentional vocabulary instruction* is essential, particularly for bilingual pupils in US schools. She will understand that her pupil, Elaina's, heritage language differs from the standard academic American English that in most American establishments functions as the dominant or sole language of instruction. She will also learn that the research shows that even in early childhood, bilingual children such as Elaina benefit from sophisticated vocabulary instruction that scaffolds conceptual development through well planned 'read alouds' (Blachowicz and Fisher 2000; Blachowicz *et al.* 2006).

Such conceptual semantic development occurs when children integrate new words into their current schemas. Student teachers on pre-service courses must learn to facilitate semantic development through instructional methods such as semantic mapping (Nagy and Scott 2000) and through meaningful communications around literature that are strategic and responsive in building discussion of word meanings across several instructional experiences (see Vivienne Smith, this volume). Consider how one pre-service teacher, Amy, reflected on her field-based experience to build new practical knowledge about engaging bilingual children in opportunities that develop their oral academic language. Amy made the following connection to the reading methods course text, *Comprehension through Conversation* (Nichols 2006):

> I was very interested when Nichols referred to the issue of some children 'dominating the talk, while other find a corner to hide in' (p. 39). This is something that I've noticed happening [in her field-based experience]. During read-alouds we have the same couple of children answering while the others gaze around or quietly listen. One way I think would be effective for allowing each student to use their voice would be the turn-and-talk technique ... Having a partner and a less pressured setting to discuss their ideas may allow children, especially those that are English language learners, to develop their ideas, and practice them before coming together as a group to discuss them. (Amy, student teacher)

Nichols (2006) does not refer specifically to children learning English, but Amy connects what she is learning about language, reading and pedagogical methods. She attends to the children's oral language development and to their engagement with academic language. She develops this practical knowledge within the space that can be afforded to reflective thinking when a reading methods course embeds a content-focus that prompts specific attention to language and literacy within field-based experiences.

Situating linguistic content with Sharon's and Amy's reading methods course supports these pre-service student teachers in learning *how* and *why* they need to intentionally pre-select, foresee and plan for the academic language needs of children. The student teachers learn to become intentional about guiding pupils in developing their knowledge of academic language functions such as seeking information, informing, describing, comparing, ordering, classifying, predicting, analysing, inferring, justifying, persuading, solving problems, synthesising, generalising, and evaluating (Achugar *et al.* 2007; Menyuk and Brisk 2005; Schleppegrell and Go 2007). At the same time, they understand how to plan reading instructional approaches such as 'read alouds', shared reading, guided reading, independent reading, and they learnt to recognise texts that offer rich contexts for developing the syntactic patterns, semantic analysis and text features that typify academic language. They learn to orchestrate children's interaction with the texts in a manner that pays attention to both language and literacy and has space to explore both children's literature and trade books to navigate the tension between an explicit focus on genre-based structure and features with an understanding of the hybridity and evolving nature of genres (Pappas 2006). Finally, Sharon and Amy can develop their own metalinguistic awareness as they learn first-hand how to apprentice children into academic language.

Semantics and morphology: developing word analysis strategies

To know a word, children must develop a complex schema of literal and figurative meanings, semantically associated words, syntactic possibilities and constraints for word usage, and morphological inflections and derivations. To efficiently and effectively develop this knowledge requires effective word-learning strategies. With instruction in semantic analysis and context clue strategies, children are able to apply these strategies to future unknown words they encounter in semantically rich contexts (Baumann *et al.* 2003; Baumann *et al.* 2002). One effective aspect of morphemic analysis is cognate instruction. Cognate instruction allows some English language learners to bridge new English vocabulary with known words in their first language whenever their first language and English share similar etymologies. This is the case with Spanish, a common first-language in the USA. Spanish speakers who are English language learners' can develop their English language schema further if they are allowed to access to their native language, whether through reading, writing, or by speaking with peers or adults who share the English language learners' first language (Carlo *et al.* 2004).

In particular, meaningful contexts for writing can potentially facilitate English language learners in developing aspects of language awareness that might impact upon reading comprehension (Green *et al.* 2003). This is due to the 'deep orthography' of English in which spelling patterns are influenced by the deeper meaning contained in morphemes, whether word roots or affixes, rather than by more immediate sound-symbol correspondence. Hence, English words might retain certain letters or letter patterns although the associated pronunciation has shifted. For example, the c in technical and technician depend upon the bound morphemes al or ian (see Apel and colleagues, this volume). In contrast, languages such as Spanish reflect a 'shallow orthography' or 'transparent orthography'. These reflect more consistently the sound-symbol correspondences, which possibly facilitates decoding fluency (Ziegler and Goswami 2005). Researchers suggest that the morphological awareness developed through writing can support children's learning of phonetically irregular spelling patterns during reading (Carlisle 1995; Green *et al.* 2003). While more research is needed in this area, evidence suggests that phonological awareness contributes to decoding, but morphological awareness contributes to comprehension (see Nunes and Bryant, this volume).

Written language: a window to language development

Both reading and writing support children's development of new linguistic knowledge and field-based experiences can mediate pre-service student teachers' learning about language development as evidenced in children's writing. In developing knowledge of a new language, children who are English language learners build upon their pre-existing understandings of how written language works. By learning to analyse the language within children's writing, pre-service teachers can better understand the children's second language development (Palmer *et al.* 2007; Schleppegrell and Go 2007). When children write in both their first and second languages, effective analysis allows the teacher to support the children's explorations of the distinctions between the two language systems (Escamilla 2000). By allowing bilingual children to draw strategically upon both languages when writing, pre-service student teachers can facilitate an awareness of the distinctions between the first and second language that the children might not have otherwise seen. Even young children can begin noting interesting similarities and differences between their two languages, and do so without linguistic confusion, as long as they are provided with meaningful opportunities to write and to reflect on their writing through rich discussions (Frey and Fisher 2006; Purcell-Gates *et al.* 2007; Rubin and Carlan 2005). Writing extended text (as opposed to writing for skills-practice activities such as copying spelling words) can allow English language learners to explore the deeper meanings of language within an engaging and authentic experience. Amy, a pre-service student teacher on a reading methods course made the following observation about Kacie, a bilingual child:

A few weeks ago the children were writing their own books and I noticed that Kacie was writing her's about flowers. She asked me to write 'pink flowers' for her and I did on a sticky-note so that she could copy it. However, I noticed that when she went back to her book she simply checked my writing with hers; apparently she had written everything correctly! I was amazed with this and even more when she presented her book when she was finally done. She sat in the author's chair and proceeded to read her book, but she read it in Spanish. (Amy, Student teacher)

By noticing and guiding children in learning about language through their writing, as Amy had with Kacie, pre-service teachers can learn about the children's language development. With peers and the guidance of a course instructor or supervisor, pre-service student teachers can realise the linguistic resources that language learners actually bring to academic literacy in a second language, resources that are often overlooked or misinterpreted as problematic for learning (Gebhard *et al.* 2008).

Conclusion

The pedagogies we have described are intended to support pre-service student teachers in developing practical knowledge by situating them in contexts that require them to link theory and practice. It is not sufficient for student teachers to simply *know* about linguistics; they must understand how and when to use this knowledge. Whether guiding pre-service teachers in the form of field-based tutoring experiences that develop practical knowledge about how to foster academic vocabulary (Pearson *et al.* 2007), or exploring the cultural and linguistic backgrounds of their students (Lee 2007), these pedagogical strategies create spaces for reflection and critical dialogue about reading teacher preparation that are essential (Hoffman and Pearson 2000).

4 Supporting children with speech, language and communication needs

Maggie Vance

Introduction

One aspect of applied linguistics is clinical linguistics, defined as 'the study of the numerous ways in which the unique human capacity for language can be disordered' (Cummings 2008: 2).

Whilst clinical linguistics might be considered to be the domain of the speech and language therapist, children with speech language and communication needs (SLCN) are present in every classroom, and, therefore, one can argue the case for teachers to have sufficient linguistic knowledge to support these pupils. This chapter is primarily about spoken language. However, mention will be made of children with dyslexia, as similar issues pertain to this group. It will describe the range of speech, language and communication difficulties experienced by children in schools, addressing policy and practice issues. Different aspects of language will be considered to identify what knowledge might be useful for teachers and how it might be applied. Issues in teaching children from a minority language background who are learning through their second language are not addressed here, but are covered in the chapter by Letts (this volume). The UK educational context will be used to illustrate the key issues.

What are speech language and communication needs?

There are a number of ways in which SLCN can be defined. A clear description has been provided by Marshall, Ralph and Palmer (2002).

a child with a speech and language difficulty/communication difficulty was defined as one who does not communicate verbally as well as other children of the same age. For example, the child may have difficulties in understanding what other people say, constructing and saying (complete) sentences, pronouncing certain sounds, using language in a socially appropriate way, using their vocal cords (voice), stuttering or stammering ... This group does *not* include those children who experience difficulties in some situations because English is not their first/main language or because they have a strong regional accent or dialect. (Marshall, Ralph and Palmer 2002: 199)

Speech, language and communication needs (SLCN) may be specific in nature such that only speech, language or communication (SLC) skills are affected, in the absence of other areas of difficulty. These specific language difficulties are sometimes called the 'hidden disability', as they are not always easily recognisable by those less experienced in this area and children can become proficient at hiding their difficulties (Hartshorne *et al.* 2002). SLC difficulties may also arise in children with other developmental disorders including autistic spectrum disorder, moderate or severe learning disabilities, hearing impairment and physical disabilities. The oral language skills of children with dyslexia and with reading comprehension difficulties may also be compromised (Plaza *et al.* 2002; Nation *et al.* 2004; Rickets *et al.*, this volume). Research has shown that many children have language delay in association with a lower socio-economic background, performing well below the level expected for their chronological age on language tasks in which their understanding of language and their formulation of utterances is assessed (Locke *et al.* 2002). Children from lower SES backgrounds have also been found to have poorer vocabularies through the early years at school (Walker *et al.* 1994).

Indeed, SLCN are considered to be the most common difficulty in young children (Law 1992). Prevalence of more specific speech and language difficulties are estimated at 6 to 8 per cent of children (Law *et al.* 1998) and a greater number of children will have SLCN in association with other difficulties. In areas of social disadvantage up to 50 per cent of children have been found to have delayed language development (Locke *et al.* 2002). Of the 2.8 per cent of the school population in England whose problems are considered to be severe enough for them to receive a statement of Special Educational Need (SEN) 23 per cent of those in primary school have a statement specifically for SLCN (DfES 2006) and most children with SEN have difficulty with some aspect of speech language or communication. Children with SLCN 'include many of the most vulnerable children, those most in need of effective support to reach their potential' (DCSF 2008a: 2).

Any and all aspects of language may be involved for children with SLCN. They may experience difficulty with speech (phonology), with vocabulary development (semantics), with utterance or sentence formulation (syntax), with tense and/or plural marking (morphology), or with language use (pragmatics). The effects may be seen in recognition (comprehension) and/or production (expression) of spoken language. Poor spoken language development will also impact on children's written language skills in that speech errors will be reflected in their spelling (Stackhouse 2006). Reduced vocabulary knowledge, grammatical difficulties or difficulties in formulating sentences will also been seen in children's' written sentences (Butler and Silliman 2002).

Difficulty in understanding spoken language will also impact on children's reading comprehension (Nation *et al.* 2004).

What do teachers know about speech, language and communication needs and linguistics?

Interviews with teachers with a child in their class identified as having a language difficulty revealed that 21 per cent either had not heard the term 'specific speech and language difficulties' or did not know what it meant (Dockrell and Lindsay 2001). A YouGov survey (2007, cited by Morgan 2008) indicated that 73 per cent of teachers had no SEN training covering SLCN; 35 per cent were confident they had skills to support children with SLCN; and 81 per cent considered they needed more training in this area. Sadler (2005) surveyed primary school teachers who had at least one child with a pre-school diagnosis of speech and language difficulties in their class. Ninety per cent of these teachers did not remember having received any input on SLCN during their initial teacher training and 50 per cent of those who reported receiving some training felt it 'adequate' in meeting their present needs. None considered it 'good'.

Mroz (2006) interviewed early years educators to identify what they felt their training needs to be in the area of speech and language. She reported difficulties in accessing training. She suggested there was a need for changes at strategic planning levels to include the area of speech and language within initial teacher training, as this would enable teachers to utilise the English Special Educational Needs Code of Practice (DfES 2001b) to enable early identification of children's SLCN.

The findings from these studies carried out in the UK are confirmed by research in other countries. Moats and Foorman (2003) in the USA argued that specific and explicit linguistic knowledge was needed to address the needs of children across the range of reading and language skills. Primary school teachers completed a survey in which they demonstrated their ability to complete a number of items such as counting phonemes in words and identifying phonemes in words when there was not a direct phoneme-grapheme match. At least one out of four teachers was reported to have difficulty with this kind of task (and see Brooks, this volume).

Research in Australia confirms that teachers may not have a good knowledge of components of language, such as phonology and syntax. Sixty-five per cent of teachers completing a questionnaire rated their knowledge as average, 15 per cent above average, and 20 per cent poor or moderate (Williams 2006). Most teachers reported gaining this knowledge post-qualification through professional development sessions, and by networking with speech and language therapy (SLT) colleagues.

Why do teachers need to know about linguistics to support children with SLCN?

Most children with SLCN are educated in mainstream settings (Lindsay 2003; 2007). Given the prevalence figures above, mainstream classes on average will contain at least two children with SLCN (Lee 2008). Importantly, children with persisting SLCN are at risk of academic failure and impacts on later social, emotional and behavioural development (Clegg *et al.* 2005). They are also particularly at risk of literacy difficulties (Snowling *et al.* 2001). As language is the main tool for learning and teaching within the classroom children with SLCN are likely to struggle to access the curriculum. They may have difficulty with curriculum vocabulary and concepts used in maths (Parsons *et al.* 2005) and science (Wellington and Wellington 2002), and difficulty in learning through conversation with teachers and other pupils. Peer relationships can also be problematic with poor social interaction and lack of understanding of others' thoughts and feelings. Difficulties in understanding language are also associated with behavioural difficulties in school (Hooper *et al.* 2003). It is, therefore, important that teachers have the knowledge and understanding of language to ensure these children are well supported within the classroom and make the best possible progress.

One might assume that speech and language therapists (SLTs), who do have specialist applied linguistic knowledge, are the professionals who will provide support for children with SLCN. However, within the UK, SLT provision for children is very variable and some children in schools will not have access to these services (Lindsay *et al.* 2002). Even where SLT services are available, the therapist is unlikely to be working directly with the child, particularly where the child is educated in a mainstream classroom. The most common model of SLT service delivery in schools is consultation with school staff (Lindsay and Dockrell 2002). There are different interpretations of what consultation means. Law *et al.* (2002) report that in educational contexts consultation was assumed to mean working indirectly with a child through another person, such as a learning support assistant, rather than directly. This is considered to embody good practice as it avoids the need to take children out of class and embeds support in the curriculum (Law *et al.* 2002). Collaborative practice is described as a dynamic system in which there is co-equal interaction between teachers and SLTs (Hartas 2004), and is considered to be 'essential for successful intervention with children and young people with speech and language difficulties' (DfES 2001b: 105–106).

In order for this approach to be successful shared knowledge and understanding are required for effective communication between the professionals involved (Lindsay and Dockrell 2002). In England, the recent Bercow Report

(DCSF 2008b) reviewed services for children and young people with SLCN, and identified joint working as a critical issue. One recommendation states that standards for Qualified Teacher Status should ensure students develop better understanding of SLCN. Knowledge of linguistics would allow teachers to work together with SLTs to support pupils, and to provide more effective support where SLT services are not available.

Children with SLCN can present a challenge to the class teacher. Here are examples of children who have great difficulty in expressing themselves.

Richard, aged 8 years, describes the first picture in a series about making gingerbread men. He is having difficulty using appropriate words to describe what he sees, which includes a rolling pin:
'The ... it's a spoon . mixing it .. and there's a knife, a/sp/a fork . a egg . sugar and salt . and the roll the salt and the roll, roll the pen .. the pen to roll the thing out . and . and the ... and the ..um.' (Lewis and Speake 1997: 80)

Gordon, nearly 6 years of age, finds it difficult to formulate compete utterances with words in the appropriate order:
'the ... girl jumper over ... a gate'; 'news me like'; 'out now?' (Bryan 1997: 146 and 148)

Not only do Richard and Gordon have difficulty in expressing what they want to say, but they will also have difficulty in formulating written sentences in writing tasks. Expressive language problems may also be accompanied by comprehension difficulties impeding understanding of what people say to them.

What is included in the Initial Teacher Training Curriculum now?

There is currently no set curriculum for initial teacher training or requirement to include material on linguistics in the UK. In the UK units of study in the field of SEN were developed for use in undergraduate Initial Teacher Training (ITT) courses for primary teachers in 2008. This material is not compulsory. The unit on speech language and communication represents about three-and-a-half hours worth of teaching material (TDA 2008a). There is an introduction to the three main elements of language: form, content and use. The unit also describes ways in which teachers can support language development through the language they use with pupils, how lessons can be adapted, and how to develop narrative skills for their pupils with SEN. This is a useful starting point, although these materials contain little opportunity to develop in-depth linguistic knowledge. Dombey (this volume) provides an example of how teaching on linguistic knowledge can be successfully included in teacher training.

What linguistic knowledge could it be useful to include in initial teacher training?

Information about ages and stages of SLC development would be useful. Some children have SLC skills at the level of development usually seen in pre-school children, which may not be an area of knowledge for teachers training to teach school-age children. This understanding supports teachers in identifying the range of normal variation in SLC development, which differences are related to local dialect or accent and which might indicate a SLC delay or more persisting difficulty. Teachers could more reliably identify children with SLCN, and refer for specialist assessment, have realistic expectations for a child who is at a particular stage of SLC development, which may not be the same as their chronological age, and target support at an appropriate level, facilitating progress to the next level.

Speech and phonology

Certain types of speech difficulty may be associated with difficulty in developing the phonological awareness skills and phonic knowledge that underpin literacy development (Gillon 2003). Sound–letter correspondences may not be accurately learnt. Children with speech difficulties may also make spelling errors that reflect their underlying speech patterns. Detailed knowledge of phonetics and phonology will enable teachers to tailor their teaching of phonological awareness and phonics to the individual child. It will enable them to work with SLTs in developing more accurate speech production for those children with ongoing speech difficulties. It will enable them to analyse spelling errors. As dyslexia may arise from phonological deficits (Snowling 2000), children with dyslexia may also benefit from support by teachers who have a good understanding of phonetics and phonology.

For example, Luke, a 6-year-old child with a history of speech difficulties, has poorly developed literacy skills. Some examples of his spellings included $pig \rightarrow$ 'Bk'; $tiger \rightarrow$ 'tk', $dog \rightarrow$ 'Dk', suggesting that he confuses voiced and voiceless sounds in writing down /b/ instead of /p/ and /k/ instead of /g/. These kinds of errors can be seen in the spellings of younger typically developing children (Treiman *et al.* 1998, cited in Nathan and Simpson 2002; and see also Apel *et al.*, this volume). In this case the errors mirrored Luke's past speech difficulties (Nathan and Simpson 2002). These authors were able to identify that Luke had difficulty with perceiving the difference between matched voiced and voiceless sounds and continued to make some errors in his speech, and this information could be used to develop a programme to improve his literacy skills. Knowledge about how speech sounds are produced and the relationships between speech sounds that are acoustically similar or that are produced in a very similar way allows this level of analysis of errors to be undertaken. In the above example the error analysis can only be fully interpreted if the particular feature that differs in both /p/ versus /b/ and /k/ versus /g/ is identified, together with knowledge of which other pairs of sounds differ on the same dimension, such as /s/ and /z/.

As well as knowledge of the development of phonological skills and the most common sound confusions found in young children, another important skill for teachers is identifying which speech sounds are in a word (as this might be quite different from the orthography of the word). An anecdotal example illustrates why this is important. A class teacher was using children's names to develop knowledge of initial sounds. Her instruction was 'Stand up if your name begins with /k/', followed by the comment 'Why didn't you stand up Charlotte?' (The first sound of Charlotte is of course 'sh', /ʃ/, not /k/.) This lack of understanding of the sounds of speech versus orthography can only lead to misunderstanding in pupils, and there will be greater confusion for children with speech, language and literacy difficulties. Brooks, in this volume, argues for teachers to be taught elements of the International Phonetic Alphabet to support the teaching of phonics for reading and spelling.

McCutchen et al. (2002) have demonstrated how developing experienced teachers' language knowledge, in particular of phonology, has an impact on classroom practice and on pupil progress in reading and writing. Spear-Swerling and Brucker (2004) provided novice teachers with word-structure instruction and this had an effect on pupil's ability to decode words, suggesting that this knowledge was important in ensuring effective teaching of word decoding. Phonetics and phonology is viewed by some teachers as being the province of the speech and language therapist (Miller 1991). However, whilst many children learn to read and write with relative ease, a teacher's knowledge of phonetics and phonology will be highly important for this group of children with SLCN, given that they are at risk for literacy difficulties and may have difficulties with their speech.

Vocabulary

Children with SLCN often have reduced vocabulary, difficulty learning new words, finding words and saying words (Chiat 2000). Phonology is one of the elements of vocabulary development and new word learning in that children need to learn what new words sound like, and how to say them. Some children with language difficulties may find learning these new phonological forms difficult.

Eamonn aged 6 years:

'I want that ....deepersiper.
.... Where deedeepsiper? I dunno deedeepsiper is. Where's the deepbersiper?
The deepdeepsiper?' Eamonn wants a deep-sea diver! (Chiat 2000: 13)

Another key aspect of word learning is developing appropriate meanings. Crystal (1987) has argued for use of a 'semantic curriculum' for teaching vocabulary to children with language difficulties. This would focus on the 'internal structure of vocabulary, using the notions of semantic fields, sense relations, and semantic features' (Crystal 1987: 40). Whilst it may be possible to provide a carefully structured vocabulary curriculum within a specialist provision, most children with SLCN are educated in mainstream classrooms and need to learn the vocabulary of the school curriculum. However, the principles of structured vocabulary teaching might be usefully applied, as children with language difficulties may make errors with words due to missing or incomplete semantic representations (McGregor *et al.* 2002). Nation *et al.* (2004) also report semantic errors made by children with poor reading comprehension. The ability to analyse semantic errors and understand the relationship between different words will enable teachers to help these children develop their vocabulary knowledge.

Sentences

Children with language impairments tend to have difficulty with understanding and using more complex sentences, such as passive sentences (Leonard *et al.* 2006). Furthermore, well-constructed sentences rely on the appropriate use of verbs. Children with language difficulties are reported to have more difficulties in learning verbs than nouns (Windfuhr *et al.* 2002). For example, Travis, aged 6 years has difficulty with using verbs. In describing some actions he says 'sugar in the pot' to describe pouring sugar into the bowl; 'fruit on floor' to describe dropping apples; and 'tip in there' to describe emptying a jar (Chiat 2000: 165, 167). These examples also illustrate how the utterances of children with language impairments are characterised by omissions of function words (Chiat 2000).

Learning to use verbs requires learning about argument structures, again an area of difficulty for children with language impairments (Thordardottir and Weismer 2002). For example, using the verb *give* requires three arguments: an agent (or giver), a theme (what is given) and a goal (the recipient). This example is from a 10-year-old boy who either uses verbs or arguments but not both together. 'My dad's boss ... house. Down lane. Not farm. Walk up' (Chiat 2000: 145).

Children with language impairments also have difficulty with morphology, to the extent that the omission of elements such as tense marking and third-person singular are considered to be characteristic of specific language impairment (e.g. Rice 2000). Knowledge of morphology has also been found to support reading and spelling in children with dyslexia (Arnbak and Elbro 2000 and see Nunes and Bryant, this volume).

Analysing the errors in a child's language in order to provide appropriate correct models and support him/her to develop their language requires at least elementary knowledge of the semantic roles of words in sentences, grammatical analysis, mapping between semantics and syntax, and morphology.

Using language

Children who have difficulty with pragmatic aspects of language may not be those who struggle with semantic and syntactic elements of language. However, difficulties with social cognition have been found in association with language impairments in some children (e.g. Marton *et al.* 2005). Other children will have pragmatic impairments associated with autistic spectrum disorder or with other developmental difficulties, such as learning disability. Difficulties in using language will affect interaction with others such as peers and teachers. Here are two examples of how conversations with children with pragmatic difficulties can go awry. The responses of each of the children are unexpected in the given context. These might appear to be difficulties in understanding the other speaker, but such responses may occur in children who have adequate comprehension of the vocabulary and structure used. Rather, the problem may arise because the child is unable to abstract the meaning within the conversational context, and/or may not be responding directly to the speaker but following his or her own train of thought.

> A young boy (F) with an ASD is looking at a picture with his SLT (T).
> T. what are they eating?
> F. cake
> T. who's holding the cake?
> F. a circle
> T. who's eating the sandwich?
> F. the bread. (Perkins 2007: 18)

> A 9-year-old boy (C) with a language impairment is in conversation with an adult (A).
> A. So what did you do when you were sick?
> C. I can't remember
> I DID though when I was run over by a car. (Bishop and Adams 1989: 250)

This is typical of the kinds of difficulties in interaction shown by children with language impairments where the various 'rules' of conversation are not followed. The conversational partner can feel somewhat confused and fail to understand the pupil's meaning. The pupil's responses may not be relevant, and may not take into account the listener's existing knowledge. They may drift from the topic of conversation or make an abrupt change in topic. The children often fail to understand the teacher's meaning. Use of non-literal language is often problematic. Children with problems in using language can become socially isolated and will benefit from support to develop their skills in interaction.

A number of frameworks can be used to analyse conversations and identify where language use is breaking down. This can include speech acts which examine the function of different utterances, Grice's maxims which consider links between utterances and how they are understood and conversational analysis examining elements such as turn-taking within conversation and repair when the conversation begins to break down.

How can teachers apply linguistic knowledge in working with children with SLCN?

Qualified Teacher Status standards in England require teachers to be able to 'adapt the language they use to meet the learner they teach' (Standard Q25(c); TDA 2008b: 9). However, the adaptation required for children with SLCN may be challenging for those who have limited linguistic knowledge. Greater knowledge of linguistics will allow teachers to develop their awareness of 'teacher talk', analysing how language is used in the classroom for learning and teaching through questioning, elaboration and so on; to monitor and adapt their own language so that children can understand; to support children's language development in their teaching of phonics/phonological awareness, vocabulary, and sentence constructions; to analyse a child's language by exploring error patterns in spelling, word confusions and syntactic complexity (and see Ellis and McCartney, this volume).

We should not underestimate the complexity of the language used in the classroom. The following examples demonstrate how challenging the language used in the classroom might be for a child with SLCN. The first is a teacher talking to a child.

What sound does /cat/ begin with? No ... that's not what I asked. I asked what sound. Good ...We have two letters that make the /k/ sound. 'k' and 'c' make the same sound. How do you know that 'cat' does not begin with 'k'? Because I didn't put 'k' on the paper ... so you know it has to begin with 'c.' (Nelson (1984: 164) cited in Wallach 2004: 49)

The second example is from a mathematics workbook used in second-grade in the USA and demonstrates the 'language load' involved in story mathematics problems:

When you subtract 3 from me, you get 10.
Who am I?
Subtract me from 7. You will get 4.Who am I?
I am 6 minus 2 minus 4.Who am I?
(Wallach 2004: 49)

Knowledge of linguistics will allow teachers to modify the language of the classroom and to adapt the curriculum for children with SLCN. For example within the Primary National Strategy (England) one objective in speaking for Year 1 children (i.e. aged from 5 to 6 years) is as follows: tell stories and describe incidents from their own experience, in an audible voice (DCSF 2009d). This will be a difficult task for many children with SLCN who may not have the expressive language skills to produce a story or description. Linguistic knowledge allows the teacher to model a story for the child at an appropriate level in terms of the child's ability to understand and remember the length or complexity of utterance and the vocabulary the child will be able to produce. They will also be able to analyse the child's speech production to judge the child's intelligibility/audibility.

Conclusion

This chapter introduces children with speech, language and communication needs. Current gaps in teacher's knowledge with regard to SLCN and linguistics are highlighted. It may not be realistic for all the aspects of linguistic knowledge presented here to be included in initial training for primary teachers. However, there should be informed debate about which areas of language knowledge would be of most use. The debate should include consideration of the needs of children with SLCN and what linguistic knowledge and skills will allow these children to be best supported in school.

5 Foreign language teaching in the primary school: meeting the demands

Daniel Tierney

Introduction

On the continent of Europe the English language dominates, so much so that I once observed an English lesson in Spain, even though I could see France out of the classroom window. If you are a teacher in most of continental Europe, then you are usually introducing children to English as part of a continuing journey of developing linguistic competence in that language, usually from age 7 through to the end of secondary education, based on the Council of Europe's (2007) Common European Framework of Reference for Languages (CEFR). For teachers in the English-speaking countries of Britain and Ireland, and in some instances in continental Europe, other foreign languages are taught and teaching Modern Languages in Primary Schools (MLPS) means different things, dependent on the model adopted. As stated in the introduction to Part I, primary teachers are often teaching a language in which they are not fluent and which they have not studied to degree level, and where children have very limited exposure to the language outside the school. This means that the purposes and models of learning require detailed consideration, and the teacher's own learning will require support. The experience of Scotland is the main example considered here.

Models of language learning

Johnstone (1994) identified five models for teaching Modern Languages in Primary Schools (MLPS):

- awareness
- encounter
- subject teaching
- embedding
- immersion.

Language awareness is where children are introduced to different languages with a view to showing them how language works rather than developing specific competence within one or more languages. The *encounter* model is where pupils encounter different languages, learn a little bit of each language and develop a degree of competence in those languages. Again, the aim is more to develop awareness of language rather than to develop specific linguistic competence per se. Both of these models could be classified within what other authors refer to as sensitisation, or what the French refer to as *sensibilisation*.

The third model, *subject teaching*, is the model most frequently to be found to date within the Scottish context. In this, the aim is to develop the child's linguistic competence in one language and to extend the provision of that language, usually from age 9 or 10 over a longer period of time, but not necessarily to the end of secondary education. Low (1999: 754) outlined the aim of a Scottish pilot project which took place in 1989–93 before MLPS were gradually introduced to all primary schools in Scotland: 'The aim was to give pupils an extra year or two in which to develop their foreign language competence rather than develop insights into general patterns and structure(s) of language or cultivate positive attitudes towards the future learning of another European language.'

The fourth model, *embedding*, is where the language work is embedded within other curricular areas. This does not mean teaching the area through the medium of the foreign language, but relating the language work to other work which is in progress. To consider the example of the study of the European Union, the language work might include European Union countries or the colours of flags of those countries. The fifth model is *immersion*, where subjects are taught through the medium of the foreign language. This method is to be found particularly in Canada where bilingual education in French and English is the norm, in Wales where bilingual education in Welsh and English is provided, and also, in Scotland and Ireland, in Gaelic-medium teaching.

The aims of MLPS also vary. For some, the primary aim may be the development of linguistic competence; for others general language awareness, or the affective aim of developing positive attitudes to languages may be most important. Add to that the development of cultural awareness, citizenship and European awareness and we have a great diversity of competing aims. Referring to those aims and the age debate over whether teaching children at younger ages is better (which thankfully is outwith the scope of this chapter), Blondin noted: 'A great deal has been written on the subject, from which it has become clear that nothing has been definitively settled' (Blondin *et al.* 1997: 1).

In England, there is no one national model and the DCSF Key Stage 2 Framework (2005), as part of the National Languages Strategy's *Languages for all: Languages for Life* (DFES 2002a) embraces a flexible approach according to local circumstances. Thus a child might learn Spanish for the last four years of primary school or encounter German and French, or look at a range of languages including those with a non-Roman script, such as Urdu, Chinese or Japanese. Given that in England, according to the Centre for Information on Language Teaching, 14.3 per cent of all primary children have a first language known or believed to be a language other than English, the need for local flexibility is obvious, not forgetting the rich language resource in those classrooms. Sir Trevor McDonald (2008), the Chair of the Nuffield Languages Inquiry, stressed that 'rather than thinking in terms of an English only culture we should be promoting English plus'. The Centre for Information on Language Teaching (CILT 2009) argued against a multilingual language awareness model in its submission to the Rose review of the primary curriculum (Rose 2009: 104) and Rose recognised the different models while coming down in favour of a more focused approach:

> The review's recommendations do not preclude schools from providing opportunities to learn about several languages, for example, as they study other countries and early civilisations. However, it is the advice of the review that more sustained attention should be given to one or two languages to ensure that children make progress over four years in keeping with the expectations of the programme of learning. (Rose 2009: 104)

Scotland embarked on primary languages in 1989, much earlier than other UK countries or Ireland. The model adopted was the linguistic competence subject-teaching model. Giovanazzi, the HMI responsible at the outset, described it as 'no mere softening up process' (Sharpe 2001: 123). That model remains in place although there is perhaps more emphasis on transferable language skills in Learning and Teaching Scotland's (2009) new Curriculum for Excellence. Whichever model is chosen, there is a greater emphasis than before on how language works. One of the failings of previous attempts at introducing languages into primary schools has been the inability of pupils to manipulate language: 'pupils were unable to transfer vocabulary and expressions learned in one context to another which varied even slightly from the one in which they were first taught' (SED 1969: 16). Children need to go beyond simple parroting of language and understand how the language works.

Linguistic knowledge and sound patterns

As outlined earlier, the linguistic knowledge required by the teacher will vary according to the model adopted. Thus teaching Spanish over four years will need more in depth knowledge of that language than teaching Spanish as one of two or three languages in the encounter model. A good starting point, whether a teacher of English on the European continent or a MLPS teacher, is accurate pronunciation of the key sounds of the foreign language. There is some consensus on the benefits of an early start in language learning for the development of pronunciation. Guberina (1991) claimed that young children appear to be especially able to acquire the sound system of a foreign language almost achieving native speaker level. Driscoll (1999) argued that there is strong empirical evidence with regard to superiority in oral/aural performance and cited Singleton (1989) in support. Tahta *et al.* (1981) and Vilke (1998) claimed that young children have more accurate pronunciation, are able to imitate sounds more accurately and become less able to do so as they grow older. Johnstone also emphasised the point: 'Provided they are exposed to good models, younger learners will have a clear advantage over older learners in the acquisition of quasi-native speaker level of pronunciation and intonation' (Low 1996: 43). Whereas Mitchell, Martin and Grenfell (1992) concluded that previous research had not demonstrated beyond doubt that young learners were more effective, except maybe in pronunciation, Low noted pronunciation as one of the benefits of an early start in the above-mentioned Scottish pilot project: 'This advantage was most evident in pronunciation, intonation, readiness to use communication strategies and ability to sustain patterns of initiation and response' (Low 1999: 755). Scottish HMI in their Standards and Quality report also noted that 'many pupils showed good mimicking ability' (SOEID 1999: 12).

I was reminded of these points from the literature as I sat observing a primary French class one morning in a deprived part of the city of Glasgow, Scotland, only a few hundred yards from the secondary school where I had been a young teacher. I witnessed, thanks to a good primary teacher, complete accuracy in pronouncing u [y] as in *du pain (some bread)* and ou [u] as in *douze* (twelve). My mind wandered back to how I had struggled as a teacher with the inability of 13- and 14-year-old boys in my class to produce these sounds accurately, and yet here were their younger counterparts doing it with ease. The primary teacher of French has many opportunities to develop these sounds in common French words, for example *bonjour (good morning)*, *salut (hello)*, *où habites-tu? (where do you live?)*, *rouge (red)*, *douze (twelve)*. The pronunciation of the [y] sound is one of the difficult ones, particularly for many young Scots and Northern Irish pupils.

The French teacher can help the young person create a number of sound patterns, written:

> r as in quatre (four), avril (April)
> é as in décembre (December), février (February)
> è as in père (father), mère (mother)
> the nasal sounds on, an, en, in as in *onze (eleven), ans (years), trente (thirty), vingt (twenty)*
> the au sound as au revoir (good-bye), de l' eau (some water)
> the qua sound as quatre, quatorze, quarante

For the Spanish teacher the following are the key sounds:

> j as in *junio (June), julio (July).* (easy for the young Scots!) (loch)
> rr as in *perro* (dog) (also easy for Scots, but not so much for the young Essex girl)

c as in cinco (five), doce (twelve), trece (thirteen) but also
c as in cinco (five), catorce (fourteen)
ñ as in señor (Mr), señora (Mrs), cumpleaños (birthday)

For German:

au as in auf Wiedersehen (good-bye), Frau (Mrs)
ch as in nacht (night)
ö as in möchte (like)
d as in und (and)
zw as in zwanzig (twenty)
v as in vor, von (before, from)
w as in wagen (car)

For Italian:

ci, ce as in cinque (five), cento (hundred)
ca, co as in cane (dog), colore (colour)
gio as in buongiorno (good morning)
uo as in uomo (man)
i as in cinque (five), dieci (ten)

Vivet (1995) pointed out how foreign languages can introduce children to a world of sounds, positive sensations, new discoveries and stimulating acquisitions which go far beyond the boundaries of monolingual and monocultural education' (Vivet 1995: 6). The young language learner starts to imitate the key sounds, but she or he only usually hears it in the classroom context and is perhaps a little more self-conscious. Thus the primary school language teacher needs to take every opportunity to expose their pupils to key sounds whether it is through greetings, such as *bonjour (good morning)*, *ciao (hello)*, use of praise *excellent*, *bravo*, through classroom instructions or through songs, games or stories. In storytelling, for example, in the story book, *Mr Gumpy's Outing* by John Burningham (1971), in the Spanish class, Mr Gumpy becomes *el señor Jímenez (Mr Jímenez)*, exposing the pupils repeatedly to certain key sounds. This development of pronunciation is actively encouraged in the National Framework in England (DCSF 2005). 'Learners need to assimilate new sound patterns and to relate them to words and meanings. This process is particularly important in the early stages of acquiring a language when learning habits are being established and with young learners who are particularly receptive to new sounds' (DCSF 2005: 6).

The primary language teacher also needs to be aware of aspects of phonetic reduction such as elision. Time is a common teaching topic in the MLPS classroom. The teacher of French needs to know that the numbers *six, dix (ten), neuf (nine)* become *il est six heures, il est dix heures, il est neuf heures (it is six, ten, nine o' clock).*

Language anxiety

Some writers argue that young learners are less self-conscious and more willing to have a go but as Rivers points out, the language classroom is 'a fertile ground for frustration, anxiety, embarrassment and humiliation' (Rivers 1964: 92) and recent research (Gregory 1996; Poole 1999; Driscoll 2000; Tierney 2009) has identified considerable language anxiety, even among younger pupils. As one young boy put it:

'I quite like speaking in French but when you have to say something out loud everybody laughs. I do not like speaking out loud ourself' (Tierney 2009: 100). The primary language teacher needs to create a stress-free environment where the pupil is not put on the spot but is speaking in a group, with a partner, or if he wishes to do so, as part of a language 'game'. Obviously, the more accurate the pronunciation the better but the aim of being native speaker-like is probably counter-productive and not necessary, as long as communication is achieved. In the national Irish pilot project, Harris and Conway (2002) noted that many pupils found the language experience to be 'fun' with lots of variety. The use of this approach is widespread throughout Europe and ludic uses of the language with games such as 'Happy Families' for family members, 'Guess Who' for descriptive language, songs and stories help to minimise the language anxiety; even primary-aged children have pointed this out to us. Because of this some writers, such as the eminent Polish linguist Komorowska, argued that children learning a foreign language should not be required to speak in the early stages. 'That is why, especially at the early stages of learning, the focus should be on listening for comprehension, accompanied by the so called 'silent period' where children are not pressurised into speaking unless they themselves attempt to do so spontaneously' (Doye and Hurrell 1997 55). Smith too argued for a silent period (Hurrell and Satchwell 1996) to allow pupils to listen and absorb the cadences of the foreign language.

Spelling and pronunciation

The language teacher also needs to develop the pupils' understanding of the phonology of the target language, to be able to link simple phonemes and spellings. The teacher of Spanish, having previously met the challenge for her pupils of pronouncing the written word '*once*' in English, now has to lead the child to understand that '*once*', the number 11 in Spanish, is pronounced '*onthay*', like the English 'th' in thin. At least Spanish is logical in that the final syllables of 12 (*doce*), 13 (*trece*), 14 (*catorce*) and 15 (*quince*) are pronounced the same way so pity the poor teacher of English in Spain meeting the English word '*once*'. The child looking at a map of France and seeing the town of '*Blois*' should be able to use previous knowledge of '*trois*' (three) to pronounce it accurately. Orthographic competence also needs to be developed in the foreign language. New 'weird' lines, symbols and so on in foreign languages are fairly straightforward but need explanation and to be demystified for the young language learner. The months of *février* (February) and *décembre (December)* should be linked for the child learning French just as *señor (Mr)*, *años (years)*, *cumpleaños (birthday)* should be for the child learning Spanish. Unless the language teacher does so, then it is hardly surprising that a girl comments: 'I don't really like reading French because the words are so different and there are weird symbols; it's quite hard to read French and pronounce the words' (Tierney 2009: 110). The child learning French or Spanish will meet many cognates such as *orange, table, hotel*, as well as silent letters in *violet, gris (grey), hotel, hola (hello)*. They need to be aware of the sound patterns to be able to pronounce these words reasonably accurately and free from mother tongue interference.

Dictionary and alphabet knowledge

Many young children are proud that they can count from one to twenty or above in a new language or recite a different alphabet. For the child learning Spanish there is the discovery of new letters in *ch, ll* and *ñ*. It is in the early language learning class that a child is introduced to the concept of a bilingual dictionary with two parts and sections with head words with such new letters.

As well as their dictionary skills, the primary language teacher will further develop children's knowledge about language. In the foreign language lesson the concepts of gender, masculine and feminine nouns and adjectival agreements will be explained. The child needs to become aware that, for example, days and months do not take capital letters in French, Italian or Spanish; that the conventions of word order might differ from English (*un triangle rouge (a red triangle), un cercle bleu (a blue circle), un carré vert (a green square))*; that punctuation may be different (*¿Cómo te llamas?* (What is your name?) *¡Estupendo!* (Wonderful!)).

Grammar knowledge

Pluralisation and negation are looked at and compared with how these are done in the native languages found in the classroom, whether that is Irish, Welsh, Urdu or Polish. Question forms too should be developed from the simple communicative *Ton nom est?* to *Quel est ton nom?*, *Comment t'appelles-tu?* to *Tu t'appelles comment?* (what is your name?) The pupils' listening skills need to be developed so they are not thrown by the simple change of word order of the question and to recognise the rising intonation in the question form. Simple connectors and modifiers should also be taught and the pupils shown how to build their language, for example *Je suis anglaise mais j'habite au Pays de Galles. (I am English but live in Wales)/Il fait assez chaud. (It is quite hot).*

The primary language teacher also needs to combine his or her knowledge of language with sociocultural competence. These include the conventions of politeness in the target language, when to use *tu/vous* (you) in French, *tú/Vd* (you) in Spanish, *tu/lei* (you) in Italian and *du/Sie* (you) in German. How does one greet people in that culture? By handshaking, bowing, by kissing on the cheeks ... oh, and how many times?

Communication strategies and confidence

The MLPS teacher should also develop strategic competence. The learner needs to learn how to be understood by the use of paralinguistic communication such as mime, gesture, rephrasing; how to repeat something to obtain confirmation from the interlocutor; how to seek assistance from the foreign speaker by asking him/her to slow down, to repeat, to rephrase. The CEFR highlights the need for existential competence; for example 'the willingness to take initiatives or even risks in face to face conversation, so as to afford oneself the opportunity to speak, to prompt assistance from the people with whom one is speaking, such as asking them to replace what they have said in simpler terms etc.' (Council of Europe 2007: 12).

Obviously, a greater knowledge of vocabulary in the foreign language helps but the language learner also needs the strategies to cope and to take initiatives and these need to be developed at the early stages. They also need to transfer their existing language resource to make sense of a reading passage in the foreign language. The CEFR points out how 'those who have learnt one language also know a great deal about many other languages without necessarily realising they do' (Council of Europe 2007: 70). They may search for clues as to a passage's meaning, identifying words such as *danger, bombes, Londres, départ, enfants, jardin* and so on in a passage about wartime evacuation, or dates, city names, accommodation on an Internet travel website.

The issue of 'language anxiety' was raised earlier. Closely linked to this is the issue of error tolerance, the need for the teacher to build confidence and communicative competence. The child saying 'I have eleven years' or '*Je suis onze ans*' has made an error but a native speaker will understand what they are trying to say. There is a need for sensitive correction or even complete tolerance, dependent on the child's stage of learning and confidence. Errors are part of the language learning process and 'language is a matter of horizontal as well as vertical progress' (Common European Framework of Reference 2007: 17). Just as with their mother tongue, children go through different stages of trial, error and correction as they communicate.

Progression

In all models considered above, there is obviously linguistic content and over four years in a subject teaching model, there will obviously be greater content. A typical programme might begin with the alphabet and numbers. The young pupil learns how to say and spell out her name and ask others their name. He or she learns greetings and farewells, not forgetting the sociocultural competence mentioned earlier. The foreign language becomes the natural language of the classroom for common instructions, for asking permission, for asking for objects such as a pencil or ruler and of course for lots of praise. The date and the weather is recorded on the class wall and/or noted in notebooks. The days, the months of the year, the seasons and the weather associated with those seasons are learned. Clothes too are a common topic and often linked in the language programme to weather and to countries. When countries and nationalities are taught, they are often within the context of a project, for example the European Union, and once again there is an opportunity to develop pronunciation, for example the underlined sections of *Angleterre, Irlande, France* (England, Ireland, France) sound similar. Another common area which can be recycled in the context of clothes is colours. The teaching of time in the foreign language lesson allows the teacher to revisit and reinforce concepts already met. The pupil is beginning to build up a new language but there is the need to go beyond 'noun pumping', the learning of ten fruits or ten colours divorced from context or understanding of how the language works. Food and drink feature too in the context of likes/dislikes (surveys), café scenarios and shopping, with many opportunities for reinforcing of numeracy as well as social skills. Town places or *le village* offer the opportunity for significant language development. Who lives there, how old are they, what do they do, what do they look like, what are the different buildings and where are they? Pupils too enjoy talking about themselves, their families, their pets, their hobbies. Transactional language received 'a bad press' in language learning after too much time was devoted in one course book to ice cream flavours and too much ice cream was obviously not good for children. Nevertheless, in the early stages of language learning, it remains important that the learner is equipped to handle situations in which he or she might find herself, such as buying a ticket, asking for directions, or even buying the odd ice cream.

Developing the linguistic skills of the primary teacher

There are many ways of developing the linguistic skills of the primary teacher. Of course, as outlined above, it depends on what the objectives are. In Scotland, because the aim is to develop linguistic competence, the teachers were given a twenty-seven-day programme of language training, designed at national level, to meet their specific needs for the primary classroom. In most of continental Europe, where the aim is development of English, teachers will follow a specialist pre-service route in English language. Where the aim is more to develop language awareness or specific skills, teachers might be given more specific short training courses to apply their existing knowledge.

The BBC-online service provides a primary French or Spanish course that covers the main topic areas and could be a useful starting point for a primary teacher wishing to refresh their language. The Centre for Information on Language Teaching offers online training: 'The Language Upskilling Specification' Its purpose is mainly to meet the needs of teachers in England as languages become a statutory requirement there from age seven and therefore 'to support the development of language upskilling courses for primary teachers and teaching assistants enabling them to move from 'beginners' to 'intermediate' or even 'advanced' levels. Although general enough to respond to the broad needs of adult language learners it includes many contexts specific to teaching and learning and so will be of particular value for those working in primary schools' (Centre for Information on Language Teaching 2009).

Conclusions

The primary school language teacher has no way of knowing which language will be required in the future, although for the non-English speaker, English is a safe bet. The primary teacher therefore, in all models, should develop pronunciation, phonemic awareness, confidence, intercultural understanding, strategic competence and some aspects of knowledge about the language(s). In doing so, the learner should be encouraged to discuss how to learn a foreign language, all of the above, but also the following: decoding skills, memorisation techniques and social conventions such as turn taking. In future, whether on a business trip to Croatia or a holiday in Slovenia, the anglophone language learner may well engage in a bilingual conversation where a mixture of the target language, English, mime and gesture is used to achieve communication. The writer would argue that the anglophone learner needs skills and strategies, combined with partial competence in two major European languages rather than attempting near-native competence in one. The development of skills in reading and listening should take greater prominence than hitherto, with some development of the productive skills of speaking and writing. The anglophone learner will understand the foreign speaker, whether spoken or written, but be able to respond in English or a combination of the two languages.

Primary school language learning means so many things to so many people. The primary school language teacher needs to choose the model that best suits and then use it to define the aims and objectives. These need to ensure progression and prepare for future language learning. In an anglophone country, there is no guarantee of continuing the same language into secondary school so there is a very clear need for effective transition. Therein lies perhaps the greatest challenge for primary languages.

Part II

The range and focus of applied linguistics research

Introduction to Part II

Sue Ellis and Elspeth McCartney

The chapters in Part II provide examples of the new knowledge that is being generated by applied linguistics research. This knowledge has implications for the primary school curricular content, for pedagogy and for policy development in the primary sector.

It would require a work of many volumes to give a comprehensive account of all the applied linguistics research that has implications for primary school teaching. These chapters, therefore, are illustrative of the range and scope of such research. The chapters represent a range of disciplines and enquiry methods. They show the different ways that research is addressing the concerns of primary teachers and policy makers, with implications that range from curriculum content to pedagogy, teacher understanding, and language and literacy policy and policy implementation.

Part II begins with two chapters describing research that challenges traditional conceptions of grammar teaching. Whereas traditional grammarians often focus on what people *should* say and write, Debra Myhill focuses on what people *could* say and write whilst Alison Sealey focuses on what they *do* actually say and write. Myhill's research asks teachers and children to focus on writers as designers, so that *how* they tell becomes as important as *what* they tell in their writing. This produces a pedagogy that promotes creative and critical understandings of language choices and their effects, and challenges traditional ways of teaching both writing and grammar. Alison Sealey develops the theme of grammar teaching and describes her research on using corpus analysis with children to provide an inquiry- and evidence-based vision of teaching grammar that can both empower and excite young learners.

The next two chapters both come from authors steeped in the background of English literature and literary criticism. Vivienne Smith takes up a theme introduced by Debra Myhill; the importance of words as more than 'carriers of the message or plot'. She challenges the dominance of picture analysis in recent writing about picture books and suggests three approaches to help teachers analyse the text of picture books, to build new understandings of the power of the text, its interrelationship with the pictures and how it can be introduced and used with children. Elspeth Jajdelska is interested in building pedagogical capacity in a different form. Her study explains how economic, technological and social changes in the late seventeenth and early eighteenth centuries changed how books were read, and led to changes in the nature of written texts. This historical narrative can help teachers today to notice and understand some of the comprehension challenges that modern children's books present for novice readers.

Two big factors that commonly impact on literacy attainment are socio-economic status and gender. Neither of these can be adequately explained by a focus that is purely on the linguistic structure of texts or on text processing skills. Gemma Moss reminds us that literacy learning is a social as well as a cognitive event and that communities 'do' literacy in different ways. She describes linguistic ethnography as an emerging area of applied linguistics research in which researchers study, often fleeting, literacy events to understand what the event means to the participants and seek to determine the potential power relations between different ways of 'doing' literacy. Her research sheds light on overlooked curriculum changes and the interactions around texts that they afford, to explain their import for different participants.

Chapters 11 and 12 both detail applied linguistics research that addresses different aspects of text processing skills. Terezinha Nunes and Peter Bryant provide a detailed account of the evidence for the role that morphological knowledge plays in learning to read and spell. Their elegant empirical studies of children show that teachers need to know about more than phonics and comprehension if they are to teach literacy efficiently and effectively; they need a deep understanding of English orthography and of how it relates to the representation of sounds and morphemes, and they need to understand the role of morphological knowledge in word reading, spelling, reading comprehension and vocabulary learning if they are to teach literacy efficiently and effectively. Jessie Ricketts and colleagues argue for a strong focus on the processes of comprehension. Their evidence is that poor comprehenders can be missed by teachers and by some of the reading tests that are commonly used in primary schools. Whether children's problems lie in discourse-level processing, oral language, working memory or a combination of factors, they need to be recognised and addressed early if they are not to disadvantage the child.

The final two chapters of this Part deal with different aspects of oral discourse as a central aspect of learning in the classroom. Adam Lefstein and Julia Snell unpick the complexities of classroom dialogue, and the implications for pupil learning. They illustrate how classroom dialogue can be analysed to help teachers understand and recognise particular styles and norms of dialogue, and the mechanisms whereby these promote or inhibit pupil learning. Angela Creese ends this Part with a timely reminder of the different linguistic backgrounds of children in a modern classroom. She identifies four principles, based on empirical research, to guide teachers' actions. Her final point, that teachers are 'agents of change and through their practice can both endorse but also challenge prevailing ideologies' is one with which, we suspect, all the chapter authors in this book will agree.

6   Grammar for designers: how grammar supports the development of writing

Debra Myhill

Introduction

The mechanic should sit down among levers, screws, wedges, wheels etc. like a poet among the letters of the alphabet, considering them as the exhibition of his thoughts, in which a new arrangement transmits a new Idea to the world. (Robert Fulton – nineteenth-century engineer)

A synergy between the work of a mechanic and the work of a writer is not the most obvious one, perhaps, yet Robert Fulton's analogy (Barlex and Givens 1995: 48) between the mechanic and the poet is an apt one. Both have to create products from the materials available, be that physical materials or linguistic resources; both have to test things out to see how they work; both have to make choices and decisions about the purpose of their work; and both have to evaluate their work critically before presenting it to the world as a new creation. At the heart of this creative activity is the concept of design. This chapter sets out to illustrate how, within a theoretical framework that conceives of writers as designers, linguistic resources and linguistic understanding play a crucial role in supporting the development of design capability in writing.

Writers as designers

I should like to lay the foundation for this chapter by elaborating the framework of writers as designers before narrowing the focus more specifically to the role of grammar and linguistics in a pedagogy of writing. The *Online Etymology Dictionary* (2009) indicates that the word, '*design*' derives from the Latin '*designare*', meaning to mark out or devise, signalling both deliberateness and intention in the activity. Its ultimate root is, of course, '*signum*', meaning a mark or a sign: historically, writing originated through marks made on stone (see, e.g., Harris 1986) and writing is intrinsically a sign-making activity. Thus the connection between writing and design is inscribed in the etymology of the word '*design*'. Moreover, the way we, as teachers and theorists, describe writing has much in common with the language of design. Pedagogically, we recognise writing both as a *process* involving generating ideas, drafting, editing and revision, and as a *product* – so we may talk about admiring the writing of Philip Pullman, meaning the novels he has written (product) or we may talk about finding writing difficult, meaning that we find it hard to transform ideas into written text (process). Similarly, that the activity of design is both a product and a process is reinforced by the function of the word as a noun or a verb, referring either to the outcome of a design process or to the design process itself. As teachers, we talk of modeling, drafts, evaluation, purpose and audience, concepts, which are equally embedded within the discourse of design, and cognitively, models of writing and models of design point to both as problem-solving activities, with plans, goals and intentions. The International Technology Education Association defines design as 'an iterative decision-making process that produces plans by which resources are converted into products' (ITEA 2009). This sits well with our pedagogical models of writing which aim to encourage writers who can draft, edit and revise, even though for many primary school writers and older low-attaining writers, writing remains very much a linear product-driven process. Developmentally, becoming a designer of writing parallels a growing command of linguistic resources, a broadening understanding of the multiple ways in which written texts communicate meaning, and a deepening sense of one's own identity as a writer.

The notion of writing as design in literacy research is not wholly new. Sharples (1999) described writing as creative design, arguing that writing is a problem-solving activity in which writers make choices in order to shape texts to fulfill their communicative goals. He maintained that 'an important part of developing the skill of writing lies in being able to understand the way we write, and how to alter it to suit the different audiences and demands of writing' (1999: 12) and suggested that the period from 10 to 14 years of age is critical to the development of writing abilities because at this age, significantly, 'children can talk about how they write as they write, rather than reading what they have written' (1999: 20). In general, however, the principle of design in relation to texts has related to multimodality and especially the visual elements of textual practices. Kress (1997: 127) argued that children's early attempts at writing are about design: young writers construct meaning from available resources in an active and transformative way which creates new meanings and new possibilities. A more sustained articulation of design is provided in Kress and van Leeuwen's (2001) exploration of the grammar of visual design, focusing on a social semiotic theory of making meaning from multi-modal texts. They note 'the incursion of the visual into many domains of public communication where formally language was the sole and dominant mode' (p. 13) and argue that the texts which children readily encounter in out-of-school contexts 'involve a complex interplay of written text, images and other graphic elements' which 'combine together into visual designs' (p. 15). Kress and van Leeuwen critique curriculum policy which ignores these influences on writing and instead preserves and valorises very conventional writing genres, dominated by verbal text. A similar point is made by QCA/UKLA (2004: 5), who observe that changed textual practices in a multi-media age relate not only to texts outside of school but also that 'Much learning in the curriculum is presented through images, often in the double-page spreads of books, which are designed to use layout, font size and shape and colour to add to the information or stories contained in the words. Such designed double-page spreads, whether in picture or information book, make use of spatial arrangements to convey ideas'. Drawing on examples from early years writers, the authors demonstrate how spatial features such as visual blocking are equivalent to the linguistic structuring achieved through paragraphing, and how visual detail and colour substitute for adjectives.

However, perhaps the most developed view of design in the context of literacy is provided by Cope and Kalantzis (2000), emerging from the thinking of the New London Group. Rooted in a view of literacy as social practice, they see the process of making meaning from texts and in creating texts as essentially transformative: 'every moment of meaning involves the transformation of the available resources of meaning' and this transformation is always 'a new use of old materials, a re-articulation and recombination of the given resources of Available Designs' (2000: 22). 'Available Designs' are the resources at hand for meaning-making, whilst 'designing' is 'the work performed on or with Available Designs in the semiotic process' (2000: 23). The consequence of this process of design is 'the re-designed', that which has been created and transformed through designing. They identify six aspects of design: linguistic, visual, multi-modal, audio, gestural, spatial, each with their own grammars. This conceptualisation of design, however, is an all-encompassing explanation of literate practice, which is not exclusive to writing.

The emphasis upon the visual and the multi-modal is dominant in almost all articulations of writing as design. Indeed, Janks (2009) states that 'design is the concept used to refer to multi-modal text production' (p. 130), implying that design is less about the writing of verbal text and much more about the final stages of text production when 'writers and publishers have to decide on the overall design of the page'. We have argued (Maun and Myhill 2005) that the notion of writing as design should embrace the verbal as well as the visual, a process in which writers shape ideas into meaningful text using linguistic resources, as well as visual or spatial resources. This design capacity gives writers creative and communicative dexterity, a way of playing with and stretching language to its limits to achieve what the writer wants the writing to do. Janks argues that control of grammar allows us as writers to 'produce the nuances we need to realise the meaning potential that language affords us. What is selected from the range of lexical and grammatical options determines how this potential is realised' (2009: 131). From the moment a child scribbles his or her first marks on a page there are elements of design evident in the choices made. In the extract below, 6-year-old Frankie is creating a Gumdrop story of his own, following a visit by Gumdrop creator, Val Biro, to his classroom. He chooses to draw on his own experience of a visit to Longleat, and the 'cheeky monkeys' he encountered, to provide the setting for the story. The choice of the sentence opener, '*If you look closely, you might see ...*' with its use of the second-person pronoun to address the reader directly, is an example of a linguistic design choice.

> *This is the nisy amazing longleat. There are some very cheeky monkeys there. If you look closely you mite see some juicy fruit and a grey rhino. Because it has ascaped. I hope he dosent see gumdrop or mr old castele or Black Horace.*

I would suggest that an effective pedagogy for writing in both primary and secondary classrooms should be built upon this idea of design, and in particular the principle of writers as designers. This foregrounds the writer at the heart of the process. Supporting the development of a design repertoire upon which the writer can draw requires attention not just to visual elements of design but also to the linguistic shaping and structuring of text. It is the creative potentiality of linguistics within this design repertoire which this chapter will explore in more detail.

The design challenge of composing writing

It is worth reminding ourselves just how challenging the act of writing is, and for very young writers, the challenges are compounded by the additional difficulties of mastering the physical aspects of writing – controlling a pencil, writing in straight lines – and the orthographic aspects of writing – shaping letters and texts. For older writers in the primary school, and in secondary too, preoccupations with spelling and with concerns about *what* to write often get in the way of considerations of *how* best to write it. Although the more superficial aspects of writing become automated with maturity, freeing the working memory to attend to higher-level issues, writing does not become easier the older you get. Growing awareness of the needs of the reader, increasing expectations of what a text can achieve, and mastering a broadening range of text types continue to make writing a demanding task into adulthood. Indeed, Kellogg (2008) likens the demand of text composition to playing chess in terms of its demand on thinking and memory, or to playing a musical instrument which involves 'mastery of both mechanical skills and creative production' (2008: 2). Children's writer, Tim Bowler, reflecting on his own writing processes asks:'Why is writing so tricky? Because it requires mastery of two conflicting skills: a creative skill and a critical skill. The former is of the imagination, the latter of the intellect, and they come from different brain hemispheres. To write well, we have to employ both to maximum effect' (Bowler 2002).

Whilst the latest developments in cognitive neuro-psychology may critique the assertion that these functions occur in different brain hemispheres, Bowler's distinction between the creative skill and the critical skill is a reminder of the competing challenges in composition and he argues that, for him, one way to reduce the demand of composition is to draw on creative and critical thinking at different points in the writing process. Cognitive theoretical perspectives have tended to frame these dual demands as 'the problem of content – what to say – and the problem of rhetoric – how to say it' (Kellogg 2008: 2). Neither the creative/critical nor the content/rhetoric dichotomies are wholly satisfactory, however. There is often a rather Romantic divide made between creativity and critical engagement, which is commonly ascribed in professional and literary thinking (see Wilson 2007 for a further discussion of this), whereas creativity and criticality frequently work together in harmony and enhance each other. Interviews with young secondary writers about their writing behaviours indicate that creative and critical thinking are frequently co-occurring during the process of composition (Myhill and Jones 2007). Equally, cognitive psychologists have a tendency to reduce writing to a set of identifiable, often measurable, processes which can gloss over the powerful interactions between processes and the social and linguistic influences which shape these processes. What is clear, as Kellogg maintains, is that 'all writers must make decisions about their texts' (2008: 2), whether that be early years writers deciding where word divisions occur, or older writers deciding how to end a text. Coleridge talked of subjecting his work to 'the ordeal of deliberation and deliberate choice' (1834: 267), which is an apt reminder of the design challenge of composition. It is also a reminder that teaching writing, at every age and stage, should support writers in becoming confident in making decisions and choices, and that those decisions and choices are not simply about content, but importantly they are about decisions at word, sentence and text level.

Grammar as a design tool

Such word-, sentence- and text-level decisions are informed by linguistic understanding. The place of linguistics, of grammar, within a literacy curriculum has historically been an uncertain one, subject to heated controversies, polemic and polarised viewpoints characterised more by ideology than pedagogy. It is not my intention to rehearse these arguments here as they have been well rehearsed elsewhere (Wyse 2001; Hudson and Walmsley 2005; Locke 2009). However, the issues raised in the 'grammar debate' point to considerable lack of clarity about what is meant by 'grammar' and even less certainty about what is meant by 'the place of grammar in the curriculum'. There is a strong tendency to adopt very traditional, conservative views of grammar (both in those who argue for and against grammar), typified by a Chomskyan view of language as innate and acquired and an emphasis on grammar in terms of correctness, fixed forms and rigid applications. Hancock (2009) summarises the tenor of the debate as 'Grammar is error and error is grammar in much of the public mind'. Significantly, Cope and Kalantzis used the word 'design' to describe literate practice because 'it is free from the negative associations for teachers of terms such as 'grammar' (2000: 20). It is also significant that I, and other authors in this book, so frequently choose to talk about 'linguistics' rather than 'grammar', thus eschewing the grammar problem.

However, in the context of developing a design repertoire in the primary writing classroom, the potentiality of grammar lies not in crude applications of prescriptive rules to correct children's writing but in opening up possibilities, patterns and ways of meaning-making. Cope and Kalantzis emphasise 'the productive and innovative potential of language as a meaning-making system', based on 'an action-oriented and generative description of language as a means of representation' (2000: 26). This is about learning that the way you write something is as important as the topic in communicating with a reader and that messages can be shaped in very different ways for different effects. Very often, these design effects are achieved by disrupting the most obvious sequence in a sentence – subject followed by verb – to create a specific effect. For example, consider the different effects in the three sentences below and the increased sense of tension and suspense in the second and third sentences created by the inversion of the subject and verb, and the positioning of the adverbial phrases at the start of the sentence. Note also that none of these sentences are intrinsically 'better' than any other (and they are all grammatically correct) but they offer different decision-making possibilities:

> The shadow moved slowly up the stairs.
> Slowly, step by step, one at a time, up the stairs moved the shadow.
> Slowly, step by step, one at a time, the shadow moved up the stairs.

Bereiter and Scardamalia's (1987) distinction between knowledge-telling and knowledge-transforming is frequently cited as a key developmental trajectory in primary writers. They observe that writers in the knowledge-telling phase move from their mental ideas to written text in a linear manner, writing down their ideas as they occur and chaining one clause and one sentence after another. Pea and Kurland evocatively described this process as a 'memory dump' (1987: 293). In the knowledge-transforming phase, however, the verbal material for the text is shaped and organised with rhetorical goals in mind. On one level, the difference between 'telling' and 'transforming' is about the shift from local to global coherence, and being able to think of the text as a whole and about its broader purposes, rather than building a text, sentence by sentence, with very local orientations. However, it is also about transformation achieved through design, which occurs at local level in terms of word choices and sentence structures, as well as at the global level of the text. Meaningful teaching of grammar which builds young writers' understanding of possible structures and their effects supports transformative writing and combines both the creative and the critical: as Ted Hughes argued, 'conscious manipulation of syntax deepens engagement and releases invention' (1987).

Linguistic development in writing

If meaningful teaching of grammar is to inform a pedagogy for teaching writing in the primary classroom, it is worth considering what research can tell us about linguistic development. In fact, there have been surprisingly few systematic analyses of linguistic development in the primary phase (and even fewer for the secondary phase). Table 6.1 summarises much of this research. The studies span over forty years and are predominantly based in the UK or the USA, although the 2002 publication from Ludo Verhoeven and his team reports on a large-scale study of linguistic development from age 9 to adulthood, which crosses both national borders (Holland, England, France, Israel and Spain) and linguistic borders (Dutch, English, French, Hebrew and Spanish). Nonetheless, there are many similarities in the respective patterns of development these studies record: in general, young writers become more adept at using longer constructions (such as clauses, noun phrases and sentences) and they use a greater range of constructions (more passives and modals, a wider variety of adverbials). There also appears to be a consensus that writers develop from dependence on co-ordination to being more able to use subordination, which is likely to reflect a growing distinction between the patterns of speech and the patterns of writing (Myhill 2009).

These studies, of course, outline linguistic development in terms of linguistic constructions which are present in children's writing. They do not consider the effectiveness of the writer's use of those constructions in the context of a specific piece of writing. The patterns of development that they illustrate may provide useful pointers for primary teachers in terms of teaching focuses for different writers at different stages of development but the studies do not address the pedagogically significant issues of how to support the creative use of language as a meaning-making resource in writing – or, in other words, how to teach children to write as designers.

Table 6.1 *A summary of research studies investigating linguistic development in the primary phase*

Author(s)	Age of children in study	Linguistic usages and constructions influenced by age
Hunt 1965	5–18	No evidence that there were linguistic constructions which acted as markers of development
Harpin 1976	7–11	Decline in use of personal pronouns; increase in clause and sentence length; increase in use of subordination
Loban 1976	5–18	Use of longer sentences; greater elaboration of subject and predicate; more embedded clauses and adjectival dependent clauses; greater variety and depth of vocabulary
Perera 1984	8–12	From dependence on co-ordination to greater use of subordination; from using simple noun phrases to longer noun phrases with more complex structures; from using predominantly active lexical verbs to making greater use of passives and modals; from temporal adverbials to a greater range; problems with ellipsis, reference and substitution
Raban 1988	5–8	Different connectives used in writing compared with speech
Kress 1994	4–8	Grasp of sentence as a textual unit not a syntactical unit; learning that writing differs from speech; early dependence on co-ordination; temporal indicators used more frequently than others
Allison, Beard and Wilcocks 2002	5–9	Dependence on co-ordination; found higher levels of subordination than in Harpin's study greater use of nominal and adverbial subclauses than relative clauses
Berman and Verhoeven 2002	9–adult	Increase in clause length
Ravid *et al.* 2002	9–adult	Subject noun phrases became more lexical with age, especially in expository texts
Ragnarsdottir *et al.* 2002	9–adult	Increase in the use of the passive
Verhoeven *et al.* 2002	9–adult	Increase in syntactic complexity

Language in action

Teaching children how to write as designers involves encouraging an active and purposeful engagement with text and an enquiring curiosity about how writers shape texts. In essence, this is about the explicit teaching of writing. Although our oral language is acquired naturally through a combination of innate capacities and meaningful social interaction, writing is always a learned activity, which is one reason why it is such a challenge. However, our language experiences as speakers, and our reading experiences do create implicit resources for meaning-making in writing. Making these implicit resources explicit is empowering for the writer because it transforms the process of writing from one of serendipity to one of active engagement. Carter argues that 'appropriate and strategic interventions by the teacher are crucial to the process of making implicit knowledge explicit' (1990: 117). But for some children, strategic interventions establish explicit knowledge where none existed before: children bring to the classroom differing language resources drawn from different linguistic experiences, particularly in terms of the range of reading experiences a child has enjoyed. The recent trend in most western English-speaking countries towards a greater emphasis on explicit teaching about text types and genres was, in part, due to a critique of personal and process writing approaches for privileging middle-class children (Martin 1985). In contrast, the teaching of genres was intended to 'enable all learners to make these genres part of their own repertoires' (Rose 2009: 162) through the processes of exploring and analysing the characteristics of these texts. I would suggest, however, that the emphasis on genres in the primary curriculum in England, and with it an emphasis on the grammatical constructions associated with genres, has tended to generate a rule-bound, even formulaic, view of texts. Instructional texts contain imperatives; narrative writing requires an abundance of adjectives, and argument texts are demarcated by *firstly, secondly, finally*. At its worst, this can result in what Kress describes as 'a subordination of the child's creative abilities to the demands of the norms of genre' (1994: 11).

Developing writers as designers is fundamentally about opening up the possibilities of choice, including creative subversive choices which break conventions, and which approaches grammar not as 'a box of labels in a dissection laboratory but a living force used every moment words are uttered' (Keith 1997: 8). It involves exploratory approaches to texts and their design and the acceptance of multiple responses and interpretations of the meanings texts evoke. It encourages active investigation of 'the rich complexity of language' (NATE 1997: 1) and an emphasis not on identification of grammatical features, but on their effect. Table 6.2 shows how the learning objectives for Writing specified in the Primary Literacy Framework for Year 4 (age 8 to 9) could be

Table 6.2 *How curricular teaching objectives can support writers in becoming designers*

Primary literacy framework: learning objectives for Year 4	Linguistic design possibilities
Creating and shaping texts Develop and refine ideas in writing using planning and problem-solving strategies	Using peer talk to reflect on design possibilities
Use settings and characterisation to engage readers' interest	Exploring how place adverbials can establish setting Exploring how nouns in apposition can establish character
Summarise and shape material and ideas from different sources to write convincing and informative non-narrative texts	Exploring the vocabulary of synthesis and contrast
Show imagination through the language used to create emphasis, humour, atmosphere or suspense	Exploring how varying sentence length can be used to create emphasis, highlight a humorous point, or build atmosphere and suspense
Choose and combine words, images and other features for particular effects	Exploring how noun phrases differ in different texts; e.g. very long noun phrases in advertisements to create market image of product and short noun phrases in fairy tales because of its roots in oral traditions
Text structure and organisation Organise text into paragraphs to distinguish between different information, events or processes	Exploring the topic sentence as a signpost for paragraph information
Use adverbs and conjunctions to establish cohesion within paragraphs	Exploring how over-use of 'and' to link ideas within sentences can cause cohesion problems within the paragraphs Exploring how an absence of adverbs and conjunctions in a paragraph can disrupt cohesion
Sentence structure and punctuation Clarify meaning and point of view by using varied sentence structure (phrases, clauses and adverbials)	Exploring how using a passive with and without the by-agent can alter the point of view
Use commas to mark clauses, and use the apostrophe for possession	Exploring how a sequence of short clauses, demarcated by commas can be used to create a sense of urgency in narrative

addressed in this way, focusing on developing writers' awareness of the linguistic design possibilities available to them.

At its simplest, developing awareness of design choices can be achieved through teaching strategies which invite the writer to make decisions and create opportunities for the writer to be aware of that decision-making. One teacher, working with 6–7-year-olds in a research project investigating the relationship between talking and writing (*From Talk to Text*), was using the strategy of oral rehearsal to support this design reflection. Oral rehearsal encourages the child to compose aloud before attempting to write the text on paper so that the phrase or sentence can be rehearsed orally, and altered if necessary, avoiding the cognitive effort of transcription and revision. In the interaction below, Zoe has been writing with a magic pencil, an imaginary pencil which writes text which only the writer can see, and she 'reads' her invisible writing to her teacher, who then encourages her to think about shaping her sentences:

TEACHER: What's your sentence going to be, Ellen?
ZOE: Mrs Zing took ... Dreamboat Zing to a castle and winded up a alarm clock and ... Dreamboat Zing ... [reading deliberately, looking at blank page and looking up]
TEACHER: This sentence is getting very long, isn't it? Think about where you want to finish your first sentence. What are you going to put in your first sentence?
ZOE: Mrs Zing and Dreamboat Zing went to a castle. Full stop.

In another classroom, working with 13-year-olds, the teacher is looking at persuasive speeches prior to the writers creating their own persuasive speech. The class has been reading Churchill's famous 'We shall fight' speech and have been experimenting with alternative ways to punctuate it to create different effects. One student offers this as a possibility:

We shall defend our island. Whatever the cost may be, we shall fight. On the beaches, we shall fight. On the landing grounds, we shall fight. In the fields and in the streets, we shall fight. ...

The teacher opens up a class discussion about this version compared with Churchill's version and tries to elicit thinking about its effect. Several of the students prefer this version because 'it's more in your face', 'more controlling' and 'more powerful'. Using an interactive whiteboard, the teacher isolates the extract quoted above from the rest of the speech and asks the class to explain in what way it is different structurally from Churchill's version, and when they struggle to articulate this, he takes just two sentences and shows both versions together:

> On the beaches, we shall fight. On the landing grounds, we shall fight.
> We shall fight on the beaches. We shall fight on the landing grounds.

At this point, the students, through this visual presentation of the contrast, recognise the reversal in sentence structure that the two versions represent and one student suggests that the adverbial phrases are less important than the idea of fighting which Churchill's version foregrounds. The discussion is ended by the ending of the lesson but at no time in this exchange does the teacher give any opinion about a 'better version', but simply works hard to get the students to think about the differing effects and emphases of the two versions. Rather than suggesting that a particular grammatical construction is 'correct' in a particular context, he fosters exploration of effects and allows individual decision-making.

Conclusion

One notable element of the teaching episode outlined above was the clear focus on syntactical structure, but the absence of the use of any grammatical terminology, such as subject or adverbial phrase. It was evident in the discussion about the difference between the two sentences that the students could see that one began with subject and verb while the other began with the adverbial phrase but they did not have the metalanguage to express this. Within the framework of teaching writers to be designers, I would suggest that the precise value of metalanguage remains ambivalent and in need of further research. On the one hand, there is no doubt that access to a metalanguage allows for more precise discussions about writing; on the other hand, good teachers can illustrate grammatical differences without using the metalanguage. Both these points were true of the episode reported above. Cope and Kalantzis argue that a metalanguage should be a 'tool kit for working on semiotic activities, not a formalism to be applied to them' (2000: 24). Any teaching of metalanguage needs to be an empowering activity which enables design discussion, rather than supporting formulaic understanding of the role of grammar in writing (such as that complex sentences are good, or that a paragraph must begin with a connective).

In many ways, the argument outlined in this chapter, that grammar can support development in writing, is premised upon principles which run counter to dominant and public views of grammar as quintessentially concerned with accuracy, correctness and, by association, propriety. Instead, this chapter proposes a pedagogical conceptualisation of grammar within a framework of creative design in which the primary benefit derived from greater awareness of linguistic constructions is not obedient adherence to accepted norms but the nurturing of a repertoire which generates infinite possibilities. It is a conceptualization which acknowledges that startling images, arising unbidden from the unconscious, sometimes surprise the writer, that the turn of a sentence in its first draft may be just right, and that through writing we often discover what we want to say. But it also recognises that for most writers, such moments of creative flow are balanced by the hard slog of generating, tuning and refining our writing.

The use of corpus-based approaches
in children's knowledge about language

Alison Sealey

Introduction: the corpus in context

This chapter explores the potential contribution of a language 'corpus' to the
knowledge and understanding about language of primary school pupils and their
teachers. In language research, a 'corpus' is the name given to an electronically
stored databank of authentic language that, with dedicated software, can be
interrogated as empirical evidence of language use, thus revealing the patterns
that emerge when large quantities of language data are gathered together in this
way. This chapter describes three examples of evidence for such patterns: the
high frequency of certain kinds of words; the mutual influence of grammar and
vocabulary on language in use; and the way in which some common words are
used differently in writing for children and for adults respectively.

Corpus work was initially developed partly because of its potential to
provide teachers and learners of English as an additional language with
more accurate accounts and examples of language in use than are available
in traditional reference books and textbooks. However, the field has contributed a great deal more than this, so that Hunston (2002), for example,
states, 'It is no exaggeration to say that corpora, and the study of corpora,
have revolutionised the study of language, and of the applications of language, over the last few decades' (Hunston 2002: 1). The tools previously
available for language analysis – introspection and assumed grammatical
categories, accepted with only minor modifications since classical times –
are superseded now that we 'have the technology to discover patterns in raw
textual data' (Stubbs 2009: 116). That is, the approach involves looking at,
and analysing, language as it is actually used, not in single texts, but in col-
lections of many texts, deriving descriptions from the evidence. One effect
of this is that, whereas vocabulary and grammar are traditionally thought

The CLLIP study was conducted by Paul Thompson and myself. Mike Scott also contributed
modifications to *WordSmith Tools* suggested by classroom experiences. This research was funded
by ESRC project grant R000223900: *An investigation into corpus-based learning about language
in the primary school.* I would like to thank Paul Thompson and Sylvia Winchester for comments
on an earlier draft of this chapter.

of as two distinct aspects of the language system, this separation has been eroded in light of the observations and analyses of the empirical data that are made possible by the developing technology – and examples are given below of some implications of this realisation for teaching and learning about language.

Contemporary lexicography relies on corpora to such an extent that no major dictionaries are compiled without reference to a corpus. Translators and interpreters use corpora routinely in their work. Teachers of foreign and additional languages benefit from a wide range of materials that are corpus based, and language learners around the world can familiarise themselves with the target variety by exploring corpus evidence. Since 1994, there has been a biennial international conference on 'Teaching and Language Corpora', and an extensive range of books and journals covers the pedagogical applications of corpus linguistics. (See, for example, in addition to numerous articles in general language learning journals, specific journals such as *Language and Computers; ReCALL* (the journal of the European Association for Computer-Assisted Language Learning), e.g. McEnery, Wilson and Barker (1997); *ICAME* (a journal linked with the International Computer Archive of Modern and Medieval English) and recent books, including the following: Aston (2001); Aston, Bernardini and Stewart (2004); Braun, Mukherjee and Kohn (2006); Burnard and McEnery (2000); Connor and Upton (2004); Granger, Hung and Petch-Tyson (2002); Hunston (2002); Sinclair (2004); Wichmann, Fligelstone, McEnery and Knowles (1997).)

However, with just a few minor exceptions, pupils and teachers in the compulsory sectors of mainstream education where English is a first language have yet to benefit from this 'revolution' in the study and description of language. This is due partly to the time it takes for developments in a field of research to reach the 'chalk-face', where practitioners are beset almost daily by a plethora of obligations and adaptations to be made in their work. It may also be due to resistance to innovation, especially certain kinds of innovation. Corpus linguistics is an empirical approach to language analysis, perhaps the epitome of the stance adopted by contemporary linguists, which seeks to observe and describe what people *do* say and write, and not to prescribe what they *should* say or write. In teaching, however, some degree of prescription is inevitable, because teaching, by definition, involves passing on to the next generation, and assessing, knowledge about what is deemed true, correct and appropriate. This no doubt accounts in part for the reservations about the utility of corpus-based teaching that are sometimes held by policy makers and teacher educators. As long ago as 1995, Hunston reviewed the potential in her article 'Grammar in teacher education: the role of a corpus', yet this potential is still far from being realised. I hope to demonstrate that there are significant rewards to be reaped if teachers, teacher educators and their pupils are indeed able to have direct access to this important resource.

r said . He could have killed him at this moment . Farimier did n't because if he did he could n't g
at on the beach and set sail . Damrod was thanking Farimier for saving him when Farimier remembers h
o climb through the entrance and failed . What was Farimier going to do ? Farimier went to find some
stayed back from the Fire Dragon , about 6m away . Farimier had a plan and hid the bucket of water b
e Fire Dragon started shooting fuming fireballs at Farimier . He dodged them all . This was the chan
into it . At the end of it was his friend Damrod . Farimier heard something coming , he turned round
ng pulled to the rocks . What was he going to do ? Farimier jumped off the ship and swam to the beac
. Damrod was thanking Farimier for saving him when Farimier remembers he left his bow on the island
oaching . The tide was high . The tide was pulling Farimier 's ship " The Black One " to an island .
athing . " The arrow must have knocked him out , " Farimier said . He could have killed him at this
arimier was confused . Nobody was on this island . Farimier saw a rocky path and started walking up
lked to the end of the path and there was a cave . Farimier walked into it . At the end of it was hi
. It was the Fire Dragon . It was hungry . It saw Farimier , walked up to Farimier and licked its l
arimier . He dodged them all . This was the chance Farimier was waiting for . Behind the Fire Dragon
an island . The rocks were as sharp as daggers and Farimier was getting pulled to the rocks . What w
arimier was curious about the uninhabited island . Farimier was confused . Nobody was on this island
next to the sharp rocks . The place was deserted . Farimier was curious about the uninhabited island
rance and failed . What was Farimier going to do ? Farimier went to find some water in the cave . He
Dragon was getting dizzy and fell to the ground . Farimier went up to the Fire Dragon . He was brea

Figure 7.1 Concordance lines for 'Farimier', from the corpus of children's writing

The corpus-based learning about language in the primary-school project (CLLIP)

The discussion and examples in this chapter are largely based on a project which researched corpus-based learning about language in the primary school (CLLIP). The research questions which we explored included: 'How do primary school pupils respond to corpus-based teaching and learning activities?' and 'What kinds of metalinguistic knowledge, understanding or misconceptions are the children prompted to articulate by the presentation of texts in a corpus format, such as concordance lines?' 'Concordance lines' are produced by the software used to analyse a corpus, and Figure 7.1 is an example of what the output looks like. In this case (which is discussed later in this chapter), the 'node' word was 'Farimier', the name of a character in a story written by one of the children in our project.

The main corpus that we used was extracted from the widely available 100-million-word British National Corpus (BNC), from which we took the texts classified as having been written for a child audience. This filtering was done because we did not want to present the children with material that would be too challenging to read, or of no intrinsic interest to them. The CLLIP corpus consists of approximately 800,000 words from forty texts, including stories, history books, a *Brownie* annual, and so on. To investigate the corpus, we used the program *WordSmith Tools* (Scott 2004). This generated various findings about patterns in the language of English written for children, on some of which we based classroom activities.

The school-based research was conducted in two phases in each of two schools, with groups of six children aged between 8 and 10 (Year 4 or Year 5 in England) whose levels of literacy made them suitable for participation in the study. Ethical procedures agreed within the University of Reading were followed, and the children and their parents gave informed consent to their involvement, as did the class teachers. The groups were withdrawn each week to work with the researchers, and detailed recordings were made (and later transcribed) of six forty-minute sessions with each group in the first phase and of three fifty-minute sessions in each school, with some different children, in the second phase.

In the following sections, some results are presented of our analysis of the corpus itself, along with examples of what the children said and did in response to their own explorations of corpus data and software. (Further examples may be found in Sealey and Thompson 2004; 2006; 2007; Sealey 2009.)

Facts and figures: investigating frequent words

Across the curriculum, policy makers and practitioners have to make decisions about which items to teach. In relation to English, one criterion for identifying the core vocabulary likely to be of high priority for young literacy learners is the frequency of particular items in the language. We have compared the frequent words in CLLIP with those prescribed for young learners in the National Literacy Strategy (DES 1998), identifying many similarities but also some significant differences (Sealey and Thompson 2006; Sealey 2009).

In addition to the common lexical items typically taught to beginning readers, evidence from many large corpora of running prose of many different types is that the most frequent items are grammatical, or function, words. The top ten most frequent words in CLLIP are *the, and, to, a, he, of, it, was, you* and *I*. When they were asked to predict which would be the most frequent words in the CLLIP corpus, the children guessed fairly accurately. For example, one child's suggested list was '*and, it, the, they, can, where, is, when, how, of*' (A7/204). With a little help, the children then used the relevant tool in the software to check their predictions. The extracts shown in Table 7.1 are from their discussion about what they could see on the computer screen as they did so.

In many ways this is an unremarkable stretch of dialogue. However, evident in it is a degree of speculation by the children and engagement with the computer and what it can tell them, which is not typical of many traditional lessons about the 'nuts and bolts' of language description. In lessons based on investigating the corpus, we found that the computer and the evidence it made available were often referred to as a kind of 'third party' in the classroom. Unlike a textbook, dictionary or worksheet, this resource is dynamic and interactive, prompting exclamations such as 'oh' and 'look', as results to their queries,

Table 7.1 *Extracts from pupil discussion about which words would be most frequent in the CLLIP corpus*

Speaker[a]	Transcribed speech[b]	Commentary
BA5	probably got *the* in it	As the children wait for the frequency list to appear, they continue to speculate about what will be at the top
BA1	*the*'s seconds look *the*'s second ah did you see that	Responding to the emerging list as it appears on the screen
GA2	yeah *the*	
PAUL	and it's given us	Paul prompts the children to notice the other highly frequent words
BA1	*the and to a*	Reading out from the list
GA3	*a*	
GA2	oh we didn't say *a*	Noticing a contrast between their predictions and the evidence

A7/237–A7/243[c]

[a] Speaker identities are made up of a first letter to indicate sex (B = Boy, G = Girl), a second letter indicating which school they attend (A or B) and a number to distinguish them within the group. Thus 'BA3' is Boy 3 at School A, etc. In the transcripts, 'BA1_name', etc. replace uses of the children's names in dialogue. The researchers appear in the transcripts as 'Alison' and 'Paul'.

[b] Transcription conventions are as follows:

Line breaks	Short pause or silent beat in the rhythm; marks speaker 'parcellings' of talk and makes long utterances readable
Italics	'Citations', including reading aloud from text on screen or paper
Bold	Stressed words or syllables
?	Utterances interpreted as questions
+	Incomplete word or utterance
-	False start
#	Filled pause: 'erm' / 'um' etc.

The degree of detail in the transcriptions is greater where a section of talk is the focus of detailed analysis. Where there is any ambiguity, the sound files have been used and punctuation added for clarification.

[c] Turns are numbered sequentially within each recorded session. The sources of examples are indicated by school, session number and turn number.

appear on the screen. In this extract, it is Paul, one of the researchers, who uses the formulation 'it's given us', but the children often produced similar structures when talking about the computer and the corpus.

Following these sessions on word frequencies, we quickly put together, at the children's suggestion, two further corpora (inevitably very small ones) comprising pieces of their own writing. When we started the next session, BA5 said, 'I want to see/I want to see how m-, what words were used the most in ours because if- I want to compare it to yours' (A9/98). This boy was impressed by the fact that the name of a character from his story, 'Farimier', was a relatively highly frequent word in this corpus. (Statistically, a high frequency of lexical, or content, words is more likely if the total number of words in the corpus is small.) By this stage in the project, the children were familiar with the concordancing function of the software, and were able to take up the researcher's suggestion to investigate this word and its patterning a little further. In response to the researcher's prompting, the children began by making some linguistic predictions, detailed in Table 7.2, which they then tested against their corpus data.

During these exchanges, the children were manipulating the display on the screen, using 'Farimier' as the 'node' word in a set of concordance lines, which they then sorted in alphabetical order of the word immediately to the right of this name. Figure 7.1, presented earlier in this chapter, shows a selection of what they could see – their findings from the rich language resource that the corpus represents.

This small-scale investigation demonstrates how the children's curiosity about language data spanned word frequencies, the application of their knowledge about word classes ('nouns', 'verbs'), and the patterns which are likely to be found in certain types of texts (e.g. in an 'action story' proper nouns are followed by verbs). Such discussion contributes to children's understanding of the properties of different word classes, but is not simply a 'naming of parts' (Mittins 1988). Rather, interaction with a corpus helps children to articulate their own questions and to see some of the predictable ways in which language behaves, including the clustering together of certain words, and types of words, in particular kinds of sequence. For example, one property of nouns is that they are often found heading groups of words that constitute the grammatical subject of clauses. So, as the children observe, a typical pattern is to find '... mostly verbs #,' '... like *walked walks # saw jumped*,' following the proper noun 'Farimier'. (Farimier is often the subject of these clauses, but not always, and the corpus evidence could, of course, be used to explore this aspect of grammar too.)

Breaking down the barriers: grammar and vocabulary

The subject of grammar, particularly in the primary school, is a particularly daunting challenge for many teachers. There are several reasons for this. One, alluded to above, is the lack of clarity about the distinction between description and prescription, where social and cultural conventions become entangled with ideas about linguistic 'correctness'. As Wardhaugh expresses it:

Most of us have learned many things about language from others, but generally the wrong things. More likely than not we have acquired ideas and beliefs that do not have

Table 7.2 *Children's predictions and observations about word patterns around the name of a main character in an 'action story'*

Speaker	Transcribed speech	Commentary
ALISON	what sort of a word do you think will come after Farimier in BA5_name's story?	
ALL	*was*	The earlier items spoken in this part of the session are predictions
GA3	*said*	
GA4	a lot of *was*	The concordance output is beginning to appear on screen
GA3	*saw remembered*	
BA1	they're highlighted them now I'll do it like that ...	The node word and the word by whose position it is sorted, in this case, the first word to the right, are highlighted on screen as BA1 manipulates the output
GA4	*jumped heard he had gone did and*	
... some turns omitted		
ALISON	is there a pattern to the word that comes straight after Farimier in BA5_name's story?	
... some turns omitted		
GA4	nouns and verbs	
GA2	mostly verbs	
GA3	yeah mostly verbs #	
GA2	because it's like *walked walks # saw jumped*	
GA4	*jumped heard*	
BA1	you you can see it all down here look	
ALISON	so they're mostly verbs could you can you think why that might be?	
GA3	because it's an action story really 'cause it's about being in a # situation where # you're in a cave with a monster and you don't know how to get out and you're fighting it and you're you want to get out so it's really an action story so *jumping* and	

facts to back them. However, we often insist on handing these on to others in the firm conviction that we are thereby handing on wisdom and perhaps even safeguarding the very language itself. (Wardhaugh 1999: viii)

A second problem in this area is a history of successive generations having themselves been taught different material, and to different levels, about the grammar of the English language. A third problem is that many of the concepts traditionally associated with 'grammar' are inherently problematic. Even on advanced courses, students of grammar often feel that the fault lies with them when authentic instances of language in use cannot be readily classified into the categories they are trying to learn. In addition to the persistence of the idea that word classes (or 'parts of speech') can be assigned to individual words semantically (so that 'doing words' must be verbs, 'naming word' nouns, and so on), grammar teaching often founders on the tendency of words to behave in ways that are not easily accounted for by notions either about 'parts of speech', or about individual words and their meaning (see Myhill 2000). An explanation for this is provided by theoretical developments that are emerging from corpus linguistics; as Sinclair observes, 'even major parts of speech are not as solidly founded as they might be' (Sinclair 1992: 14).

I have witnessed the confidence of many teachers, and student teachers ('trainees'), shaken by lessons in which the patterns they were trying to convey to pupils are undermined by the examples generated in the classroom. A sequence on a training video for the *National Literacy Strategy* in England (DfEE 1998a) has the teacher inviting a class to suggest adjectives to describe a dog. One of the suggestions is 'sausage' (to give 'sausage dog', a common nickname in the UK for the dacshund breed of dog), and this illustrates the discrepancy between the idea that it is 'adjectives [that] describe nouns' and the fact that nouns are themselves often used as modifiers in just this way. The obverse of this problem arises when classroom exercises involve substitutions of items which seem to share characteristics, but which somehow fail to fit into the designated slots. A potential reason for such problems is summarised by Stubbs (1996: 40) in these terms: 'Any grammatical structure restricts the lexis that occurs in it; and conversely, any lexical item can be specified in terms of the structures in which it occurs ... Words are systematically co-selected: the normal use of language is to select more than one word at a time.' In other words, authentic instances of language production frequently disrupt the supposed structures and 'rules' about grammar which teachers may be trying to impart.

Once out of the relative safety zone of nouns, verbs and adjectives, lessons on the grammatical classes such as prepositions and conjunctions are often particularly fraught. A prescribed item in the literacy curriculum in England is 'to search for, identify and classify a range of prepositions: *back, up, down, across, through, on*, etc.; experiment with substituting different prepositions

Table 7.3 *Children talking about concordance lines of prepositions*

Speaker	Transcribed speech	Commentary
GB1	is *underneath* an adverb or a preposition?	*Underneath* can be used as either, depending on the context. In the concordance line under discussion, it was followed by a noun phrase, and so had been classified as a preposition, and colour-coded accordingly
BB1	mm#	
GB1	it's a preposition because it tells you	The 'it' which 'tells' the reader that *underneath* is a preposition refers to the screen, or the software – i.e. the clue is in the colour-coding. See comment above about the attribution of agency to the corpus and software.
GB3	yeah yeah I think it's a preposition	
GB2	well if it didn't tell you then how would you know?	GB2 seems to be pushing her peers to articulate what the characteristics of prepositions are, rather than depending on the visual clue of the colour-coding
GB1	#	
GB2	because you're going underneath something that's in accordance to the thing that's going over you	This contribution, together with others in the discussions, seems to be drawing on ideas from previous work on the subject with their usual teacher.

B5/144–B5/151

and their effect on meaning. Understand and use the term *preposition*' (DfEE 1998d: Year 5, Term 3).

I suggest that it is more challenging than it may appear to provide children with a really helpful definition of this category of word. The fact that the authors have included *back* in this list, when, given its distribution, it is not usually classified as a preposition, supports this claim. To illustrate some of the problems, Table 7.3 presents an extract from one CLLIP session in which the children worked with concordance lines of prepositions, using corpus output that was colour coded in accordance with the automated part-of-speech tagging available with the British National Corpus.

Conceptually, as GB2's final turn suggests, prepositions are identified with relationships of time or space, while syntactically they typically occur before noun phrases. But to what extent can different prepositions be substituted for each other, and what are the constraints?

```
use you want to go. It will mean giving   up a lot and --' she gave the ghost of
, merely picking at her meal, Karl kept    up a lively alert manner which belied
ul was dragged from his retreat to wash    up, a little work was done, and then,
st. 'For Christ's sake, I brought you       up!' All right, all right, Bodo said.
the bulk of a church where he pulled        up, although wisely keeping the engine r
et the business of the accident cleared    up and then, although he did not norma
a nip and, as Erika volunteered to wash    up, Frau Nordern, not to be outdone, h
frown. 'Werner?' Frau Nordern heaved        up her brief-case and let it fall on to
agical hours until, at 10.00, she stood    up. 'Home time,' she said. 'No,' cutt
but I know that she is keeping the bar      up. However, we'll see about that -- i
right.' Frau Nordern forced her window     up.  'I didn't believe you anyway.'
   . 'O.K.,' Bodo climbed into his pick_up. 'I'll be in touch. Just --' he hesit
ut Hans, tell me, have you been mixed       up in any rackets?' Herr Nordern almo
e ordered a taxi .' Karl was muffled        up in his luxurious overcoat. He kissed
hed in his merry way. 'But I was tucked     up in bed early -- not difficult in Dr
! I'm joking. And I'm off.' He stood        up, shrugging his broad shoulders into a
And so am I, she thought, as she ran        up the stairs. Only Omi was in, and s
until a small group of musicians struck     up the opening bars of the first hymn.
u wonder what the Security Police are       up to not knowing that -- and Steinmark
ncentration, and then .' Erika stood        up, too, and gave a rueful shrug. 'Conce
```

Figure 7.2 Concordance lines for 'up' in the CLLIP corpus

If we select *up* as an example, a definition of its meaning would probably involve the notion of orientation in space, contrasted with *down*. To illustrate its characteristics as a preposition, a teacher might well provide an example such as 'The man went up the stairs'. As an alternative approach to teaching about this word and its patterns, empirical evidence of how *up* is actually used can be provided by a corpus. A search on any sizeable corpus generates thousands of instances, so the output here, from the CLLIP corpus, has been restricted to twenty examples, randomly selected by the software from a range of source texts. It is displayed as it appeared when the concordance lines were sorted alphabetically, first by the first word to the right, and then by the first to the left. (See Figure 7.2.)

In only one of these lines do we find a prototypical construction of the type 'she ran up the stairs'. Many of the other examples illustrate that *up* is functioning as part of a longer string, particularly closely linked to a verb. Furthermore, although there is perhaps a vestigial hint of directionality in saying that something is *kept up*, at least metaphorically, this is less obvious with *struck up*, while with *clear up*, *wash up*, *mix up*, *muffle up* and *tuck up*, this 'core' meaning seems largely irrelevant, as it does with *be up to* something.

Illustrated by this brief exploration of an apparently simple, and very common, English word, is a phenomenon which corpus linguistics has done a great deal to illuminate, namely that '[i]ndividual words often do not correspond

come back the next day and find them all mixed up again. Books on whales sneaked their way into the 'OP
he told himself. 'That Simon had her all mixed up. She didn't know what she was doing.' Watching her no
right, up, down, forwards and backwards mixed up. It was bad enough trying to get to a classroom and h
I'm a farmer -- and if I do happen to be mixed up in other people' s extraordinary affairs, it's no fau
w that. But Hans, tell me, have you been mixed up in any rackets?' Herr Nordern almost dropped his glas
light. Somehow, she had let herself get mixed up. 'Stupid bitch!' she told herself. But he had shown h
olour-blind, only it's not colours I get mixed up, it's objects. I've tried seventy-one different docto
to Endill. 'And you! I told you gettitng mixed up. I meant the salt and the the the other one.' 'why di
thing. 'Oh yes. I'm sorry. I was getting mixed up with that boy was trouble.' 'But it was' started End
charge. 'But I'm serious. You've not got mixed up in any fiddles?' 'What fiddles could I be in?' Herr N
ed around.' Endill found out later that mixing up the signposts was a favourite pastime of the more mis
section. Books on Scottish History were mixed up with those on Volcanoes, and a particular book on Wor

Figure 7.3 Concordance lines for 'mix* up' in the CLLIP corpus

point of a knife. Wine was carefully mixed with water, because drinking undiluted wine was
silent and full of secrets, rarely mixing with strangers. People believed they knew things
to get cold. She wasn't allowed to mix with other children. 'They say she's very suscep
nyway they'd be pretty disgusting, mixed with the bits in his pocket. He could hear someone
know the type so I can't tell. Don't mix with nobs much. Well-dressed though, and I wouldn'

Figure 7.4 Concordance lines for 'mix* with' in the CLLIP corpus

to units of meaning' (Stubbs 2001: 49). Like many other words which a traditional part-of-speech approach would classify as either prepositions or adverbs, or perhaps as particles in phrasal verbs, *up* occurs very frequently in longer sequences where items are co-selected. Classroom activities could easily include explorations by the children of the kinds of pattern to be found, so that rather than worrying about whether *up* is a preposition or an adverb in *mix up*, they could investigate how this string is used in the CLLIP corpus. Instructed to list all instances of 'mix [+ inflection] + up' (represented in the command for the software as *mix* up*), Figure 7.3 shows the concordance lines which were found by *WordSmith* in CLLIP.

These lines illustrate another finding common in corpus investigations: that certain forms of a particular lemma are often much more frequent than others. Here, 'mixed' is much more frequent than 'mix' or 'mixes', and the constructions in which it appears connote passivity: people 'get mixed up' – by others, specified or not, but also by themselves. As for substitutions ('mix + other prepositions'), there are no instances of *mix* down, mix* over, mix* along* and so on in this corpus. Figure 7.4 shows that the few instances of *mix* with* pattern rather differently, and, again, children could be challenged to identify what the differences are, perhaps focusing on the words to the right of the node.

Table 7.4 *Types of entities premodified by 'sad' in the CLLIP corpus*

Human entity sad +	(Product of) (part of) body sad +	Emotion sad +	Cognitive / perceptive entity sad +	Textual entity sad +	Event / passage of time sad +
child	*eyes*	*happiness*	*memories*	*song*	*mishap*
lady	*heart*		*sight*	*story*	*pause*
	mouth		*thoughts*		*time*
	voice				

Developing vocabulary: frequent words in different contexts

A final illustration, in this brief chapter, of corpus-based evidence likely to be useful in teaching also involves the overlapping nature of words and structures. Common sense suggests that development in the use of vocabulary equates to knowledge of larger numbers of words. Our research comparing the CLLIP corpus with a larger corpus of fiction written for adults highlights another dimension: the ability to deploy familiar words in new contexts, and in particular a progression from using words to denote more literal meanings towards the exploitation of their more figurative connotations.

This has been reported more extensively in Thompson and Sealey (2007), where we noted how simple words for body parts, such as *neck* and *finger* are used differently in children's and adults' fiction (see also Sealey 2009). A similar finding occurs with *face*, which is frequent in both corpora (CLLIP and the adult fiction texts from the British National Corpus), but, unlike the adult texts, the children's corpus contains no instances of strings such as 'in the face of' or 'to face up to'. It is not more words, or longer words, that account for a sense of greater sophistication in writing where these idiomatic uses are found.

The more sophisticated tone of the adult texts can also be demonstrated by comparing how a core adjective such as *sad* is used in each of these corpora. For ease of comparison, I have extracted just those lines in which *sad* is used as an attributive adjective immediately preceding the noun it modifies. This is the list from CLLIP, which I have classified into rough semantic categories, which readers may evaluate for themselves (Table 7.4).

We would expect the equivalent list from the corpus of adult fiction, which is much larger, to be more extensive, and indeed it is. Using the same semantic groups, which are, of course, fairly 'fuzzy', we find similar kinds of things being described as *sad*, but these nouns denote (and connote) a more nuanced range of concepts (Table 7.5).

Table 7.5 *Types of entities premodified by 'sad' in the adult fiction corpus*

Human entity sad +	(Product of) (part of) body sad +	Emotion sad +	Cognitive / perceptive entity sad +	Textual entity sad +	Event / passage of time sad +
character	bits of cut-off hair	boredom	appearance	answer	aftermath
clown	body	disappointment	echoes	description	day
dancer	bosom	disgust	decision	document	deed
couple	cry	disillusionment	gaze	news	departure
family	expression	excitement	memory	note	end
figure	eyes	feeling	recognition	picture	event(s)
girl	face	humility	scent		errand
man	features	longing	secrecy	poem	experience
Mancunian	kind of demeanour	resentment	seriousness	reading	homecoming
pair	laugh	sorrow	sound	soliloquies	moment
people	look		truth	song(s)	time(s)
sort of a boy	shake of her head			story	trial
victim	sigh			strains of [a piece of music]	
woman / women	smile			tale	
wretches	tones			text	
	voice			words	
	wails				

In addition, nouns denoting semantic domains beyond those found in the children's texts are described as 'sad'; these include *alchemy, associations, attempts at cultivation, business, case, chore, circumstances, condition, decline, decrepitude, disarray, discrepancies, disrepair, dresses, effect, fact, gas-lamps, ghosts, life, light, lighting, load, loss, object, place, reflection, regularity, remains, sack, side, silence, sort of way, state of affairs, state to be in, sun, thing, vacancy, wall(s), world.*

The significance of this evidence is that it adds to our understanding of what may be most indicative of progression and development in writers' use of vocabulary – not simply the addition of more single items to the stock of known words (replacing *sad* with polysyllabic synonyms), but the ability to use common words in a wider range of contexts and combinations.

Conclusion

In this chapter I have provided a brief indication of the extent of the impact of corpus techniques on linguistic description. Our small-scale classroom project demonstrates that children are quite capable of using this resource, as they do many other kinds of technology and software, to gather and evaluate evidence about the subject they are learning about, rather than relying solely on intuition or the authority of teachers and textbooks. Our own research into the characteristics of writing intended for children highlights some patterns in both grammar and vocabulary, and reinforces insights about the way these two dimensions are much more interlinked than was previously believed.

I suggest that an applied linguistics curriculum for primary teachers could usefully make them more aware of these resources, including existing corpora, tools for making their own corpora, and the software for analysis. It could give them opportunities to explore their own preconceptions and intuitions about language, and also provide many potential lines of investigation for their pupils in the language classroom.

8   Words and pictures: towards a linguistic understanding of picture books and reading pedagogy

Vivienne Smith

Introduction: picture books and pedagogy

Picture books have long had a place in the primary classroom. Bright colours, pleasing formats and good stories have attracted both teachers and children. Teachers have recognised their usefulness in convincing children that reading is worth the effort it involves, and children have delighted in the possibilities of play they offer: they have readily engaged visually, emotionally and intellectually with the ideas on the pages.

For some years, in some infant classrooms, picture books took on a central place in the pedagogy of reading. Waterland (1985) and Ellis and Barrs (1996) showed how skilful teachers might construct from picture books a programme for initial reading tuition, and Meek (1988) went some way in explaining how this worked at a theoretical as well as a practical level. She wrote of the rich, but untaught 'lessons in reading' that were afforded by the best books that readers read, and showed how texts such as *Rosie's Walk* (Hutchins 1969) and *Each Peach Pear Plum* (Ahlberg 1976) taught children not just how to read the words, but how to think like a reader.

One might have expected that by 2009, a complete and systematic pedagogy for learning to read with picture books would have been developed, but this has not happened. Changing priorities in educational policy in England, for example The *National Literacy Strategy* (DfEE 1998c), focused attention on reading skills and measurable progression in reading and these ideas sat uneasily with Meek's less tangible concepts of developing an understanding of irony and entering into conspiratorial pacts with authors. Picture books stayed in classrooms, but too often their status was diminished. They were good for fun. They made delightful end-of-day stories and provided excellent adjuncts to topic work. They proved to children that reading could be enjoyable; but the serious business of learning to read and to progress as a reader went on elsewhere in the curriculum, and with other sorts of texts.

This chapter seeks to reconsider the role of picture books in reading pedagogy. It begins with a review of some of the recent scholarship in the field and concludes that increasingly, attention has been given to the pictures in the text over and above the words that accompany them. It argues that words are important too, especially in teaching children the habits of mind that young readers need to develop if they are to become engaged and committed readers. This chapter distinguishes between words as 'carrier of story' and words as 'tesserae of language'. It argues that it is this second category that teachers and educators need to work on if they are to uncover the potential of picture books as an educational tool, and to use them profitably in the classroom.

Picture books and academic discipline

At much the same time that picture books began to be side-lined in so many classrooms, they started to develop an importance elsewhere in academic thinking. In the growing field of children's literature – a discipline sometimes located in the education departments in universities and sometimes in litera-ture departments – academics started to notice that some picture books were really something special. Talented author/illustrators, such as Maurice Sendak, John Burningham and Anthony Browne, had elevated the form. Sendak, for example, with *Where the Wild Things Are* (1963), showed how, by manipulat-ing the balance of picture, white space and words on a double spread, the reader could be guided in and out of taking control of an imaginative narrative space. Burningham, with *Granpa* (1984), demonstrated that serious matters, such as the death of a grandparent could be explored subtly and sensitively through the careful juxtaposition of minimal text, white space and simple, almost sketchy drawings. And Browne, in many of his books (perhaps most noticeably, *Gorilla* 1983; *Changes* 1990; *Hansel and Gretel* 1981) introduced readers to visual intertextuality, surrealism and postmodernism. His work showed readers how rich and multilayered a detailed reading of a good picture book could be. There could be no doubt, after this, that picture books were more than simple, illus-trated children's stories.

Academic interest developed in a number of directions. Some academics (for example, Nodelman 1988; Sipe 1998; Agosto 1999; Nikolajeva and Scott 2000) became interested in the picture book as a phenomenon. What was it about the interaction and interdependence of words and pictures that made the best picture books work? These and other writers spent time describing how in particular books, word and image 'rub up alongside each other' (Lewis 2001: 40) and they developed categories to explain them. Although writers dif-fer in the number of categories they identify and in the names they give these categories, they broadly agree that in some books (or parts of books), the words and pictures reflect each other, and appear to do much the same job. In others, pictures enrich and enhance a sparse text, or, conversely, thin illustrations are explained by detailed written narrative. In more complex books, they notice how pictures and words enjoy a contrapuntal relationship, at times working against each other in order to create harmonious effects. Finally, they show that sometimes the words and pictures seem actually to contradict. According to Nikolajeva and Scott (2000), it is the 'dynamic interaction' of the words and pictures in all of these relationships that makes the best picture books successful.

This is a powerful idea, and one might expect as a result of it to find a strand of picture book research that explores this dynamic interaction fully, and gives detailed attention to what both words and pictures *do* in particular texts. But this research is hard to find. It is not that the words are altogether ignored. Nikolajeva and Scott (2000), for example, write about the written text in the books they describe, but they look at the text in terms of what it says rather than how it says it. They show for example, how words might contribute to the reader's understanding of character or setting and viewpoint. Nikolajeva (2003: 41) writes about words as 'verbal guidance', that help the reader understand what the pictures cannot show. She explains how in characterisation they provide, for example, a nominative function, give information about abstract characteristics such as gender and explain concrete relationships, such as friendship alliances or family ties. The contribution of language in this dynamic relationship then, appears to depend on its content rather than its constructedness. Few academics seem to be interested in how the way the language has been put together might affect the meanings that can be made.

It may be that reading language has become so natural a function for many adult readers of picture books that they simply *can* take it for granted. A second strand of thinking in picture book research has assumed this is the case. It takes as a tenet that because so many adults have spent their lives developing a facility for understanding *words*, what they need to do now is to learn how to read pictures. Doonan (1992) has been influential here. She has shown readers how pictures in books might be read as images and provided them with a vocabulary derived from art appreciation, rather than literature, to articulate what they see and describe how what they see is effective. She has explained how composition, how choices of colour, tone, line and viewpoint all influence the way that readers interpret what they see on the page. Further help came from Kress and van Leeuwen (1996). Drawing on functional linguistics and mostly media texts, they developed a grammar of visual design, which, together with Doonan, has been widely used by those who have wished to explore exactly how images in picture books are composed and how they communicate to readers. Lewis (2001), Smith (2001) and Hall (2008) have all used these tools to provide close readings of images in some picture books. So useful have they become in revealing the complexity and subtlety of visual texts that the words have been marginalised still further. A measure of this, perhaps, is that at the *Second International Symposium on New Impulses in Picturebook*

Research (Glasgow University 2009), two of the books which elicited most interest and enthusiasm among the delegates were David Wiesner's *Flotsam* and Shaun Tan's *The Arrival*. Neither book has a verbal text.

If literate adults find pictures challenging to read, then the question of what children, who are by definition less experienced readers, make of them arises. A third strand of picture book research has explored this question. Arizpe and Styles (2003) and the teachers they worked with presented a selection of multi-layered picture books to primary school children. They monitored the children's understanding after initial readings and again, later, when the texts were revisited. They asked the children to draw as well as talk in response to the texts and what emerged was a sensitivity and sophistication of response in even the youngest children's understanding that astonished the adult researchers. The children saw more and understood more than the researchers thought possible: it seemed that pictures communicated to them in a way that overcame the disadvantage of youth, inexperience and the relatively limited language and literary resources that were available to the children because of youth and inexperience.

Researchers developed this thinking in two ways. Some explored how other (often older) children responded to and negotiated the complex and postmodern picture books that were increasingly available (Evans *et al.* 2009). Others investigated how the pictures in these books might communicate to children when language itself was difficult. Arizpe (2009), for example, worked with immigrant children in investigating how pictures and picture books might help them to make sense of issues of place and cultural identity. Walsh (2009) looked at teenage refugees to Australia and asked what they made of postmodern picture books, such as *Flotsam*. For these teenagers especially, the lack of written language was important: many of them were still engaged in the process of learning English. So, in this strand of research too, the visual took precedence over the verbal.

This brief summary of current research into picture books brings into focus two clear points that are relevant to the thinking of this chapter. The first is that research has moved far from the concerns of those days in the 1980s, when the books were seen as delightful texts for helping children learn to read. Then, they were a pedagogic tool for teachers. Now they are not. These days, we are more likely to read about children's natural ability to interpret complex images than to consider their use in teaching children anything. Secondly, the gradual diminution of the importance of the verbal text is apparent. When learning to read words mattered, then the language in which those words were constructed was important (Perera 1993). When this ceased to matter to adult readers of picture books, words became little more than carriers of story and story structure. Furthermore, when it became apparent that some very skilled artist/storytellers, such as David Wiesner and Shaun Tan could tell complex and subtle stories in pictures alone, then words could be sidelined altogether. This chapter argues for a return to thinking about words and about pedagogy in picture book research.

Words: carriers of story or tesserae of language?

A difficulty in writing about language per se is that it is generally hard to distinguish between the medium and the message. It is always much easier to see what is being said than to identify how a message is put across. This is my problem with scholars such as Nikolajeva and Scott (2000), who claim to explore the interplay of words and pictures in the picture book, when, in fact, their work deals mostly with the message the words contain. For them words are carriers of plot, or story structure or characterisation – not a focus of interest in their own right. They consider what the words tell, but not, in detail how they tell it.

A similar problem used to exist with pictures. Readers could see what they did, but many could not, or did not, explain how they did it. In those days, pictures were overlooked and readers were encouraged to concentrate on hearing the story. As we have seen, the work of Doonan (1992) and Kress and van Leeuwen (1996) addressed this. They provided a vocabulary and a system of analysis that helped readers to see the medium as well as to read the message. They made it possible for close readings of the pictures to be made. What I argue here is that we need to be able to make similar close readings of the words in picture books, and that if we learn to do this, our understanding of how picture books work will be significantly improved. For this to be possible, we need to look at the tesserae of language in individual texts: to explore how it is made, how the words are put together and the effect of these choices on the ear as well as the mind of the reader (for just as art is visual, language is aural).

The benefits of such an approach for teachers would be tangible. An understanding of the craftedness of prose would enable them to appreciate more fully the likely effect of that prose on readers. They would be better able to assess the challenge that differently constructed phrases pose to inexperienced readers, and better able to understand the affordances of changes in modality, tone and even rhythm to the stance a reader needs to adopt in interpreting any text. They would be better at helping children understand that all language, and written language especially, is never a neutral tool for transparent communication, but is planned, purposeful and situated and the product of a writer's conscious effort.

Language, just like pictures is deliberately made. It deserves equal attention.

Towards a systematic framework for considering language in picture books

There is no single system of linguistic analysis that meets the needs of teachers who might wish to understand the language in picture books better and so develop a useful pedagogy. What I offer here are three different approaches – none of which is sufficient in itself – that might be useful to teachers who wish to develop tools for looking more closely at what the language in the books they wish to use with the children in their classes is doing. The first approach is from the tradition of reading pedagogy and looks at how the way the language of a text is organised (rather than merely the vocabulary or content) might support beginning readers. The second approach is a more literary one and looks at how an understanding of prosody might support an appreciation of the quality of text. The third, which draws on critical language study, considers how the language of a text positions the reader, how it develops and maintains social understandings, and how the reader can use this to unpick the assumptions that govern the world in the text.

The pedagogic function: how words support the reader

Perera (1993) argued that a number of linguistic features were important in texts for beginning readers. She explained that a recognisable and coherent structure was important. There should be no sudden shifts in time or setting. Rhythmic language was good, and also language that children regularly heard or used themselves, rather than the artificial language of the literary story or stilted reading scheme. Repetition, if it was sustained but appropriate, was also useful. The idea was that these structures supported inexperienced readers. They provided frameworks that helped them hang on to story shape and anticipate likely events and vocabulary.

These are useful ideas and a close analysis of the language of the opening pages of two texts for very young readers demonstrates how a consideration of coherence, for example, might make a real difference. Consider the example in Table 8.1.

The texts are superficially very similar. They both set up stories in which young readers are invited to open flaps to discover something (or someone) who is missing. They both begin with questions and conclude with statements. But they are different in the way the reader is supported.

Where's Spot? seems to me to be highly ambiguous. If I were coming to this book for the first time I might not be sure who or what Spot was. The empty bowl on the page and the mention of dinner-time suggests he is a dog – but there is a dog on the page already. Who is this dog on the page? Who is saying the words? Is it the dog or an invisible narrator – perhaps the owner of the

Table 8.1 *Comparison of text in* Where's Spot *and* In Wibbly's Garden

	Where's Spot (Hill 1980)	*In Wibbly's Garden* (Inkpen 2000)
Text	*Where's Spot?* *Naughty Spot!* *It's dinner time. Where can he be?*	*Have you seen Wibbly Pig?* *He's in the garden looking for Pigley*
Image/ layout	Left: initial question top. Beneath it, two dog dishes – one with Sally written on it, one with Spot. Sally's is empty. Centre spread: armchair and dog facing right. Looks sideways towards reader. Right: words at top.	Left: toy car under leafy canopy. Apples on ground. Initial question below. Right: green door with hole that shows pig tail. Door opens to reveal pig, who looks up at reader. Words on reverse of flap.

armchair? Who are the words addressed to? Is it the reader or the dog? What has Spot done that is naughty? Neither the words or the pictures help the new reader know any of this.

The Inkpen book conversely makes reading much safer. Here the narrator addresses the reader directly and demands a relationship with him: 'Have *you* seen Wibbly Pig?' When Wibbly has been discovered behind the gate, he confirms the understanding: 'He's in the garden ...' A kindly, parental voice is set up that guides the young reader through the book and supports his intertextual thinking as the story unfolds ('the bean was one of those magic ones' (p. 6); 'A giant's castle – of course there is!' (p.10)).

Clearly, a child who has had few experiences with books is more likely to find the second text more coherent and rewarding than the first, and the teacher who is able to recognise this is in a strong position. An understanding of how the narrative voice might support or confuse the reader empowers the teacher to make well-informed pedagogic decisions. How might reading pedagogy change, I wonder, if all teachers looked at the texts of the books they read with children in this way?

Literary quality: how has the writer crafted this text?

Language, like art, is the product of a creative process. Good writing does not flow unconsciously from the writer's pen or keyboard. It is honed and crafted, deliberately tempered, until the writer has achieved the exact effect he or she wants. A second framework that we might wish to use to explore the written language of picture books would look at this craftedness. It might focus on the originality of language choices, the virtuosity through which pace or tone is achieved, the effect and quality of imagery. A metalanguage borrowed from literary criticism can be employed here.

Especially useful for considering language in picture books is prosody. Text in picture books is generally short. Because of this, like poetry, it often has a special quality – a spareness, an elusive allusiveness – that makes it distinctive from the prose of other sorts of writing. Furthermore, picture books for very young children often rhyme and are rhythmic. A knowledge of prosody would enable a teacher to identify and explore the extent and the effect of poetic devices in the texts she uses with the children she teaches.

I want to look here at two short extracts from picture books, one for very young children and one for older readers and show how an examination of the language from a literary point of view highlights the power of the prose. First, from Martin Waddell's *Owl Babies* (1992):

The three baby owls have been jumping about in their tree worrying about the absence of their mother. The new opening shows an adult owl flying across the gutter of the spread towards the bottom right. The words 'AND SHE CAME.' Written in white against a black background are positioned at the top, to the left. The next opening shows a panoramic view of her descent towards the chicks. The words: 'Soft and silent she swooped through the trees to Sarah and Percy and Bill' are placed again in the top left corner, this time in blue.

There are several things to notice here. First, there are the changing rhythms; the three strong stresses of the opening words and the contrast with the lyrical, lilting phrase that follows. The reader can hear the flapping of the mother owl's wings or the undulation of her flight as the cadence, accentuated by alliteration, carries her to her chicks. It is significant that the alliteration is on the 's' sound. There is a sigh of relief in its repetition and a gentleness that is perhaps a reflection of the soft sound of wind in feathers. Finally, the litany of the three owl baby names brings her home, with a reassuring echo of what has been established as normal in this text. All is right with the world. Much of the emotional power of *Owl Babies* is charged in these two short sentences.

The second passage comes from Kevin Crossley-Holland's Christmas book *How Many Miles to Bethlehem?* (2004), illustrated by Peter Malone. The book begins with a single spread on the right hand side of the opening. The reader sees Mary, a realistic young woman, centre page. She is obviously pregnant, and rests a hand on her unborn child. Above her, to the left a stylised moon is shown, and at her feet, to the right, a robust angel beats a large drum. The text above her reads:

> I am Mary.
> Tight as a drum.
> Round as the lady moon calling out to me.
> (Crossley-Holland 2004: 1)

Again, the strength of the rhythm arrests the reader: the strong insistent stress of a drum beat in the monosyllabic first two lines. Does it signify that Mary's time is near? Is it a hint of tension, of danger to come? There is certainly tension in the imagery. One fears that from the bursting of this drum will come more than a harmless baby. And then the beat relents. The drum relaxes into a moon and the language becomes expansive and languid. There is a yawn in the full vowel sounds, and a yielding to the persuasive call of nature. We move from masculine, military imagery to one more feminine, a concern with the moon, with mother earth and fertility.

All this in just sixteen words. What is important about it is the way these few words set up the tone and tenor of this book. They signal to the reader that this retelling will not present a simpering, sentimental stable scene, but an ambiguous, allusive text that needs to be worked at. The reader who can unpick the language of this text is not engaging in a form of literary acrobatics. Rather, he or she is showing a nuanced awareness of language. Surely we need a pedagogy that will help children develop this.

It might be that a way to develop out thinking in this area is to move towards an understanding of music as well as poetry. Heald (2008) writes persuasively about the musicality of many texts for young children. He shows how the rhymes, rhythms and refrains of many picture books enchant the children he works with and how the sounds of the language reinforce the message of the text: 'the legato sounding soft B consonants, perhaps subconsciously, informs his readers that a sense of symmetry and equality exists' (2008: 229). He writes too of the sensory pleasure that the language of musical texts affords to the reader.

Critical language study

Finally, we might use a framework from Fairclough's (1989) work on critical language study to explore the way words work in picture books. Fairclough's system assumes a sociological slant and explores the link between language and power. For example, it considers language as a means of establishing and maintaining social relations. It unpicks the unexpressed ideological assumptions that govern the world as it is presented in text and it explores author choices in vocabulary and sentence structure. It takes account, where possible, of what is omitted from a text as well as what is included, and it examines how texts position readers in relation to the authority of the writer.

To some extent, Lewis (2001: 162) takes on a critical language stance in his discussion of modality in the opening lines of *The Jolly Postman* (Ahlberg and Ahlberg: 1986). The text begins: 'Once upon a bicycle/ *So they say/* A Jolly Postman came one day' (Lewis' emphasis). Lewis explains how the parenthesised phrase distances the storyteller from the absolute truth of what he is about to tell (it is only what I have heard!) and thus prepares the reader for the fictionality of the story. He might also comment (though he does not) on the use of 'Once upon a bicycle' rather than the expected 'Once upon a time'. This construction too alerts the reader to the teasing playfulness of the text that is to come. There is a slipperiness of language and reportage here that sets the reader up as an active interpreter of text rather than a passive receiver of story.

A text that will help make clear how critical language study might help readers explore the ideological underpinnings of picture books is David McKee's *The Conquerors* (2004). The story begins like this:

> There was once a large country that was ruled by a General. The people believed that their way of life was best. They had a very strong army and they had the cannon. From time to time the General would take his army and attack a nearby country. 'It's for their own good,' he said. 'So they can be like us.' (McKee 2004: 1)

I want to comment on the dissonance between content and language in the first three sentences here, and to describe the effect of this dissonance. The passage begins simply, with an opening phrase that echoes traditional folk tales ('There was once an old woman who lived in a vinegar bottle' (MacDonald 1995), for example). This sets up two expectations in the reader; one of cosy familiarity – this story will follow a typical pattern, and perhaps play out a moral, and two, that it will be set in a distant time and/or place, where the unusual (possibly magical) can happen. It is interesting that the subject of the first sentence is the country itself rather than the ruler who governs it, but noticeable that the phrase, 'ruled by a General' is given weight by its place at the end of the sentence, and that the General is made important by capitalisation. The reader might wish to wonder about this, but is given no time to think. Instead the second sentence returns attention to 'the people'. The verb 'believed' comes as a surprise. With glib confidence the reader is told that 'the people' all believed the same. Language here, like the General, it seems, does not admit the possibility of dissent. Then the grounds for this belief are given: it is not an assurance based on prosperity or freedom, but on a strong army and *the* cannon. Here again, the language seems simple, but the emphasis of the end of the sentence and an unexpected definite article alert the reader to the understanding that more is going on here that might initially meet the eye or the ear. The reader is jolted into reading against the grain of the language. Who is this General? In what sort of a society is the cannon a guarantee of happiness?

Like the prose, the illustrations confirm that simplicity is merely a surface feature here. The style is consciously naive. 'The people' drawn and coloured with childlike simplicity, are shown at the top of the left side of the spread. All the women have yellow hair and orange tops. All the men have blue jumpers and red hats. Everyone is smiling and all have their hands raised in the air. What they are cheering at is 'the cannon'. It sits in the centre of the page and is dragged along by a proud looking soldier on a proud white horse. To the right, across the gutter, ranks of soldiers march, or possibly goosestep, past the General, who wears golden epaulettes and a posh hat. The soldiers too are identical: they march in step and their eyes look straight ahead, but like 'the people', their face *shapes* are different. The realisation that individuality is possible but, for whatever reason, is unexpressed, undermines the assuredness of the image.

With both words and pictures here, it is not what is said or shown that unsettles the reader, so much as how what is said and shown hints at something more complex. Together they convince the astute reader that beneath the simple surface features of language and illustration is a less simple and less uniform truth. The text works as a lesson in the unreliability of rhetoric, and this surely is a lesson that is worth helping children learn.

Conclusion: picture books and pedagogy

I hope that in this chapter I have shown two things: first that language in picture books deserves attention in its own right, just as pictures deserve attention. I hope I have shown that affording language that attention is rewarding and interesting. It enriches our reading of texts.

I hope I have shown too, that there are pedagogical implications of paying the texts of picture books attention that are more subtle, and I might say more important, than just teaching children to decode words. A careful evaluation of the language will help teachers match texts to the linguistic and emotional needs of the children they teach, and so help them find the right texts for the right child. What better way is there to help children understand that reading is worthwhile than to give them wonderful texts that fully meet their needs? A literary and musical understanding of what language is doing is important too. Teachers who can hear and analyse what a text is doing are well placed to help children get the most out of what they read. They can point children to texts that are well written as well as well designed, and help them to learn, through experience, what the best texts and the best language can do. Finally, a critical analysis of text and how it works can help teachers raise children into a greater awareness of how text works in the political world in which we all live.

Meek (1988) famously showed us that texts teach readers how to read. Looking closely at the part language plays in this process is not reductive: rather it enriches and enhances our understanding of how meaning is made and how fortunate we are to have such wonderfully complex texts to work with.

9   From storytellers to narrators: how can the history of reading help with understanding reading comprehension?

Elspeth Jajdelska

Introduction

Reading can be a sensitive and politicised topic. The debate in the public sphere often concentrates on phonics and the different methods for teaching decoding. Yet it is well known that decoding is not the whole story of the reading curriculum. Efficient decoders can still be poor comprehenders when reading silently, for a variety of reasons (see, e.g., Ricketts *et al.*, this volume; Emmott 1999 [1997]: 9; Cornoldi and Oakhill 1996). Knowledge of comprehension problems that do not result from decoding problems arises from many disciplines, including psychology and linguistics. This chapter suggests that narrative history can illustrate linguistics findings about silent reading comprehension (some of them discussed elsewhere in this volume) in a vivid and accessible way. My own research in the history of reading suggests that style, sentence structure and textual organisation all altered in response to a swift increase in silent reading in the early eighteenth century (Jajdelska 2007). Understanding this historical process can help teachers to recognise comprehension challenges in texts and perhaps to diagnose problems more accurately, showing pupils that silent reading is a complex, comparatively recent and historically rare accomplishment, one of which they can be proud.

The chapter starts with an explanation of an unusual set of conditions which coincided at the end of the seventeenth century to permit, for the first time, a critical mass of readers to move beyond reading as a verbal performance to become fluent, silent readers in childhood. This critical mass created demand for a new kind of text, written in new ways which catered for silent readers. As a result, style and narrative structure underwent radical changes in this period. I go on to discuss three of these changes in more detail: punctuation; sentence structure; and the roles of 'writer' and 'reader'. I show that all three are relatively remote from 'natural' language and therefore likely to present challenges as learners become silent readers.

I wish to thank the AHRC and Sue Ellis, as well as the East Ayrshire teachers and Learning-Teaching Scotland, who participated in the knowledge exchange study.

118

The rise of silent reading in the eighteenth century

Records of silent reading date back at least to antiquity. Perhaps the most famous account from the ancient world is that given by St Augustine of his patron and teacher St Ambrose:

> When he was reading, his eyes ran over the page and his heart perceived the sense, but his voice and tongue were silent. He did not restrict access to anyone coming in, nor was it customary even for a visitor to be announced. Very often when we were there, we saw him silently reading and never otherwise ... We wondered if he read silently perhaps to protect himself in case he had a hearer interested and intent on the matter, to whom he might have to expound the text being read if it contained difficulties, or who might wish to debate some difficult questions. If his time were used up in that way, he would get through fewer books than he wished. Besides, the need to preserve his voice, which used easily to become hoarse, could have been a very fair reason for silent reading. (Saint Augustine, trans. Chadwick 1992, VI.iii (3), pp. 92–93).

At first sight, an account like this might seem to undermine my claim that silent reading did not influence text structure until the eighteenth century (for a detailed account of my historical claims in this chapter see Jajdelska 2007). Yet Augustine's point is that something needs to be explained about Ambrose's choice to read silently; he must have been avoiding a conversation or protecting his voice. This implies that the normal model in this period for reading was reading aloud.

The same is true for medieval reading models. Saenger has shown that silent reading in monasteries increased in the Middle Ages and was associated with the introduction of spaces between words in manuscripts (Saenger 1997). However, there was still no sign that the default model of a reader was one who read silently. So even though some individuals in all ages have chosen, for a range of reasons, to read silently, the dominance of silent reading, the almost unconscious assumption by most writers that their reader will be silent, is far more recent. 'Reading' was routinely understood as performing a text aloud. Memorisation was central to all reading instruction as this would allow the reader to perform even more effectively. So texts were written assuming a model of 'the reader as a speaker', as though they were scripts. Students were taught to memorise and perform texts aloud as part of rhetoric, a subject which dominated the early modern curriculum.

Teachers will know better than most that becoming a fluent silent reader requires many years of engaged reading in childhood. In their OECD study, Kirsch et al. show that 'engagement in reading ... (time spent reading for pleasure, time spent reading a diversity of material, high motivation and interest in reading)' is a powerful predictor of success in silent reading comprehension (Kirsch et al. 2002: 106). In the present day we take it for granted that children in the developed world will have sufficient access to books and texts to allow this; even the most impoverished children in western societies can in theory encounter a wide range of attractive texts in libraries and elsewhere (in practice, of course, not all children will come from homes which encourage this).

But for the greater part of history, the conditions for engaged reading were rare. These conditions are as follows:

- disposable income to buy or borrow a range books which children can read without supervision;
- leisure time for children to read at will and for pleasure;
- an ideology which encourages reading for pleasure;
- freedom from pressure to memorise text.

Although the invention of the printing press exponentially increased the production of books in the early modern period, for most readers books were still expensive consumer goods and owning enough of them for engaged reading in childhood was rare. However for an elite group, this began to change in the late seventeenth and early eighteenth centuries. Disposable incomes among what we now call the middle class increased sharply, and their houses filled with all kinds of consumer goods – china, pictures, tea and coffee as well as books (Weatherill 1996).

Children of this class also had, for the first time, the opportunity to read for pleasure. Seventeenth-century educationalists had been suspicious of reading for pleasure. Reading was seen as a solemn affair undertaken to improve the soul or provide practical advantages in life. Readers of fiction (such as cheap romances and plays) were disparaged by preachers. This ideology, as well as the cost of books, meant that children were expected to read in order to memorise. A typical father advised his son:

Let not thy Books be many, but of the best. Thou art never the worse Scholar, if thy Library lay in thy head. Thou hast no more Learning than what thou carriest about thee, that which lies by, is the Authors, not thine. If Books would make a Scholar, the Bookseller might bear the Bell. (Anon. 1688: 16)

So most children in the early seventeenth century lacked both sufficient texts and encouragement to become engaged readers. They also lacked leisure. One reader, a merchant's son, wrote of his enthusiasm for reading romances, but in doing so revealed how difficult it was to find the time. He used, 'all the time I had from school' to read these books, which turned out to be Thursdays in the afternoon and Saturdays; reading in the evenings was curtailed by the cost of candles (quoted in Wright 1935: 86–87). This forms a striking contrast with well-off children a generation later whose parents' increased wealth bought more leisure and candles, as well as more books.

Educational thinking was also changing. The traditional emphasis on memorisation was challenged by thinkers such as Locke (1693: 63, 183, 186 and elsewhere). In the world of classical rhetoric, memorisation was central both to allow effective performance of texts and to allow the maximum number of people to benefit from rare and expensive books and scrolls. But in Locke's day, for the first time in history, and for an elite group, the conditions for engaged reading in childhood were in place: disposable incomes, leisure, permission to read at will and for pleasure, and freedom from the need to memorise. As a result, within a generation the number of fluent, silent readers was sufficient to support the printing of texts tailored to their needs. A typical text of this kind was Addison's *Spectator* which had a circulation of around 3,000 and a readership of perhaps 60,000 in London (Addison 1998: 88).

This led to what the *Cambridge History of the English Language* has called a 'sea change' in prose style in the period (Adamson 1999: 604–605) as well as a radical break with the past in narrative structure. These new textual features became permanent features of narrative prose, presenting challenges which today's young readers still encounter. In the rest of this article I discuss three of these features in more detail: punctuation, sentence structure and the roles of 'writer' and 'reader'.

Sentences are not 'natural'

In most linguistic writing today, the concept of the sentence is assumed to be fundamental. Yet Crystal has pointed out that there are 'innumerable definitions' of the sentence (Crystal 1992: 313). The history of silent reading suggests that one way of understanding sentences is as autonomous units whose syntactic scope is bounded by pauses (Jajdelska 2007: 80–81). Units of this kind are the product not of natural language but of changes in prose style brought about by a surge in silent reading.

This becomes clearer when we consider the role of silence in communication. Pausing in speech is a form of communication. Pauses can indicate a very wide range of meanings, such as incomprehension, disagreement, anger and patience among others (Jaworski 1993). So for centuries, when writing was understood as a script for oral performance, pauses were avoided, because their communicative role makes them prone to misinterpretation. Even today, a live performer (such as a comedian) will be careful to avoid long pauses in case they are interpreted as an invitation to heckle or as a failure of memory. Early modern writers used long strings of clauses and minimal punctuation to avoid pauses and their potential misinterpretation by a live audience. As a result, writing from earlier periods cannot be analysed in sentences as they are understood today:

Honored S^r.
'Tis 12 months since I had the favour of a line from you, wch. I willingly attribute to ye great throng you hav had about matters of greater moment, I had the ill hap to

enquire of y^r friend D^r W: wheth^e the Lett^e with the Roman Monum^{ts}. had appeared at Gresham Col: because if it had miscarryed (wch. I was afraid of because of your silence) I could not retrieve a Coppy of it, and hav rec'd such an ill natured return (because not addressed to himself) as I never had from any Gent^m. but this only to your self.

(Ralph Thoresby, letter to Hans Sloane, MS 4039, f. 136, British Library)

This letter by the merchant and antiquary Ralph Thoresby was written in the 1690s, and a present-day reader is immediately struck by his reluctance to use a full stop. In fact at this period in his life, Thoresby virtually never used the full stop (later on he tried to adapt his style to the changes brought about by silent reading). Present-day readers will also find Thoresby's approach rather breathless and at times ambiguous, because modern-day readers have ceased to notice their own skills as fluent, silent readers. But Thoresby's readers, used to thinking of reading as a kind of speaking, would find the avoidance of poten-tially confusing pauses quite natural. This style – strings of loosely connected clauses – may also be familiar to teachers of young children who are used to reading the writing of their young learners.

So why do we find the sentence (with full stop) indispensable nowadays, and why might young readers be closer to accomplished readers of Thoresby's era than to their fluent counterparts today? The answer is that with silent reading there is no danger of misinterpreting a live performer. As a result, writers in the era of silent reading began to use longer pauses more freely for the sole and newly unambiguous purpose of clarifying syntax. Joseph Addison, a pioneer of the new style, corrected his own writing using just this technique:

Manuscript version

Of all <u>Disparities that</u> in humour makes the most unhappy <u>Marriages yet</u> scarce enters into our thoughts at the contracting of them.

(Addison, n.d.), Extract from drafts of the *Spectator*, MS Don. d. 112, f. 20, Bodleian Library)

Printed version

Of all <u>Disparities, that</u> in Humour makes the most unhappy <u>Marriages, yet</u> scarce enters into our Thoughts at the contracting of them.

(Addison 1965, vol. I, p. 515)

Here, Addison has noticed that his first version could be read as 'all the dispar-ities that make the most unhappy marriages in humour'. Had he been writing a decade or two earlier, he might have hesitated before adding the comma lest his (oral) reader be misinterpreted as having lost his or her place, or inviting an interruption. But the silent reader who pauses at a comma knows that he or she is not inviting interruption, because there can be no meaningful interruptions to a silent reader. So Addison is free to use a pause to clarify his syntax. For the same reason he can use a comma to clarify that it is the disparity in humour and not the unhappy marriages which 'scarce enter our thoughts'.

The same approach to sentences in the era of oral reading can explain some of the syntactic choices at the time. Here is Ralph Thoresby once more:

Sir *John Osborne* of *Kelmarsh* in the County of *Northampton*, had an only Daughter married to Sir *John Peyton* of *Islam* in the County of *Cambridge*, with whom all the Estate went from the Family of the *Osborne's*, except about *600l. per Annum* in *Essex*, and an House called *Parstow*, which were settled upon *Richard Osborne*, younger Brother of the said Sir *John*, which *Richard* I take to be the first in the preceding Pedigree, which was enter'd in the Heralds Office, (*E. 1. Folio* 190.) when Sir *Hewet Osborne* was but one Year and … Days old. (Thoresby 1715: 3)

Again, a present-day editor or teacher would split this string of relative clauses into a sequence of shorter sentences. But a writer who thinks of reading as speaking will organise syntax in order to avoid pausing, often, as here, by using subordination. Again, long sequences of loosely connected subordinate clauses are found spontaneously in the writing of less experienced writers today. But whereas nowadays this is treated as a fault, in Thoresby's day it was a perfectly sensible strategy to avoid potentially ambiguous pauses when the text was performed aloud. Otherwise the hearers might mistakenly think that the speaker/writer had finished speaking.

So both the punctuation patterns and the syntactic structures that we associate with a failure to understand sentences, are in fact very sensible strategies for writers whose readers will perform their texts orally. Sentences, in other words, are a long distance from spontaneous or natural language, and learning them requires some rather artificial role-play.

Storytellers and narrators

Teachers are used to introducing the concept of a 'narrator'. Some aspects of narrators are quite easy to understand. For example, most learners will not struggle to give a description of a narrator's character ('friendly', 'distant' and so on). However, the ease with which these aspects of narrators can be understood may lead to underestimating their stranger qualities. This can be illuminated by comparing 'storytellers' with 'narrators'. Storytelling is an innately human activity – there are no societies which do not tell stories. But there are many societies whose stories do not have 'narrators', as they are understood today. Storytelling is intensely social and draws on a 'shared space' between storyteller and audience. This is so even when we tell each other very brief and simple stories. For example, without being aware of it, speakers use their hands to indicate the directions of 'in' and 'out' when they tell stories to an audience in the same room (Özyürek 2002: 702). And, of course they also use facial expressions and a wide range of vocal effects to clarify the events in their stories.

Explicating events which involve movements in time or space are particularly crucial to the audience's understanding of a narrative. In signed languages, changes in point of view are even marked by a 'referential shift' (Emmorey 1996: 184). Moreover, in many cultures, including that of early modern England, there exist a wide range of conventional gestures to clarify movements and time changes (Roach 1985: 34; Bulwer 1644; Stern 2000).

It should be clear, then, that transferring stories from live performance to the written word can potentially cause confusion. In the early centuries of print this was less of a problem. This is because readers learned to perform texts rather than read them internally; that is they treated them as scripts. Any given text might be read and prepared many times, so that initial ambiguities could be cleared up through performative tools like gesture and tone of voice. The reader's job was to prepare the text for enactment to a live audience.

The real change came with the rise of texts written for a silent, rather than an oral, reader. It is a commonplace of modern stories that third-person narrators have a 'God's eye view' of events. But it is rare to analyse exactly what that involves. Research by psychologists suggests that understanding this kind of narrator is surprisingly complex. Rall and Harris (2000) looked at how children made sense of comparatively simple narratives with narrators of this kind:

They [the children] might adopt an 'external' view of the scene being described by mentally locating themselves outside the space as an observer. Once the protagonist or the protagonist's location is identified, they treat that location as a landmark or 'anchor'. Children then code any displacement that is described in the narrative in terms of whether it consists of an approach toward the anchor or a retreat away from it. (Rall and Harris 2000: 206)

Understanding a narrator, then, involves creating a mental 'anchor' outside the imagined space where events are taking place. This anchor is fixed to some extent in time and space, but it is notional insofar as no real person could ever inhabit it. This anchor enables changes in location within the story.

Emmott has suggested that the problems encountered by even good decoders in comprehending narrative can be explained, at least in part, by the difficulties in imagining movements from one mental model of the story's context to another (Emmott 1999 [1997]). So the narrator's 'anchor' must be flexible enough to allow him or her to change between locations, but at the same time fixed enough to allow readers to interpret changes *within* any given location. These complex requirements were simply not needed by learners in the period before widespread silent reading.

The contrast between storytellers and narrators can be illustrated through extracts from two famous eighteenth-century narratives. The first paragraph is the opening of Defoe's pioneering novel, now known as *Robinson Crusoe*. It was written at the point of transition from an assumption that reading is oral to an assumption that reading is silent. Defoe is still using the older style, suited to oral reading. The second extract is from another giant text of the eighteenth century, Samuel Richardson's novel *Pamela*. This paragraph was inserted by an anonymous editor into a pirated version. Pirate editions were very popular in an era when copyright law was still evolving and pirate editors would often add new material so that they could claim it was a 'new' version. In this case, the opening paragraph is *not* by Richardson, but by a writer who has adapted to the new style suitable to silent readers.

Extract from Robinson Crusoe
I Was born in the Year 1632, in the City of *York*, of a good Family, tho' not of that Country, my Father being a Foreigner of *Bremen*, who settled first at *Hull*: He got a good Estate by Merchandise, and leaving off his Trade, lived afterward at *York*, from whence he had married my Mother, whose Relations were named *Robinson*, a very good Family in that Country. (Defoe 1719: 1)

The difficulties in this text for a present-day reader can be explained by Defoe's reliance on a storyteller rather than a narrator. An oral reader, for example, could easily clarify the very swift movements in place (between York, Bremen and Hull) and time (his father's early years in Bremen, the move to Hull, his son's birth in York) by using gesture and other tools within a shared space. A silent reader however might struggle with these rapid (and non-chronological) changes in mental model. For such a reader, the approach taken by the pirate editor of *Pamela* is more suitable:

Extract from pirated edition of Richardson's *Pamela*
IT was in that ever memorable Year 1720, when one half of the Island of *Great Britain* seemed under a strong Infatuation, and were precipitantly running on their own Ruin, that Mr. *John Andrews*, a very honest and worthy Man, who liv'd in a yeomanly way, partly as a Gentleman, and partly as a Farmer, upon a slender Estate of his own, in the County of *Bedford*, was over persuaded to sell his small Patrimony, to adventure what he received for the Purchase of it, in the *South Sea* Stock, with Hopes of raising a Fortune, that might enable him to support his Family, consisting only of himself, his Wife and one Daughter, without being obliged to follow that laborious Part of his Business himself, which took him too much off from that studious and contemplative way of living that he greatly desired his latter Days might be Crowned with. (Richardson 1741, vol. I: 1–2)

To replace the oral storyteller assumed by Defoe, this anonymous pirate editor has created a narrator, one who is located somewhere outside the action not only of the story at this point (Pamela's birth in Bedford) but outside the island of Great Britain. And unlike a real human being (such as a storyteller) this narrator is able simultaneously to observe the behaviour of particular individuals (John Andrews) and of the whole country (one half of the island of Great Britain). The narrator's physical location outside the action is mirrored by his location in time. The 'present' of the story is during Pamela's adult position as a servant in a great man's home, but the narrator can move backwards to the earlier time of her birth with ease.

Conclusion

Understanding the history of reading can yield surprising insights into technical issues in reading comprehension. The transition to ubiquitous and fluent silent reading happened relatively late in the history of literacy, and involved the creation of a new and artificial approach to sentence structure, as well as the invention of an unnatural being, 'the narrator'. Those teaching young children need to appreciate how artificial and strange these aspects of reading might appear to those new to reading. Perhaps the most useful application of this historical narrative is to turn it into a personal one, so that learners are understood as experiencing an accelerated version of the historical transition from a reader who speaks the text to an audience to a silent reader. Some work on this has already begun. Elspeth Jajdelska and Sue Ellis collaborated with teachers and the curriculum advice body for Scotland, Learning and Teaching Scotland (LTS), on a knowledge exchange project which was funded by the Arts and Humanities Research Council (AHRC). This explored how understanding the history of reading gave primary teachers new insights into the comprehension challenges that texts pose young readers aged 5–12.

10   Talk about text: the discursive construction of what it means to be a reader

Gemma Moss

By focusing on the literacy event, this chapter will use perspectives which combine linguistics with ethnography to explore how children talk about texts in both formal and informal social settings. What might analysis of such talk contribute to teachers' understanding of the literacy curriculum and its role in fostering children's development as readers?

Introduction

In a discussion paper outlining the distinctive characteristics of linguistic ethnography Rampton and colleagues define what sets it apart from other research traditions that are concerned with studying language in context, such as applied linguistics and sociolinguistics, in these terms: 'linguistic ethnography generally holds that to a considerable degree, language and the social world are mutually shaping, and that close analysis of situated language use can provide both fundamental and distinctive insights into the mechanisms and dynamics of social and cultural production in everyday activity' (Rampton *et al.* 2004).

If applied linguistics and sociolinguistics give primacy to understanding the role of language in specific contexts, linguistic ethnographers explore the ways in which an ensemble of linguistic, material and cultural resources shape social interaction. Linguistic ethnography is very much attuned to the way in which the social world in its many facets is continuously remade in particular encounters which are both shaped by the past but also have the potential to transform how things stand. Change and continuities are equally important with an accent on individual agency, tempered by an understanding of the social history which structures how any social interaction takes place and the resources which constrain as well as enable the choices individuals can make. Whilst the term 'linguistic ethnography' is still in its infancy and may to-date have limited circulation outside the UK (see special issue, *Journal of Sociolinguistics* (2007) Vol. 11: 5), these defining characteristics underpin this chapter and its analysis of talk about text.

Talk about text: speech genre or literacy event?

One of the main areas in which perspectives from ethnography have been successfully allied with perspectives from linguistics is in the study of literacy. For some while now ethnographers interested in understanding how the use of literacy varies within and across communities have employed the concept of the literacy event in their studies (Heath 1983; Street 1984). Broadly speaking, literacy events can be defined as any occasion where a piece of written text plays an integral part in whatever is going on. Heath comments that literacy events 'have social interactional rules which regulate the type and amount of talk about what is written, and define ways in which oral language reinforces, denies, extends or sets aside the written material' (Heath 1983: 386). Studying literacy via the literacy event places the written text firmly in its context of use. Researchers pay attention to the nature of the occasion where literacy is used, the relations between any participants and the meanings and intentions that shape what they do, alongside the precise role reading and writing play in that interaction. To a greater or lesser extent this becomes available for study via the talk that accompanies the use of written texts.

Amongst the literacy events that have been studied are those that participants themselves label and recognise as particularly salient. An obvious example here would be the bedtime story – an event that happens outside of school and is both recognised and accorded considerable significance within particular communities (Heath 1982). Within-school examples would include 'reading aloud', 'story time' or 'show and tell'. But literacy events may also be of a more fleeting character, less directly remarked upon by their participants and occur in contexts where literacy is more closely woven into other aspects of everyday life – navigating official forms or seeking help with specialised texts such as legal documents would be good examples (Baynham 1995). The range and diversity of the events such research has uncovered have challenged some of the normative descriptions and prescriptions of literacy's point and purpose which derive from other historically more dominant traditions within education and psychology.

As it has become more apparent from such work that what it *means* to read and to be a reader or to write and to be a writer varies within and across cultures, so questions about how children acquire culturally specific versions of literacy through participating in particular kinds of literacy events have followed. In line with sociolinguistics, this had led to questions for education about whether and how far literacy events within the school curriculum share features with literacy events that happen elsewhere, or whether they omit and overrule understandings and intentions that belong to other domains. Just as with sociolinguistics, the potential power relations between different ways of doing literacy become part of the object of study. By asking 'what counts as literacy' (Heap 1991), researchers pay particular attention to who holds the rights to define the answer in the context of particular events. Apply this question to literacy events in school and procedurally teachers hold more rights to define what counts as reading and writing: they are the experts, their pupils the novices who are inducted into the school's way of doing things.

Focusing on the social occasion in which literacy is embedded rather than the written text and its individual reader or writer is not to deny that there is an alphabetic or iconic principle at work when encoding or decoding written languages, or that grappling with language written down makes different demands on those who undertake this task than dealing with speech, including through the semantic and linguistic forms that are particular to written language. But it also asserts that learning to read and write are profoundly social acts tied to social purposes and understandings. Literacy events demonstrate these social understandings. They encode social relations alongside features of the written text that their readers or writers may focus on. For researchers adopting this approach, analysis of the talk about text that occurs within specific literacy events is integrated with analysis of the purposes and intentions that shape the occasion in which reading and writing take place, and which will colour the meanings that will be made from the text itself. Part of the peculiarity of schooled literacy that becomes visible via this route is that the uses of reading and writing in schooled settings are explicitly regulated – there are clear rules about who can access which kinds of texts under what conditions, and what they can be taken to mean. Children are directly inducted into these rules through the literacy events teachers orchestrate as part of the school day and this has a profound influence on their sense of themselves as readers (Moss 2007).

Studying literacy development through a focus on literacy events: the bedtime story

What are the advantages of studying literacy in this way? Certainly there is a very sharp contrast with the study of literacy from (mainstream) psychological perspectives. Most psychological traditions treat literacy primarily as a set of cognitive skills which the individual child needs to acquire and will do so predominantly through a process of direct instruction. Issues of debate within the field include: how the various skills involved can be defined; the precise sequence in which they should be taught; the most appropriate forms of pedagogy to ensure the maximum number of children acquire the right skill set; and how to remediate those who struggle to develop the relevant skills within the expected time frame. Whilst the quality of interaction between the teacher and the child may be of interest, the social structure of the event in which such interaction takes place is widely overlooked. Talk about texts, particularly the child's talk about the text, is largely regarded as a transparent window onto an internal and cognitive interaction between the child and the text which will have already taken place and which the talk brings to light. Answers to comprehension questions thus represent the level of understanding that the child has achieved through prior internal mental activity. Talk about texts has a key function in the assessment of individual competence, but the social relations between participants as the talk unfolds can be safely bracketed off.

A focus on literacy events rather than the skills associated with text processing or the linguistic structures the text represents is more compatible with social psychology and in particular the work of Lev Vygotsky. Vygotsky observed that: 'Every function in the child's cultural development appears twice: first on the social level, and later on the individual level' (Vygotsky 1978). In contrast with other psychological traditions, for Vygotskians the talk with adults or significant others which accompanies reading and writing has a vital role to play in constructing and making visible the competencies that later children will exercise individually and is a key part of the process by which they make such competencies their own.

Henrietta Dombey provides a useful example of this approach in her study of the 'bedtime story' (Dombey 1992). A ubiquitous feature of some communities' social interactions round literacy, such events are often regarded as playing a key role in children's literacy development. Dombey set out to analyse why this might be so, and what the nature of the event adds to children's development as readers. The example in Figure 10.1 stems from a literacy event in which a mother reads the picture book, *Rosie's Walk*, to her 3½-year-old daughter, Anna. The initial exchange between mother and her daughter makes clear that the event is embedded in the wider flow of domestic time, and in this instance depends upon the daughter capturing her mother's attention away from other routine activities in order for the two of them to read together. This is the last in a series of books the pair have read together – whilst the mother would clearly like to retreat to supper, Anna prolongs the reading.

The way in which Dombey lays up the transcript makes clear that the full meaning of the text rests as much with the pictures and their sequencing as it does with the writing. Indeed, the single sentence that makes up the written text includes no reference to the main action in the story and the question which drives the narrative: whether the fox will manage to catch the hen as she makes her way around the farmyard and before she returns to the coop. In this event all the decoding of the written text is undertaken by the mother. Anna's role is not to join in with this aspect of reading. Rather the sequence of questions she poses show that her attention is on the story grammar as it unfolds in the pictures and the words she hears and through the ways in which they counterpoint each other. Both mother and child supply sound effects for pictures that have no accompanying written text – Boum; Splash – but which highlight the

M	C' mon 'cos I want to go and have my supper.	ROSIE'S WALK By
		PAT HUTCHINS
	Hurry up.	*Picture of carefree hen walking*
	Rosie's Walk	*through cluttered rural scene,*
		followed by watchful fox
		Cover
M	Rosie the hen went for a walk	*Picture of hen setting out*
		across picturesque farmyard
A	A fox is following her	*with fox eyeing her greedily*
		from under the hen-house
M	Oh!	Rosie the hen went for a
		walk
M	Across the yard	*Picture of hen walking past*
		fruit trees, unaware of fox
		jumping after her
		across the yard
M	Boum ****	*Picture of hen walking on*
		unaware while fox bumps his
		nose on rake he has landed on
M	Around the pond	*Picture of hen walking beside*
		pond, unaware of fox jumping
		after her.
A	**** fish in the pond	*No fish in picture.*
		around the pond
A	Splash! How they, how the fox just don't get out?	*Picture of hen walking on*
		unaware of fox landing in the
		pond. No fish in the picture
M	Oh I expect he'll climb out	
A	Why?	
M	Why will he climb out?	
A	Yeah	
M	Well, why do you think he'll climb out?	
A	Like when he wants, when he, the hen to eat	
M	Yes, he wants to eat Rosie	

(Dombey, 1992, pp. 30–31)

Figure 10.1 A mother reads the picture book, *Rosie's Walk*, to her 3½-year-old daughter, Anna (Source: Dombey 1992)

plight of the unfortunate fox. The questions that Anna asks orientate to the present in the story as it unfolds: how will the fox get out of the pond; why is the fox so determined to keep on following the hen? The legitimacy of these kinds of questions is reinforced by the mother's answers, which keep the focus steadily within the narrative structure. Dombey comments 'Through their conversational talk mother and child are creating a story world and moving about inside it, making judgments on its elements and exploring its possibilities and laws' (Dombey 1992: 33). She is very clear on the value of this kind of talk, arising in relation to but also reanimating the particular sequence of words and pictures that make up the tale:

> Paradoxically, the loose and shifting structures of conversation permit mother and child to actualise the tighter and more complex structures of narrative. The discourse structures Anna is familiar with, and in which she plays the leading role, serve to elaborate and articulate the less familiar structures of the narrative, where her mother has control of the discourse. What is new is not merely juxtaposed with what is familiar: it is through the familiar that the new is given its coherence and significance and enters Anna's possession. (Dombey 1992: 34)

Dombey's analysis focuses on the way in which the social interaction that accompanies this bedtime story produces a deep understanding of story grammar and thus lays the ground rules for reading in its fuller sense. This happens in a sustained partnership as mother and daughter focus on the same text, with the mother both supporting and enabling her daughter to reach well beyond the competence as a reader that she could muster on her own. Dombey argues that in this way and through these kinds of events, this child will come to understand what it means to read and engage with narrative structures, long before the responsibility for decoding text falls to her.

'Did you see?' Literacy events that map less easily onto concepts of literacy development

It is harder to know how to respond to literacy events whose pedagogic value or purpose is much less immediately clear. Take the following example of small group talk collected as part of a project designed to map children's competence in television literacy.

GLORIA: Did you watch *Beadles About*? Fat people going into the tent?
RANJIT: Oh yeah
NATALIE: Break dancing (laughing)
CAROL: And she had to pull up her skirt, to get into the tent (Everybody laughs)
GLORIA: See them funny knickers, boy

I would argue that this can usefully be regarded as a literacy event, even if the text under discussion is a partly scripted TV programme rather than print or writing. The text that the group recall, *Beadles About*, was a popular television programme which used hidden cameras to film interactions designed to amuse and provoke. It was screened at peak time, during a period when most

The example of Gloria, Ranjit, Natalie and Carol discussing television viewing was collected for the Television Literacy project, funded by the ESRC, 1989–91. The research team members were David Buckingham, Valerie Hey and Gemma Moss.

households still could only receive terrestrial rather than satellite or cable TV. This is the entire sequence of talk about this particular text which occurs in the midst of a much longer sequence of similar moments in which this group of 11–12-year-olds recount to each other the highlights of particular programmes they have enjoyed, or list favourite programmes.

The open-ended interview from which this extract comes was designed to elicit what children knew and understood about TV as part of a research project intended to inform the media literacy curriculum for schools (see Buckingham 1993). The interviewer's brief was to encourage the five participants to talk about what they liked and disliked about watching television, as far as possible allowing the group to set their own agenda. This proved disconcertingly easy to do. After some talk about the soap opera, *Home and Away*, largely steered by the interviewer, one of the participants, Gloria, in effect wrested control over the direction of the conversation by asking the interviewer 'Don't you like any other programmes?'. This allowed the conversation to move on from what Gloria clearly regarded as too prolonged a focus on soaps to a more free-flowing discussion from then on. The extract above was fairly typical. Whilst some exchanges sustained the talk about a particular programme for a little bit longer, none of them provided the kind of detailed reflection on aspects of what these young people had seen that might have counted as conceptual knowledge of genre, industry, audience or even plot and character. On the contrary, the talk was organised around two key phrases, 'I like' and 'Did you see?', which would be followed by either a rough list of programme titles or, as in the extract quoted above, a brief resume of part of a programme – just enough to spark off a reaction amongst others in the group, and then the talk would move on.

This kind of talk is clearly familiar to these participants. They create the dynamic to the conversation and its pace and flow using strategies that they bring from elsewhere. What they say is not a product of the structured intentions of the interviewer, or indeed the interviewer's check-list of formal features or kinds of knowledge about television that might be worth recording. In the published account of the project (Buckingham 1993), this group's treatment of the opportunity to talk about their favourite television programmes is quoted as an example of small group interviews where social talk dominated, turning it into 'an 'anti-educational' event, as a chance to get out of lessons and let off some steam' (Buckingham 1993: 65). Whilst the dynamic of the event is clearly regarded as having a social purpose for its participants, from an analytic point of view what they have to say is treated as disappointing. The social function gets in the way of an exploration of the underlying cognitive competencies that children might bring to making sense of television: 'there is generally very little attempt to explain the reasons for their preferences, although evaluative comments … may be offered in passing. Typically, the children seem to perceive little point in being equivocal, or offering more nuanced judg-ments'. And 'Some retellings took the form of very brief references ... if you missed that episode, the reference will probably be meaningless' (Buckingham 1993: 66).

Yet in a sense this is to prioritise the interests of the adult as evaluator over those of the children, for whom recall of text in this implicit fashion is clearly quite sufficient. In part this is to do with the way the texts they refer to have come to be shared property. The question 'Did you see?' signals this quite precisely. This exchange depends upon the audience having watched the same programme, something which is characteristic of a broadcast medium with few channels. This remains one way of exploiting the medium now. Despite the explosion of multi-channel TV, popular programmes bind the audience into experiencing the same moment in the same timeframe. Part of the pleasure is talking about it afterwards in precisely this kind of way. If you saw those 'fat people going into the tent' then you do indeed know what this means. The conversation as a whole can and does disregard those experiences that have not been shared. The question 'Did you see?' allows the audience to focus pre-cisely on what they hold in common.

That this is to do with the social means through which the text is encoun-tered rather than the medium per se is underlined by the way in which children talked about videos they had watched. Unable to rely on others' familiarity with the text, speakers would expect to hold the floor for longer, and were much more likely to launch into more detailed narrative accounts, in which they attempted to sequence key elements in the plot whilst trying to clarify for others what made it interesting.

STEWART: I like Kickboxer
GEMMA: Kickboxer? What's that?
STEWART: It's a video, it's about this um,/
? Kickboxer [one?
STEWART: [there's this, yeah, and there's this man, he's the champion of kickboxing, and this other, like, he's a much better person, kick breaks his spine, and he can only move his top half, and his brother swe, swears revenge on the other man, and um, the man's like, men, um, kidnap his girlfriend and the man, so he won't beat the other men, he said if you win I, um your sister and that will get, girlfriend will get killed, and so his teacher goes off and saves them but it's not like, all like that and then he comes, when they come back he kills the person/

Here the narrative that Stewart constructs provides the sequence of events that drive the plot – the injury and the quest for revenge – but also highlights charged elements of the action – 'kick breaks his spine'; 'swears revenge'; 'kidnap'; 'girlfriend will get killed'; 'kills the person'. These stand out even if precisely who does what to whom is not entirely clear.

Both kinds of talk quoted above, whether implicitly or explicitly, invoke the texts' content and situate the speaker(s) and their audience in relation to the text. In contrast with the practice Dombey records in her study of the bedtime story, this talk happens off-text and away from the site of the first reading: the text may be being invoked in the talk, either retrospectively or prospectively, but it is not immediately present. I have commented elsewhere on the role such talk about text has in creating and sustaining interest in different kinds of media texts (Maybin and Moss 1993; Moss 1993). I turn now to the role this kind of social talk about text has in relation to book reading.

Literacy events and the social distribution of texts

Prior to the use of cable and satellite as a means of streaming programmes at a time and place that suit the individual consumer, the social organisation of terrestrial television made it highly likely that a large audience would have seen the same programmes at the same time. To some extent scheduling ensures this is still possible. By contrast, children's book reading is less likely to generate this pattern of a large number of individuals holding in common a relatively small selection of texts, whose reading has in effect been synchronised. On the contrary the available evidence suggests that individual's book preferences are quite diverse and where particular texts are held in common they are most likely to have been read in very different timeframes (Moss and McDonald 2004). An obvious exception outside of school would be *Harry Potter*. Avid collectors, who purchased the books in sequence as they were published and then read them as fast as they could within a few days, could bank on finishing the story at roughly the same time as their friends, and would then be able to share the content of the text with other fans, through recall and selection of 'best bits', before settling down to wait for the next volume.

This kind of synchronised experience of the written text would have been far more familiar during the nineteenth century. Dickens' novels mostly became available in monthly instalments and might well have been read in a group as well as individually, in a way that mimics more closely the ongoing engagement of the modern audience with soap operas or popular television series rather than contemporary forms of book-reading. Inside school, the class reader provides access to texts under broadly similar conditions. However, the extended pacing of such activity over say a half-term, the little use of cliff-hangers or charged moments to structure how the reading is chunked, and the very different ways in which the text itself becomes embedded in a range of school tasks make it hard to replicate this kind of sustained interest and excitement.

The mode of distribution of the text colours the possibilities for talk. So too does the dynamic of the event in which any text is recalled. Interviews structured around book reading seldom get the anarchic charge seen in the first extract above. They do yield more lengthy re-tellings on the part of a single individual, which more closely follow the pattern of the video recount. The following example, collected from an interview with two Year 5 students aged 10, is not untypical:

DAVID: My favourite book that I've ever, ever read has to be *Dinotopia*
INTERVIEWER: Yeah? Go on tell me about *Dinotopia*
DAVID: *Dinotopia*'s about this island where there's dinosaurs and people live together, [and it starts off
PETER: [And there's two people who are stranded on the island
DAVID: Yeah, Will and Arthur Denston and Will is, Arthur is Will's father, and there's this coral reef all the way round, going round Dinotopia and they smacked into it and they got stranded on Dinotopia and then all these dinosaurs swirled round them and they all, no they see a dinosaur comes out the bush and he throws a stone at it and then all these other dinosaurs, big ones, come out.

It is hard to know how far this kind of blow-by-blow account mimics or is influenced by the criteria for recalling narrative texts in classroom settings. Certainly the level of detail that David seeks to muster here, including the relationship between the key characters, the setting, how they got there and their reaction to the first encounter with the dinosaurs, leads to a good deal of self-correction and addition in pursuit of accuracy and explicitness.

This is not to say that this inevitably happens round book reading. In the extract below from the same interview, both boys are able to focus on the best bits in Roald Dahl's *Matilda*, a book they both know:

INTERVIEWER: And which is your best one of all the Dahls?
PETER: ... it would have to be Matilda
INTERVIEWER: Mhm, because, what do you like about that one? ...
PETER: [it's really funny and because Matilda just puts lizards everywhere
INTERVIEWER: She does what?
PETER: She has lizards and she put one in the teacher's drink
DAVID: No that was the boy, another girl, not Matilda
PETER: I thought it was Matilda
DAVID: No, it was Matilda's best little friend. He scooped it up, she scooped it up from her pond and then put it in her pencil case and brought it to school, and she tips it into Miss Trunchbull's (...)
INTERVIEWER: What happens in the end to Miss Trunchbull?
DAVID: Miss Trunchbull, does she get killed or does she get sent to jail?
PETER: Sent to jail.

In general there are far fewer opportunities for children to recall jointly books they are all familiar with, and the relationship of such talk to on-going engagement in the text is quite different. These 'best bits' act as mini-summaries, complete and sufficient in themselves, rather than embedded in an unfolding drama, signalling what will come next.

The ways in which children talk about texts varies according to the dynamic of the social setting in which the talk takes place, as well as the mode of distribution of the text itself, and its formal features. To explore this relationship further I will turn now to another kind of literacy event which takes place within the primary curriculum and provides an opportunity for both informal and social talk to take place alongside the act of reading.

Sharing texts in real time: the formation of reading networks?

The extract below was collected from a Year 3 classroom in an English primary school one year before the introduction of the National Literacy Strategy. The transcript shows a group of 7–8-year-old boys sitting at the same table and talking together as they read during a session known in class as 'Quiet Reading Time'. The extract below starts as the researcher joins the group. The books they have on their table are a copy of the non-fiction book, *EyeWitness Guides: Desert*; a copy of the traditional tale, *Tattercoats*, in this version a paperback picture book; and a copy of Dr. Seuss' poem, *I Can Read with My Eyes Shut.*

INTERVIEWER: What was it you were just drawing my attention to, Miles?

MILES: That/ It's a lady or man, died in a desert in about cos you can see there's all sand {Miles is pointing to a picture of a mummified corpse on page 12 of the Dorling Kindersley *EyeWitness Guides: Desert*}

INTERVIEWER: Yeah, all dried up, yeah

MILES: (She) dried, Blip! Aghh {Miles makes a choking sound. He turns over to the next page} Look poisonous, poisonous, Aghh {Miles acts as if he is choking and dying. He is looking at a picture of a cobra on p. 15 *EyeWitness Guides: Desert*}

JOSH: Look (...) Miles, Miles, Miles, shall I tell you something, tell you what, I'm looking, they look like {pointing to a picture of tadpole shrimps on p. 14}

MILES: What?

JOSH: like egg burgers,

MILES: Egg burgers?

JOSH: Yes, yes you could make a sausage chip (mountain) {laughter}

ALAN: Look, look, read this, you can read about anchors and all about (ants), you can read about (ankles?) and crocodile (pants)

MILES: Oh, what, I've read that one before

ALAN: yeah it's brilliant

JOSH: {reading to self} *She had a wide b* {hesitates} *a boy*

MILES: Read that/ look, I'll show you a really good one, over there, look you can see it's dead {pointing to a picture of a lizard?, page 28?}

ALAN: Yeah, you know what that is?// That is odd isn't it

JOSH: I need a new book now

Before the introduction of the National Literacy Strategy to England, 'Quiet Reading Time' was a ubiquitous feature of the literacy curriculum. While teachers listened to individual readers read aloud, other children in the class would have the opportunity to read to themselves or with others in contexts that were lightly monitored. The transcript above captures something of these possibilities. Three boys on this table have each chosen different books. Miles has been making his way through the Dorling Kindersley *EyeWitness Guides: Desert*, a large hardback non-fiction book, sixty-four pages long and divided into a sequence of double-spreads each covering a separate theme – birds, mammals, seas of sand and so on – through a combination of image and writing. Miles moves rapidly from page to page, steering by the pictures and pausing to exclaim over items that catch his interest, and seeking to bring them to someone else's attention. Josh has been intermittently reading aloud to himself from *Tattercoats*, a thirty-two-page paperback picture book re-telling the Cinderella story. From time to time he turns from this book to *Deserts* as Miles attracts his attention and scans the page it is open on. At the end of this episode Josh decides to change *Tattercoats* for something else from the class library. Alan has been reading a paperback version of the Dr. Seuss' poem *I Can Read with My Eyes Shut*. He alternates between reading silently to himself and reading bits and pieces aloud to the others, finally inviting Miles to join in a joint recitation as he gets to the end of the poem, shortly after this extract finishes. He then hands the book on to Miles who wants to read it for himself.

The transcript captures the rapid shifts in attention of these three participants as they at times compete to bring something from a particular text to the notice of the rest of the group. Whilst it is possible to form a judgement that Josh struggles more with the mechanics of reading than the other two, given the hesitant way in which he reads aloud and to himself rather than for the others, the transcript also highlights the social purposes that reading has in this context for all three children. Different kinds of text content gain social currency under these conditions and are actively brought to others' notice. The texts that lend themselves most easily to being shared in this way are the non-fiction text and the poem. In both cases it is possible to detach either short extracts or individual images from their place in the longer text and relocate them into a new context where they gain new meanings. This is particularly true of the images selected from *Desert*. (See Moss 2007 for an extended discussion on the design characteristics of these kinds of non-fiction texts and the reading paths they create.) This kind of reading looks very different from the sustained solitary attention that individuals are more generally expected to give under other conditions. It also provides one key way in which individual readers network their way to new texts.

Conclusion

Social talk about texts in informal settings looks very different from the kind of talk about text that is valued and expected in more formal pedagogic settings.

It is less immediately attuned to the acquisition of particular skills, may rely on implicit rather than explicit references to the texts themselves and disregard what might in other contexts be seen as key elements in the text. At a time when much classroom practice is dominated by explicit pedagogy driven by precise learning objectives designed to generate measurable and auditable outcomes, it is hard to incorporate opportunities for this kind of social interaction in school. In making space for talk in English lessons, schools prioritise: accurate and well-focused recall of the text's contents; clear demonstrations that children understand what they have read and can identify literary conventions including plot, character, aspects of language and genre; or talk that guides children into new knowledge. What gets overlooked is the ways in which texts are shared in different contexts through talk, either in real-time or retrospectively; the role talk about texts has in the formation of reader networks, and in instilling the motivation to read on or read more; and how this can cement friendships or even encourage competitive one-upmanship. These are not aspects of reading that could or should be audited or measured. But they do have a place in classrooms.

Teachers can use talk about text to instruct and assess children's reading. Children can use talk about text to do social identity work, develop their interests *and* learn more about what it means to read and to be a reader. Both have a place in classroom settings.

11 Why we need to know about more than phonics to teach English literacy

Terezinha Nunes and Peter Bryant

Introduction

The triangle formed by the relationship between a teacher, a learner, and the object to be learned is a common way of representing what teachers need to know when teaching their pupils. Teachers' knowledge of the content to be learned is referred to as *subject matter knowledge*; their knowledge of how students learn about this object, of their conceptions (or misconceptions) before they are taught and how their knowledge changes through instruction, is known as *pedagogical content knowledge* (Schulman 1986; Strauss *et al.* 1999). Schulman argued that subject-matter knowledge for teaching is more than what is expected of the subject major who is not preparing for teaching. 'We expect the teacher to understand why a given topic is particularly central to a discipline whereas another may be somewhat peripheral. This will be important in subsequent pedagogical judgments regarding relative curricular emphasis' (Schulman 1986: 9). Schulman proposed that pedagogical content knowledge must include knowledge of 'the most useful forms of representation of those ideas [to be taught], the most powerful analogies, illustrations, examples, explanations, and demonstrations – in a word, the ways of representing and formulating the subject that make it comprehensible to others' (Schulman 1986: 9). Schulman's distinction between these two forms of knowledge, and the emphasis on the connections between them, is a landmark for many who are concerned with teacher education. Two decades later, researchers are still working on defining and measuring subject matter knowledge for teaching and pedagogical content knowledge (e.g. Hill, Rowan and Ball 2005; Hill, Schilling and Ball 2004; Kahan, Cooper and Betha 2003; Krauss *et al.* 2008).

In the case of teaching English literacy, subject-matter knowledge can be defined as knowledge of how written English works, and pedagogical content knowledge as knowledge of how children learn how to read and write in

We are very grateful to the ESRC-Teaching and Learning Research Programme, whose generous support (through grant number L139251015) made our research reported here possible. Their support also enabled the review of research that forms the basis for this chapter.

140

English, what is difficult and what is easy, how the more difficult aspects can be mastered, and what predicts their further progress in reading comprehension and writing skills. In the first section of this chapter, we summarise significant points about English orthography and some aspects of written language vocabulary. In the second section, we review research that shows how morphological knowledge is used in spelling and reading. This research represents crucial aspects of pedagogical knowledge and shows why teachers must know about more than phonics to teach English literacy. The third section discusses the educational implications of the research reviewed in the chapter.

English orthography and written English

'Reading is jointly defined by a language and by the writing system that encodes the language. The language part is to be taken seriously and cannot be identified simply with strings of spoken phonemes' (Perfetti 2003: 4). Perfetti lists three components of language that must be considered in the connection between language and reading: grammar, phonology and pragmatics, and includes under grammar two subcomponents, syntax and morphology. He stresses that 'the components of the system of most importance for reading are phonology and grammar, in particular the morphological subcomponent of grammar' (2003: 4); he does not dwell on the importance of pragmatics, which affects language use. Thus, even though elsewhere he defines English orthography as an example of the family of alphabetic writing systems (Perfetti and Liu 2005), he stressed in this paper that knowing about phonics is not sufficient for understanding reading. It has become increasingly common to refer to English orthography as being 'morphophonemic' (Venezky 1995), because in English orthography two principles operate simultaneously: the representation of sounds by letters (the phonographic principle, according to Jaffré 1997) and the 'visual identity of meaningful parts' (Venezky 1999) or the semiographic principle (Jaffré 1997). Put simply, English represents the sounds of words but also their structures in terms of meaning components, called morphemes.

Morphemes are the smallest units of meaning in a language. The word 'books', for example, has two morphemes, the stem 'book' and the suffix 's', which indicates plurality. In many words in English, when the representation of morphemes in spelling conflicts with the representation of sounds, the morphological representation prevails. For example, the plural of nouns is written with 's' irrespective of whether it sounds as /s/, as in 'books', or as /z/, as in 'bees'. Similarly, regular verbs in the past are spelled with the suffix 'ed' irrespective of whether their ending sounds are /t/, as in 'kissed' or /d/ as in 'killed'. Suffixes as well as stems have a fixed spelling in English. The spelling of a stem is conserved across words even when the pronunciation changes: for example, in the word 'magician', the representation of the stem 'magic' is conserved even though the stem's pronunciation changes.

We (Nunes and Bryant 2009) have argued that the semiographic principle can also lead to differences in spelling where there are no differences in the sounds of words. For example, we spell the end sound /ks/ differently in different words: 'fox' and 'socks', 'mix' and 'tricks', 'tax' and 'tracks' all end in the same sound, /ks/, but we spell this ending sometimes with 'x' and sometimes with 'ks' (or 'kes', if the word has a split digraph, as in 'jokes' and 'makes'). If we were simply trying to represent the sounds of oral language, we would have no reason to spell these word endings differently. However, these spellings, which are entirely predictable, represent grammatical and morphological relations. The /ks/ sound at the end of words in English is most often represented by the letter 'x', as in 'fox', 'mix' and 'tax', but this rule does not apply to words that can be decomposed into two morphemes, the stem plus an affix, as in 'sock+s', 'trick+s' and 'track+s'. Another example of a distinction made in spelling, but not in oral language, is the spelling of schwa vowels in the endings of words such as 'confession' and 'magician'. Both words end in the same sounds and their endings are often spelled by children in the same, incorrect way: 'shen' or 'shon'. Although these words continue to cause problems for children when they are 9 years old and thus have been learning to read and spell for about three or four years in England, their spelling is completely predictable from the semiographic principle. 'Confession' is composed of the stem 'confess' and the suffix 'ion', which forms abstract nouns, and 'magician' is composed by the stem 'magic' and the suffix 'ian', which forms agents.

Venezky (1995) argued that morphology is important both for spelling and word reading, as morpheme boundaries are often essential to determine the boundaries of a grapheme. The letters 'ph', 'th' and 'sh' are often a single grapheme in English and correspond to a single phoneme: 'photography', 'weather' and 'dishwasher' exemplify these digraphs. However, these letters may have to be defined as parts of a different unit, if they are in different morphemes: 'uphill', 'hotheaded' and 'dishonour' exemplify the need to define these sequences as two letters, not a single grapheme. His view is that, if we were to treat these examples as exceptions, we would end up with an uneconomical system, which would offer a poor characterisation of how English is read.

If we go beyond orthography to think of written English texts, a second reason to think about morphology is immediately apparent. There are important differences between the use of language in oral and written form, and one of them is the size of vocabulary used. Estimates of the size of vocabulary required for everyday conversation and for reading text indicate that the latter exceeds the former by tens of thousands of words (Nagy and Anderson 1984). So reading text requires children to read words that they do not know from their previous encounters with oral language, and one must wonder how this is possible. Nagy and Anderson (1984) analysed printed school English and noted that, for every word learned, there are at least three derivatives (i.e. words such as 'magician' and 'confession', formed by a stem plus a derivational suffix) whose meanings are recognisably related to the stem. Thus, if children realise that English represents morphemes and know how morphemes relate to meaning, they may be able to utilise morphological information and work out for themselves the meaning of words that they encounter in print for the first time.

In summary, English orthography represents phonemes, which are units of sound, and morphemes, which are units of meaning. It is based on two principles, the phonographic and the semiographic principles. Written English uses a vocabulary that is considerably larger than oral English. Many of the new words that children encounter in print in primary school texts are derivatives, whose meanings are recognisably related to the word's stem. Thus teachers' subject knowledge of English for teaching literacy should include an understanding of the role of phonology and morphology in English orthography. Teachers' pedagogical knowledge should include the consequences of this view of orthography for the study of psychological processes involved in literacy learning.

The role of morphology in literacy

The theoretical refinements in the analysis of English orthography in the last two decades stimulated new research about the processes involved in the development of children's reading and spelling. In this section we sample some of this research, considering spelling, word recognition, reading comprehension and finally vocabulary learning.

Spelling

Nunes and Bryant (2006; 2009) summarised much of the research relevant to the importance of morphemes for spelling carried out in the last twenty years. Their review strongly suggests that children beginning to learn to read and spell find it difficult to coordinate the representation of sounds with the representation of morphemes in spelling. For example, they spell regular verbs in the past predominantly by representing the end sounds, /t/ or /d/, rather than using the 'ed' ending. Figure 11.1 shows the number of correct responses, out of ten, for endings of words that had to be spelled phonetically and for regular verbs in the past, which should have the 'ed' ending. The words that should be spelled phonetically were either non-verbs, such as 'field' or 'soft', or irregular verbs in the past, such as 'sold' or 'left'. The study was longitudinal; the children

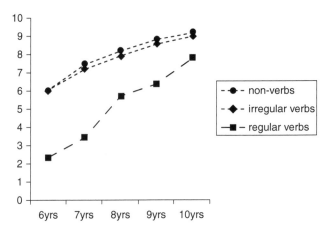

Figure 11.1 Mean number of correctly spelled word endings (out of 10) by age level (from Nunes, Bryant and Bindman 1997)

were first seen when they were about 6 years of age, and followed until they were about 10 years. The words were dictated in the context of sentences so that it was clear to the children what the target word was. As can be seen in Figure 11.1, the children were much better at spelling word endings phonetically than morphologically, and the difference persisted until age 10.

The difficulty that children seem to have in adopting an apparently simple spelling rule based on morphology might be related to the teaching that they receive, which tends to focus their attention on phonics. However, it is also possible that the rule is not so simple: children need to use the concept of grammatical category, verbs vs. non-verbs, and also elaborate on the category verbs, and restrict the 'ed' spelling to regular past verbs. It is perhaps instructive to think of another case where children must make another, perhaps simpler, distinction, which also impacts on spelling using morphological rules. The difference between nouns ending in 'ian', which are person words, and nouns ending in 'ion', which are not person words, might seem simple. Nunes and Bryant (2006) obtained data on 200 children aged 9 and 10 years in four different schools. The children were asked to spell words, such as 'magician', 'electrician', 'confession' and 'discussion', and also pseudowords, such as 'lagician' and 'denassion'. The pseudowords were presented in sentences so that the children could find out what they were supposed to mean; for example, 'someone who does lagic is a lagician' and 'when people denass they are having a denassion'. The reason we used pseudowords was that it was quite possible that many 9- and 10-year-olds would spell some of the words we dictated, which were quite common, from memory, but they might not realise why 'magician' is spelled with 'ian' and 'confession' with 'ion', even though

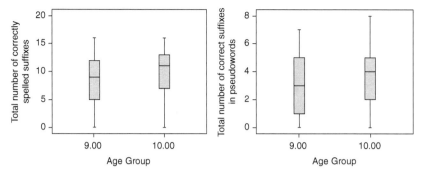

Figure 11.2 Median number of suffixes spelled correctly in words (out of 16) and pseudowords (out of 8) and range of scores by age level

their ending sounds are the same. We dictated to the children sixteen words, eight of which ended in 'ian' and the other eight in 'ion'. We dictated eight pseudowords, again half ending in 'ian' and the other half in 'ion'. There were also eight other words and four pseudowords in the list which did not involve using this morphological distinction (e.g. 'termite' and 'lemonade'). We only scored in this assessment whether the child had spelled the suffix correctly and entirely disregarded errors in the word stem. The results of this assessment are presented in Figure 11.2.

The darker lines in the middle of the bars indicate the median for each of the groups; the lines that extend beyond the bars indicate the range of scores. The median for number of suffixes spelled correctly for the 9-year-olds is less than half of the words, and also less than half of the pseudowords. The 10-year-olds' median is slightly above half of the suffixes in words and pseudowords being correct. It is also possible to see from the graph that scores ranged from zero to all suffixes spelled correctly at both age levels. Thus, there is considerable variation in children's performance, but on the whole most 9- and 10-year olds do not find this morphological spelling easy.

In summary, words in which the spelling dictated by phonological rules clashes with the morphological spelling, and the morphological rules prevail, cause great difficulty to many children, even though they have been learning to read and spell for four to five years.

Word recognition

Fluent reading is not a letter-by-letter process: people parse words into units that are larger than a single letter but smaller than the word. Leong (1989) made use of this process of parsing, which takes place rapidly and unconsciously, in an ingenious experiment designed to test whether people parse words into morphemes during word recognition. He reasoned that if he mixed lower- and upper-case letters in a word, this mixture would disrupt reading if the mixture crossed the boundaries of the readers' way of parsing the word, but that it would facilitate reading if the mixture coincided with these boundaries. He showed Canadian children, aged from 10 to 12 years, words that contained different mixtures of upper- and lower-case letters. When this mixture is random, it makes word reading more difficult: 'mAcHInE' is more difficult to read than 'machine' or 'MACHINE'. He showed children two types of upper- and lower-case letter-mixes; for example, 'tractOR', in which the word is parsed into morphemes, and 'tracTOR', where the boundaries correspond to sequences of sounds that can be pronounced together. The children were asked to indicate whether the letter sequences on the screen were words or not by pressing a key in a computer keyboard, a task known as lexical decision task. Children's reaction times were faster when the boundaries of the upper and lower case letter groups coincided with the morphemes. This shows that children use morphemes as units during word recognition. This facilitating effect was larger for older children and also for those with higher reading ability within their grade level. So, the better children are at word recognition, the more they rely on morphemes. Further experimental evidence for the role of morphemes in word recognition in experimental studies with adults has been provided by Caramazza, Laudana and Romani (1988) and Taft (1988; 2003), among others.

Other studies have explored the effect of morphological knowledge on word reading using a different approach, by investigating whether morphological awareness predicts children's word reading. Singson, Mahony and Mann (2000), for example, gave children in grades three through six (mean ages from 9 years 1 month to 12 years 4 months) three different types of measures: they assessed their general intelligence, their verbal short-term memory, and their awareness of suffixes. These were the tasks that they used in order to predict how well the children would perform in a test of their word reading ability. They used a statistical technique, called regression analysis, which allows the investigators to find out whether the children's awareness of morphemes predicts how well they do in a word reading task, after taking into account their general intelligence and their short-term memory. They found that the children's knowledge of morphemes made a statistically significant contribution to the prediction of their word reading skill after controlling for the effects of intelligence and short-term memory. In a second study with children of the same grade levels, they assessed the children on a vocabulary test, phonological awareness and morphological awareness, and used these measures to predict their word reading. They wanted to know whether the children's awareness of the sounds of words would be more important for word reading than their awareness of morphemes. They found that, for the younger children, in grade

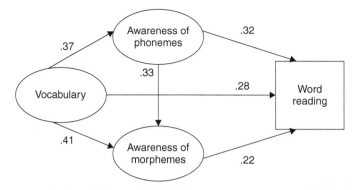

Figure 11.3 A theoretical model of the relationships between vocabulary, phonological awareness, morphological awareness and word recognition for children aged 10 (adapted from Singson, Mahony and Mann 2000)

3, awareness of sounds was indeed more important than their awareness of morphemes. However, from about age 10, the children's awareness of morphemes continued to be a statistically significant predictor of word reading, even after controlling for the effects of vocabulary and awareness of phonemes. They proposed a theoretical model of what contributes to word reading; an adaptation of this model is presented in Figure 11.3.

The figure shows that there are connections between children's vocabulary, their awareness of phonemes and their awareness of morphemes, and word reading ability. The numbers next to the arrows are coefficients (β) that can vary from 0 to 1; the larger the value, the greater its importance for predicting the children's word reading. The direct connections between vocabulary, phoneme awareness and morpheme awareness with word reading are similar. There are also relationships between the three predictors of word reading: the children's vocabulary is related both to their awareness of phonemes and to their awareness of morphemes.

These interconnections between children's linguistic ability are expected: after all, they are linguistic abilities. The important result illustrated in Figure 11.3 is that, although these abilities are inter-related, each one makes an independent contribution to the children's word reading ability. This means that, in order to improve children's word reading, teachers should find ways of strengthening their awareness of phonemes and morphemes, and also their vocabulary.

Reading comprehension

Considering that there is such a clear connection between children's awareness of morphology and word reading, one inevitably wishes to find out whether there is also a connection between morphological awareness and reading comprehension. Nagy, Berninger and Abbott (2006) reason that it must be so. Their view is that the effects of morphological awareness on reading comprehension are related to the children's ability to understand words in text even when they have not encountered these words previously. They argue that

morphologically complex words are more common in written language (and especially academic language) than in spoken language (Chafe and Danielewicz 1987), and the proportion of such words increases as frequency decreases (Nagy and Anderson 1984). Thus, with each grade children encounter an increasing number of morphologically complex words. The majority of these have meanings that can be inferred from the meanings of their component parts (Nagy and Anderson 1984), and so recognizing the morphological structure of words should aid children in interpreting and learning them. (Nagy, Berninger and Abbott 2006: 134)

Thus, according to their analysis, it is necessary to investigate the relationships between morphological awareness, vocabulary and reading comprehension in order to see whether morphological awareness makes a significant contribution to reading comprehension, above and beyond what it has in common with vocabulary. The reason to consider vocabulary in these analyses is that children who have a larger vocabulary will know more of the printed words than those with smaller vocabularies; so they would have an advantage in reading comprehension. This advantage should be considered in the analysis of the relationships between morphological awareness, vocabulary and reading comprehension.

Nagy, Berninger and Abbott (2006) studied three samples of children in the USA: one group was in grades four and five, the second in grades six and seven, and the third in grades eight and nine (approximate age range from 10 to 15 years). They used statistical techniques similar to those just described for the study by Singson, Mahony and Mann (2000), which allow for the investigation of whether morphological awareness makes a statistically significant contribution to predicting reading comprehension, after controlling for the children's vocabulary. Their results for children in grades four to five and six to seven are presented in Figures 11.4 and 11.5.

The numbers next to the arrows indicate the strength of the connections between vocabulary, morphological awareness and reading comprehension. The comparison between the two sets of results suggests that, when the children are younger and the link between vocabulary and morphological awareness is stronger, it is not possible to demonstrate a direct connection between vocabulary and reading comprehension, independent of morphological awareness. In contrast, the direct connection between morphological awareness and reading comprehension is quite strong. As the children progress through primary school, vocabulary does make a significant contribution to predicting reading comprehension, independently of their morphological awareness,

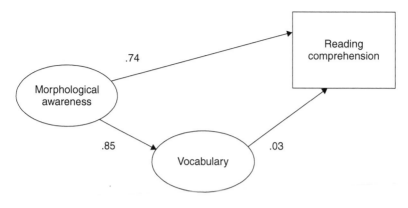

Results for grades 4–5

Figure 11.4 A model of the relationships between vocabulary, morphological awareness and reading comprehension for children in grades 4 and 5, aged approximately 9–10 years (adapted from Nagy, Berninger and Abbott 2006)

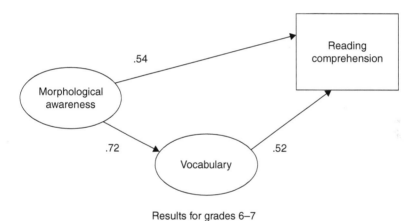

Results for grades 6–7

Figure 11.5 A model of the relationships between vocabulary, morphological awareness and reading comprehension for children in grades 6 and 7, aged approximately 11–12 years (adapted from Nagy, Berninger and Abbott 2006)

which continues to make a significant and independent contribution to reading comprehension.

Deacon and Kirby (2004) also examined the role of morphological awareness in reading comprehension, using a longitudinal design. They first assessed the children when they were in second grade and predicted their reading comprehension in fourth and fifth grade. They included in their study a measure of

the children's general intelligence and a measure of their phonological awareness, as well as a measure of morphological awareness. They found that morphological awareness made a statistically significant contribution to predicting
reading comprehension two and three years later, even after controlling for the
children's reading comprehension levels when they were in second grade, their
intelligence and their phonological awareness.

This finding has a very important educational implication: it suggests that
improving children's morphological awareness early on can have long-term
effects on their reading comprehension progress.

Vocabulary learning

Morphemes play a part in the recognition of words that children already
know: could they also play a part in learning new words?

In order to learn a word, children must do two things: (1) they must be able
to remember the sequences of sounds that form the word (i.e. must use their
phonological short-term memory) and (2) they must attribute meaning to this
sequence of sounds. There is evidence that morphemes play a part in both of
these steps.

The classical task for assessing phonological short-term memory in connection with vocabulary learning was developed by Gathercole and Baddeley
(1989); it is known as the non-word repetition test. In this test, children are
asked to listen to some made-up words and to repeat them. By choosing
made-up words, Gathercole and Baddeley are certain that the children have not
heard them before. Examples of the non-words used in their test are 'hampent',
'stopograttic', 'woogalamic' and 'dopelate'. They found that the children's
performance on the non-word repetition task correlated with a measure of their
vocabulary taken at the same time as the non-word repetition test, and also with
another measure of vocabulary that was given to the children about one year
later. Gathercole and her colleagues have since produced further evidence to
show that children's phonological short-term memory is strongly associated
with their ability to learn new words (Gathercole, Hitch, Service and Martin
1997; Gathercole *et al.* 1992).

Later, Gathercole (1995) reasoned that long-term memory might also play
a role in this task. If some of the non-words were more word-like than others,
they would be remembered more easily: in other words, there should be a
familiarity effect. She asked twenty adults to judge the non-words in word-
likeness in a general way, not thinking of whether they were like specific
words, and used the mean score obtained from these judgements to represent
the non-word word-likeness. Just as she predicted, the children (in the age
range 2 to 5 years) were better at repeating the non-words that had higher
word-likeness scores.

Nunes and Bryant (2009) used the same reasoning but extended it to consider the role of morphemes in non-word repetition. Almost all of the non-words in Gathercole's non-word repetition task cannot be analysed into morphemes. So we created a new set of non-words, composed with morphemes in non-existing combinations, such as 'concentrationist', 'unsausagish', 'winteriser' and 'computerist'. Our non-words were matched in number of syllables to Gathercole's non-words but the number of morphemes in some is actually smaller than the number of syllables; for example, 'unsausagish' has four syllables but only three morphemes. If the children remember the non-words by identifying their morphemes, they would have fewer items to remember, and thus would perform better in our non-words. We also predicted that the children's morphological awareness would correlate with their performance in repeating non-words with a morphological structure, even after controlling for their phonological awareness. However, their morphological awareness should not correlate with performance on Gathercole's task, after controlling for phonological awareness.

Both of these predictions were confirmed: the children did better when they repeated non-words with a morphological structure and their performance correlated with the measure of morphological awareness, after controlling for phonological awareness. We conclude that morphological awareness must play a role in remembering the sounds of a new, real word when it is made by morphemes that we already know.

The second step in learning a new word is to give it meaning. We tested this hypothesis in a teaching study (Nunes and Bryant 2006). We reasoned that, if morphological awareness helps children identify the morphological structure in a new word and have a good stab at its meaning, then improving their morphological awareness would also improve their ability to define pseudowords made with real morphemes. So we asked children to define a set of pseudowords before and after they participated in a programme designed to improve their morphological awareness, and compared their performance with that of an untaught, comparison group. The children (170 in the taught group and 104 in an untaught group) were in grades three through six and their ages ranged from about 7 to 12. Examples of the pseudowords that we asked them to define are 'unclimb', 'biheaded', 'resleep' and 'chickener'. The comparison between the taught and untaught groups used their performance at pre-test as a control so that the children were being compared at post-test with those who had similar performance at pre-test. The children who had been taught about morphemes performed significantly better in the pseudoword definition test at post-test than the untaught group. Their mean was about one-third of a standard deviation above the mean for the control group, a level of improvement that is considerable as the outcome of a teaching programme delivered by the teachers in the classroom.

So we can safely conclude that children's awareness of morphemes helps them with both tasks that they need to carry out to learn a new word: if it is a multi-morphemic word, morphological awareness helps them remember the word and it helps them give some meaning to the word.

Educational implications

In this chapter, we have argued that learning to read and to write English is learning about a morphophonemic orthography (Venezky 1995), in which letters are used to represent sounds and morphemes. Thus teachers' subject knowledge should involve a deep understanding of the complexities of representing sounds and morphemes in English, and how these affect word reading and spelling. Their pedagogical knowledge must encompass a deep understanding of what children learn when learning literacy. Perfetti (2003) suggests that 'what a child learns is how his or her writing system works – both its basic principles and the details of its orthographic implementation. We know this learning has occurred when the child can identify printed words as words in his or her spoken language in a way consistent with the writing system' (Perfetti 2003: 16). We have added to this basic definition the remark that children will encounter in print words that they have not encountered in oral language. They might actually mispronounce some of these, for example by stressing the wrong syllable: I was told by the father of an avid 6-year-old reader that in their house everyone stresses the final syllable in 'processor' as a family joke because of the way his daughter read the word on the box of the newly purchased food processor. However, there was no doubt that she understood what was in the box when she read the label, and knew that it would be a machine to process food.

The significance of morphemes for children's literacy development has attracted interest for some time. Beers and Henderson (1977) indicated its importance in children's developing concepts of orthography and Henderson and Templeton (1986) underlined the importance of helping children see how meaning is represented by letters in spelling instruction. There was then not as much systematic evidence as there is now for the importance of morphological awareness, as measures of morphological awareness had not been developed and validated. Evidence is no longer sparse and unsystematic: there is a solid body of evidence to show the significance of morphological knowledge for word reading, spelling, reading comprehension and vocabulary learning. This does not mean that all the answers are known; for example, there is a need for further research on the long-term impact of early teaching of morphology to children. There is also room for developing methods, even if some solid programmes have been created and assessed (see, e.g., www.education.ox.ac. uk/research/resgroup/cl/clr.php). We know relatively less about whether and how children with serious reading and spelling problems profit from this type of teaching. However, there is no longer any reason to hesitate about including morphology in programmes for teacher education and literacy instruction.

The success in the development of phonological awareness measures and the demonstration that it plays a causal role in literacy development (e.g. Bradley and Bryant 1983) did not have an immediate impact on teacher education and policy development in the UK, but it did eventually influence both. It is now time for teacher educators and policy makers to refresh their ideas about how teachers should be prepared to teach children how to read and write and how to conceive of literacy instruction in the future.

12   Understanding children's reading comprehension difficulties

Jessie Ricketts, Joanne Cocksey and Kate Nation

Introduction

In the early stages of learning to read, children must learn to map letters onto sounds so that they can decode and recognise words. However, the ultimate goal of reading is to understand the messages conveyed by text, and simply being able to read words and texts accurately is not sufficient for comprehension to occur. As children move through the school years, access to the curriculum will increasingly rely on reading comprehension. Children with poor reading comprehension skills will struggle to learn from what they read, placing them at a disadvantage that may have wide-ranging educational consequences. The aims of this chapter are to raise awareness of children's reading comprehension difficulties, indicate some of the applied linguistic knowledge that can help primary teachers better understand them and emphasise the importance of monitoring and supporting reading comprehension skills in the classroom. In the first section, we review research on some of the factors that underpin reading comprehension, with particular reference to 'poor comprehenders', children who show impaired reading comprehension despite age-appropriate word recognition abilities. We then consider the educational implications of being a poor comprehender and present some recommendations for the assessment of reading comprehension abilities in school settings.

Explaining children's reading comprehension difficulties

The Simple View of Reading (Gough and Tunmer 1986) describes two potential barriers to reading success: difficulties with decoding and difficulties with language comprehension. Children's skills can vary continuously across these two dimensions, resulting in four extreme reading profiles. Figure 12.1 depicts these dimensions, with decoding skills ranging from poor to good on the horizontal axis and comprehension skills ranging from poor to good on the vertical axis (see also Bishop and Snowling 2004; Nation and Norbury 2005). The Simple View of Reading provides a useful framework for literacy education (Stuart, Stainthorp and Snowling 2008), emphasising the importance of both

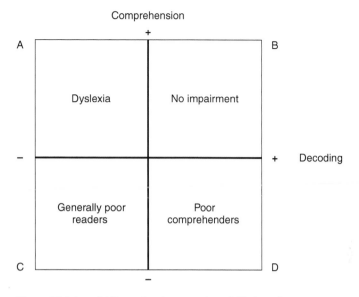

Figure 12.1 A multidimensional approach to skilled reading

language comprehension and decoding in reading success. Each component requires teachers to understand different areas of applied linguistics. It is worth noting that the term 'simple view' might be unfortunate in that it could be interpreted as suggesting that learning to read (and teaching children to learn to read) is a simple matter. This is not the case: all must surely agree that reading is a complex skill that takes time to master, involving within-child factors in interaction with many environmental influences. The simplicity of the model comes from the straightforward fact that skilled reading, by which we mean reading for meaning, depends on children developing two sets of skills (decoding and comprehension) that must work together: both components are necessary and neither component on its own is sufficient for skilled reading to occur.

There is good evidence to support the relative independence of the two components. First, decoding and comprehension are dependent on different linguistic and cognitive abilities. Progress in decoding and word-level reading is predicted by children's phonological skills, amongst other things, whereas progress in comprehension is more related to factors such as vocabulary and grammatical understanding (e.g. Muter, Hulme, Snowling and Stevenson 2004; Oakhill, Cain and Bryant 2003). A second important source of evidence comes from examining the profiles of children with different patterns of strengths and weaknesses in reading. Reference to the Simple View of

Reading (Figure 12.1) tells us that there are three reasons why reading for meaning may be difficult for a particular child. If decoding is poor, as in children with developmental dyslexia (Snowling 2000), difficulties with text reading accuracy and fluency will constrain reading comprehension (quadrant A). In contrast to those children with dyslexia, approximately 10 per cent of primary school children show a profile of comprehension deficits relative to age-appropriate accuracy (Nation 2005; Yuill and Oakhill 1991). Children with this profile are usually referred to as 'poor' or 'less-skilled' comprehenders (quadrant D). Finally, a child might have difficulties with both decoding and language comprehension, placing them in quadrant C of multidimensional space.

Since poor comprehenders have age-appropriate reading accuracy skills, their difficulties with reading comprehension cannot be explained in terms of poor reading accuracy. Therefore, research with this group of children has shed light on the factors that contribute to reading comprehension, beyond those associated with decoding and reading accuracy. Poor comprehenders have been studied by a number of research groups within the UK (Cain and Oakhill 2007; Nation 2005; Stothard and Hulme 1992; Yuill and Oakhill 1991) and elsewhere (Carretti, Cornoldi, De Beni and Romanò 2005; Catts, Adlof, and Weismer 2006; Johnson-Glenberg 2005). There is a growing literature describing poor comprehenders and attempting to address why they find it difficult to extract meaning from text. We review some of this literature next; for more comprehensive reviews see Cain and Oakhill (2007) and Nation (2005).

Research by Oakhill, Cain and colleagues has identified a number of discourse-level processes that play an important role in reading comprehension development (for a recent review see Cain and Oakhill 2007). These include factors such as comprehension monitoring, knowledge of story structure and the ability to make inferences. For example, Cain (2003) presented poor and skilled comprehenders with a prompt (a topic, title, or series of pictures) and asked them to tell a story. Whilst poor comprehenders produced oral narratives that were similar in length to those produced by skilled comprehenders, their stories were rated as being less well structured because they lacked coherence and cohesion. Cragg and Nation (2006) extended this work, showing that poor comprehenders have difficulty producing written as well as oral narrative. Another area that has received particular attention is the failure of many poor comprehenders to make spontaneous inferences from connected text (Cain and Oakhill 1999; Cain, Oakhill and Lemmon 2004; Oakhill 1994; Yuill and Oakhill 1988). To fully understand the intended meaning of connected text, the reader often needs to go beyond what is literally stated in the text, and make inferences. For example, a cohesive inference is when a reader must make an inference in order to integrate information across parts of the text. If children have difficulty in making inferences, they will have difficulty in comprehending what they read or hear.

Our own research has focused on poor comprehenders' oral language weaknesses. Given the clear need to understand the individual words that are included in a text in order to fully comprehend it, it is not surprising that poor comprehenders' vocabulary skills have been investigated thoroughly (for a review, see Nation 2009). Receptive and expressive oral vocabulary impairments have been observed in poor comprehenders (Nation, Clarke, Marshall and Durand 2004; Nation and Snowling 1998; Ricketts, Nation and Bishop 2007; but see Stothard and Hulme 1992). Further, poor comprehenders seem to have difficulty with a wide range of tasks that involve meaning. In a series of studies, Nation and Snowling (1998) investigated semantic skills in groups of poor and skilled comprehenders that were matched in terms of chronological age, decoding level and nonverbal ability. Children completed a semantic judgement task, in which they were asked to judge whether pairs of words were synonymous or not (e.g. boat-ship), and a semantic fluency task, in which they generated exemplars in response to a category label (e.g. animals: lion, tiger, etc.). Children also completed equivalent tasks tapping phonological skills. For these, they judged whether pairs of words rhymed (e.g. rope-hope) and generated rhyming words in response to a target (e.g. plate: mate, straight, etc.). Compared to skilled comprehenders, poor comprehenders were slower and less accurate when making semantic judgements and generated fewer category members in the semantic fluency task. In contrast, groups did not differ on the phonological tasks.

Although poor comprehenders exhibit semantic impairments that encompass poor oral vocabulary, their oral language deficits are not limited to semantic tasks. Poor comprehenders also have difficulty with tasks that require grammatical processing and broader comprehension skills, such as marking tense and understanding syntactically complex sentences and discourse (Catts et al. 2006; Cragg and Nation 2006; Nation et al. 2004; Nation and Snowling 2000; Nation, Snowling and Clarke 2005). Notably, some children identified as poor comprehenders on the basis of their reading profile have significant problems with aspects of oral language processing, consistent with a diagnosis of Specific Language Impairment (Catts et al. 2006; Nation et al. 2004). For example, Nation et al. (2004) reported a detailed assessment of the language skills of a group of twenty-five poor comprehenders. The assessment battery included multiple measures of phonology, semantics, morphosyntax and language comprehension. Between five and nineteen of the poor comprehenders met criteria for Specific Language Impairment, depending on the criteria adopted.

In summary, detailed investigation of oral language skills in poor comprehenders has demonstrated that with the exception of good phonological skills, poor comprehenders show a range of oral language weaknesses (Nation *et al.* 2004). In particular, poor comprehenders have difficulty with language comprehension and the components of language that predict reading comprehension most strongly in typically developing readers, namely vocabulary and grammar. Longitudinal studies with typically developing readers have shown that reading comprehension scores are predicted by earlier performance on tasks that assess oral vocabulary knowledge, the ability to use morphology to mark plurals and tense, knowledge of word order and comprehension of syntactically complex sentences (Muter *et al.* 2004; Nation and Snowling 2004; Oakhill *et al.* 2003). While it is tempting to suggest that poor comprehenders' difficulties with oral language place them at risk of reading comprehension difficulties, the association could go the other way: the mild-to-moderate weaknesses in spoken language seen in poor comprehenders in mid-childhood might be a consequence of their reading comprehension impairments. On this view, poor comprehenders may read less, and also benefit less from their reading experiences than control children. This may lead to relative weaknesses in spoken language emerging over time as a downstream consequence of their reading impairment.

Prospective longitudinal studies, however, offer support for the claim that children who go on to have poor reading comprehension, start school with lower levels of oral language skill. Catts *et al.* (2006) found that poor comprehenders selected at age 13 years showed deficits in language comprehension measured earlier in time at ages 5, 7 and 9 years. Similar findings have been reported in a recent UK study (Nation, Cocksey, Taylor and Bishop 2010). Notwithstanding this clear evidence of early language problems in children who go on to have poor reading comprehension, it seems likely that relationships between oral language and reading will be reciprocal across development. For example, as reading skills develop, engagement with texts will provide an opportunity for children to learn new vocabulary (e.g. Beck, Perfetti and McKeown 1982). A number of studies have now demonstrated that children with reading comprehension difficulties show poor new word learning, suggesting that vocabulary development in these children will be slow (Cain, Oakhill and Elbro 2003; Cain *et al.* 2004; Nation, Snowling and Clarke 2007; Ricketts, Bishop and Nation 2008).

One cognitive factor that has been explored in children with poor reading comprehension is working memory. Working memory is defined as the capacity to process and simultaneously store information in memory. It is easy to see why working memory is critical for reading comprehension: to build an effective representation of a text while reading it, a child must hold online in temporary memory a mental model of the situation described by that text, as well as dynamically update it as new information becomes available. It is not surprising to learn therefore that children's performance on verbal working memory tasks predicts reading comprehension both concurrently and longitudinally (e.g. Oakhill *et al.* 2003), and that poor comprehenders perform less well than control children on measures of working memory, especially when the task involves processing and storing linguistic information (Nation, Adams, Bowyer-Crane and Snowling 1999; Yuill, Oakhill and Parkin 1989). However, the precise nature of the relationship between working memory and reading comprehension in poor comprehenders remains controversial. Nation and colleagues (1999) proposed that poor verbal abilities constrain performance on both working memory and reading comprehension tasks (for a similar argument see Stothard and Hulme 1992). In contrast, Cain (2006) suggested that working memory impairments may underpin difficulties with discourse-level processes, which in turn give rise to poor reading comprehension.

In summary, reading comprehension difficulties in poor comprehenders may be caused by impairments in discourse-level processing, oral language, working memory or a combination of factors. Strong conclusions from previous research have been limited because intervention and longitudinal studies with this group are lacking (for notable exceptions see Cain and Oakhill 2006; Catts *et al.* 2006; Clarke *et al* 2010; Johnson-Glenberg 2005; Nation *et al.* 2010; Yuill and Oakhill 1988). Nonetheless, findings from research with poor comprehenders are consistent with longitudinal studies from typically developing readers showing that reading comprehension scores are significantly predicted by earlier performance on measures of oral vocabulary, grammar, listening comprehension, text integration, comprehension monitoring and working memory (Muter *et al.* 2004; Nation and Snowling 2004; Oakhill *et al.* 2003).

Educational implications of being a poor comprehender

The existing literature on poor comprehenders has focused on children in the middle-to-late primary school years. As children move from 'learning to read' in the early primary years to 'reading to learn', however, reading skills will increasingly determine how well they access the school curriculum. Thus, if poor comprehenders continue to struggle with understanding text it is likely that their learning and educational achievement will be compromised.

Across schools in England, Standard Assessment Tests (SATs) are administered to assess children's educational performance. These tests allow schools to establish whether children are working at, above or below the expectation for their age. One longitudinal study has used performance on SATs to investigate educational attainment in poor comprehenders. Cain and Oakhill (2006) identified twenty-three poor comprehenders at age 8 years and compared them with twenty-three skilled comprehenders over a period of three years. At age 8, groups differed in reading comprehension scores but were well matched for chronological age, performance IQ and text reading accuracy. Cain and Oakhill went on to explore comprehension scores and SATs results when children were aged 11 years. At this point, the poor comprehender group obtained significantly lower reading and listening comprehension scores than their skilled peers, with the majority of poor comprehenders showing persistent comprehension impairments. Mean SATs scores indicated that poor and skilled comprehenders were working at an age-appropriate level across curriculum subjects. However, it is important to note that as a group the poor comprehenders performed less well than the skilled comprehenders.

Recently, we had the opportunity to revisit a group of children initially described at ages 9 and 10 years by Ricketts, Nation and Bishop (2007). At age 11 years, we re-assessed their reading comprehension and examined their performance on SATs. Our results replicate Cain and Oakhill (2006) by finding that the poor comprehender profile is relatively stable over time, and that poor comprehenders perform less well than skilled comprehenders on SATs tests at age 11 years. However, in contrast to Cain and Oakhill, we found that poor comprehenders were less likely to perform at an age-appropriate level on SATs. Taken together, these studies suggest that at the end of primary school, poor comprehenders show poorer performance on school tests than skilled comprehenders of the same age, and some may be at risk of educational failure. Further, this is likely to become more pronounced in secondary and tertiary education when access to the curriculum becomes increasingly dependent on reading.

The early identification of children at risk of later educational difficulties is an important goal. Nation and Angell (2006) contended that poor comprehenders' reading comprehension difficulties often go unnoticed by teachers in the classroom and that they seldom come to the attention of specialist professionals. This is likely a consequence of the enormous demands placed on teachers in the classroom – for instance, they cannot routinely conduct the detailed individual assessments needed to identify discourse-level difficulties (see next section). In addition, poor comprehenders' strong word-level reading skills no doubt serve to mask their comprehension difficulties, especially given the strong emphasis on decoding highlighted by England's literacy curriculum (the *National Literacy Strategy*) over recent years. We suggest that raising awareness of the Simple View of Reading, which places an emphasis on comprehension as well as word recognition, might in turn raise awareness of the existence of poor comprehenders. Early identification is an important first step towards intervention and instruction that is appropriately geared towards improving children's reading comprehension. Research with poor comprehenders suggests that good word recognition does not guarantee comprehension and also indicates some markers that could alert teachers to reading comprehension difficulties. For example, given that poor comprehenders struggle with oral language and producing narrative (e.g. Catts *et al.* 2006;

Cragg and Nation 2006), limited language skills and poorly structured written work may indicate difficulties with reading comprehension. However, an important focus for future research will be to consider whether there are easily identifiable behaviours that reliably indicate the poor comprehender profile. Importantly though, in all cases careful assessment is needed to establish whether a child has impaired reading comprehension.

Recommendations for assessment

A large number of reading comprehension assessments are available. Our intention here is not to provide a detailed review of each assessment; instead, we offer some general discussion about the nature of reading comprehension assessment. This is followed by a description of a new assessment that we hope will prove useful to teachers.

As discussed earlier, the Simple View of Reading shows that children may be at risk of reading comprehension failure due to difficulties with word-level decoding accuracy and fluency, with linguistic comprehension, or with both. A thorough assessment should include tests designed to measure both decoding and comprehension. Decoding is much simpler to assess than comprehension and certainly, without a reasonable level of decoding skill, a child will struggle to comprehend text. However, it is important to remember that successful decoding is no guarantee that successful comprehension will follow.

In contrast to the ease of measuring a child's word-level reading skill, comprehension is very difficult to measure because reading comprehension is not a unitary construct. It is a complex skill dependent on a number of cognitive processes: to understand written text, words need to be recognised and their meanings accessed, relevant background knowledge also needs to be activated, and inferences generated as information is integrated during the course of reading. In addition, control processes monitor both ongoing comprehension and the internal consistency of text, allowing the reader to initiate repair strategies (e.g. re-reading) if comprehension breakdown is detected. This complexity presents challenges for assessment, especially as many of the cognitive processes that contribute to reading comprehension are covert and therefore cannot be directly observed or measured.

Tests of reading comprehension vary enormously in terms of the nature of the text that the child reads, and the response format via which comprehension is inferred. Some texts are as short as a single sentence whereas others contain extended passages comprising a number of paragraphs. Some texts are read silently whereas others are read aloud. Of those that are read aloud, some allow for reading errors to be corrected by the tester. Different response formats include multiple-choice, true–false judgements, sentence completion, open-ended questions and story-retell. Across all response formats, the nature of the question varies substantially with some items being more or less dependent on decoding, specific vocabulary, background knowledge and the particular type of inference needed. Tests also vary with respect to the load they place on cognitive resources such as working memory.

It follows from this that the nature of the assessment determines which aspects of comprehension are being measured. In turn, this may influence the children who are identified, or not, as having comprehension impairments. Some tests that seem at first glance to provide a measure of reading comprehension might in fact be very highly dependent on decoding. For example, Nation and Snowling (1997) found that a multiple-choice cloze task (the Suffolk Reading Scale, Hagley 1987) was more a measure of decoding and word-level reading skill than of comprehension. In their study, some children performed very well on the cloze test despite showing quite substantial comprehension impairments when reading extended discourse and answering open-ended questions (for similar findings, see Cutting and Scarborough 2006; Keenan, Betjemann and Olson 2008; Spooner, Baddeley and Gathercole 2004). Other tests are problematic as many of the questions can be answered via background knowledge without the text needing to be read (Keenan and Betjemann 2006). Thus, children with low levels of background knowledge may be falsely identified as having reading comprehension impairments and conversely, some children's reading comprehension difficulties may be masked, if they can rely too heavily on background knowledge to answer the comprehension questions.

In research studies in the UK, poor comprehenders have usually been defined using the Neale Analysis of Reading Ability II (Neale 1997), published by NFER. In this task children read a series of narrative texts that range from 26 to 141 words aloud, and any reading errors are corrected by the assessor so that comprehension can be maintained. Following reading, the child answers four or eight open-ended questions tapping both literal understanding and inference. This test yields measures of text reading accuracy, text reading rate and reading comprehension and includes normative data collected in 1996 for children aged from 6 to 12 years.

In 2009 and 2010, GL Assessment (formerly NFER) published two versions of the York Assessment of Reading for Comprehension (YARC, Snowling *et al.* 2009; Stothard *et al.* 2010), one for primary school pupils (aged five to 11 years) and one for secondary school pupils (aged 12 to 16 years). The YARC assessments include passage reading and comprehension components. These tests follow essentially the same structure as the *Neale Analysis of Reading Ability II* (Neale 1997): children read passages and answer open-ended questions. However, they provide more recent normative data (from 2008 and 2009) for children aged five to 16 years and include some important developments. First, the passages that children read are determined by their word reading accuracy (performance on the *Single Word Reading Test 6-16*, Foster, 2007) rather than their chronological age. This ensures that passages are at an appropriate level of difficulty and, therefore, the examiner can avoid administering a large number of passages to provide a sensitive measure. Second, both versions of the YARC assess the ability to read a range of materials by including non-fiction as well as fiction texts. Third, in the primary school version, the beginner passage is a shared reading task and sections of this text are read by the examiner as well as the child. Half of the comprehension questions are based on text that the child has read (reading comprehension), and half on text that the child has heard (listening comprehension). This means that the test can be used with children who are in the first stages of reading connected text. Performance on the remaining passages of both tests relies exclusively on reading comprehension. We hope that the publication of these tests will allow for improved identification, monitoring and instruction of children and adolescents with reading comprehension difficulties.

Time constraints make it difficult for individual assessments to be conducted in the school setting. Poor oral language or written work (e.g. limited use of vocabulary or grammar, poor organisation) will, in some cases, indicate reading comprehension difficulties. In addition, children with weak reading comprehension skills may find it difficult to answer questions about texts when working in groups, giving 'don't know' responses or inappropriate answers. If a child's reading comprehension raises concern in the classroom, every effort should be made to assess comprehension of extended text or discourse, not just word- or sentence-level comprehension. Since the YARC passage reading tests (Snowling *et al.* 2009, Stothard *et al.*) take only ten minutes, they provide an efficient first step for establishing whether a child has difficulty with text reading accuracy, fluency and/or reading comprehension. Further, the test manual includes an analysis of the comprehension questions that children are asked. Each question is classified according to the type of information that is needed to provide a correct answer. For children who obtain low comprehension scores, this information can be used as a starting point to guide teaching and further assessment. Given the complexity of comprehension, it seems likely that children may fail to understand what they have read for a variety of different reasons. Thus, if a more comprehensive assessment is warranted – and possible given time and financial constraints – it should include assessments of oral language, general cognitive resources and working memory as well as reading comprehension.

Summary and conclusions

Poor comprehenders are children who have reading comprehension difficulties despite being able to read words and texts effectively. The existence of children with this reading profile reminds us that there is more to skilled reading than the ability to read isolated words accurately. Research with this group has focused on whether and how discourse-level processes, oral language abilities and working memory skills underpin reading comprehension. Although further longitudinal studies are needed in order to tease apart causal mechanisms, recent findings lend support to the proposal that early oral language impairments in poor comprehenders contribute to their reading comprehension difficulties later on in development (Catts *et al.* 2006; Nation *et al.* 2010). Reading comprehension impairments in this group appear to be relatively persistent over time (Cain and Oakhill 2006), and their difficulties can go unnoticed in the school setting. Thus, efforts need to be made to identify these children at a young age, and to put in place appropriate interventions (for example, see Clarke *et al.* 2010) with the aim of fostering comprehension skills as children move through adolescence and into adulthood. Using the Simple View of Reading to guide educational practice provides an important step in this endeavour, emphasising the need for teachers to consider two components of reading skill – decoding and comprehension. This might serve to raise awareness of the poor comprehender profile, and guide literacy support for all children.

13 Classroom discourse: the promise and complexity of dialogic practice

Adam Lefstein and Julia Snell

Introduction

We estimate that, on average, an English primary teacher poses over 60,000 questions and follows up pupil responses with over 30,000 evaluations in every year of classroom lessons. This talk is shaped by deeply ingrained habits, resulting in part from an estimated 13,000 hours spent as a pupil watching others' teaching practice (Lortie 1975). However, a recent resurgence of interest in classroom discourse among educational researchers and policy makers is focusing attention on patterns of teacher talk. This attention, in turn, is placing demands upon teachers that they transform their talk, making conscious and informed choices about what had heretofore normally been second nature.

How should teachers and teacher educators respond to these demands? What do they need to know and understand about classroom discourse? In addressing these questions we review a broad consensus emerging from three decades of research on the topic, according to which (i) the way teachers and pupils talk in the classroom is crucially important, but (ii) the dominant pattern of classroom discourse is problematically monologic, so (iii) it should be replaced with more dialogic models. While we find much merit in this conventional wisdom, in this chapter we also show its limitations, arguing that teaching and classroom interaction are far more complicated and problematic than is typically captured by descriptions of and prescriptions for dialogue.

One note about the scope of our discussion: pupils and teachers talk in multiple classroom settings and configurations, including, for example, whole-class lecture or discussion, pupils talking in pairs, one-on-one teacher–pupil conferencing, and small group work (with and without teacher guidance). Here we focus primarily on discourse in the whole–class setting, partly on account of space limitations, but also because the complexities we examine are most pronounced in this configuration. We caution, however, that this focus should not be interpreted as in any way detracting from the importance of alternative settings; indeed, good pedagogy draws upon a broad repertoire of teacher and pupil discourse and interactive forms (Alexander 2005).

Classroom talk matters

Intuitively, how teachers and pupils communicate must be important: after all, talk is central to most of what happens in classrooms. Through talk, for example, concepts are explained, tasks demonstrated, questions posed and ideas discussed; indeed, one is hard-pressed to think of any significant school activities that do not involve talk in some way. But talk's ubiquity in classrooms is a rather weak argument for its importance. Perhaps children would be better served by lessons with less talk, thereby allowing each to get on with their own work, individually, without the distractions of teacher guidance, pupil chatter and other noise. However, a strong argument ties talk and language to pupil thinking, learning and development. In a famous passage, Vygotsky asserts the primacy of social interaction in human development: 'Every function in the child's cultural development appears twice: first, on the social level, and later, on the individual level; first, *between* people (*interpsychological*) and then inside the child (*intrapsychological*) ... All the higher mental functions originate as actual relations between people' (Vygotsky 1978: 57).

Vygotsky argues that thinking originates in social interaction – that discourse between people is internalised as individual cognition. There are at least three ways in which internalised talk can advance thinking. First, language is a cognitive resource: by being exposed to and participating in certain ways of using language, one becomes a 'fluent speaker' of that language, able to use and understand its key concepts and expressions (cf. Lemke 1990). Second, through talk participants are exposed to alternative voices and perspectives that challenge or elaborate their own world-view. Third, habitual interactional patterns – e.g. providing all participants opportunity to voice their views, demanding and providing justification for arguments, questioning assumptions, clarifying concepts, and so on – are internalised as habitual ways of thinking. Indeed, Sfard (2008) argues that the similarities between interpersonal communication and individual cognition are such that they can usefully be thought of as different manifestations of the same processes.

In short, the ways of talking into which we are socialised shape both the cognitive tools at our disposal and the habits of mind whereby we put those tools to use. This idea is supported by numerous studies of the relationship between classroom talk and pupil learning (see Mercer 2008 for a succinct review). This raises the question: What ways of talking do children most commonly encounter in classrooms?

Conventional patterns of classroom talk

It is difficult to generalise about classroom talk, since different classroom cultures have developed in different national contexts (cf. Alexander 2001); schools, teachers and pupils differ within contexts; and indeed patterns of talk in the same class may vary with changing topics, aims and activities. Nevertheless, over three decades of research in a wide variety of Anglo-American schools have found relatively consistent patterns in the whole class teaching observed (e.g. Cazden 2001; Edwards and Westgate 1994; Galton, Hargreaves, Comber and Pell 1999; Mehan 1979; Sinclair and Coulthard 1975; Smith, Hardman, Wall and Mroz 2004). Teachers dominate classroom interaction, talking most of the time, controlling topics and allocation of turns, judging the acceptability of pupil contributions and policing inappropriate behaviour. Pupils talk much less than the teacher, for shorter durations and in most cases only in response to teacher prompts. Whole class discourse is typically structured in Initiation-Response-Evaluation (IRE) cycles: teachers *initiate* topics, primarily by asking predictable, closed questions that test pupils' recall of previously transmitted information; pupils *respond* with brief answers; and teachers *evaluate* pupil responses, praising correct answers ('well done!') and/or censuring error ('you haven't been paying attention!'). (Some researchers prefer IRF [Initiation-Response-Feedback] to IRE, thereby signalling the multiple functions that can be performed in the third move [Wells 1993]. However, given the actual frequency of evaluation, we find IRE to be a more fitting description.)

To illustrate these patterns, consider the segment in Extract 1, which was recorded during a Year 5 lesson (pupils aged from 9 to 10 years) on apostrophes in southern England in April 2004 (for details about the study from which this episode was extracted see Lefstein 2005; 2008). Prior to this segment the pupils completed a worksheet of exercises involving placement of missing apostrophes. The teacher, Ms Goodwin, then orally reviewed their answers sentence by sentence.

1	Ms Goodwin:	next sentence
2		sh:h (2)
3		'Its made (.) of hundreds (.) of animals (.) bones' (.)
4		lots of 's'-es in there (.)
5		Drew
6	Drew:	bones
7		(2)
8	Ms Goodwin:	is it just telling you
9		there's more than one bone
10		or is it telling you that
11		something belongs to those bones
12		(7)
13	Ms Goodwin:	does anything <u>belong</u> to those bones

14	Drew:	no
15	Ms Goodwin:	no (.)
16		it's not one
17		that's just an 's' to show
18		that it's more than one (.)
19		Beatrice
20	Beatrice:	its
21	Ms Goodwin:	its is the first one
22		which is short for (.)
23	Pupil:	it is
24	Ms Goodwin:	it is made (.) of hundreds (.) of animals (.) bones
25		Keith
26	Keith:	hundreds
27		(1)
28	Keith:	no
29	Ms Goodwin:	what belongs to the hundreds
30	Keith:	no (.) animals
31	Ms Goodwin:	animals (.) good

Figure 13.1 Extract 1 – 'Hundreds of animal bones'

Ms Goodwin introduces the problem by restating the sentence, 'It's made of hundreds of animals bones' (line 3). Since the class have already reviewed a number of similar exercises, this restatement of the problem is understood by the pupils as a prompt to provide the answer. This initiation elicits three responses, each of which is further probed by Ms Goodwin. See Figure 13.2 for a schematic summary of the segment's structure.

Response 1: Drew responds with 'bones', which is incorrect. Ms Goodwin does not explicitly evaluate this response, though her rejection of his answer is palpable in the two second pause in line 7 – correct responses in Ms Goodwin's classroom are immediately accepted – and in her probing of his answer (in lines 8–13). In following up Drew's response, Ms Goodwin questions whether the 's' in bones signifies the plural form or possession (lines 8–11). This initiation is met with seven seconds of silence, after which she reformulates her question with the more straightforward 'does anything belong to those bones?' (line 13). Drew responds, 'no', which Ms Goodwin confirms by repeating it (line 15). She then draws out the implication – '[bones] is not one [of the correct answers]' (line 16) – and then elaborates upon his one-word answer by explaining the function of the 's' that presumably confused him (lines 17–18).

Response 2: Since Drew's response has been rejected, the floor is now open to other guesses. Beatrice responds with 'it's', which is positively evaluated by her teacher (in line 21). Ms Goodwin then follows up with a new initiation, asking what 'it's' is short for (line 22). An unidentified pupil offers the correct response, which is also positively evaluated through repetition of the sentence with the contraction spelled out.

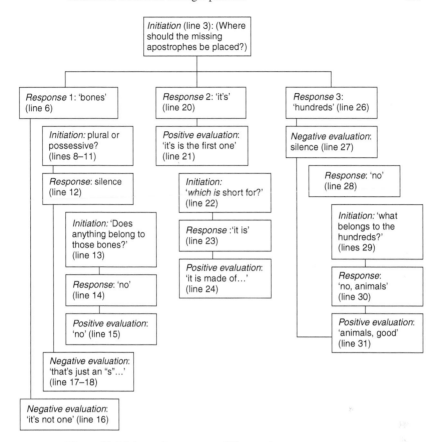

Figure 13.2 Schematic structure of Extract 1

Response 3: For each of these problems two apostrophes were missing, so, now that the first one has been located, the (unstated) question is where the second apostrophe should be placed. In line 26 Keith offers 'hundreds', but then retracts this answer one second later, after it was not ratified as correct. Ms Goodwin begins to probe his response (in line 29) – an additional sign that it is incorrect – and Keith changes his response to 'animals' (line 30), which is indeed praised as correct (in line 31).

In addition to the IRE structure, the segment exhibits the other discourse features reviewed above: the teacher controls the topic, allocates turns, and talks more often and for longer durations than the pupils, who respond with one or two word answers. Ms Goodwin poses 'closed questions', that is, questions for which the teacher has one correct answer in mind. Repeated investigations have found a much higher rate of closed than open questions in teacher discourse.

For example, in a major study of classroom interaction in English classrooms, Galton and colleagues (1999) found that 59.3 per cent of all teacher questions were closed questions, either requiring a factual answer or one correct solution to a problem, while only 9.9 per cent were open questions, in which more than one response was acceptable; the remaining 30.8 per cent of questions posed were concerned with task supervision and classroom routine (see Galton, Croll and Simon 1980; Alexander 1995; and Smith and colleagues 2004 for other studies yielding very similar results with different groups of English primary teachers and at different historical moments).

This high rate of closed questioning, and the IRE structure of which it is a part, have been widely criticised as detrimental to pupil independent thinking and learning. First, the structure positions teachers (and textbooks) as the sole legitimate sources of knowledge: the pupils' role is to recall and recite for evaluation what they have previously read or been told. Second, the structure tends to produce a rather disjointed lesson overall, with teachers moving from topic to topic with little or no clear line of reasoning. A third criticism is that, to the extent that participants do engage in more demanding cognitive activities (e.g. explaining concepts, relating ideas to one another, challenging and/or justifying positions), the bulk of the work is performed by the teacher.

With regard to extract 1, while the activity is not highly demanding, the division of labour is noteworthy: Ms Goodwin does most of the academic work, posing the problems, judging responses and elaborating the justifications for pupil answers (both right and wrong). Pupils' efforts are focused on figuring out what their teacher wants to hear, and many of them employ ingenious strategies to accomplish this task without necessarily attending to the substantive issues raised by the problems posed. Consider, for example, Keith's responses in lines 26–30. He first guesses 'hundreds', but when this response is not immediately accepted, he takes back his response (line 28), and changes it to 'animals' (line 30). How did he divine this new answer? The pupils have already been cued (in line 4) that the right answers will be words that end with an 's', so by process of elimination – 'bones', 'it's', and 'hundreds' having already been considered – the remaining correct answer must be and indeed is 'animals'. Throughout the lesson, a number of pupils employed this strategy of guessing one answer and switching if it was not immediately accepted. The strategy is enabled by Ms Goodwin, of course, by the nature of the questions she asks and by the very predictable ways in which she evaluates responses (see Street, Lefstein and Pahl 2007 for further examples and discussion of this phenomenon).

To summarise our argument up to this point: language and interaction play crucial roles in learning and development, but the structures of classroom discourse in which most pupils regularly participate are not well suited for mediating pupil learning or for shaping positive habits of mind. Such talk focuses pupils on divining what is in the teacher's mind, rather than thinking for themselves; promotes uncritical acceptance of teacher and textual authority; and limits the potential range of perspectives pupils encounter. What are the possible alternatives to this state of affairs? In the next section we look at recent efforts to make classroom discourse more dialogic.

Dialogic alternatives

Researchers and educators from a range of disciplinary and practical contexts have sought to transform conventional classroom discourse patterns, recommending in their stead alternative models of talk and interaction. 'Dialogue' is often invoked in discussions of preferred modes of classroom talk: for example, relevant book titles include *Dialogue in Teaching* (Burbules 1993), *Opening Dialogue* (Nystrand, Gamoran, Kachur and Prendergast 1997), *Dialogic Inquiry* (Wells 1999), *Towards Dialogic Teaching* (Alexander 2005) and *Educational Dialogues* (Littleton and Howe 2010). Likewise, the UK government has recently begun to champion 'dialogic' practice (DfES 2003; QCA 2005), though this official adoption of the term has been severely criticised. In this regard, Alexander (2004) warns of the danger 'that a powerful idea will be jargonised before it is even understood, let alone implemented, and that practice claiming to be "dialogic" will be little more than re-branded chalk and talk or ill-focused discussion'.

A wide variety of ideas are attached to dialogue, owing to the concept's rich and long history, which includes uses across a broad range of disciplines, including philosophy (e.g. Plato, Buber), literary theory (e.g. Bakhtin), critical pedagogy (e.g. Freire) and psychology (e.g. Rommetveit). The various dialogic approaches differ in many respects, depending on their educational and social aims, and the dimensions of talk and social interaction upon which they focus. In what follows we briefly review five of the key dimensions addressed, noting with regard to each dimension the relevant critique of traditional classroom practice and examples of alternative, dialogic practices proposed.

Structural dimension: many dialogic models seek to replace teacher-dominated IRE with more equitable interactional structures, in which participants freely exchange ideas (rather than all communication being mediated by the teacher), discursive rights and responsibilities are more evenly distributed, and all voices are given an opportunity to be heard. Approaches that emphasise this structural dimension often enumerate rules for teachers to follow. For example, the 'teacher talk' section in a government handbook (DfES 2003: 22) includes a list of dos and don'ts, excerpts of which are reproduced in Figure 13.3.

Epistemic dimension: many dialogic models seek to replace traditional reliance on teacher and textbook with a more critical stance towards knowledge. In such a stance, pupils and teachers take an active role in meaning-

DO	DON'T
• choose questions and topics that are likely to challenge children cognitively	• merely ask children to guess what you are thinking or to recall simple and predictable facts
• expect children to provide extended answers which will interest others in the class	• tolerate limited, short answers which are of little interest to other children
• expect children to speak for all to hear	• routinely repeat or reformulate what children have said
• signal whether you want children to **offer** to answer (hands up) or to **prepare** an answer in case you invite them to speak	• habitually use the competitive 'hands up' model of question and answer work
• when children give wrong answers ask them to explain their thinking and then resolve misunderstandings	• praise every answer whether it is right or wrong

Figure 13.3 Excerpts from DfES (2003) advice on 'teacher talk'

making, are authorised to contribute perspectives (and their perspectives are deemed worthy of being taken seriously), and focus on questions that are open to genuine inquiry. Scott, Mortimer and Aguiar (2006) capture this idea well in their contrast of *authoritative* and *dialogic* facets of discourse: in the former 'the teacher's purpose is to focus the students' full attention on just one meaning', while in the latter 'the teacher recognizes and attempts to take into account a range of students', and others', ideas' (Scott *et al.* 2006: 610).

Interpersonal dimension: many dialogic models seek to develop a collaborative and supportive learning community instead of the individualistic, competitive and impersonal environment commonly found in contemporary classrooms. Relationships are seen as key to building and maintaining such a community:

[D]ialogue is not fundamentally a specific communicative form of question and response, but at heart a kind of social relation that engages its participants. A successful dialogue involves a willing partnership and cooperation in the face of likely disagreements, confusions, failures, and misunderstandings. Persisting in this process requires a relation of mutual respect, trust, and concern – and part of the dialogical interchange often must relate to the establishment and maintenance of these bonds. (Burbules 1993: 19–20)

This interpersonal dimension is also emphasised, for example, in Alexander's (2005) notion of dialogue as *supportive*: 'children articulate their ideas freely, without fear of embarrassment over 'wrong' answers; and they help each other to reach common understandings' (Alexander: 34). Similarly, interpersonal concerns are central to Mercer's (2000) distinction between disputational, cumulative and exploratory forms of talk. *Disputational talk* is characterised by high levels of competitiveness and criticality as participants defend their own positions; *cumulative talk* is characterised by high levels of solidarity as participants desist from criticising one another; only in *exploratory talk* are relationships conducive to participants' critical yet constructive engagement with each other's ideas.

Substantive dimension: dialogic models seek to replace the often disjointed nature of classroom discourse, in which the teacher leads the class through a series of unrelated IRE cycles, to discussions characterised by what Alexander (2005) refers to as dialogic teaching's *cumulative* feature: 'teachers and children build on their own and each others' ideas and chain them into coherent lines of thinking and enquiry' (Alexander 2005: 34). Similarly, this dimension is central to Michaels, O'Connor and Resnick's (2008) *Accountable Talk* framework, which guides pupils and teachers to talk in ways that are accountable to the learning community ('attending seriously to and building on the ideas of others'), to standards of reasoning ('emphasizing logical connections and the drawing of reasonable conclusions') and to knowledge ('making an effort to get their facts right and making explicit the evidence behind their claims or explanations').

Political dimension: underlying many dialogic models are political concerns, including, for example, seeking ways of giving pupils greater agency and voice in the conduct of classroom life, empowering traditionally disenfranchised groups, and transforming schools into 'places where students learn the knowledge and skills necessary to live in a critical democracy' (Giroux and McLaren 1986: 224). Dialogue is promoted as a means of subverting often authoritarian and alienating classroom power relations, granting pupils greater freedom and self-determination.

How do these different dimensions play out in actual classroom discourse? We spent two-and-a-half terms last year exploring possibilities for whole-class dialogue with a group of primary teachers in an East London school as part of the ESRC-funded, 'Towards Dialogue: a Linguistic Ethnographic Study of Classroom Interaction and Change' project (RES-061–25–0363). As part of this study we facilitated teacher group discussions of video-recorded lesson excerpts, including the following extract which was recorded during a Year 6 literacy lesson (pupils aged from 10 to 11 years) in late November 2008. We invite the reader to consider this extract in relation to the dimensions outlined above. The class have been reading and discussing C. S. Lewis' *The Lion, the Witch and the Wardrobe*. In this particular lesson, they look at Chapter 14, in which Aslan (the Lion) surrenders himself to the White Witch. Extract 2 occurs about 40 minutes into the lesson. The pupils had been working in groups, each group addressing a different question arising from the text. In the segment captured below in Figure 13.4, the teacher, Ms James, leads the class in discussion of one of these questions, regarding why the gateway to Narnia was not always open.

1	Ms James:	when they went in there again
2		it was all blocked up wasn't it
3		they [couldn't get through
4	Sean:	[((nods emphatically))
5	Ms James:	why is that
6		why- why did that happen (.)
7		this group why do you think that happens
8	Sean:	becau:[s:e
9	Ben:	[erm
10	Ms James:	right Sean was just about to say something then
11		(3)
12	Sean:	I don't know
13	Ms James:	you're not sure
14		o:ka:y
15		maybe you can add something in a moment
16		Ben
17	Ben:	I think
18		maybe it's because erm
19		they only let people in at certain times (1)
20		like (1)
21		like when they- Aslan was back
22		they let Peter and Susan in
23	Ms James:	okay
24		do you think that maybe the wardrobe only lets in
25		good people
26	Anon:	(nope)
27	Anon:	why did (they)
28	Julie:	but she let in Edmund- they let in Edmund
29	Ms James:	so we're not saying it-
30		we- we're disagreeing with that then
31	Sean:	they only let certain people in
32	Ms James:	only let certain people in
33		bu:t if there's some-
34		we're saying they only let good people in
35		why do they let Edmund in
36		what do you think Brian
37	Brian:	I think it's if they believe in it
38	Vanessa:	yeah that's what I think
39		because (.)
40		erm Lucy-
41		Lucy wou- didn't know about it and then she (.)
42		went in Narnia and then she found out that it was there and she
43		believed in it

Figure 13.4 Extract 2 – Getting in to Narnia

44	Ms James:	but can I just disagree with Brian-
45		do you mind if I disagree with you Brian
46		right
47		the rest of the children
48		they didn't really believe in it did they
49		Peter and Susan
50		they thought that Lucy was ju:st
51		being silly be- because of her age
52		and they all rushed into the wardrobe didn't they
53		when Mrs McCreedy was showing these people
54		around the house
55	Julie:	((whispering)) they were with Lucy ((this pupil has her hand up and
56		appears eager to contribute))
57	Ms James:	and they suddenly went in
58	Julie:	because they were [with Lucy
59	Ms James:	[but they didn't believe in it (.)
60		what do you think about that
61	Julie:	because they were with Lucy
62	Ms James:	sorry
63	Julie:	because they were with Lucy
64	Ms James:	so they were <u>with</u> somebody that <u>did</u> believe (1)
65		ah so you think you've got to have a <u>belief</u> in Narnia
66	Pupils:	yeah
67	Ms James:	to be able to get in
68	Deborah:	((nods))
69	Pupils:	yeah
70	Ms James:	okay
71		((shrugs her shoulders))
72	Deborah:	yeah but what about Edmund
73	Ms James:	but what about Edmund
74		ah Deborah just said
75	Deborah:	because he went in after Lucy (.)
76		not while-
77		he didn't go in <u>with</u> Lucy
78		(2)
79	Ms James:	so what do we think about that now (1)
80	Pupils:	yeah
81	Anon:	(okay maybe you were wrong)
82	Ms James:	okay maybe you're wrong
83		so you have to sort of back down on that argument
84		okay that's- that could be an interesting one to discuss in more detail
85		later but (.)
86		I want to go onto <u>your</u> question now

Figure 13.4 (cont.)

What is happening in this episode? To what extent and in what ways might it be considered dialogic? In discussing this episode we begin with a brief overview and then analyse it according to four of the five dimensions of dialogue outlined above. (We have not included the political dimension in this discussion, owing to its limited salience to this strip of interaction.) In the final section, we conclude with some comments on the limitations of our analysis, the complexities of dialogue in the whole class setting and implications for changing practice.

At the beginning of the extract the teacher, Ms James, reviews the question that has been previously posed – 'Why is it that sometimes the children couldn't get through to Narnia?' – and asks the group to which the question had been assigned to respond (lines 1–7). Following some uncertainty about which individual group member should answer (lines 8–16, to be discussed in detail below), Ben offers an idea: 'maybe it's because they only let certain people in at certain times' (lines 18–19). This idea forms the first of five conjectures that are discussed throughout the episode (see Figure 13.5). These conjectures are ignored, contested, elaborated, supported and/or refuted such that at the end of the episode the class remains without an answer to the question, but with the sense, perhaps, that this issue 'could be an interesting one to discuss in more detail' (lines 84–85). We have ended the extract at line 86, in which Ms James closes the discussion of this question by moving on to the next group's question.

Structural dimension: while talk in this episode is largely mediated (and dominated) by the teacher, this is not exclusively the case. Pupils give extended responses – longer, at least, than the 1–2 words typical in whole-class discussion – for example in lines 17–22, 38–43 and 75–77. Pupils participate in the discussion outside of the accepted IRE slots: for example, Vanessa follows on from Brian's response (lines 38–43); Julie repeatedly interjects, 'because they were with Lucy' during Ms James' turns; and Deborah challenges, 'Yeah, what about Edmund?' after Ms James appears to have concluded the topic (line 72). Likewise, Ms James deviates from IRE conventions: her questions tend to be more authentically open than is conventional in IRE (the question with which she opened the episode is a prime example), and her use of the feedback move is more probing and challenging than strictly evaluative as right or wrong. Finally, multiple voices are brought to bear on the topic, with four pupils and Ms James contributing conjectures, and another three pupils and Ms James elaborating, supporting and/or refuting those conjectures.

Epistemic dimension: there are at least five ways in which this episode is dialogic in its approach to knowledge. First, the question discussed is authentically open in the sense that, based on Ms James' responses to pupil contributions, she does not appear to have an answer in mind. Indeed, and this is the second point, it would seem that the question is also open in the sense that it does not allow for a definitive answer – it is *in principle* unknowable (cf. Harpaz and Lefstein 2000). Thus, the class do not resolve the problem, and Ms James concludes the discussion by saying that they need to think and discuss further. Third, while Ms James plays a central role in managing the interaction, she does not assume a privileged role with regard to knowing the answer to the question she has posed. She offers a conjecture (in the form of a question, in lines 24–25), but then backs off of this five lines later when presented with evidence refuting it. Likewise, note how she respectfully disagrees with Brian, as a peer, rather than evaluating his comment in an authoritative, teacherly manner (lines 44–54). Fourth, as noted above, multiple pupil and teacher perspectives are voiced in the extract, and the participants critically engage with most of the ideas brought forward.

Interpersonal dimension: while it is difficult to comment on classroom relationships, which take shape over long durations, on the basis of a short segment, we offer the following tentative remarks about dialogic relations in the extract (which draw also on other recordings and observations of this class). First, as noted above, Ms James models respectful disagreement with Brian (in lines 44–45), posing her ideas as a question and offering Brian the opportunity to respond to her refutation with 'what do you think about that?' (line 60). It is perhaps no coincidence, then, that pupils themselves start to question ideas that arise during the discussion. Deborah, for instance, appears at first to agree with conjecture 5 (line 68), but after giving it further thought engages more critically: 'But what about Edmund?' Second, Ms James attempts to draw in pupils, such as Sean (line 10), who are normally on the periphery of classroom discussion (see below for further discussion of this interaction), thus fostering a supportive, inclusive classroom environment.

Substantive dimension: the cumulative nature of the episode is graphically represented in Figure 13.5, which demonstrates its underlying logic of inquiry – of conjectures and refutations – and how most of the participants' contributions are attended to and treated seriously. Participants build upon one another's ideas: conjectures 3 and 5, for example, appear to emerge out of ideas that immediately preceded them. For the most part, the episode also adheres to the criteria of accountable talk: participants respond to one another's ideas (accountability to the community), bring in evidence from the story (accountability to knowledge) and appeal to standards of logical consistency when refuting and/or supporting one another's ideas (accountability to reason). It is worth noting, however, some exceptions to these generalisations. For example, it is not entirely clear to us whether Ms James' question, 'Do you think the wardrobe only lets in good people?' (lines 24–25) is a probe of Ben's conjecture or an attempt to replace it with a different idea (hence the broken arrow connecting conjectures 1 and 2). Either way, Ben's idea that the wardrobe only opened

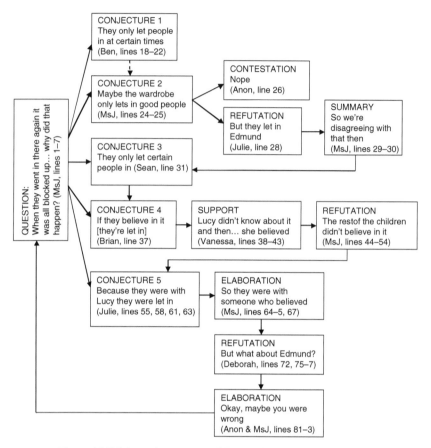

Figure 13.5 Schematic structure of Extract 2

at certain times fell out of the conversation, which subsequently focused on the possibility that the wardrobe only opened for certain people.

Problematising classroom dialogue

In light of the preceding section, we feel relatively secure in our judgement that extract 2 exhibits a number of desirable, dialogic features (that is, after all, why we chose it), but less comfortable about concluding our analysis on that note. In this final section we draw attention to the limitations of our perspective, data and interpretations. We problematise some of the assumptions underlying our previous analysis – not necessarily arguing that they are wrong, rather inserting question marks where we had previously placed full stops. In particular, we explore the partial and bounded nature of the data considered, the resulting analytic foci, and the complexities and problematic nature of dialogue in the whole class setting. We conclude the chapter by returning to the question of what teachers need to understand about classroom discourse.

Data limitations: what we call 'data' – the recordings, notes, artefacts and impressions we bring with us from the field – are necessarily partial, a particular slice of experience, cut at a particular angle, and at a particular moment in time. Consider the partialness (and partiality) of the data we have discussed above: it is less than two minutes of an hour-long lesson, occurring about three months into the school year, ten years into Ms James' teaching career, and in the eleventh year of the pupils' lives. It was shot at a certain angle: from the back corner of the room, opposite where the teacher stood, thereby capturing the teacher's face but mostly the sides or backs of the children's heads. The audio catches loud and well-projected voices, but misses comments pupils mumble or whisper under their breath. Participants experienced the episode through all five senses; in transcribing it we have reduced the sounds, sights and smells to a relatively flat record of the audible words spoken, with minimal indication of pauses and non-verbal communication. Finally, we have not supplemented the video record and our field notes with interviews or other materials that might help us fill in gaps in our knowledge about the participants, their past experiences, present intentions, future hopes and so forth.

Analytic foci and perspectives: the nature of the data collected shapes what we can and cannot readily perceive to be happening. In what follows we outline some of the key ways in which the data, along with our theoretical perspectives and assumptions about dialogue, have shaped our gaze:

a) *Focus on discourse moves*. The very brief duration of the extract makes it easier to appreciate discourse moves – e.g. questions and responses – than processes that happen over longer periods: a curricular unit or even pupil task; learning a concept; development of relationships and identities; or evolution of classroom culture. All of these longer processes bear upon the way participants make sense of the shorter events that in turn contribute to them. So, for example, how we (and the participants) make sense of Ms James' question, 'Do you mind if I disagree with you, Brian?', depends upon our assessment of Ms James' tone, which in turn depends on an implicit understanding of her character, which is based on our previous experiences with her.

Furthermore, the focus on discourse moves is problematically narrow if one's aim is to change the nature of talk. Discourse moves are embedded in activities and institutions, which crucially constrain possibilities for what can legitimately be said, in what ways and how it will be understood (Levinson 1979). Examples of relevant activities include pupil tasks, assessment frameworks and the curricular unit as a whole. Relevant school institutions include the national tests, performance management and Ofsted inspections. Changing activity and institutions exerts pressure on talk; any attempt to change talk without accounting for the way it is shaped by activities and institutions is likely to encounter enormous difficulties.

b) *Focus on the linguistic mode.* Representing interaction by means of a written transcript privileges the spoken word over the non-verbal gesture and silent glare. As such, it can obscure the facts that the quiet participants tend to outnumber the vocal ones, and that there is a lot more communication and other social activity going on off-stage than is captured by a running account of the centre-stage teacher–pupil talk. Viewing the video without audio, or listening to radio microphone recordings of pupils talking under their breath, provides a very different perspective on 'what is happening' in the lesson.

c) *Privileging the teacher's perspective.* The focus on the linguistic mode, and the way the camera angle places the teacher in the centre of the frame, tend to privilege the teacher's perspective on the lesson. Likewise, owing to our relative proximity to the teacher in age and interests we tend to identify more readily with her, and to look at the lesson from her perspective. How might such a perspective differ from those of the pupils? In a major study of classroom discourse, Galton and colleagues' (1980; 1999) found that the average teacher spent most of their class time interacting with pupils, but the average pupil spent nearly two-thirds of their time interacting neither with the teacher nor with other pupils. So, only a small number of pupils are involved in the whole-class discourse events that dominate lesson transcripts. When alternative research methods are employed we see that pupils who are relatively 'passive' vis-à-vis the whole class discussion (and are thus absent from the transcript) are actively engaged in other pursuits. For example, radio-microphones pinned to individual pupils capture the hushed side comments that are made in response to official classroom talk; discussions of extracurricular experiences, popular culture and peer relations; and pupils working hard to manage multiple (and often conflicting) classroom identities (e.g. projecting the image of obedient pupil to the teacher while displaying an anti-school stance to one's peers) (Rampton 1995; 2006; Maybin 2006; Snell 2008).

How might the episode examined in extract 2 have been differently experienced by individual pupils? To illustrate how a different set of analytic foci and perspectives can lead to a different account of the episode, we revisit lines 6–16 of the extract. This segment highlights pupil identities, an issue central to dialogic concerns such as relationships, power and voice, but which has heretofore not entered our analysis. Since much of the communication in this segment is non-verbal, we use still images from the video recording to illustrate our analysis.

Figure 13.6 *Nominating Ben* – Ms James: 'This group, why do you think that happens?' (line 7)

Ms James opens this sequence by asking the relevant pupil group to share their response to the question they have been working on (lines 6–7). As she nominates 'this group' she turns to face Ben (Figure 13.6). Ben is a member of the group that was tasked with answering this question, but he is not the only member; Deborah to his right, and Sean and Rob, who are sitting in front of him, were also part of the group. Based on teacher targets and our observations, we know that Ben is perceived to be an able pupil who often participates positively in class discussions, while Sean and Rob, who are seated at the front row of desks directly in front of the teacher, are viewed as low ability. Even though Ms James verbally addresses the question to the whole group ('this group', line 7), her body language suggests that she expects the answer to come from Ben, the higher ability pupil. Ben acts as if the role of group spokesperson has been allocated to him, and begins to formulate his response, buying time with the filler 'erm' (line 9), but in doing so, he overlaps Sean who has already begun what appears to be an answer ('becau:s:e', line 8). At this point Ms James stops Ben's utterance rather abruptly and offers the floor to Sean ('right Sean was just about to say something then') (Figure 13.7). Three seconds of silence follows, after which Sean replies, 'I don't know'. Rob has now raised his hand, but Ms James reverts back to Ben, who can usually be relied upon to give an answer that will move the discussion forward (Figure 13.8).

Figure 13.7 *Giving the floor to Sean* – Ms James: 'Right, Sean was just about to say something then.' (line 10)

Figure 13.8 *Returning to Ben* (line 16)

This short sequence raises a number of questions. Was Sean genuinely begin-ning to formulate an answer on line 8? Or was he trying to feign participation in this lesson without actually having to take a turn? After all, the teacher had already turned away from Sean and seemed to be directly addressing another pupil (see McDermott and Tylbor 1983 for a description of a pupil who adopts a similar strategy). If so, does Ms James collude with this pseudo-participation by letting him off the hook too easily ('you're not sure ... okay') and by keep-ing alive the possibility that he will be able to participate later: 'maybe you can add something in a moment'? Notice also how Ms James reformulates Sean's 'I don't know' to 'You're not sure', giving the impression that Sean is still formulating his ideas and thus downgrading the seriousness of Sean's admis-sion (and protecting Sean's 'face' in front of the other pupils) – it is not lack of knowledge but lack of certainty. Further, what roles are played by the other pupils in his group? Consider Ben, for instance, who is ready to step into the role of speaker/group spokesperson at a moment's notice. Sean's identity as a low-ability pupil emerges in an interactive process between his own actions and the way he is identified by others, both teacher and peers (Maybin 2006; McDermott and Raley 2008).

Finally, what are the implications of this episode for our analysis of classroom discourse and dialogue? In our previous discussion of Extract 2 we glossed over this section, treating it as insignificant, momentary noise sandwiched between the substantive question, conjectures and refutations. However, our reanalysis of this episode shows that a more complete understanding of class-room discourse needs to go beyond tracking the exchange of information (and thus focusing on who does or does not have it); that the focus needs to be on the pupils rather than just the teacher, and that 'pupils' should not be treated as an undifferentiated entity but as individuals; that individual pupil identities are often constructed and reinforced in interaction with others; and that this has implications for how pupils see themselves and how they participate in classroom activities.

Conclusion: dialogue as a problem ... worth confronting

In this chapter we have argued for the importance of classroom discourse as a key mediator of pupil learning, and contrasted conventional classroom pat-terns with more dialogic approaches. We have presented a multidimensional approach to dialogue, which brings together structural, epistemic, interper-sonal, substantive and political concerns, and illustrated such an approach in the analysis of a lesson extract. We have problematised this analysis, showing the limitations of our data and analytic perspectives, and demonstrating how the extract might have been experienced by a pupil who was only marginally involved in the episode.

We hope that our discussion of multiple dimensions, perspectives and concerns that are brought into play in classroom discourse has impressed upon readers some of the complexities of conducting dialogue in the whole-class setting. These complexities have important implications for how we think about dialogic classroom practice. According to a common view of teaching (and dialogue), there is a right or wrong answer to every situation: 'best practice' can be identified, prescribed and implemented. Acknowledging the complex web of competing concerns and tensions inherent to dialogue, however, gives way to a view of dialogic practice as a set of problems or dilemmas. Confronting these dilemmas is usually not a matter of choosing between dialogue or monologue, but between competing dialogic concerns. Moreover, while a (dialogic) move may encourage, empower and foster growth for some participants, it may also silence and alienate others (Lefstein 2010).

Consider, for example, some of the dilemmas that emerge in extract 2: Should Ms James have stayed with Sean, insisting that he participate in the discussion and/or heavily 'scaffolding' his answer? Or was turning to Ben in order to move the discussion forward the best course of action? Should she have focused more attention on Ben's conjecture (1), by opening it up for discussion? Or was the injection of a second conjecture the best way to ignite the conversation? What about explicitly disagreeing with Brian? Did that advance the dialogue, as we have suggested, by modelling respectful disagreement and by effacing her teacherly authority, or did it ruin Brian's day?

These and countless other dilemmas arise from the conflicting demands teachers face, which are rooted in the disparate needs of the many individuals in the classroom (think both Sean and Ben) and the different concerns raised by the five dimensions of dialogue [see Lefstein (2010) for elaboration of teacher roles according to different dialogic dimensions].

In conclusion, we return to the question with which we opened the chapter: what do teachers need to understand about classroom discourse? Teachers need to understand the importance of talk in teaching and learning; be sensitive to the ways in which conventional discourse norms can be detrimental to pupil thinking and learning; and appreciate the promise – and complexity – of dialogic practice. Such understanding would go a long way towards improving classroom discourse, but we should emphasise that teacher knowledge is a necessary but insufficient condition, for talk is embedded in activities and institutions, and needs to be considered alongside related facets of pedagogy and educational organisation.

Transcription notations

(text)   Transcription uncertainty
(.)   Brief pause (under one second)

(1)   Longer pause (number indicates length to nearest second)
(( ))   Description of prosody or non-verbal activity
[Overlapping talk or action
[
text   Emphasised relative to surrounding talk (underlined words)
te:xt   Stretched sounds
sh-   Word cut off

14 Pedagogy and bilingual pupils in primary schools: certainties from applied linguistics

Angela Creese

Introduction

During the annual half-day session devoted to learning about English as an additional language (EAL) on a crowded initial teacher training curriculum at the University of Birmingham, one trainee teacher approached me at the end of my guest lecture. She wanted to check that she had understood my endorsement of her bilingualism in the primary school classroom. She wanted confirmation that she could and should use Urdu alongside her English. Unlike many of my responses to the complex questions students ask, I was able to give a clear unambiguous answer 'Yes'. Using the linguistic resources of teachers and pupils in the endeavour of learning and teaching to engage and facilitate is to be endorsed and supported in our school classrooms. In this chapter, I draw on a body of research to consider how teacher and pupil languages and varieties of languages can serve as resources in the primary school classroom. I show how pupil and teacher bilingualism can be used in multilingual class-rooms drawing on two different contexts. The first is a Gujarati complementary school in Leicester while the second is a Birmingham primary school. I make the argument that we should be encouraging code-switching as a pedagogic resource for teaching and learning and suggest that our initial and continuing teacher development programmes need to offer support and strategies to teachers to implement such an approach.

Multilingual and bilingual education: certainties, realities and principles

In a recent article, Hornberger (2009) articulates ten certainties about multi-lingual education based on empirical research in 'many corners of the world' (2009: 198). Hornberger defines multilingual education at its best when it values more than one language in teaching and learning; recognises and values understanding and dialogue across different lived experiences and cultural world views; and draws out the knowledge which children bring to the class-room. According to Hornberger, the children themselves should be viewed as full and indispensable actors in society – locally, nationally and globally. Others have made similar points. De Jong and Freeman Field (2010) argue that educators can achieve quality schooling for bilingual learners through the use of three principles: affirming linguistic and cultural identities; promoting additive bilingualism; and fostering integration. Harper *et al.* (2010) illustrate the importance of activating and developing children's multilingual background knowledge to increase participation and make connections in learning. Conteh (2007a), researching English primary schools, highlights the skills and knowledge of bilingual teachers in primary school classrooms. She outlines three theoretical, practical and policy implications for education in the UK's culturally and linguistically diverse society:

- the need to develop models of teacher professionalism and standards for teacher development which recognise the diversity of knowledge and experience which teachers bring to their work;
- the need to promote bilingualism as a normal aspect of learning for many pupils in our classrooms and additive bilingualism as a valuable achievement in mainstream classrooms;
- the need to understand and acknowledge more fully the links between teaching and learning in mainstream and complementary contexts. (Conteh 2007a: 469)

Bilingualism in education

García and colleagues (2009) define bilingual education as education using two or more languages in instruction during which acquisition of a second language does not impede first or 'native' languages (Muir, Morales, Falchi and Garcia 2009: 390). According to Garcia, multilingual schools, 'Exert educational effort that takes into account and builds further on the diversity of languages and literacy practices that children and youth bring to school' (Garcia *et al.* 2006: 14). The US context described by García above does not easily map onto the UK context where 'bilingual education' means something very different. In England and Scotland, we do not have 'bilingual education' in the US sense which sees programme models developed to 'balance' the different languages during the school day. Rather in our mainstream schools we 'celebrate' multilingualism and multiculturalism but do not explicitly set out to learn and teach bilingually. We work with linguistic diversity but do not enforce models of bilingual education. The Welsh context is perhaps the exception here – although the focus on Welsh as an indigenous and national language differs from the context of multilingualism described by Garcia above. Thus, when Garcia (2009) describes bilingual education she is describing more than the tolerance of other languages or even the celebration of other languages as is often manifested in our UK primary and secondary schools. She is arguing for much more. According to Garcia bilingual education means going beyond acceptance or tolerance of children's languages to 'cultivation' of languages through their use of teaching and learning. It also means going beyond the safeness and rhetorical comfort zone of 'celebratory' bilingualism which discursively values young people's multilingualism but does not include these languages in teaching and learning processes in any sustained and meaningful way. Bourne (2001) has described the dangers of 'celebratory discourses' which keep other languages 'outside and incidental to the learning process' (Bourne 2001: 251). Conteh (2007a) finds that government policy related to language diversity in mainstream schools has been motivated by a tacit, but strongly stated, concern to 'contain' bilingualism, and to prepare pupils for a monolingual rather than a multilingual future in society.

Bilingual pedagogy

For many years educationalists running bilingual education programmes particularly in the USA have insisted on the separation of the two languages arguing that this avoids linguistic contamination (Jacobson and Faltis 1990: 4). However, the research evidence shows that such a policy stance is problematic resulting in what Cummins calls the 'two solitudes' (2005: 588); Heller calls 'parallel monolingualism' (1999: 271), and what Blackledge and Creese (2010) describe as 'separate bilingualism'.

García (2009: 5) argues that we need an integrated and plural vision for bilingual education, 'by which bilingualism is not simply seen as two separate monolingual codes', but 'depends upon the reconceptualization of understanding about language and bilingualism'. According to Garcia, we need to move away from 'monoglossic' ideologies of bilingualism which 'view the two languages as bounded autonomous systems' (2009: 7) to heteroglossic ones which views bilingualism as dynamic. Creese and Blackledge (2010) use the term 'flexible bilingualism' to describe how teachers in complementary schools in England use their languages to connect to the young people they are teaching. In a study of complementary schools in four English cities they show how bilingual teachers and children move between their languages which goes 'unnoticed' and is 'unproblematic' to the participants themselves as they engage in task completion (Martin *et al.* 2006; Creese and Blackledge 2010). For them, their 'languages' appear not to be separate but rather act as resource to negotiate meanings.

Conteh (2007a; 2007b) has made a similar point. She describes how bilingual teachers – in both primary and complementary schools – use codeswitching to create a culturally responsive pedagogy while Martin-Jones and Saxena (2003) describe how bilingual adults in primary classrooms use their linguistic, personal and cultural histories as funds of knowledge for teaching and learning. Anderson (2008) has recently called for flexible pedagogic approaches for responding to bilingual contexts which do not fit easily into existing paradigms and argues for using the bilingual skills which bilingual teachers bring to the classroom. The pedagogic potential of code-switching is also examined more recently by Martin and colleagues (Lin and Martin 2005; Arthur and Martin 2006). Code-switching, these authors argue, increases the inclusion, participation and understandings of pupils in learning processes; it creates less formal relationships between partici-pants allowing for ideas to be more easily conveyed, and lessons 'accom-plished'. Arthur and Martin (2006: 197) speak of the 'pedagogic validity of code-switching' and consider ways in which research might contribute to a 'teachable' pedagogic resource.

García (2007) makes a similar point but proposes that we abandon the term code switching to describe what bilinguals do with their language and adopt the term 'translanguaging' to describe how languages seep into one another. She has shown in her work in New York schools that languages are not her-metically sealed units; rather they leak into one another so that it is not always clear or helpful to view languages as separate. The term translanguaging, she argues, shifts the focus from the actual language code to how the speaker uses the language. It puts the multilingual speaker at the centre of the frame rather than language(s). According to García 'translanguagings are *multiple discur-sive practices* in which bilinguals engage in order to *make sense of their bilin-gual worlds*' (2009: 45 – emphasis in original).

Conceptualising a bilingual pedagogy in UK schools

This view of code-switching as positive rather than 'suspicious' holds promise for primary and secondary school participants. I wish to explore this possi-bility further in this chapter. The intention behind the seminar that originally brought this collection of chapters together was to develop a vision of what an applied linguistics curriculum for pre-service primary school teachers might look like. In the BAAL seminar, we were asked to reflect on: *what do primary teachers need to understand, and how*? In the section below, my contribution to addressing this question is to further exemplify the points made from the lit-erature reviewed earlier in this chapter. I do this drawing on research recently conducted on complementary schools. Like Conteh (2007b: 469), I believe we need to understand and acknowledge more fully the links between teach-ing and learning in mainstream and complementary contexts so that we might learn more about the possibilities of bilingual pedagogies and strategies (Bhatt *et al.* 2004). In considering the links between the two sectors I draw out four principles based on the empirical research described above.

Principle 1: Teachers should feel confident in drawing on the full linguistic repertoire of classroom participants as a learning and teaching resource

In other words teachers should not feel guilty about using their own bilingualism or their pupils' bilingualism, or the bilingualism of other teachers or parents in classroom practices. Shin (2005: 18) describes attitudes towards code-switching as negative, noting that bilinguals themselves 'may feel embarrassed about their code switching and attribute it to careless language habits'. Setati *et al.* (2002: 147, in Martin 2005: 90) make reference to the 'dilemma-filled' nature of code-switching in their study of South African classrooms. Martin (2005) describes attitudes to code-switching in Malaysia: 'The use of a local language alongside the "official" language of the lesson is a well-known phenomenon and yet, for a variety of reasons, it is often lambasted as "bad practice", blamed on teachers' lack of English-language competence … or put to one side and/or swept under the carpet' (Martin 2005: 88).

Moving between languages has traditionally been frowned upon in educational settings across different contexts, with teachers and chidlren often feeling guilty about its practice. Code-switching is rarely institutionally endorsed or pedagogically underpinned. Rather, when it is used, it becomes a 'pragmatic' response to the local classroom context rather than a 'planned' response. Martin suggests that we need to consider moving beyond the pragmatic towards a more formal endorsement of this pedagogic strategy. Arthur and Martin (2006: 197) suggest that code-switching might be considered as a 'teachable pedagogic strategy' while Conteh (2007a: 457) encourages us to think about it as a 'culturally responsive pedagogy'.

I now turn to some data to illustrate the pedagogic potential of translanguaging. I show how this approach of mixing languages is endorsed by teachers working in two very different examples. The first data set includes extracts from a complementary school teaching Gujarati in Leicester, while the second data set comes from a Birmingham primary school. Rather than describing guilt or disapproval about the mixing or blending of languages, there is explicit institutional endorsement of this in both the complementary and primary school context. The first three extracts below come from teachers in classrooms in which Gujarati is being taught in a Leicester complementary school.

We're always comparing – it is nice to do things in Gujarati but we love you to do things in English as well … How are we going to separate those things? No. Actually we are giving more. You don't have to change the way you are to mix with others. You can enjoy both worlds, both lives. (Interview with head teacher, Gujarati school)

The languages are getting mixed so a new language is emerging – the language of Leicester! (Interview with teacher, Gujarati school)

Since this is a Gujarati school, I will mix English and Gujarati … if you don't understand you can raise your hand and I will explain it. (Field notes, Gujarati school assembly)

In all three extracts the teachers in the Gujarati schools endorse the mixing of Gujarati and English. The teachers recognise the importance of drawing on the young people's bilingualism. They flag up the potential of mixing languages rather than the more usual position of enforcing boundaries between languages by insisting that only certain languages can be used in the classroom domain.

In an example from a different context, a Birmingham primary school, we hear a similar position put forward by the assistant head teacher. In the following extract, the teacher is describing how she wants the children to view their primary school as a place where they can move 'unproblematically' (Martin *et al.* 2006) between languages.

We talked about wanting children to be able to switch in and out. Wanting children to choose a preferred language and switch in and out. We said where are we going and what do we actually want? I mean you do hear children do that … just switch in and out. But there are also children who still have not got the confidence to do that but I think it depends where they are, who they are working with. (Assistant head)

The assistant head recognises that the school needs to work with rather than against existing practices. The reason for this approach is described below:

We want to talk about language – pupil talk, bilingualism – developing language – whatever the language because the strategy that we have is to develop all children's language whether they are bilingual or monolingual children – not to exclude children. We have a lot of children who have several languages. (Assistant head)

The aim to develop pupil's 'language' is understood by this Year 6 child at the same school.

My feelings towards my own language is happy because the whole time I do it I feel confident to do it and I feel happy when I am doing it and English is the same … there are a lot of people in this school that use both languages most … because some schools don't really use the two languages. This school uses both languages and I feel confident with both of them and happy when I am using both. (Pupil, Year 6)

The pupil above endorses the position put forward by the assistant head that using both languages in an asset in the school. The school had a policy of employing bilingual teachers and working with their monolingual teachers to develop strategies for using the languages of their pupils. Language development was placed at the centre of the school's objectives and they were inclusive of both monolingual and bilingual teachers in developing strategies for working with their multilingual pupils.

Below are two vignettes drawing on observations of the same Birmingham primary school. The first illustrates a monolingual teacher working with a group of Year 5 children while the second illustrates a bilingual teacher working with a Year 6 group. The vignette below shows a monolingual teacher creating a multilingual awareness ethos in her class and facilitating pupils' use and development of their funds of knowledge (Moll *et al.* 1992), in a way that enhances the experience of all learners.

> ### Vignette: Year 5 classroom. This week in the school is Literacy Art week.
>
> This is a Year 5 class with twenty-six pupils in attendance and three absent. The class is ethnically and linguistically diverse. Their teacher is Miss West, an English speaking monolingual teacher.
>
> The class focus is extension work on a Chinese folk story they have been reading. The teacher speaks about respecting and listening to others. Pupils work in pairs for around 20 minutes working on the task to write a short dialogue for one scene of the folk story. They do this by discussing in pairs and providing feedback to the teacher. Sometime they do this in their home language. When this happens Miss West asks for an interpretation from another student. This requires other children to listen out for the translation into English. Miss West stresses to the whole class the importance of producing 'powerful language' in the dialogues.
>
> The children then break into group still with their home language pairs. There are Sylheti, English, Pushto, Arabic, Mirpuri groups. The children work and are lively in their discussions. Their aim is to produce a piece of dialogue in English. They do this discussing in different combinations of language(s). The pupils are then encouraged to perform their dialogues to the whole class. They do not hesitate. Some perform in English, some in the home languages and some bilingually with one person playing one part in one language and the other in another. One pair gets stuck with the word 'promise' and does not know the Mirpuri for it. Her partner says, 'don't worry, just say it in English'.
>
> One pair of girls perform in Mirpuri and another group of children ask them to do it again in English. They do this without any problem. After the English version, Miss West questions the girls about the scene itself – whether it has come from the storyline. After watching the performances the teacher asks for improvement points from the audience. Miss West makes the point that the language could have been even more powerful.
>
> On the wall is a display which shows photos of paired talk partners/groups under which is a short extract about how they use their home languages in class.
>
> We use our home language to extend our vocabulary
>
> We like working together to improve our home language.

The following vignette is from the same school but a different classroom in which a bilingual teacher works with her Year 6 class. In the vignette we see that the pupils' languages are 'central to learning and teaching'. Pupils demonstrate the process of skills and knowledge transfer between languages, and the teacher consistently provides 'affirmative messages' to the pupils about their language skills.

Vignette: Year 6. This week in the school is Literacy Art week.

This Year 6 classroom is a bright cheerful place with pupils' work all round the walls. The teacher's name is Miss Rashid. The class is 'high tech' and the teacher moves between the computer, the flip chart and the board. Children are grouped on the mat. There are many teacher compliments and these are also used to enforce classroom behaviour.

Miss Rashid reminds the children about a folk story from Japan. Children are encouraged to help one another. 'Ahmed help Asha'. The teacher comments that there are not enough hands up and this triggers a movement into paired talk in the children's home languages. 'Not enough hands up. Discuss in pairs'. She encourages pupils to think through her teaching and their learning rationale, 'Why do you think I am doing this?' Their task is to write a Haiku poem. Miss Rashid presents a model to them and works on English vocabulary enrichment asking for alternative synonyms and antonyms from her pupils. She also works on parts of speech and uses a diagram which requires pupils to place parts of speech in the correct box. They then write a class Haiku all together before being asked to write one in their pairs.

There are several particularly noticeable features in this class. First, how much pupils have to listen to each other in order to advance the task. Miss Rashid often calls upon students to interpret or extend what a previous pupil has said. The pattern of 'home language' into 'English' sets up a routine which requires all students to listen. The teacher's request for translation/interpretation means that all pupils need to listen carefully to other pupils. Second, this multilingual teacher appears to be extending some home languages through a focus on new/key vocabulary in the community languages. Third, pupils are encouraged to take collective responsibility while an individual has been asked a question. So while a particular pupil is thinking about an answer Miss Rashid tells the rest of the class 'Everybody think about how you would explain a noun'.

After the paired whole class 'mat work' the children move to their language groups where they must write a group Haiku poem. Language groups represented are Mirpuri/Kashmiri, Sylheti, Urdu, and English. The pupils all write in English with discussions in home and English language.

These schools' endorsement of translanguaging in both the Birmingham primary school above and Leicester complementary school is actually rather unusual in educational contexts where teachers more often indicate their disapproval of 'mixing' languages in the classroom. This is reflected in a quotation from one of the teachers in Zentella's well-known study of US schools. 'When they don't understand something in one language, they'll go to the other, which is easier for them … and like, then sometimes I have to be bouncing from one language to the other, which is wrong' (Puerto Rican teacher; in Zentella 1981). This brings us to the second principle described here.

Principle 2: A pedagogy which emphasises the overlapping of languages and literacies in the child is to be preferred to one which argues for the separation of languages for learning and teaching

Examples of pedagogies which explicitly seek to develop bilingual and biliterate strategies do exist. In terms of optimising pedagogy, Hornberger suggests, 'bi/multilinguals' learning is maximized when they are allowed and enabled to draw from across all their existing language skills (in two+ languages), rather than being constrained and inhibited from doing so by monolingual instructional assumptions and practices' (Hornberger 2005: 607).

Cummins (2005: 588) also makes some explicit suggestions for developing bilingual strategies. He suggests,

(a) systematic attention to cognate relationships across languages; (b) creation of student-authored dual language books by means of translation from the initial language of writing to the L2 [second language]; other multimedia and multilingual projects can also be implemented (e.g. creation of iMovies, PowerPoint presentations, etc); (c) sister class projects where students from different language backgrounds collaborate using two or more languages. (Cummins 2005: 588)

In the UK, research has shown how bilingual children do not view their literacies and languages as separate, bur rather experience them as 'simultaneous' (Kenner 2004; Robertson 2006; Sneddon 2000). Kenner (2004) notes how children growing up bilingual and attending community languages classes experience their worlds as 'simultaneous' rather than as separate linguistic and cultural entities. In a more recent study Kenner and colleagues (Kenner *et al.* 2007, Al-Azami *et al.* 2010) show the sophisticated skills which bilingual pupils bring to their literacy practices. In particular Al-Azami *et al.* illustrate how bilingual pupils can use transliteration in which primary school pupils write Bengali (Bangla) words using the English alphabet. They exemplify how pupils use their linguistic and conceptual knowledge from each of their languages to accomplish bilingual learning. They found that children understood the idea of transliteration. For example, when their teacher checked with them what it meant, they said: 'in Bangla, writing in English, but Bangla words'. They discussed together how to represent Bangla sounds, and transferred their phonetic knowledge from English. Al-Azami *et al.* argue that transliteration is both liberating and empowering for children and serves as an essential bridge between languages and learning in several key ways: as a communicative bridge between children, bilingual parents and monolingual teachers; as a conceptual bridge enabling reflection on the ideas and language structures that have been written down; as a bridge to the Bengali script itself, since children can use the transliteration to work out the corresponding Bengali letters; and as a bridge to new learner identities, because children have the chance to develop their confidence as bilingual writers. Al-Azami *et al.* suggest that transliteration is particularly advantageous for second and third generation children, who have had less opportunity to learn Bengali script, because it enables children to maximise the cognitive and linguistic benefits of bilingualism.

Similarly, in our work on complementary schools, we show how bilingual teachers in complementary schools use their linguistic resources to keep the task moving while simultaneously offering a model of translanguaging as institutionally acceptable (Creese *et al.* 2008). As I explained above recent research on complementary classrooms show their classrooms as spaces which draw on code-switching and translanguaging as usual practice. Recordings of classroom interaction in complementary schools abound with examples of moving between languages for teaching and learning purposes. In the following extract the teacher PB has asked children to describe their 'daily routine'. We provide the English translation in square brackets.

PB: mari dincharya, daily routine … Medha ane Jaimini, mane shu thawu game
   [My daily routine … Medha and Jaimini, what I'd like to be]
S: what is it? [chat]
PB: … bai jana decide karo … only five minute j apu chhu … je awde e bolwanu
   [both of you decide … giving you only five minutes … speak what you can]
S: Miss, basically shu karwanu … discussion karya pachhi?
   [basically what do we have to do? After discussion, what?]
PB: bolwanu
   [speak]
S: shu bolwanu?
   [speak what?]
PB: je discuss karyu hoi
   [what you discussed]
S: oh … <chat> … etle we discuss it and then decide what we gonna say … miss ame ek bijanu kaie ke ek ek …
   [so we discuss it … miss, do we speak about each other or one by one …]
PB: tame decide karo ke kone bolwu chhe …
   [you decide who speaks]

This short extract illustrates how teachers and children draw on their languages to engage in the task. In many ways, there is nothing remarkable about this bilingual interaction. The constant movement between languages goes unnoticed to the participants themselves as they engage in task completion. For them, their 'languages' appear not to be separate but rather act as resource to negotiate the nature of the task. We can view this as an example of translanguaging in which pupils uses their languages in a pedagogic context to understand what is expected of them by the teacher. We might think of Gujarati and English not as distinct languages here, but rather as a set of signs which speakers use to undertake the task at hand. Even in this short extract we see that translanguaging is not only permitted, but expected. In this way translanguaging contributes to the production of a language ideological world which sees pupil and teacher heteroglossia as pedagogically productive and creative.

Translanguaging exemplifies typical bilingual linguistic practice. Below is a further example of language use in the home in which a bilingual English/ Gujarati young person is working on his homework with a relative.

R: Shlok! Can you come here? <sound of piano in background> *Fur Lise tara pac-chalnu lai aaw,* [bring the back of your book] I'll have a look with you. What have you done at the back?
SH: all the religion and that …
to hu wanchu [ok, I'll read] … *aa anthi wanchyu* [I haven't read this]
<reads with hesitations> *saslae oonda chit … chit..*
R: [helps SH to read] *saslae inda chitarya* [the rabbit painted the eggs]
SH: <repeats> … *lamba kan walo saslo wagdama raheto. E bhare chabrak* [the long eared rabbit lived in a jungle. He was very clever] *chabrak etle?* [what is 'chabrak'?]
R: clever, *chalak, tara jewo* [clever, like you]
SH: <laughs and continues to read>
        (Home recording: Student (SH) and relative working together on homework task)

In the above extract we see the participants English and Gujarati is used to accomplish the task. The reading activity requires the foregrounding of Gujarati with English used mostly for the instrumental activity of discussing the task. The translation of the word *chabrak* into clever and back again allows the participants to bring a lightness to the homework task. There is nothing particularly significant about this extract. It is a typical example of translanguaging which is a typical feature of bilinguals language use. We know that bilinguals code switch in many different contexts including home and school. However, mainstream primary and secondary schools may view this linguistic behaviour with suspicion and make little use of it pedagogically. This brings us to a third principle.

Principle 3: A recognition that bilingual teachers/assistants bring a set of unique resources, knowledge and skills to learning and teaching

In a recent study, Conteh (2007b) asked two bilingual teachers two questions: what were the teacher's purposes in codeswitching? And, what were its effects on the children? Conteh found that most of the teachers' code-switching was aimed at providing support for individual children, or for checking that the children understood what was going on. Conteh also argued that bilingual teachers extended the thinking of the pupils they were working with using code-switching in particular to ensure that important concepts were understood by the children. In addition, Conteh found that the bilingual teachers used code-switching as a practice in performing their professional identity. This was important to the bilingual teachers as it allowed them to draw on funds of knowledge which they used as 'cultural bridging between life in Bradford and Pakistan (Conteh 2007b: 196). Conteh draws on Cummins (2001: 1–2) to remind us of the potential transformative power of the conversations between teachers and learners. Specifically she argues that code-switching, 'is a distinctive feature of being bilingual, which very clearly links social, cultural and linguistic factors' (2007a: 466) and she suggests that this is a particularly important resource in working with second- and third-generation ethnic minority children from different heritage backgrounds.

This returns us to the opening paragraph of this chapter and allows me to again make the point that bilingual teachers should feel able to draw on their linguistic resources to include, engage and teach their pupils. This brings us to the last of the fourth principles discussed in this chapter.

> *Principle 4: A need for teacher training and development*
> *in how to employ these translanguaging resources for the*
> *wellbeing of the child*

Despite the endorsement in this chapter of bilingual strategies/pedagogies based on flexible methods there is also need for caution. Martin (2005: 90) writes,

And yet we need to question whether bilingual interaction strategies 'work' in the classroom context ... [D]o they facilitate learning? Can classroom code-switching support communication, particularly the exploratory talk which is such an essential part of the learning process? A corollary to this is whether teacher-training programmes (both pre-service and in-service), in multilingual contexts take into account the realities and pragmatics of classroom language use in such contexts.

Lin (1999) acknowledged that switching between English and Cantonese in her study ensured understanding and motivation but warned against notions of easy transferability to other classrooms in other contexts. Further, the development of pedagogies which respond to the research literature will not work in any 'mechanistic generalisable way' (Arthur and Martin 2006: 197). The above research emphasises the importance of responding to local circumstances rather than it applying carte blanche. Although we can acknowledge that across all linguistically diverse contexts moving between languages is natural, how to harness and build on this will depend on the socio-political and historical environment in which such practice is embedded, and the local ecologies of schools and classrooms.

We know from both research (IOE 2009), media (*Guardian* 2008), government reports (Dearing and King 2007) and professional organisations (Naldic 2009) that the number of teachers specialising in languages is falling. This is both true of those teaching English as an additional language as well as teachers of foreign languages. Teachers receive very little input on EAL or community languages, or indeed the role of language in teaching and learning across the curriculum. There is even less provision for bilingual classroom teachers or bilingual EAL teachers or bilingual subject-specific curriculum teachers. Although specific programmes of study do exist for teachers' continuing professional development in the area of EAL, there is little specialised training available for bilingual teachers. If we are to develop innovative pedagogies which reflect the lives of multilingual young people attending schools in the UK we will need better provision for training our teachers for working in linguistically diverse contexts.

Conclusion

Teachers are agents of change and through their practice can both endorse but also challenge prevailing ideologies. Teachers can and do work towards more equitable educational policies and practices for linguistically diverse pupils through their classroom practices. As Hornberger and Skilton-Sylvester suggest, 'In looking at the ways in which power is constructed through language and in interaction, actors can begin to see themselves as agents who have the power to transform practices and not merely as recipients of already decided upon norms' (Hornberger and Skilton-Sylvester 2000: 100).

This quote offers those of us working in educational contexts a positive and proactive view of the way in which we shape our classrooms. It emphasises the ability of practitioners to change and transform settings. It asks us to think local and consider how our own practices as teachers and researchers will figure in the lives of the children we work with. This chapter has suggested that we need to find ways which endorse the typical and usual practices of our bilingual participants in our schools. Rather than thinking monolingually and insisting that languages be kept separate in the teaching and learning processes or that lip service only is paid to languages other than English in our primary school classrooms, we need to find ways that our pupils and our bilingual teachers can draw on the full range of the linguistic resources without feeling guilty about doing so.

Part III

Empowering teachers and teachers'
use of knowledge

Introduction to Part III

Sue Ellis and Elspeth McCartney

Authors in Part III have applied linguistic knowledge in ways that are directly useful to teachers in the classroom to support their understandings of children's language and literacy development. For all authors, the common aim is for linguistic understandings to become part of teachers' professional knowledge, to be used as practical and functional analyses and teaching methodologies.

To these ends, Henrietta Dombey and Jane Briggs outline the *Knowledge about Language* strand at the University of Brighton, introducing student teachers to linguistic knowledge in the context of texts used by and with children, aiming to provide powerful tools for graduates to develop children's language, reading and writing. Greg Brooks makes the case for teachers understanding the rudiments of the internationally recognised phonetic alphabet, in order to appreciate, discuss and analyse the complexities of English phoneme-grapheme correspondences. Kenn Apel and his colleagues deal with word-level literacy, teaching to develop children's phonemic, orthographic morphological and semantic awareness and mental imagery in order to spell, and pinpointing the precise learning needs of children with language-learning difficulties. Mary Hartshorne notes that teachers are one group amongst the wider children's workforce who require extensive knowledge about speech, language and communication. She outlines the development and use of a self-assessment *Speech, Language and Communication Framework* that allows individuals to assess their own level of competence in these areas, from a universal level needed by the whole workforce to a postgraduate, extension level. Sue Ellis and Elspeth McCartney describe a research-based model of language support for teachers working with therapists to support children with persisting language impairment, where linguistic principles and language-learning activities are offered to teachers 'just in time' to implement change in classrooms. Carolyn Letts gives practical advice for teachers on observing, identifying and supporting children whose problems with language acquisition can be masked by the use of two or more languages. Viv Ellis and Jane Briggs conclude the book with a timely reminder that many factors other than linguistic knowledge impact upon effective teaching, and whilst teacher education has to value learning about language highly, it has to ensure that learning is fit for the purpose of improving schools as places for children to learn.

The authors in this Part recognise that teachers and student teachers have little time to learn linguistics. Dombey and Briggs also suggest that students may need to be persuaded of the value of doing so, and Brooks cites earlier examples of inappropriate linguistic information being offered to teachers. Apel and colleagues note that a common model of spelling as a memorisation task acts against the development of linguistic approaches, and Hartshorne recognises the scale of the need to equip and develop language understandings across the whole children's workforce. Ellis and McCartney stress the competing and intense demands upon teachers in pre-service education, and Letts the difficulties presented when a child is secure in none of their languages. Ellis and Briggs fear fragmented, tick-box lists of linguistic 'knowledge' being demanded from teachers, which do not recognise teachers' learning across boundaries.

The link amongst authors here is their response to such challenges, offering the application of linguistic knowledge in a focused and practical way. They do not propose a model of 'learn then apply' linguistics, but rather outline linguistic understandings, knowledges and resulting procedures that have been mediated for teacher use. The suggestion running in common through the chapters is that it is through practical application that such linguistic frameworks will become an integral part of teacher knowledge, and be used in the classroom to enhance child learning. Their approaches have been developed to empower teachers to do a big part of their job, helping children to master the complexities of language and literacy.

15 Building knowledge about language into a primary teacher education course

Henrietta Dombey and Jane Briggs

Introduction

In this chapter we set out the subject matter that student teachers encounter in the *Knowledge about Language* strand of the four-year BA course at the University of Brighton, UK. This course leads to Qualified Teacher Status, entitling graduates to apply for posts as probationary teachers in England's primary schools (TDA 2009c). We show how this content sits in the course as a whole and how it is related to pedagogical issues and to classroom concerns.

Wider background

It is not clear what is the relation of explicit linguistic knowledge to teachers' effectiveness as teachers of reading and writing. In the USA, despite extensive research into reading-teacher education, there is no answer. In a critical analysis published recently in *Reading Research Quarterly*, eighty-two empirical investigations carried out in the USA, meeting rigorous acceptability criteria, are evaluated by Victoria Risko and colleagues on the Teacher Education Task Force of the International Reading Association (Risko *et al.* 2008). Not one of them concerns explicit linguistic knowledge. There is one relevant study published in the UK, but it is not recent. This is the *Effective Teachers of Literacy* project, commissioned by England's Teacher Training Agency and carried out by a team led by David Wray and Jane Medwell at the University of Exeter over ten years ago (Medwell *et al.* 1998).

That study contrasts teachers of proven effectiveness with a validation group chosen to represent teachers with a typical range of effectiveness, and aims to identify the knowledge and beliefs that distinguish the two groups. The results of a quiz on linguistic terms show that the effective teachers were more likely to be able to identify word classes in a sentence, but few could pick out more than nouns, verbs and some adjectives. Both groups were largely unsuccessful in identifying phonemes or onsets and rimes, with the effective teachers scoring slightly worse than the others. Both groups found great difficulty in expanding an inadequate definition of a verb. The effective teachers were more successful at naming distinguishing aspects of non-standard accents or dialects, but avoided linguistic terminology in doing so. The effective teachers also showed a greater awareness of children's authors than the comparison group teachers.

But the differences between the groups appear to be less a matter of de-contextualised knowledge than of operational focus in a teaching context. Asked to compare two pieces of children's writing on the same task, the effective group focused first on the text as a whole – its content and detail, genre and so forth. Nearly all in the comparison group put spelling and punctuation before such matters. And while the effective group judged the success of a piece of writing primarily in relation to its intended function, a large proportion of the validation group considered the use of capital letters and sentence length to be the key indicators of quality. Similarly, in commenting on children's reading and re-telling of a story, the effective teachers used more criteria and made more inferences about children's strategies and understanding, while the comparison teachers commented on items of vocabulary used. The authors comment:

What our data cannot show, of course, is how much more effective the effective teachers might have been if their knowledge of linguistic concepts had been more extensive and more explicit (Medwell *et al.* 1998: 24).

So our *Knowledge about Language* strand at the University of Brighton cannot be said to be based on research evidence. Instead, it is founded on an unsupported belief that increasing student teachers' explicit knowledge about language, if approached in the context of a concern to help children become more effective language users, might well help them become more effective teachers of literacy.

Institutional background

The University of Brighton is a major provider of initial primary teacher education in England. Over the last fifteen years, we have scored well on various statutory inspections of the relevant courses in general and the English components in particular (Ofsted 2005; 2008).

Although we are pleased to have this approval, it has not been the shaping force of our planning or teaching. Rather than aiming for high inspection scores and setting our course by the official directives, we have, over the years, built our own principled approach to literacy education, based on theoretical and empirical research of children learning to talk, read and write, and informed by our own experience of working with children and student teachers. This has shaped our course design, our module writing, the planning of school experience placements, and, of course, the teaching transactions we engage in. All of these have continued to evolve as our knowledge and understanding of this complex area develops.

To the extent that we consider that there is an important body of linguistic knowledge we would like our student teachers to acquire, we can be said to take a positivist view of this aspect of teacher education. But we also recognise the need for student teachers to make connections to their own prior knowledge and to engage in collaborative dialogic learning activities that generate connections between theory, their own beliefs, prior knowledge and practice. We recognise too that knowledge acquisition requires intentionality of the learner. In this sense the learning and teaching can be said to be coloured by a constructivist approach.

This paper focuses on the university's four-year BA with Qualified Teacher Status (QTS) degree course, but the subject matter presented below is also included in our one-year Postgraduate Certificate of Education (Primary) course. Most of our new entrants to the BA course are fairly proficient users of language, both spoken and written. But their knowledge of language is tacit and operational, rather than explicit and consciously organised. They can do things with language, but are unfamiliar with the technical terms that label what they do. Few starting their courses can readily identify (much less define) subordinate clauses, although all can use them with skill, and have probably been doing so since they were about 4 years old. This immediately places learning about language in a different category from most other learning. We have to be clear about this and about our reasons for teaching such knowledge, and communicate these effectively.

The principal aim of our teaching in literacy has been to help our student teachers become effective teachers of literacy in the primary school. We see this as enabling their pupils to talk, read and write in order to construct and communicate meaning effectively, with a range of partners, to a range of audiences, for a range of purposes. To achieve this most fully, we see that both student teachers and children need a rich experience of children's literature to develop their awareness of the possibilities of making meaning through language – of what words can do. This approach is not just a set of abstractions or pious hopes: the team of English specialists includes great expertise in such practices as writing workshops, shared reading and literature circles. To this extent our approach to primary education in literacy can be summed up as experiencing powerful language, and learning to put it to use.

However, for well over ten years, phonics has played an increasingly important role in our teaching of reading and writing at Brighton. We are persuaded by the evidence of the positive contribution that explicit phonics teaching makes to children's literacy learning. Indeed we would argue that knowledge of phonics is essential for all those learning to read and write in an alphabetic writing system. So we see it as necessary that student teachers should learn something about the segmental phonology of English if they are to become effective teachers of reading. They need to know how the spoken sounds of English map onto their representations in written words.

But to be effective, primary teachers need to understand more than this about the English language. If they are to enable their pupils to construct and communicate meaning effectively through talk, reading and writing, they need to enlarge their understanding of what language is and how it works. They need this, together with some understanding of educational psychology, if they are to construct key informing principles, as well as a repertoire of productive classroom practices. We see an understanding of the processes of language acquisition as fundamental to the construction of these informing principles.

To acquire an appreciation of children's spoken and written language and how these develop, most student teachers need to extend their technical knowledge of language – what it is and how it works – at the levels of text structure, morphology and syntax, as well as segmental phonology. So our subject matter includes all these aspects of language study to some degree.

We do not aim to improve student teachers' own use of language through this work, nor to enable them to transmit similar lessons about language to primary school children. Instead our aim is for them to understand something of how effects are achieved through language. We also aim to help them appreciate the complexity of children's implicit learning of discourse structure, syntax and morphology (in addition to lexis), that enables them to use spoken language effectively and to write coherent texts, expressing fine shades of meaning and complex relationships. This, then, provides a necessary foundation for our student teachers to study language acquisition, the facilitation of spoken language in school and the teaching of reading and writing.

So we have developed a *Knowledge about Language* strand that runs through the four-year BA (Ed.) course. Students explore some topics through self-study materials and others as part of modules on the learning and teaching of language and literacy. In the section that follows we set out the content of this strand. The section after that shows how this subject matter is contextualised and developed in the various English modules.

The content of our 'Knowledge about Language' strand

We aim to introduce much of this knowledge in Year 1 of the BA course, principally in two key contexts: through booklets that the students work through, on their own (or preferably, in pairs) and through a module on early literacy development, which involves aspects of segmental phonology. The idea is that this knowledge will inform subsequent study of children's language and literacy development in and out of school and in turn be deepened and extended. For example, later modules on early language development and the teaching of writing build on and extend knowledge of syntax.

Word classes

The aim of this element is to enable student teachers to talk more easily about language and to appreciate something of the choices that skilled authors make. On entry, most of our student teachers admit to only shaky knowledge of word classes. Early in the first semester they are given a sixteen-page, A4 University of Brighton booklet, to work through in a set time. This treats the word classes in turn with examples, explanations and tasks for each. (See Figure 15.1.)

Word classes are described semantically, with additional syntactic and morphological clues. Students who find sections of the booklet insufficient are directed to relevant pages in David Crystal's *Discover Grammar* (1996).

There are eighteen tasks, ranging from '1. List 10 nouns of your own choice' to '18. List all the interjections and determiners in the passage below'. Texts from children's literature are used for these.

Where the question is an open one, student teachers are asked to check with a friend, while answers to 'closed' questions are given at the back. The booklet culminates in a final test (also self-corrected) in which they have to locate a number of examples of each word class from a given text.

Task 5: List ten varied adjectives of your own, including some ending in the suffixes listed above. Compare your answer with a friend's.

    Adjective   *red, nice, fragrant, appalling, tedious, Chinese*

- An adjective tells you more about a noun.
  Yellow pages, dirty plates, kind Ada

- You can slot an adjective in between 'a' or 'the' and a noun.
  A green apple, the big dog, the last straw, a nice day

- You can put an adjective after 'I am' or 'it is'.
  I am lonely. It is juicy.

  But beware! This also works for some nouns.

- You can put an adjective after 'more' or 'most' or 'very'.
  More beautiful, most kind, very sincere

  But beware! This also works for some adverbs.

- Some adjectives end in 'ous', 'ful' or 'ent'.
  'luscious', 'fruitful', 'silent'.

Figure 15.1 Example of how the word class 'adjective' is presented

Text structure, syntax and morphology

As student teachers find these topics challenging, this subject matter was initially taught through a separate module, with six two-hour sessions for classes of thirty or so. However, time constraints have meant that this is no longer a taught part of the course. Hence, the University of Brighton booklet that accompanied the module is now distributed in Year Two and, like the word classes work, is completed through individual or group study. This study is contextualised in Curriculum English sessions. In this booklet, each topic is addressed in turn, with most time and emphasis given to syntax. The booklet includes, as material for analysis, many extracts from texts written for children, as well as four key texts written by children, with original spelling and punctuation.

We aim to enable the student teachers to understand better how these texts work and what linguistic forms the child writers have learned. It is quite some time before they are able to identify all the forms used in the text, an extract of which appears as Figure 15.2, particularly those in the last sentence of the second paragraph and the last sentence of the extract. Student teachers are also asked to reflect on how they think the child authors might have acquired their repertoires of linguistic forms.

To complete the booklet, student teachers also need to use David Crystal's *Discover Grammar* (1996) and, for the work on text structure, David Wray and Jane Medwell's *English for Primary Teachers* (1997).

Chapter one written by Humble the cat

       I heard the Wolves again last night, howling at the tops of their voices, long and loud big and bold.

       I went to my secret hunting field just now, I stayed out there for ages. I came in through the window, like the ghost of the cat next door, whose life was meant to end.

I've come in for warmth and comfort by the fire and up against the dog.

       Alice is fidgeting in her cradle she can smell mouse on me. The dog lies near the fire with her belly facing the centre of the sparks. I hear noises and turn my head, I thought it might have been Alice, but it was the Dog wandering over to Alice's cradle, wobbling with her belly so big.

Figure 15.2 Part of one of the four texts by primary children used in the booklet, the opening part of a piece written by a 10-year-old girl in the role as the cat in Henrietta Branford's *Fire, Bed and Bone*

The booklet is divided into sub-topics, which are introduced and explained through a number of examples. These are followed by a series of tasks for the student teachers to complete. As with the work on word classes, they are asked to check with a friend where the question is an open one, and consult the answers at the back for 'closed' questions.

Students complete a test paper involving all three topics, but with most attention given to syntax. (See Figure 15.3.) The test is based on a passage from a book for children. As well as answering questions on morphology and text

---

Syntax Topic 2 Simple and Compound Sentences

What is a clause? A clause is a central unit for making meaning through language-
that is for saying something about something. Each clause is made up of a number of
different elements, one of which must be a Verb. In the following sentence there are
two clauses: [Luckily midnight struck] and [Prince Cinders changed back into himself].

A simple sentence has only one clause. A compound sentence (or multiple
sentence) is made up of clauses joined together in sequence, usually by a conjunction
such as 'and', 'but' or 'then'. This type of joining together is called co-ordination.
Each clause is equally important. You can increase the length of a compound sentence
by adding more and more clauses. But beware! Sentences made like this can become
boring.

| 1 | Simple sentence | [The dog chased the cat furiously]. |
| 2 | Compound sentence | [The dog chased the cat] and [he tackled the rat] but [then he got hurt]. |

Task 1:   **Make up a simple sentence, and a compound one. Mark the
beginning and end of each clause with square brackets.**

Task 2 :   **In the sentences below, all taken from books written for children, try
to identify the clauses, marking them as above. Two have already
been done for you.**

1   From *Charlotte's Web* by EB White

[Wilbur liked Charlotte better and better each day.] [Her campaign against

insects seemed sensible and useful.] Hardly anybody around the farm had a

good word to say for a fly. Flies spent their time pestering others. The cows

hated them. The horses detested them. Mr and Mrs Zuckerman were always

complaining about them, and putting up screens.

From White, EB *Charlotte's Web* (Puffin 1963)

Figure 15.3 How simple and compound sentences are introduced

structure, the student teachers have to identify and label particular sentence and clause structures and comment on their use. Reflecting on their results, students identify areas still in need of development which are then tracked by their professional development tutors.

Phonology

Phonology is tackled in all curriculum English modules, in relation to the teaching of reading and writing. It is approached through taught sessions, including workshops and student presentations, handouts, close examination of recorded classroom practice, further reading, and teaching practice preparation. It may also feature in discussion about particular lessons in school. When the topic is initially introduced in taught sessions, student teachers are often asked how many phonemes there are in English. Some fifteen years ago, many offered numbers that ranged from ten to several hundred. More recently they have tended to suggest around 40 to 50, showing a greater awareness than their predecessors. Before starting on the process of identifying the phonemes of English, they are asked to 'read' aloud a number of nonsense words that follow English spelling patterns (see Figure 15.4 for examples).

plag	crench	glame
gatter	clure	mald
grance	octuce	graduction
poctation	snopple	rebbage
plaughter	shrief	crall

Figure 15.4 Nonsense words following English spelling patterns

When they have pronounced the 'words' in chorus (with some differences in the 'words' *mald*, *grance* and *crall*, determined by accents north or south of England's <a> divide) the student teachers are asked whether they sounded them out, letter by letter. Most are aware of using analogy with familiar words such as *bald*, *cabbage* and *daughter*, rather than building the words up one letter or phoneme at a time. However, it is stressed that they are highly experienced readers of English, not 5-year-olds learning to read.

Through lectures and self-study materials, student teachers are taught or reminded of the following:

1. what a phoneme is (defined as the smallest unit of speech sound that makes a difference to a word's meaning, e.g. /s/a/t/ vs. /c/a/t/, /s/i/t/, /s/a/d/);
2. how many phonemes there are in English, with emphasis on the high number of vowels and the low number of letters representing them;
3. to identify phonemes in spoken words;
4. something of the complex relation of phonemes to graphemes in English, including terms such as diphthong, digraph, blend, grapheme;
5. that the spelling of very many words in English involves other principles besides single phoneme/grapheme correspondences (rime units, morphological spellings and fossilised spellings);
6. patterns of progression in the development of children's phonological awareness;
7. the important role of rhyme in both English spelling patterns and the development of children's phonological awareness;
8. the importance of analogy in learning to recognise words in English;
9. how to complement phonics programmes that focus solely on synthetic phonics and neglect the other principles that govern English spelling besides single phoneme/grapheme correspondences;
10. that very many of the commonest words in English defy a synthetic phonic approach;
11. how to develop balance in their teaching, between different approaches to word recognition and between word recognition and reading for meaning in a broad and rich literacy curriculum;
12. how to make phonics teaching systematic, but also fun, active, creative and effective, in the context of a reading programme focused on reading for meaning. (See Figure 15.5.)

How this learning is contextualised in English modules in the BA course

Year 1

In Year 1 of the BA course, the first Curriculum English module is *The Development of Language and Literacy*, which is provided for those taking both the Foundation Stage (teaching children aged 3 to 5) route, or Key Stage 1 or 2 (teaching children aged 5 to 11) route. This is approached within the context of the students' own experiences as readers, writers, speakers and listeners. The students bring to the module a language autobiography, detailing what they remember about their own language and literacy development.

We consider it imperative to establish early on that language, both spoken and written, is seen as a social process concerned with meaning-making. So students engage in a range of activities whereby they explore, first hand, what

---

Key Characteristics of Effective Phonics Teaching

a) **Characteristics shown in the TTA research project** *Effective Teachers of Literacy*:

1.   There is a high emphasis on the construction of meaning - in all phonics teaching.

2.   Phonics is taught not as an end in itself, but as a means to children becoming independent readers – making sense of text for themselves.

3.   Teaching is clear, explicit and communicated as purposeful.

4.   Phonics teaching is contextualised in meaningful texts.

5.   There is a strong emphasis on developmental spelling.

Figure 15.5 A sample handout on effective phonics teaching

it means to be a reader and a writer and how this relates to oral language. They are introduced to theories of language acquisition and also the role of the adult in facilitating children's language development. There is a strong emphasis on the role of high quality literature in introducing children to literacy and enabling them to develop as readers and writers. Explicit connections are made between the students' own experiences and theories of language and literacy development, which are then related to classroom practices. They are also introduced to the importance of the teacher's role in developing phonological awareness and the explicit teaching of phonics in relation to reading and writing.

Within this module, students begin the process of compiling their individual bibliographies of children's literature. By the end of the four-year course they are required to read a broad range of children's literature, evaluating each book at text, sentence and word level, as well as identifying how children might relate to the text, and why. In this module they also begin working independently with the word classes booklet, as part of their directed self-study. This aspect of their knowledge about language is contextualised in taught sessions, for example, when analysing children's literature.

The students are also given the phonics booklet, as well as *Letters and Sounds* (Primary National Strategy 2007), for further independent study. Towards the end of the module a phonics evaluation exercise enables them to assess their knowledge of phonics at this stage in the course. The assignment for this module requires the students to select an appropriate text for a developing reader and to analyse it, justifying the reason for their choice and identifying ways in which they might work with this text in a Foundation Stage, Key Stage 1 or

Key Stage 2 setting. On their first block placement at school, the students are required to work with this text and to plan activities related to the book, including drama/role play; shared and guided reading; literature circles and explicit phonics teaching.

Year 2

In Year 2, in their second Curriculum English module, the students continue working on their children's literature bibliographies and phonics self-study materials and begin working on the booklet on text structure, syntax and morphology. Tutors contextualise this, particularly in relation to the study of shared reading and writing. Every week, the knowledge about language addressed in each section of the booklet is explored within the context of the teaching of reading and writing.

The first assessment task for this module is a detailed analysis of a child's writing, using Eve Bearne's writing miscue framework (Bearne 1998). The booklet on text structure, syntax and morphology supports the students' analysis and helps them talk explicitly about the effectiveness of the child's written language, identifying strengths and areas for development.

The second task is an essay in which students explore the effect of engagement with high quality literature, through drama and writing in role, on the quality of children's writing. Both tasks require students to articulate their analysis of written texts and their understanding of how writers use language to have an impact on readers.

Explicit teaching of phonics in relation to reading and writing is an ongoing strand throughout the module. At the end of the module students complete a phonics test paper and a grammar paper, both intended to highlight areas for development that students can work on independently during Year 3 of the course. Progress on this is tracked by the students' professional development tutor.

Year 3

There is no Curriculum English in Year 3 as this year is devoted to a complementary placement in an out-of-school educational setting. However, all students undertake an Education Studies double module in Child Development. Half of this module focuses on early language learning and development and is taught by members of the English team. The intention is to extend student teachers' understanding of first and second language acquisition. Using transcripts of children's talk at different stages of development, students analyse children's language, supported by their self-study booklets and additional materials.

As assessment, students carry out a series of observations of a very young child and present their analysis of the child's development, considering the theories explored in the module and identifying implications for inclusive classroom practice. Analysis of the child's language requires them to understand not just the structures and forms of oral language but how language is used, and what the child's language use tells us about their thinking and cognitive development.

Year 4

In the final Curriculum English module in Year 4, *Teaching and Assessing Language and Literacy*, students taking both the Foundation Stage/Key Stage 1 or the Key Stage 1 or 2 routes submit their peer-assessed children's literature bibliographies and their phonics and grammar papers with a self evaluation of these aspects of their subject knowledge. The taught element of the module focuses on preparation for the students' final school placement and analysis of their teaching and learning afterwards. The second assessment task is for students to present an exploration of key principles for effective English teaching, as exemplified on final block school placement, and underpinned by reference to appropriate theory and research evidence. This final task is intended to enable the students to demonstrate their subject knowledge within the context of their own classroom practice.

Conclusion

As has been outlined, we attempt to present aspects of linguistic knowledge in the context of texts used by and with children, aiming to demonstrate how such knowledge can illumine the study of literacy, enabling student teachers to become more powerful in teaching children to read and write. We try to tailor our presentations to the professional needs of our students, who have not come to study linguistics and who need to be convinced of the relevance of linguistic knowledge to their professional concerns. But there is a real problem in the students' propensity to forget this way of looking at language when their attention turns to other concerns.

And there is an enduring uncertainty about the relation of explicit knowledge about language to skill in its use. While there is a clear case that knowledge of phonics contributes positively to learning to read, there is no clear body of evidence to show that knowledge of syntax, for example, makes a positive contribution to children's effectiveness as speakers and writers. Nor is there clear evidence to show that knowledge about language makes student teachers more effective teachers of literacy.

But it does seem to give them the confidence to talk about key features of text and help them to think about what they see in children's writing and in shared writing and about their relation to texts read by and to children. It seems to enable them to talk about a wider range of aspects of children's development as writers and readers with parents, colleagues, advisors and inspectors.

Above all, this study seems to give student teachers a respect for the evolving language of the children they teach. And we think it helps them to see its complexity, so that they do not see language development as a simple matter of acquiring a set of techniques.

16   Using the International Phonetic Alphabet to support accurate phonics teaching

Greg Brooks

Introduction

The orthography of English is far from transparent, and how phonemes relate to graphemes is an essential part of teachers' professional knowledge to underpin phonics. This knowledge should be applied from the earliest stages of teaching reading and spelling in order to understand the system and children's confusions, and to give more accurate guidance on where generalisations apply and (just as crucially) where they do not. This chapter argues that teachers need a way of 'talking about phonemes' and their relationships with graphemes, and discusses the case for using relevant International Phonetic Alphabet (IPA) symbols as a means of simplifying and systematising teachers' understandings.

To my mind, the aspect of linguistics that is most essential for primary teachers to know is the International Phonetic Alphabet (IPA). To back up this statement, I am going to do the following:

- provide some account of previous attempts to define which aspects of linguistics teachers need to know;
- summarise the case for using phonics in the initial teaching of reading and spelling;
- put the case for teachers needing to know (a bit of) phonetics and IPA to underpin accurate phonics teaching;
- answer some objections;
- suggest how much teachers might need to know in this area; and
- along the way, provide some worked examples of the application of IPA.

A personal history

In somewhat over forty years' experience in the field, I have encountered at least three attempts to provide teachers with linguistic knowledge. All arose

Many thanks to Maxine Burton for allowing me to quote several passages verbatim from Burton and Brooks (2005), and to Henrietta Dombey for permission to use her vignette and for checking my account of it.

from the best of motives, the desire to provide teachers with more theoretical understanding of some aspect(s) of the English language, in order that they might teach it more accurately and efficiently.

The first encounter came while I was doing my one-year Post-Graduate Certificate of Education at the University of Leeds (UK) in 1966–67. An earnest young linguist gave a few lectures on transformational-generative grammar, then the hottest thing around. But it was not long before rumblings of discontent grew into open rebellion: hardly any of us could see why English needed to be analysed this way or how transformational grammar was supposed to help us teach English, still less any other language (despite there being amongst our number several intending teachers of modern foreign languages and classics).

For the second encounter I cannot give the exact date or place, but I think it was in Leicester (UK) some time in the early 1980s; certainly it was a large seminar devoted to much the same question as the two-part seminar at the University of Strathclyde which gave rise to this volume. I recall that luminaries from both the British Association for Applied Linguistics (BAAL) and the Linguistic Association of Great Britain (LAGB) proposed a very detailed syllabus for intending teachers of English language at primary and secondary levels, and foreign languages. Many of those attending, including me, soon became convinced it was so comprehensive that it would have filled an entire first-degree course in linguistics, and that hardly any of it could be accommodated even within three- or four-year B.Ed. degree courses, let alone one-year Post Graduate Certificate of Education (PGCE) courses.

My third close encounter of the linguistic kind occurred in the period in the 1990s when I was the BAAL representative on CLIE, the Committee for Linguistics in Education, a joint venture of BAAL and LAGB, with representatives of a few other interested organisations such as the UK Reading Association (now the UK Literacy Association), the National Association for the Teaching of English, and the National Association for Teaching English and other Community Languages to Adults (NATECLA). I seem to remember that recommendations for initial teacher training syllabuses were made, but I am not sure they were implemented.

If these episodes have a common theme, it is that they contained either too much content, or over-complex detail, or both. It is therefore no surprise that they have sunk without trace. The lesson for the joint University of Strathclyde/ BAAL/Cambridge University Press endeavour is therefore pellucid: keep it simple, and directly practical. My proposal for IPA is intended to be both.

The case for phonics

Within the last ten years two systematic reviews of the use of phonics instruction with children have appeared, one in the USA led by Linnea Ehri for the

Table 16.1 *Research questions addressed by two systematic reviews of phonics instruction*

Research question	Answer given by Ehri *et al.* (2001)	Answer given by Torgerson *et al.* (2006)
Does systematic phonics instruction enable children to make better progress in reading *accuracy* than unsystematic or no phonics?	Yes	Yes
Does systematic phonics instruction enable both typically-developing children and those at risk of failure to make better progress in reading *accuracy* than unsystematic or no phonics?	Yes	Yes
Does systematic phonics instruction enable children to make better progress in reading *comprehension* than unsystematic or no phonics?	Yes	Not clear
Does systematic phonics instruction enable children to make better progress in *spelling* than unsystematic or no phonics?	Yes	Not clear
Does systematic **synthetic** phonics instruction enable children to make better progress in reading *accuracy* than systematic **analytic** phonics?	(Not addressed)	Not clear

National Reading Panel (Ehri *et al.* 2001), the other in this country (Torgerson *et al.* 2006). Table 16.1 lists the main research questions that either or both reviews addressed, and the conclusions reached.

The main reason for the differences in conclusions is that Ehri *et al.* (2001) used evidence from thirty-eight experimental or quasi-experimental studies (that is, randomised and non-randomised controlled trials respectively), whereas Torgerson *et al.* (2006) used only evidence from twelve randomised controlled trials (RCTs). The principal conclusion that can reliably be drawn, in my opinion, is that systematic phonics instruction enables children to make better progress in reading *accuracy* (that is, the recognition/reading aloud of single words) than unsystematic or no phonics. And since we know that accurate word identification is a prerequisite for comprehension, teachers' phonetic knowledge underpinning their phonics teaching must be accurate, whatever variety of phonics they use to teach word identification and spelling.

The case for some phonetics

I am not going to argue that all teachers of language need to learn a lot of phonetics (e.g. exactly where the airstream is obstructed to produce different types of consonant, or how many click consonants there are in various languages of southern Africa, or how to use the full panoply of IPA to represent every subtle difference between English accents) – that would be to commit the same error as the previous attempts to define what teachers need to know. And of course I am not suggesting that teachers use IPA with children – in fact, they should be forbidden to. But I do maintain that they need to know and be able to use a broad transcription of the predominant English accent used in Britain, namely received pronunciation (RP), and a few variants.

Why RP? Not just because it's the most widely understood British accent, and certainly not as a disguised attempt at elocution lessons, but because it is the most studied accent and its features and transcription are widely agreed, and because it or a very similar accent will be used by virtually all the teachers learning to use IPA to transcribe it (but not, of course, by some of their pupils – more on this later).

The case for IPA

First, an example: how many phonemes are there in *confusing*? Answer: nine, as in the top row of this analysis:

/k	ə	n	'f	j u:	z	ɪ	ŋ/
↓	↓	↓	↓	↘↙	↓	↓	↙↘
c	o	n	f	u	s	i	n g

But what the arrows show is that, although there are nine phonemes and nine letters, only six of each map one-to-one. The last phoneme, the sound spelt jointly by the two letters <ng> here and in many other words, is symbolised /ŋ/. There are many other two-letter graphemes (digraphs) in English spelling, and some trigraphs (e.g. <tch> in *match*), and even a few four-letter graphemes (e.g. <ough> in *through*).

Conversely, the fifth and sixth phonemes, /j/ representing the sound mostly spelt <y> in word-initial position, as in *yell*, and /u:/ representing the sound of the exclamation 'Oo!', are jointly spelt by one letter, <u>. There are many other two-phoneme graphemes in English but <u> spelling the sequence /ju:/ (which is its letter name), and <x> spelling /ks/ are by far the commonest.

If English had a consistent orthography the example just given would be redundant – it is because English orthography is so variable that a separate, consistent symbolisation is needed for talking accurately about the relationships between sounds and spellings.

This has long been recognised by teachers of English as a foreign language and by publishers of dictionaries (and especially by publishers of dictionaries for foreign learners), and the *Letters and Sounds* (DCSF 2007b) materials incorporate a (very nearly) consistent symbolisation.

But which system should be used? Many lexicographers, and the devisers of *Letters and Sounds*, make up their own. They generally do this by choosing graphemes from the ordinary spelling system which they hope are sufficiently unambiguous, and provide a key with examples. A quick glance through just a few dictionaries, books about English spelling, and so on, which purport to show pronunciations will reveal that hardly any two use exactly the same system – despite the existence, for over 100 years, of an internationally agreed and consistent one, the International Phonetic Alphabet.

Textbooks on the phonetics of English, on the other hand, even the most elementary ones designed for those with no previous knowledge of the subject, use IPA symbols for their transcription of the sounds of English. This is done without comment or justification and is taken to be the self-evident *modus operandi*; indeed IPA is used as the only vehicle of instruction. IPA uses a set of symbols mainly derived from the letters of the Roman alphabet with some additions – see below. Using these symbols, any word of the established vocabulary of the English language can be written unambiguously and with one-to-one correspondence between IPA symbols and sounds.

The main advantage of such a system is that it provides a clear basis for analysing and discussing variant spelling choices for the same phoneme, and differing pronunciations for the same grapheme – essential underpinning knowledge for teaching phonics. It also helps to explain why some well-organised phonics schemes start with the six letters <s a t p i n> and their most frequently corresponding phonemes /s æ t p ɪ n/ – this set gives immediate access to about fifty familiar and regularly spelled words.

Effective delivery of phonics as a strategy for teaching reading and spelling seems to me to demand a sound knowledge of the phonemes and phonetic transcription of the language. Native 'intuition' is insufficient and at times misleading, as I will illustrate below.

Objections

However, there seems to be great resistance to the use of IPA in order to achieve proficiency in the relevant aspects of phonetics. In order to bolster the case for using IPA, I now set out some of the reasons that are often given for this resistance and show the extent to which they are unfounded.

Table 16.2 *The International Phonetic Alphabet symbols for the twenty-four consonant phonemes of the received pronunciation accent of English*

/b/	as in the first sound of	*by*	/baɪ/
/d/	as in the first sound of	*dye*	/daɪ/
/f/	as in the first sound of	*few*	/fjuː/
/g/	as in the first sound of	*goo*	/guː/
/h/	as in the first sound of	*who*	/huː/
/k/	as in the first sound of	*coo*	/kuː/
/l/	as in the first sound of	*loo*	/luː/
/m/	as in the first sound of	*my*	/maɪ/
/n/	as in the first sound of	*nigh*	/naɪ/
/p/	as in the first sound of	*pie*	/paɪ/
/r/	as in the first sound of	*rye*	/raɪ/
/s/	as in the first sound of	*sue*	/suː/
/t/	as in the first sound of	*tie*	/taɪ/
/v/	as in the first sound of	*view*	/vjuː/
/w/	as in the first sound of	*well*	/wel/
/z/	as in the first sound of	*zoo*	/zuː/
/ʧ/	as in the first sound of	*chew*	/ʧuː/
/Ʊ/	as in the first sound of	*jaw*	/dʒ/
/ʃ/	as in the **third** sound of	*fission*	/ˈfɪʃən/
/ʒ/	as in the **third** sound of	*vision*	/ˈvɪʒən/
/θ/	as in the first sound of	*thigh*	/θaɪ/
/ð/	as in the first sound of	*thy*	/ðaɪ/
/ŋ/	as in the **last** sound of	*ring*	/rɪŋ/
/j/	as in the first sound of	*yell, union*	/jel, ˈjuːnjən/

Objection 1: IPA is difficult, like learning another language with a different script

A broad transcription of RP is actually easy to learn – when I was an 18-year-old English language assistant in a French secondary school in 1963 it was used in all the textbooks for teaching English as a guide to pronunciation, and I taught myself the system in a couple of weeks. Tables 16.2 (consonants) and 16.3 (vowels) present the IPA symbols for the forty-four phonemes of RP; in both, sample words exemplifying the phonemes and their symbols are transcribed in full to show how the system operates. All transcriptions are shown between forward slashes, this being the international convention, and the only extra symbols to note are the stress mark /ˈ/, which is placed before the stressed syllable in words of more than one syllable, and the 'pointy colon' /ː/, which marks a long pure vowel. The system set out here is identical to that in the *Cambridge English Pronouncing Dictionary* (16th edn, Cambridge University Press, 2003).

Table 16.3 *The International Phonetic Alphabet symbols for the twenty vowel phonemes of the received pronunciation accent of English*

Short pure vowels			
/æ/	as in the first sound of	*ant*	/ænt/
/e/	as in the first sound of	*end*	/end/
/ɪ/	as in the first sound of	*ink*	/ɪŋk/
/ɒ/	as in the first sound of	*ox*	/ɒks/
/ʌ/	as in the first sound of	*up*	/ʌp/
/ʊ/	as in the **second** sound of	*pull*	/pʊl/
/ə/	as in the first sound of	*about*	/ə'baʊt/
Long pure vowels			
/ɑː/	as in the first sound of	*aardvark*	/'ɑːdvɑːk/
/iː/	as in the first sound of	*eel*	/iːl/
/ɜː/	as in the first sound of	*earl*	/ɜːl/
/ɔː/	as in the **whole** sound of	*awe*	/ɔː/
/uː/	as in the first sound of	*ooze*	/uːz/
Diphthongs			
/eɪ/	as in the first sound of	*aim*	/eɪm/
/aɪ/	as in the first sound of	*ice*	/aɪs/
/əʊ/	as in the first sound of	*oath*	/əʊθ/
/aʊ/	as in the first sound of	*ouch*	/aʊtʃ/
/ɔɪ/	as in the first sound of	*oyster*	/'ɔɪstə/
/eə/	as in the **whole** sound of	*air*	/eə/
/ɪə/	as in the **whole** sound of	*ear*	/ɪə/
/ʊə/	as in the **second** sound of	*rural*	/'rʊərəl/

Most of the symbols for consonants are familiar letters of the Roman alphabet – /b d f g h k l m n p r s t v w z/ are all used with their familiar consonantal sound values, and most of the others are distinctive enough to learn quickly. The only tricky one is /j/, which is used for the initial sound in *yell* – if you know any German, you will be familiar with this – and not for the phoneme at the beginning and end of *judge* – the symbol for that is /dʒ/. Fewer vowel symbols are familiar letters (/e/ and /ɑː iː uː/ with their long vowel marks), but /ɪ/ is obvious enough, and /æ/ (known as 'ash') was used in old English. For the rest, practice makes perfect.

> *Objection 2: It is perfectly possible to transcribe the sounds of English using the letters of the alphabet, either on their own or in various combinations*

This may be perfectly feasible for languages with regular phoneme–grapheme correspondences. English is not such a language. It is not just a case of there being more sounds (forty-four) than letters (twenty-six) but that the values of the letters themselves are not consistent. For example, <th> represents two distinct phonemes, as in *thick* and *that*. Those who try to represent these phonemes differently using ordinary letters mainly retain /th/ for the voiceless sound in *thick* and use /dh/ for the voiced sound in *that* – even though in the very few words in which <dh> occurs in English it always represents /d/, as in *dhoti, dhow, Gandhi, jodhpurs*, and despite the perfectly learnable nature of /θ, ð/ for the voiceless and voiced sounds respectively.

It is especially difficult to represent the vowel and diphthong phonemes in an unambiguous way, as the following example shows. In *Letters and Sounds* <igh> is used for the diphthong /aɪ/ as in *night*, and so on, though this is only one, and not even the most obvious, way of representing this diphthong. Consider its other spellings in *duiker, eye, feisty, height, hide, item, maestro, my, rye, shanghai, type.*

Objection 3: It is irrelevant when you have native speakers teaching other native speakers; it may be appropriate only for EAL/ESOL

But being a native speaker of a language does not guarantee phonemic awareness on the part of either teacher or learner. Consider these examples, taken from a study of the teaching of reading to adult learners (Besser *et al.* 2004):

(1) The tutor demonstrates breaking words into syllables – 'marr-i-ed', 'temp-er-a-ture'. She sets the learner a task: to change letters to change the sound, e.g. ee to ea.

   The examples are poor, since in normal pronunciation *married* has two syllables and *temperature* three, and <ee> and <ea> sometimes represent the same sound.

(2) Learner D. and a volunteer have a box of lower-case alphabet letters.

   They are working on <oo> and the chosen words are *poor, floor, flood, blood*. The volunteer sets the words up, then takes some letters away, leaving <oo>. The volunteer calls out the words and D. arranges the consonant letters around the vowels. The volunteer asks, 'What do you hear at the end of the word *floor*?' to try to help D. use the <r>.

   At the end, this example shows the volunteer, because of incomplete phonetic knowledge, misleading herself and probably also the learner in an attempt to be helpful. In almost all British accents, there is no further sound to be heard at the end of words like *poor, floor* beyond the sound represented by <oo>. More accurately, the letters <oor> form one grapheme representing either the same sound as <or> in *for* or, in *poor*, possibly (though this phoneme is rapidly disappearing) the second sound in *rural*, /ʊə/. It would probably have been more helpful to deal with <oor> separately from other examples of <oo>. The tutor could then have pointed out that the pronunciation /ʌ/ for <oo> in *flood, blood* is highly unusual – it occurs only in those two words – and that the two most frequent pronunciations for <oo> are those in *mood* and *look* (in their southern English versions). This is a clear case where more precise knowledge would have enabled this teacher to be aware of, and teach a limitation on, phonics.

Objection 4: It would be yet another burden on hard-pressed teachers

It would be less difficult to learn for those who have an English language/ linguistics degree background, but possibly more difficult for others. But the whole point of learning the system is to reduce confusion and make phonics teaching more accurate and efficient, which would be a saving all round.

For example, at the British Association for Applied Linguistics seminar at Strathclyde University in Glasgow 2008, the author of the previous chapter, Henrietta Dombey, retold an incident she had observed. A teacher was trying to get her Year 1 class to generate the pronunciation of 'treasure' by over-zealous application of synthetic phonics. The children correctly supplied /t/ for the <t> and /r/ for the first <r> but then pronounced the <ea> as /iː/, as in *eat*, at which point the teacher said 'No, it's like *head*'. The children continued bravely on, venturing both /s/ and /z/ for the <s>, and looking quite bemused when their teacher told them that this <s> actually represented the phoneme /ʒ/. Not wanting to give up, the teacher pressed on, asking them about the <ur>, but this time eliciting no responses from the increasingly puzzled children. After she had supplied the necessary schwa, the teacher pointed to the final <e>, saying in desperation 'I do not know why that's there!'

There are only four words in the language that end in /eʒə/: *measure, pleasure, treasure, leisure*. These children were already familiar with *measure*, so, as Henrietta observed, the most productive approach would have been to teach *treasure* by analogy with *measure* (and add *pleasure* later, and *leisure* when the children were ready for the exception). On the way to teaching <easure> pronounced /eʒə/ by analogy the teacher could validly have asked the children to sound out <t, r> as /t, r/, but should have stopped here, where synthetic phonics breaks down. My point is that teachers need to know both the benefits and the limitations of phonics, and I am arguing that they will be helped by IPA and the more exact knowledge of grapheme–phoneme and phoneme–grapheme correspondences it can underpin.

Objection 5: It only applies to RP and fails to account for other accents

In principle, IPA can be used to represent any accent, and this flexibility is one of its great strengths. Most people in Britain speak with accents which either have very similar phoneme inventories to RP, or which require only a few small differentiations in the symbols. For example, the mostly northern English /ʊ, æ/ in place of mostly southern /ʌ, ɑː/ in words like *butter, path* require only the use of the appropriate symbols.

I once helped a colleague analyse a short story a boy had written and titled 'A dog I wons new' (for the full text and more analysis see Gubb 1982). If I had been this child's teacher I would first have praised his entirely accurate transcription of his pronunciation of *once*, /wɒns/ – each of the four phonemes is written with the letter most frequently used to spell it. It is just that *once* is one of the trickiest words in English – the initial /w/ appears not to be represented in the spelling at all (the only other such word being *one*), and the final /s/ is spelt <ce>. This is the regular spelling of /s/ word-finally in monosyllables after /n/, knowledge that the teacher should have but should not confuse the child with. On the other hand, the child's non-RP /ɒ/ vowel has enabled him to write <o> rather than <u>, as children with RP accents might. I would also have praised the child for spelling *new* meaning 'not old' correctly, but pointed out that when you want to write 'I knew that' the /n/ at the beginning is written <kn>.

How much do teachers need to know?

In order to analyse and understand English spelling accurately they need to know and be able to use the IPA symbols for the forty-four phonemes of RP and similar accents. When it comes to the phoneme–grapheme and grapheme–phoneme correspondences, there is no need for them to know all the 280 graphemes and 500+ correspondences that I have uncovered while analysing the English spelling system. They would need to understand and know how to look up and deploy the eighty-nine graphemes that I think constitute the main system of English spelling, and their 136 correspondences with the forty-four phonemes, plus some common words which have rare correspondences – these are words which it would be more sensible to teach by analogy or even, in a few cases, as units. We've seen an example of a word that yields better to analogy – *treasure* – and one that needs to be taught as a unit is *choir*, where after the initial /k/ spelt <ch> the remaining /ˈwaɪə/ (the sound of the word *wire*) appears to be spelt by <oir> as an unanalysable unit. Tables 16.4 and 16.5 list the correspondences I would expect teachers to be able to deploy, with some of those 'tricky' words alongside. (Reverse tables could be shown for grapheme–phoneme correspondences, but these are enough to make the point.)

Within the Tables there are three sequences of two phonemes spelt with one letter: /ks/ spelt <x>, /əl/ spelt <le>, and /juː/ spelt <u ew ue u.e>. <u.e> is an example of a 'split digraph', in which two vowel letters either side of one consonant letter (or very occasionally two) spell a vowel phoneme. There are six split digraphs in English orthography, the others being: <a.e e.e i.e o.e y.e>.

Table 16.4 *The main consonant phoneme–grapheme correspondences of British English spelling, with some common words with rare graphemes for the phonemes*

| Phoneme | Grapheme(s) | | As in … | Common words with rare graphemes for the phoneme |
	Basic	Other		
/b/	b	bb	bed rabbit	\<bu\> buy
/k/	c	ck k q ch	come back look queen Christmas	\<cu\> biscuit
/tʃ/	ch	tch	children match	\<t\> picture
/d/	d	dd ed	dad teddy called	
/f/	f	ff ph	from off elephant	\<gh\> cough enough laugh rough tough
/g/	g	gg	get jogging	\<gh\> ghost \<gu\> guy
/h/	h		horse	\<wh\> who whole
/dʒ/	j	dg(e) g ge	just budgie bridge giant orange	
/l/	l	ll	leg ball	
/m/	m	mm	my mummy	\<mb\> climb lamb thumb \<me\> come some \<mn\> autumn
/n/	n	nn	now dinner	\<ne\> done engine none \<kn\> knife knot know
/ŋ/	ng	n	sing sink	
/p/	p	pp	pen apple	\<ph\> shepherd
/r/	r	rr	red berry	\<wr\> write
/s/	s	c ce se ss	sit city once horse grass	\<st\> castle Christmas listen
/ʃ/	sh	ti	ship station	\<ch\> machine \<ci\> special \<s\> sugar sure \<ssi\> permission
/ʒ/	si		vision	\<s\> treasure usual
/t/	t	tt ed	but little looked	\<th\> Thomas \<tw\> two
/θ/	th		thing	
/ð/	th		that	\<the\> breathe
/v/	v	ve	very have	\<f\> of
/w/	w	u	went queen	\<wh\> what when (etc.)
/ks/	x		box	
/j/	y		yellow	\<i\> onion
/z/	z	s se ze zz	zoo is please sneeze puzzle	\<ss\> scissors

Note: The two-phoneme sequence /kw/ is almost always spelt \<qu\> and should also be taught as a unit.

Table 16.5 *The main vowel phoneme–grapheme correspondences of British English spelling, with some common words with rare graphemes for the phonemes*

Phoneme	Grapheme(s)		As in …	Common words with rare graphemes for the phoneme
	Basic	Other		
/æ/	a		and	
/ə/	a	e er o re	a the butter button centre	\<ar\> sugar \<i\> possible \<our\> colour \<ure\> picture
/eɪ/	a.e	a ai ay	came bacon paint day	\<aigh\> straight \<ea\> break great \<eigh\> eight \<ey\> they
/eə/	air	are ar	fair fare parent	\<ear\> bear pear tear wear \<ere\> there where \<eir\> their
/ɑː/	ar	a	far ask	\<al\> half \<are\> are \<au\> aunt laugh \<ear\> heart
/e/	e	ea	went bread	\<a\> any many \<ai\> said \<ay\> says \<ie\> friend
/iː/	ee	e ea ey ie y	see he beach key field city	\<e.e\> these \<eo\> people
/ɪə/	eer	ear er ere	cheer hear hero here	\<ier\> fierce
/ɜː/	er	ir or ur	her girl worm fur	\<ear\> early earth heard learn \<ere\> were \<our\> journey
/ɪ/	i	e y	is England gym	\<a\> sausage
/aɪ/	i.e	i igh y	like I night my	\<eigh\> height \<eye\> eye
/əl/	le (only word-final)		little	
/ɒ/	o	a	not was	\<au\> because sausage \<ou\> cough
/əʊ/	o	o.e ow	so bone blow	\<oa\> boat \<oh\> oh
/ɔɪ/	oi	oy	boil boy	
/ʊ/	oo	u	book put	\<oul\> could should would
/uː/	oo	ew u u.e	too blew super rule	\<oe\> shoe \<o\> do to two who \<ou\> you \<ough\> through \<ue\> blue \<ui\> fruit
/ʊə/	oor	ure	poor sure	\<our\> tour
/ɔː/	or	a ar au aw ore	for all warn sauce saw before	\<augh\> caught naughty \<oor\> door floor \<ough\> bought \<our\> four your
/aʊ/	ou	ow	out down	
/ʌ/	u	o	but some	\<ou\> country young
/juː/	u	ew ue u.e	union few argue cute	

Beyond all this children teach themselves the rest, and teachers have to learn when to intervene, and mostly when not to.

Conclusion

I consider that the case for the use of IPA in these contexts is strong and the objections weak or misplaced, and therefore strongly recommend the incorporation of instruction in basic phonetic analysis and transcription, and knowledge of the main phoneme–grapheme and grapheme–phoneme correspondences, into the training of all teachers of initial reading and spelling.

17 Developing word-level literacy skills in children with and without typical communication skills

Kenn Apel, Elizabeth B. Wilson-Fowler and Julie J. Masterson

Introduction

Words have power. Spoken words convey meaning and intent. Without an understanding and facility with spoken words, face-to-face communication can be impeded. Written words are equally powerful. Successful reading and writing require strong knowledge of the written word. Children must know how to read words to access meaning at the word, sentence and text level. Equally important, children also must be able to spell words correctly to convey accurate and appropriate information to their readers.

In the USA, teachers provide instruction in word-level reading (i.e. decoding and recognition abilities) during the early primary years (e.g. Darling-Hammond 2000) although the amount of time focused specifically on decoding may be variable (e.g. Juel and Minden-Cupp 2000). Even less time is spent on spelling instruction. Graham *et al.* (2008) reported that 90 per cent of the primary-grade teachers they surveyed taught spelling. However, there was quite a bit of variability in teachers' responses, with some spending less than twenty minutes per week and a few not teaching spelling at all. It seems educators assume that children should quickly develop good word-level reading and spelling skills, and, therefore, provide little focused instruction in these areas, especially beyond the early primary years. While the majority of children acquire word-level reading with minimal instruction, a substantial number do not (Lyon 1998). Estimates are that almost 18 per cent of children in the USA encounter significant reading problems in the first three years of school (NAEP 2005). Perhaps more alarming, research suggests that children who continue to struggle with word-level reading receive far less, if any, decoding instruction as they progress through later academic years (Catone and Brady 2005). Additionally, many children, both those with typical learning (TL) abilities and

Authors Masterson and Apel are authors of *SPELL-2: Spelling Performance Evaluation for Language and Literacy and Spell-Links to Reading and Writing* and have a financial interest in these products.

those with language-learning impairment (LLI) struggle with spelling. Some schools may not emphasise spelling because of the desire to spend maximum time on reading instruction. Others may follow a teaching philosophy that minimises the importance of correct spelling in final drafts of written work. Regardless of the reason, it is likely that the problems that some children have with spelling are due to the amount and quality of instruction they received.

The purpose of this chapter is first to provide a brief overview of typical instructional procedures used in the USA to develop children's word-level literacy skills, and then to offer an alternative conceptual framework for building word-level reading and spelling skills. Finally, we provide suggestions for implementing such a framework in whole classrooms with children with TL skills and in smaller group settings for children with LLI.

Common instructional strategies for teaching word-level literacy skills

In the USA, instruction in word-level reading ability (i.e. how to decode or 'sound out' words) does not occur regularly, yet when instruction does take place, decoding skills improve (Pullen *et al.* 2005). When children do not recognise a written word, it is not uncommon for educators to suggest they either use the context of the written material or make a guess after being given the first letter or two. Both of these strategies often result in failure. The former strategy typically is unsuccessful because children are reading books that contain new information; thus, they are less knowledgeable about the context and cannot make the needed predictions. Using the second strategy is equally unproductive for the same reason; in the majority of situations, children guess the wrong word because of their lack of contextual knowledge.

For most of the last century, spelling instruction in US classrooms has generally taken the same format: children are provided a list of words on Monday and then tested on those words on Friday. This 'Friday Test' approach often encourages rote memorisation of the words and may involve words that follow a theme (e.g. 'space words', such as <u>moon</u>, <u>rocket</u>, <u>launch</u>, <u>astronaut</u>, <u>gravity</u> when reading about moon expeditions), or are based on a specific orthographic pattern (e.g. all words contain within-word doubled letters, such as <u>ladder</u> and <u>letter</u>) (Graham *et al.* 2008). Even if there is a reasonable rationale for grouping the list of words, children still are encouraged to memorise them, with little attention given to helping them to discover and learn the patterns that govern why words are written the way they are. Additionally, although some sort of spelling instruction, or at least, attention to spelling, occurs in the early primary years, the amount of spelling instructional time varies considerably across classrooms, with some children receiving less than thirty minutes of instruction per week (Graham *et al.* 2008). When teachers focus primarily on reading to improve both reading and spelling skills, research demonstrates that improvements in reading are accompanied by a drop in spelling ability (Mehta *et al.* 2005).

The 'Friday Test' approach to spelling instruction teaches children that the written word must be memorised. Such an approach contradicts more recent theories about spelling development (e.g. Apel *et al.* 2004), which elevate the importance of teaching specific linguistic knowledge that contributes to word-level reading and spelling abilities. In fact, a growing body of evidence supports word-level literacy instruction that targets five language skills, and results suggest this *multi-linguistic approach* to word-level literacy instruction improves spelling and word-level reading performance (e.g. Apel *et al.* 2004; Kelman and Apel 2004; Kirk and Gillon 2008; Roberts and Meiring 2006), even demonstrating changes in brain function (Richards *et al.* 2006; Richards and Berninger 2007).

An alternative conceptual framework for teaching word-level literacy skills: the multi-linguistic approach

Contrary to popular belief, most written words are written the way they are because of specific phonological (sound), orthographic (letters and letter patterns), semantic (word meaning), and morphological (word meaning relations) rules (Apel and Masterson 2001; Masterson and Crede 1999). Children must tap into all of these linguistic knowledge bases to become successful word-level readers and writers. With knowledge about sound, letters and meaning, most children will improve in their word-level literacy skills.

Perhaps not surprising to most educators in the twenty-first century, children must develop adequate *phonemic awareness* skills as they acquire word-level reading and spelling abilities (e.g. Gillon 2005; National Reading Panel 1997). Phonemic awareness is the conscious awareness of the sounds of language, and the ability to talk about and manipulate those sounds. In particular, the ability to segment words into their individual phonemes or sounds is important for spelling. Conversely, phonemic or sound blending is highly important for decoding unknown words. *Orthographic awareness* also impacts upon reading and spelling development, because children must understand the conventions or rules used to translate speech sounds into print. Orthographic knowledge includes an understanding of letter–sound correspondence (for example, letter b̲ represents the /b/ sound; generally, long vowel sounds in one-syllable words typically require two vowel letters); rules for which letters can be combined to represent sounds (for example, only letter combinations c̲r̲ or c̲h̲r̲ can be used to represent the initial /kr/ phoneme blend) or which can occur in certain situations (e.g. English words cannot start with the letters n̲g̲).

The manner in which words are written is also affected by meaning. *Morphological awareness* is required to understand the importance and uniformity of spelling affixes as they are placed onto simple base words. For example, the letter s̲ added to the word *car* signals more than one and it is always spelled as an s̲ even though it sounds like a /z/. (And see Nunes and Bryant, this volume.) Morphological awareness also aids readers and writers by helping them to understand modification rules when affixes are added to base words (e.g. we double the p̲ in sh̲o̲p̲ before adding the i̲n̲g̲), as well as increasing their knowledge of meaning relations, and shared spelling, among words that are derivations of a base word (e.g. a̲c̲t̲, a̲c̲t̲o̲r̲, a̲c̲t̲i̲o̲n̲, a̲c̲t̲i̲v̲i̲t̲y̲). In the latter case, understanding the shared meaning, or morphological relations, among words can aid spelling of more complex words that contain neutral vowels (e.g. o̲p̲p̲o̲s̲i̲t̲i̲o̲n̲); the second, neutral vowel in o̲p̲p̲o̲s̲i̲t̲i̲o̲n̲ is spelled with the letter o̲ because the word is derived from o̲p̲p̲o̲s̲e̲. A word's definition also dictates its spelling. Applying *semantic awareness* helps readers and writers to know that the word s̲o̲n̲ represents a family member, while the word s̲u̲n̲ represents a celestial body. Without this semantic awareness, the incorrect meaning may be conveyed in writing or obtained during reading.

While many English words are spelled according to specific sound, letter, or meaning rules, some words and parts of words are spelled simply by convention. In other words, phonemic, orthographic, morphological, and semantic aspects of a word do not explain completely the reason why the word is spelled the way it is. For example, when a child reads or spells the word b̲r̲e̲a̲d̲, he or she can apply knowledge of phonology to realise there are four sounds in the word, and knowledge of orthography to understand how three of those sounds (/b/, /r/, and /d/) are spelled or decoded. However, the fourth sound, written e̲a̲, must be learned specifically, as the /E/ sound can be read or spelled with the letters e̲ or e̲a̲, and e̲a̲ can be read or spelled as the long 'e' sound, such as in b̲e̲a̲d̲. Thus, children develop a fifth knowledge base called *mental graphemic representations* (Apel and Masterson 2001), which are the images of written words or parts of words stored in the mental lexicon.

Collectively, these five knowledge resources aid readers and writers as they recognise and produce written words. We refer to these knowledge sources as the *five building blocks of word-level literacy*. Historically, little attention has been given to assessment and instruction that simultaneously account for all five blocks. Over the last decade, we have been applying this knowledge to determine how best to assess children's word-level literacy skills (e.g. Apel and Masterson 2001; Apel, Masterson and Niessen 2004; Masterson and Apel 2000; Masterson, Apel, and Wasowicz 2006) and provide theoretically grounded instruction to children with TL and LLI (Apel and Masterson 2001; Kelman and Apel 2004; Masterson and Crede 1999; Wasowicz *et al.* 2004). In the next section, we discuss how educators and speech–language pathologists can implement a multi-linguistic approach to word-level literacy instruction for classrooms of primary-school children, and in individualised instruction for children with LLI.

A classroom model for the multi-linguistic approach to word-level literacy instruction

During the primary years, educators are focused intently on improving children's literacy skills, as without adequate word-level skills, children will not obtain or provide meaning at the text level. We, along with others, have found a multi-linguistic approach to word-level literacy results in both improved word-level reading and spelling (Apel and Masterson 2001; Apel, Masterson and Hart 2004; Butyniec-Thomas and Woloshyn, 1997; Kelman and Apel 2004; Kirk and Gillon 2008; Roberts and Meiring 2006). The key element of this approach is to provide children with strategies for gaining and using the five building blocks of word-level literacy.

Typically, at the class level, we assume all children require sufficient instruction in these five blocks to improve their word-level literacy skills. Even if children have some knowledge of the five blocks, further instruction provides a stronger base from which to draw when attempting to read or spell complex words. We typically provide explicit instruction and focused and continuous practice on one block (e.g. phonemic awareness) for approximately two to three weeks (e.g. Apel, Masterson and Hart 2004), then introduce a second block which is practised for a similar amount of time. Presenting the multi-linguistic approach in this sequential manner provides directed learning experiences in all five blocks across a relatively short amount of time. Importantly, sessions are scheduled periodically to review and revisit the patterns and skills learned during earlier sessions, with the focus on helping children understand they have a repertoire of skills and knowledge to employ when reading and spelling (Apel, Masterson and Hart 2004). In general, we use the following structure to guide our daily lessons:

1. Review the previous lesson and introduce the new target pattern to be taught.
2. Model the strategy used to highlight the target pattern via a chalk board, white board, magnetic board, or overhead projector.
3. Request the children to practise the strategy by following subsequent models.
4. Provide additional practice through small group or individual activities. Often, these activities provide children with an opportunity to understand or continue to discover the target pattern.
5. Engage in a whole-class discussion regarding the target pattern learned. Request children to verbalise the pattern learned, how the strategy enabled

them to discover or learn the pattern, and how they can apply the new knowledge to other reading and writing activities across the curriculum.

6. Require children to write the pattern learned in a spelling journal along with examples of the pattern.
7. Send home an activity similar to the class activity that permits the children to demonstrate their new knowledge to their families. An additional or alternative home assignment can be actively to search books and magazines to find words containing the target pattern.

When planning, we choose carefully the words used within the lessons. First, the words chosen clearly represent the pattern being taught (e.g. words representing long 'a' vowel sound using the range of long vowel 'a' letter patterns). Secondly, the words chosen are developmentally appropriate and, when possible, represent frequently occurring words in the English language. This second factor increases the likelihood that children will encounter the words used in the lesson when they read or are asked to write compositions. We use the SPELL-Links curriculum lessons (Wasowicz *et al.* 2004) which provide lists of words and recommendations for activities to practice the strategy being taught for each unit. The word lists are separated into words that teachers can use while demonstrating the strategy and word lists for the children to use as they practice the strategy. Additionally, the *SPELL Links to Reading and Writing Word List Maker* (2008) is a tool that allows a teacher to develop a list that contains words that match the target skills and occur frequently, starting at the kindergarten level (roughly 5 years of age) and going beyond sixth grade (12 years of age and older). We also include words taken from the existing curriculum, as long as they meet the knowledge or skill targeted.

A wide variety of activities can be implemented within the aforementioned lesson structure. In interest of space, we provide an example activity for only three of the five building blocks: phonemic awareness, orthographic knowledge, and morphological awareness. Further ideas are discussed elsewhere (Masterson and Apel 2007; Wasowicz *et al.* 2004).

Phonemic awareness

We often use Sound Strings (Apel and Masterson 2001; Wasowicz *et al.* 2004) when targeting children's phonemic awareness. The purpose of the activity is to increase children's awareness of the number of sounds in a word and then to mark each sound with a letter (or letters). Sound Strings are short strings of leather (e.g. a shoe lace) containing approximately nine different coloured beads. Through modelling, we demonstrate that a child should move one bead per sound heard in a word (e.g. moving five beads for the word <u>stomp</u>). Once the beads are moved, the children are shown how to place the sound string on paper, draw a line for each sound in the word, and then write at least one letter on each line. Thus, Sound Strings create a need to attend to the number of sounds in a word and represent that number of sounds in print. When children are attempting Sound Strings on their own, we provide feedback on the accuracy of beads moved and whether there is at least one letter representing each sound noted. One aspect of Sound Strings we believe is useful for classroom instruction is that a teacher can quickly visually check whether each child has moved the correct number of beads (by determining which colour bead is the final one moved), and so help struggling children without other children being explicitly aware of a particular child's error.

Orthographic knowledge

Developmentally, rules for letter-sound correspondence for consonants (e.g. that letters <u>c</u>, <u>k</u>, <u>ck</u>, and <u>ch</u> can represent the /k/ sound), followed by vowels and digraphs are targeted earlier than rules for within-word positional rules (e.g. consonants that can be doubled at the end of base words). To address the numerous orthographic rules and patterns that govern spelling of base words (which are words without affixes), several activities can be used. Commonly, we use Word Sorts to help children discover the target rule (Apel and Masterson 2001; Masterson and Crede 1999; Wasowicz *et al.* 2004).

In the early primary years, children can struggle when attempting to spell words containing long vowel sounds. Using a Word Sort activity, we model and then require children to sort word cards, with each card containing either a long vowel word (e.g. <u>rain</u>, <u>bike</u>) or a short vowel word (e.g. <u>ran</u>, <u>bit</u>). The children are encouraged to sort the cards into two piles, each set or pile containing words that seem to follow a pattern. Verbal scaffolding is used to help them during the sorting process, using statements such as, 'Hmm, that card says ran. Ran. That has a short vowel sound. Bit. That card says bit, and bit also has a short vowel sound in it. Now, that card says rain. Rain. That word has a long vowel sound. Ok, you decide which cards go in which piles.' The goal is to guide the children so that they sort the words according to the contrasting rules present in the example words.

After sorting, we engage children in a discussion about their discovery. In this discussion, the children are encouraged to state what makes the words in each pile different. Again, we sometimes use verbal guidance to help them discover the differences between the piles. Extending the example given above, we might say, 'Hmm, you said all of these words in this pile have short vowel sounds in them. How many vowel letters do you see in each word? And these words in this pile, you said they all had long vowel sounds. How many vowel letters are in those words? Now, can you tell me a rule or pattern you see that tells you how to spell long vowels?'

Once the rule has been identified, the children write the pattern or rule they have learned in spelling journals and generate additional words that match the pattern using their own examples. They also conduct word searches, exploring their class texts or other reading material to find other words that contain the target pattern.

Morphological awareness

Morphological awareness activities include lessons that focus on a variety of rules and strategies involving additional morphemes (affixes) added to base words, as well as an understanding of how base words and their inflected (e.g. cat, cats) and derived forms (e.g. busy, business) are related. One activity is called *Word Relatives* (Apel, Masterson and Hart 2004; Wasowicz *et al.* 2004). The goal is to help children understand that they can use the spelling of familiar, base words to help them spell less familiar, affixed words that are related to, or derived from, that base word.

The typical word relative activity involves discussing how family members often look and/or sound like each other because they are related, but some family members, though related, do not sound or look like other relatives. Using this analogy, we then discuss how words also have relatives that share a similar meaning. These word relatives may resemble a family member by sound (silly/silliness), look (magic/magician), or both (friend, friendly). Word relatives also may not sound or look completely like a family member, yet still be related (e.g. busy, business).

After establishing the concept of relatedness, we provide a word representing a family of meaning (e.g. continue) and ask children to brainstorm relatives of that word (for example, continuous, continually, continuity). We discuss whether these relatives share meaning with the original member, and then use that member (continue) to help spell the relative (continuity), even if the relative does not sound exactly like the family member. When suffixes must be added to a base word, we model and discuss the necessary modification rule required to correctly change the base word spelling. For example, when changing continue to continuity, a modification rule dictates that the final e in continue be dropped before adding the ity suffix. For individual practice, children are given a list of base words, prefixes and suffixes and instructed to write as many new word relatives as they can. They are told to underline the letters that are shared by a base word and newly created word, thus highlighting the portion that 'looks the same' and the portion that changes from base word to its inflected or derived form.

Using a multi-linguistic approach to improve word-level literacy skills of children with LLI

Children with LLI often struggle with word-level literacy skills (e.g. Catts *et al.* 2001). A growing body of research supports a multi-linguistic approach to improving these children's deficient skills (Apel, Masterson and Hart 2004; Kelman and Apel 2004; Kirk and Gillon 2008; Masterson and Crede, 1999). While the aforementioned classroom-based, multi-linguistic approach undoubtedly can be implemented in classrooms containing children with LLI, we have found that more individualised, tailored instruction can result in great gains for children for whom a typical amount of instruction does not lead to adequate abilities. When working with children with LLI, we attempt to tailor or individualise the instruction to their specific needs. By pinpointing the exact difficulties they demonstrate in each of the five building blocks of literacy, we can structure instruction to target these deficits, providing for optimal and focused learning experiences.

Tailoring word-level literacy instruction for children with LLI

Given that there are numerous factors that contribute to children's spelling and word-level reading skills, an optimal approach to individualised instruction must do more than simply determine whether words are spelled or read correctly or not. We have outlined this multi-linguistic approach to word-level literacy assessment in several recent publications (Apel, Masterson and Niessen 2004; Masterson and Apel 2000; 2007). Because children's spellings provide an optimal view of what they know about the linguistic underpinnings, or five building blocks, of word-level reading and spelling, we begin with an analysis of their spelling ability.

Our first step is to collect a sufficient sample of words that are (a) developmentally appropriate for the child and (b) contain sufficient exemplars of important orthographic patterns (e.g. short/long vowels, consonant digraphs, clusters, unstressed vowels, inflections, derivations). The second step is to identify the error patterns that have not been mastered and flag them for potential instruction. We typically use 60 per cent accuracy as our mastery criterion. The third step is likely the most distinctive feature of our approach. The spellings for the sound associated with each individual orthographic pattern are examined to determine why the child is making the error. If the sound is not represented by a letter, the error is categorised as a deficiency in phonemic awareness, for example with gn for gain, the vowel sound is not represented. If the sound is represented, but spelled illegally, the error is due to limited orthographic knowledge. For example, with GAN for gain the child does not know that the long /a/ sound is typically not spelled with a single vowel letter in monosyllabic words. If the word is multi-morphemic, an affix may be misspelled (e.g. *'walkt'* for walked) or the modification of the base form in the derived form may be incorrect (*'pennyless'*for penniless). Such errors would be classified as problems in morphological knowledge. Finally, if the misspellings are plausible, or legal, yet incorrect, the error is categorised as a deficiency in storage of mental graphemic representations (e.g. *'gane''*for gain). Once the reasons for the errors have been identified, tailored instruction can be provided.

This approach to identifying children's specific weaknesses may be performed by hand. However, we have developed an automated version that allows for optimal sample elicitation and instant error analysis. The *SPELL-2: Spelling Performance Evaluation for Language and Literacy* (Masterson *et al.* 2006) is administered via a microcomputer and samples ranging from eighty-two to 182 words are collected from the child. Instant error analysis and follow-up modules yield reports that identify potential orthographic targets and their associated error sources.

We also have recently begun using a metric, the *Spelling Sensitivity Score (SSS)* (Apel *et al.* 2008; Masterson and Apel 2007), that is based upon the five building-block classification system to best characterise performance at baseline levels and/or measure children's response to intervention (e.g. Masterson and Apel 2000; 2007). Consistent with the approach outlined that identifies potential sources of errors for instructional planning, points are awarded in the *SSS* system based on the nature of the spelling error. The spelling for each segment (phoneme or affix) is scored as 0 if it is missing, 1 if it is spelled illegally, 2 if spelled legally, and 3 if correct. The scores are averaged to determine the *SSS*. An overall *SSS* of less than 1.00 indicates that the child is not capturing the phonological structure of words in his or her spellings. An *SSS* between 1.00 and 2.00 means that phonological structure is basically intact but the child's orthographic skills are not adequate. An *SSS* between 2.00 and 3.00 indicates that the child's phonemic and orthographic skills are sufficient; however, he or she has failed to develop sufficient mental graphemic representations. Based on pilot data we have collected so far, the *SSS* appears to be sensitive to gains due to development as well as instruction (Apel *et al.* 2008; Masterson *et al.* 2008).

Although the above procedure enables us to determine which one or more of the five building blocks of word-level literacy are deficient, for children who struggle with word-level reading, we also conduct a *miscue analysis* (Masterson and Apel 2007; McGuinness 1997; Nelson 1994). This analysis allows us to determine how deficient linguistic knowledge identified through the analyses described above may be specifically impacting upon word-level reading. When conducting a miscue analysis, we require the children to read a portion of at least two texts: a text that the child states is easy to read, and one he or she believes is difficult to read. Our purpose is threefold. First, we aim to determine if the child is aware that some texts are more challenging than others and to ascertain whether those perceptions are accurate. That is, we want to establish whether more successful reading occurs on the easier book. Secondly, we want to determine whether the texts differ in content, structure (e.g. formal vs. less formal writing, including vocabulary) and genre (e.g. narrative vs. expository). At times, the text itself can lead to poor word-level reading abilities. Finally, we want to examine the child's word-level reading abilities with more than one text in an attempt to get a better representation of his or her true abilities.

In miscue analysis, the child reads each text aloud while we note any errors that occur. This allows us to determine the source of possible decoding problems. For example, a child may substitute a word that shares meaning with a word in the text, reading apple as orange. Such a strategy may suggest the child is using background knowledge related to the text's content instead of decoding the actual words present. While the use of background knowledge is important for comprehending text (Kintsch and Rawson 2007), one must apply it in a confirmatory manner, after reading the word, rather than as a substitution for what is presented in the text. A child who substitutes one word for another with similar meaning may not have, or know how to use, semantic awareness that deals with the effect of word spelling on meaning and vice versa. Another common miscue or error during reading includes omitting words when reading or incompletely decoding a word (e.g. reading the first two letters of apostrophe, /ap/, and then moving to the next word). These two types of miscues add to the data gathered from the spelling analysis, and suggest that the child does not have the orthographic and phonemic awareness skills required to recognise sounds corresponding to letters or letter patterns in words and then phonemically blend those sounds together to access understanding of the word.

Finally, another common error or miscue that occurs with children with LLI includes substituting a word for another word in the text because the two share similar visual characteristics (e.g. reading bottle as bother). We call this the 'guess and go' strategy (Masterson and Apel 2007). This strategy typically is used, similar to the miscue discussed above, when the child does not have sufficient orthographic and phonemic awareness skill to blend sounds consistently and effectively across the word to capture meaning.

The results of a spelling analysis and the outcome of a miscue analysis allow us to identify specific linguistic deficits in the knowledge children with LLI demonstrate, and to develop individual goals for improving word-level literacy skills. Once deficient areas are identified, the activities discussed above for classroom instruction in the five building blocks can be modified and used for individual or small group instruction. The difference between classroom and individualised instruction is primarily the degree to which it can be tailored to meet the needs of each child. Either classroom or individualised instruction focuses on the multiple linguistic knowledge resources that aid word-level reading and spelling.

When a child is identified as demonstrating poor word-level reading skills, we sometimes supplement the multi-linguistic approach with specific attention to decoding practice. Using the term *continuous voicing*, an expression we use with children for phonological recoding (Masterson and Apel 2007), we model and then encourage children to 'leave their voice on' (i.e. blend sounds across a word) as they attempt to sound out an unknown word. This approach is contrary to what many children have experienced; often they are told to sound out each letter with a voice break in between (e.g., /d/ – /o/ – /g/). By encouraging children to actively blend the sounds as they sound them out, opportunities to recognise the word are enhanced. Thus, we encourage children to blend across the word without stopping voicing and/or stopping and starting the decoding again. Once a child has successfully blended across the word, he or she is asked whether the blended information 'rings a bell'. In other words, we encourage the child to determine whether the word just read matches a known word in their mental lexicon. If it does, we congratulate the child for successful continuous voicing, and move on. If it does not, we instruct the child to consider alternative ways to pronounce certain consonant or vowel sounds and then use continuous voicing again.

There are two focal points of the continuous voicing approach. First, it should lead to successful identification of the word being decoded. Secondly, with subsequent attempts, it should lead to a more solid, retrievable mental graphemic representation of that word. In essence, we tell children that the more continuous voicing is used, the less likely it will be needed, because clear and strong mental graphemic representations are constructed. To help emphasise this notion, we re-present words that have been successfully decoded using continuous voicing several times during a session or two. Typically, by the third or fourth presentation, the child no longer needs to apply continuous voicing; rather, the word is recognised instantaneously. We use these experiences to help the child understand the importance and worth of continuous voicing as a means to developing strong word-level reading abilities.

Conclusion

Word-level literacy skills are important. Strong word-level reading and spelling abilities help children gain information from texts and provide new information to their reading audience when they write. To be successful with word-level literacy, children should have a solid knowledge of five linguistic building blocks that support word-level reading and spelling. The multi-linguistic approach to classroom and individual instruction emphasises these five building blocks and increases children's word-level literacy skills. Armed with phonological, orthographic, semantic, and morphological knowledge, as well as solid mental graphemic representations, children will experience the power of words as they read and write.

18　The development of the Speech, Language and Communication Framework (SLCF)

Mary Hartshorne

Introduction

This chapter will note how the entire children's workforce requires a clear, comprehensive framework of skills and knowledge about speech, language and communication. It outlines the development in England of such a framework, which has been constructed by The Communication Trust for online use, and illustrates its practical application with case studies. The *Speech, Language and Communication Framework* (SLCF) allows any practitioner working with children, such as teachers, psychologists or speech and language therapists to evaluate their own knowledge and identify gaps and areas for further development. It signposts training and other ways of gaining skills and knowledge relevant to the individual's profile, and suggests ways of transferring these into practice. The SLCF is designed to give teachers, including student and practising teachers, clear pathways for professional development in speech, language and communication.

The need for the children's workforce to support speech, language and communication

Speech, language and communication skills are fundamentally important to many areas of children's development, underpinning the current government national frameworks in the UK (HM Government 2004; Scottish Government 2006; Welsh Assembly Government 2005). The central importance of spoken language in relation to other areas of learning, as well as to social and emotional wellbeing has been emphasised in recent reports (DCSF 2008c; 2009b). Given this, the need for the whole of the children's workforce to know about speech, language and communication and be able to support the speech, language and communication development of all children and young people has been highlighted and strengthened (Morgan 2008).

This has particular relevance for primary school teachers. Effective language skills are essential for children to engage with the curriculum; in the

242

classroom spoken language is the primary medium through which teachers teach and pupils learn. Children and young people need to be able to understand what is being said, express themselves clearly, share their feelings and make their needs known. They not only need to understand the demands placed on them within the classroom, they also need to be understood in order to be active participants in their education (Lee 2008: 3). This requires a certain level of proficiency in spoken language.

It is suggested that the ways in which teachers talk to children can influence learning, memory, understanding and the motivation to learn (Goswami and Bryant 2007) – but also that there are enormous individual differences in language skills of children in primary schools. In some parts of the country, particularly in areas of social disadvantage, around half of children starting school do so without adequate speech, language and communication skills for their age (Locke *et al.* 2002). More recent surveys in similar areas have shown that, if unsupported, this difficulty with language continues well into primary education (Leyden *et al.* 2007). Given the right support, children may make good progress; however, some children and young people in our schools have more persistent speech, language and communication needs (SLCN). It is estimated that this is around 10 per cent of all children and young people (Law *et al.* 2002), including around 7 per cent of all children who have SLCN as their main area of difficulty (Tomblin *et al.* 1997); this group is likely to need more specialist support to reach their full potential.

This places a huge responsibility on primary school teachers as well-developed language and subsequent literacy skills are crucial factors in ensuring access to the whole of the curriculum, later academic success, positive self-esteem and improved life chances (Snow and Powell 2004). Children with SLCN are at risk of low attainment, as well as associated social, behavioural and emotional difficulties (Hartshorne 2006).

The need for training and professional development for school staff

The Cambridge Primary Review (Alexander 2009; Howe and Mercer 2007) highlighted the fact that, despite a current focus on speaking and listening in statutory frameworks and guidance (DCSF 2009a), in many classrooms children seldom have the opportunity to interact productively. Further, that primary school teachers can be unaware of the need to actively promote the skills needed for communication in classrooms (Howe and Mercer 2007). As the majority of children with SLCN are in mainstream schools, there is a crucial need for school staff to understand language difficulty, children's needs and how to support them. Although teachers are often aware of the importance of communication and are concerned about levels of children's language, many express their anxiety and lack of knowledge in being able to support them. A recent investigation into levels of teacher knowledge about SLCN and development showed that over 60 per cent lacked confidence in the ability to meet their children's needs (Sadler 2005). Others identify a limited input on speech, language and communication in initial teacher training (Marshall *et al*. 2002).

Addressing the need; developing a framework

The need for education staff to be skilled in supporting children's language has long been acknowledged. A report in 2002 (DfEE 2002), detailed the results of a national survey of provision for children with SLCN and recommended joint training between speech and language therapists (SLTs) and teachers. As a result of this, a major collaborative project endorsed by both health and education was funded to develop the *Joint Professional Development Framework* (JPDF) (I CAN 2001). Developed by a team of cross-sector experts in the field of SLCN this described learning objectives related to areas of professional competence for teachers and SLTs to support the development of skills and knowledge collaboratively. Endorsed by the then TTA and RCSLT, it reflected the impact of SLCN on education across all levels of language: speech, grammatical structure of language, meaning of words, processing of information and using language appropriately.

Although not a training course in itself, the JPDF proved valuable for teaching and speech and language therapy professionals and training providers in outlining what needed to be included in continuing professional development (CPD) so that both professional groups felt more confident in supporting children with SLCN in school settings. A review of the JPDF in 2006 showed that the framework has been used in a range of ways: to audit and plan the range and level of training required within schools and services; as an audit tool to focus the agenda of multi-professional learning sets within local authorities; to support the development of courses at post graduate level by academic institutions and local services – and in particular a 'collaborative master's' pathway with both an education and speech and language focus run jointly by City University and the London Institute of Education.

The review also identified reasons why the JPDF had not been more widely adopted. Many practitioners considered it to be too theoretical, at times too high level, and offering limited reference to the curriculum. The frequent developments to children's services, changes to the curriculum, and new initiatives meant that the framework was rapidly becoming out of date. The original laudable intention was for training to be jointly delivered and received by teachers and speech and language therapists (SLTs), but in reality this meant huge challenges, both in meeting the shared needs, but also in organising training events.

A key message was that the uptake and strategic support received would be greatly enhanced if the training was accredited.

The conclusions of the review recognised an ongoing role for the JPDF. At the time there was nothing similar available that gave such a developmental overview and structure. However, it needed to be updated, extended and expanded in response to the review findings, in relation to the changing climate and policy context and the increasing knowledge and awareness of the importance of language and impact of SLCN.

A major driver for change was the growing awareness of the fundamental importance of speech, language and communication resulting from campaigns by organisations such as I CAN, who ran the *Make Chatter Matter* campaign (I CAN 2009), and the National Literacy Trust's *Talk to your baby* campaign (NLT 2006). This meant that competence in supporting children's language was important not just for specialist professionals, but for the whole of the children's workforce. In England, this heightened awareness culminated in establishing the *Communication Trust*, funded in 2007 by the Department for Children, Schools and Families (DCSF 2007a), The Communication Trust brings together the experience and expertise of a number of different organisations, committed to effecting real and systematic positive change in the skills and knowledge in speech, language and communication across the children's workforce in England. Underpinning the work of the Trust was the development of the Speech, Language and Communication Framework (SLCF); in effect a revised, extended and updated JPDF.

Introducing the Speech, Language and Communication Framework (SLCF)

Following the review of the JPDF, the SLCF was designed with some key developments in mind. It recognises the importance of speech, language and communication to the whole children's workforce and provides a universal level, focusing on introductory skills and knowledge to support typical speech, language and communication development effectively, rather than just SLCN. The SLCF takes into account recent increased knowledge around the link between language and social disadvantage (Clegg and Ginsborg 2006), behaviour (Stringer and Clegg 2006: 93) and literacy (DCSF 2009b: 3), with greater focus on these areas. It defines competences, rather than learning objectives, reflecting the wish for skills and knowledge to be in place in practice. The SLCF remains strongly committed to the collaborative approach to professional development identified as best practice (Wright 1992), but recognises the practical challenges this can provide. Developed by an expert group with the support of a wide reference group from the field of speech, language and communication, the relevance and integrity of the SLCF was assured through

A – Typical speech, language and communication development and use

B – Identifying and assessing SLCN

C – Positive practice

D – Speech, language and communication and behaviour, and emotional and social development

E – Roles and responsibilities and how services are structured

F – Special educational needs in educational settings

G – Parents, carers, families, peers and friends

H – The effects of professional development in speech, language and communication

Figure 18.1 The eight strands of the Universal, Enhanced and Specialist compentences describing the speech, language and communication skills and knowledge needed by the children's workforce

oversight from strategic and professional bodies from education (Qualifications and Curriculum Authority (QCA), General Teaching Council (GTC), Training and Development Agency (TDA), speech and language therapy (Royal College of Speech and Language Therapists (RCSLT), National Association of Professionals working with Language Impaired Children (NAPLIC)) and the wider children's workforce (Children's Workforce Development Council (CWDC)). The SLCF also links to the Integrated Qualifications Framework (IQF) and relevant professional standards.

The SLCF therefore sets out the skills and knowledge needed by the children's workforce in speech, language and communication, describing around 150 competences in all. The competences cover four stages from Universal (for the whole workforce and focusing on typical development) through to Enhanced, then Specialist for those working in specialised roles with children and young people with SLCN. In each of the first three stages, competences are organised into the eight strands, shown in Figure 18.1. The fourth stage of the SLCF, Extension, focuses on specific skills developed through postgraduate levels of study and follows a slightly different structure.

As well as a set of competences, the SLCF has been developed as an interactive online tool on Communication Help Point (www.communicationhelppoint.org. uk), which means it can be used to do the following:

• *self-evaluate* current levels of skills and knowledge through the completion of an online questionnaire, where practitioners rate their confidence in each area;

• *profile* current skills through collating the questionnaire information. This recognises existing areas of confidence and becomes a learning development

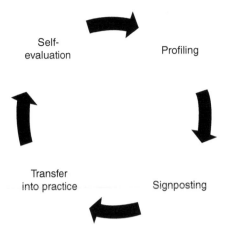

Figure 18.2 Using the Speech, Language and Communication Framework

plan which highlights areas in which practitioners may wish to develop further;
• *signpost* relevant training and professional development opportunities to extend skills and knowledge in the right areas and emphasise the transfer of training into practice. (See Figure 18.2.)

Primary school teachers support speech, language and communication development as a major part of their role and are likely to be involved in helping to identify those children who may have SLCN; therefore *the enhanced stage* sets out relevant skills and knowledge. Competence at the enhanced stage presupposes competence at the universal level as an essential foundation.

Wider applications of the SLCF

In a recent discussion paper (Morgan 2008) a number of issues were identified as being important in ensuring a workforce skilled and confident in supporting children's language. The SLCF seeks to address many of the issues identified.

The effectiveness and benefits of training and CPD

Sustained, collaborative continuing professional development has been identified as the most effective for changing teacher behaviours and impact on learners (Cordingley *et al.* 2003). However, evaluation of training and continuing professional development may not always be robust. In schools, training and professional development may take many forms but there is a lack of comprehensive information about which is most effective and has the most impact on pupils (Ofsted 2006). This is also the case for children's speech, language and communication (Dockrell 2008).

With best results reported to occur where CPD was central to schools' improvement planning (Ofsted 2006), through the Communication Help Point the SLCF can be of great benefit to school managers. It can be used to demonstrate the existing levels of skills and knowledge of individual practitioners and groups. The online design means it is possible to collate results quickly and efficiently, which can greatly help to plan and prioritise future professional development in speech, language and communication for individuals, teams or a whole school. The SLCF may also be useful in monitoring changes in confidence or practice following training or professional development.

Example: planning and evaluating training in Somerset

Bowlish Infant school in Shepton Mallet used the SLCF for two main reasons: to identify whole-staff CPD requirements and then to evaluate change in skills and competences post-training. The SLCF enabled details to be obtained rapidly on whole-staff knowledge around speech, language and communication, which led to the development of a clear, targeted training plan. Good use was made of staff time as they were not duplicating training, but building on existing knowledge and developing their skills further.

The SLCF enabled the success of the training to be evaluated not only by the school leadership team looking at whole-staff change but also providing individuals with a tool to reflect on their own improved skills. Post-training evaluation led to the formulation of a further targeted training programme.

The SLCF enabled the development of a whole-school approach to speech, language and communication.

Transferring training to practice

Learning is based upon a cycle of experiences, reflection, conclusions and subsequent plans to change practice in the future; concrete experience being central to the learning process (Kolb 1984), and in ensuring that learning results in changes to practice – 'transformative learning' (Moon 2004). Supporting the transferal of learning into practice can be supported though guided learning books or action plans (I CAN 2008), but needs this specific focus.

As the SLCF is competence-based, the importance of practitioners transferring skills and knowledge acquired through training or CPD into positive practice with children and young people is highlighted throughout. The SLCF therefore can support the full cycle of professional development, from evaluation, access to CPD, transfer to practice and re-evaluation.

Limited overview of existing knowledge, skills and opportunities for CPD

Across the UK, a wide range of professional development in speech, language and communication exists, but there is currently no cohesive approach outlining what opportunities are available, for whom and at what level (Morgan 2008). A major review of services for children with SLCN in England reported 'little evidence of areas systematically considering the skills which ... people would need or how they would acquire them' (DCSF 2008c: 34–42). Training includes diverse content across a whole range of topics in speech, language and communication development and needs. This is differentially available for various practitioners and offered by a raft of providers including academic institutions, speech and language therapy departments, local authority teams and private and voluntary organisations. It can be confusing for the practitioner who wants to further their knowledge in speech, language and communication.

Communication Help Point hosts a growing database of local and national training in speech, language and communication, which can be searched according to practitioner group, training provider or keyword. Training providers map their courses against the SLCF so that practitioners can clearly see what development opportunities will meet their needs, providing clear routes for professional development in speech, language and communication.

Example: mapping training in Barking and Dagenham

The Speech and Language Needs Team, part of the Quality and School Improvement Service in Barking and Dagenham are using the Speech, Language and Communication Framework to support and develop further their comprehensive training in speech, language and communication needs across the borough. The team has provided universal training to all schools in the authority, reaching forty-nine mainstream primary schools. This training is supported by a locally developed handbook on SLCN for all teachers and assistants. Each school has two to three link practitioners, one of whom is a teacher, to access a more detailed level of training and develop action plans to support speech, language and communication in their schools. The team has now mapped their existing training and identified current strengths and areas for further development. These will be included as part of new enhanced stage training and CPD activities, ensuring detailed coverage of skills and knowledge across the SLCF at enhanced stage. The SLCF will also be useful to support the evaluation of the effectiveness and impact of training. The overall aim is to equip all professionals working with children and young people with the confidence and competence to enhance the communication skills of all children and young people.

Quality assurance and accreditation

There is currently in England, no standardised quality assurance system across the range of training offered in speech, language and communication development and needs, and although a number of training providers have achieved accreditation this is not the case for the majority of training. This is at odds with that government's push for accreditation (DCSF 2008c).

In recognition of the importance of accredited qualifications, the Communication Trust has developed seven accredited units of qualification relevant for practitioners across the children's workforce, which focus on supporting children's speech, language and communication. These Level 3 units have been accepted onto the Qualifications and Credits Framework (QCF) and also form part of the new *Children and Young People's Diploma*, including a mandatory unit for all early years practitioners to undertake. This work has supported the embedding of the SLCF and its component skills effectively within the children's workforce.

Training 'overload'

Government policy initiatives around inclusion have a key impact on training needs both in terms of teachers being adequately prepared for changes to working practice, and being able to support children with different types of need (Johnson, Dunn and Coldron 2005). Identified as a national priority for teachers' continuing professional development as part of the personalisation agenda (TDA 2007), and recommended by the select committee committee (House of Commons Education and Skills Committee (2006), there is a requirement for training in special needs, resulting in a need for prioritisation of training. Training in speech, language and communication has to compete with other training needs. The choice of SLCN for the initial module of the national programme for professional development in SEN, the Inclusion Development Programme (DCSF 2007a) is pleasing, but school managers report difficulty in coping with the numbers of training initiatives with which they are required to engage (DCSF 2008c).

The SLCF describes a system of competences which provides the practitioner and manager with guidance as to how individual training and development initiatives may overlap or complement each other. The focus of *competences* rather than *content* provides a framework on which to base professional development.

Example: Mapping National training and CPD initiatives

The Communication Trust has used the SLCF to map a range of existing nationally available training programmes and initiatives. The learning outcomes and course materials are cross-referenced to the SLCF, providing a profile of the level and range of skills and knowledge which the training may support. This information has been collated across a number of programmes such as the *Including young people with speech and language impairments in secondary school* (Afasic Scotland and Edinburgh City Council 2007) and *Speech and language in the Classroom* training (Elklan 2009), highlighting areas of coverage and identifying potential gaps. This can help practitioners and managers to select training which is most likely to target their specific learning and development needs and support training providers in the development of new training.

The SLCF was being used to support the roll out of the *Inclusion Development Programme* (DCSF 2007a) through its use as an evaluation tool for practitioner confidence before and after training. In the pathfinders programme, four different methods of delivery were used – cascade training, direct delivery, a web–based forum and a buddy model. Information was being analysed from each model using data from the SLCF.

Recent developments: links with university courses

The flexibility and wide application of speech, language and communication framework illustrated above through case studies shows how it has been designed to respond to both local and national need. Feedback from the initial pilot year has resulted in refinements to the original version. Work with the Plain English Campaign has made it more accessible to a wider range of professionals and there are plans to align it to further national occupational standards such as those within the Youth Justice sector. The SLCF also has application to initial teacher education.

The primary Initial Teacher Education programmes at the University of Derby (UK) are auditing their BEd and PGCE programmes using the SLCF to see where current practice sits in relation to the framework and to identify possible areas of development that could be improved in collaboration with the Communication Trust. In this way, the SLCF can be seen to support the inclusion of speech, language and communication issues within initial teacher education programmes.

Summary

The SLCF has been designed to be a comprehensive set of competences to clearly set out the expectations for knowledge and skills in speech, language and communication across the children's workforce. It has a number of different applications as a dynamic tool to enhance the training and professional development opportunities for a wide range of professionals, not least primary school teachers, who clearly have such a vital role in supporting the speech, language and communication development of all the children they work with at a crucial time in their development.

19 How to empower teachers working with children with language impairments: why a 'just-in-time' model might work

Sue Ellis and Elspeth McCartney

Introduction

Children who experience any form of language difficulty or delay are a highly vulnerable group in mainstream schools. Language difficulties can affect social and emotional development (Botting and Conti-Ramsden 2000) and academic achievement (Conti-Ramsden *et al.* 2009), including literacy achievement (Snowling *et al.* 2001), and they may result in lowered social self-esteem, at least until the end of compulsory schooling (Lindsay, Dockrell and Palikara 2010). Difficulties with language often impact on children's educational achievement because of the role played by expressive and receptive language skills in understanding oral and written language, and because of the importance of efficient phonological processing in learning to decode and encode writing.

Social inclusion policies in the UK, and in many other countries, mean that children with language difficulties are now spending most of their schooling in mainstream classes rather than in specialist language provision (DfEE 1998b; Scottish Executive 2002). These policies are premised on the belief that children who struggle with language will make best progress if they are immersed in the linguistically and socially rich learning environment of the classroom, and that the 'dense and varied' language experiences offered by the mainstream context will benefit such pupils.

There are large numbers of children with language, communication and/or speech difficulties, whether developmental difficulties or secondary to factors such as hearing loss or physical disability: 'on average, every primary school classroom in the UK will have two or three children who have some form of speech language and communication needs (SLCN)' (Lee 2008 : 7).

Increasingly, legislative programmes are charging education services with developing the potential of, and educating, all such children. Examples are as follows: 'No Child Left Behind' (USA); 'Better Outcomes for Children' (New Zealand); 'Getting It Right for Every Child' (Scotland); and 'Every Child Matters' (England). For these countries, the legal responsibility for the education and language development of children with language and communication difficulties rests with the education service. Teachers and head teachers are required to know the type of language support that children need, and they have a specific legal responsibility to ensure appropriate provision. Further, in countries such as the UK, cross-public-sector and co-professional working practices are mandated to ensure holistic and appropriate provision. In particular, primary school staff members are often supported by speech and language therapists (SLTs) in meeting the language-learning needs of children with speech, language and communication needs (SLCN). The SLTs advise and support class teachers, schools and parents, and they may also work directly with the children. In the UK, SLTs usually work for the National Health Service, which is separate from the education service, although service integration is progressing.

The legal responsibility of education staff underlines the strong partnership required between school staff and SLTs. It also necessitates classroom teachers having sufficient applied linguistics knowledge and skills so that children with language difficulties are properly supported in the classroom and receive the kind of continuous, contextualised intervention that will positively promote their language development. However, determining the specific knowledge that is necessary, and deciding how it might best be framed, is a complex task. Vance (Chapter 4, this volume) outlines the complexity of language difficulties and the complex linguistic knowledge that teachers might be required to access. She highlights some current gaps in teachers' linguistic knowledge and experience and discusses the difficulties of accommodating this gap.

Teachers are responsible for educating children with SLCN and obviously need a clear and evidence-based understanding of the forms of classroom support and the intervention programmes that are likely to be effective for particular children. A deep understanding of the linguistic principles that underpin such programmes would help to ensure their sensitive deployment, adaptation and implementation in the classroom. However, whilst it is crucial that primary teachers' underpinning knowledge is accurate, appropriate and accessible, it is both unrealistic and unreasonable to insist that teachers simply import the knowledge-base and frameworks of SLTs. New knowledge that is not framed in ways that teachers welcome as 'useful' for the classroom is difficult to apply easily and efficiently in practice. Nor is such knowledge likely to be integrated into teachers' existing knowledge sets, or impact on how they think about their wider curricular provision in the context of children's learning. Both teachers' and the SLTs' knowledge needs to be transformed if it is to become useful in co-working contexts. Professionals need to consider for individual children: 'which knowledge is needed by whom, to what extent and at which stages in the cycle of support' (Forbes 2008: 152).

The new knowledge and skills which teachers require should be constructed in ways that take account of two important aspects: first, how teachers already frame and apply their professional and craft knowledge in the classroom; and secondly how school systems and wider policy systems affect this. We argue this is necessary if the education system is to be equipped to meet its legal and moral obligations to provide effective support and development for vulnerable SLCN children in mainstream schools.

This chapter focuses on research with children who have specific language impairments, and considers some aspects of the contrasting frameworks that SLTs and primary teachers bring to their work. It outlines three studies, focused on intervention, which begin to unpick some of the problematic issues that arise from differences in SLT and teacher knowledge, and it considers some of the wider influences on how teachers interpret and use evidence and advice.

Applied linguistic frameworks: initial education of SLTs and primary teachers in the UK

Working with detailed applied linguistic frameworks is a central part of the SLT's job. Much SLT pre-service education is focused on providing the necessary knowledge-base to do this and ensuring that student SLTs can apply knowledge appropriately. The Royal College of Speech and Language Therapists provides curriculum guidance for qualifying SLTs that includes many of the applied linguistics frameworks covered in this volume: phonetics, general linguistics, conversation/discourse analysis, psycho-linguistics, sociolinguistics and bi/multilingualism, with their clinical applications. The guidance also specifically includes language and literacy, covering theoretical models, language in the school curriculum, typical and atypical development of literacy and the relationship between spoken and written language abilities (RCSLT 2010). This gives a specific slant towards work with teachers, sharing interests in reading and writing.

SLTs will graduate having completed placements on which they were required to apply linguistic knowledge to diagnostic investigations of children's communication and language abilities, and they will have completed university assignments in which they debated both the theoretical and practical implications of applied linguistic perspectives. They will have a firm understanding of applied linguistics research and of the evidence-base and that has informed the design and content of many diagnostic assessments and language interventions. However, whilst they will have a broad understanding of educational models, contexts and the curriculum, they are unlikely to understand the complexity and breadth of the primary curriculum, nor have knowledge of its underpinning disciplines.

Initial teacher education courses to qualify as a primary teacher are quite different. They are necessarily broad, and primary teachers have much less exposure to applied linguistics frameworks during their pre-service education. Language and literacy programmes compete for time with other important subjects, including mathematics and numeracy, health, expressive arts, social subjects and science. In Scotland, all primary teachers train to teach children aged from 3 to 12 years, and a would-be teacher must cover the appropriate developmental progression and pedagogical approaches for each age/stage in each curricular area. As in many other countries, UK primary teachers frequently work with teaching pedagogies and content that have explicitly emerged from applied linguistics research; for example, when teaching reading they will use phonics-based approaches and take running records to analyse reading strategies, and they will use genre-based approaches to teach non-fiction writing (see Dombey and Briggs, this volume, for examples of how this is used in training). But the context of primary teaching means that the primary student teachers' attention is often on the application of the pedagogical approach rather than on understanding the theoretical frameworks or the detailed evidence-base from which the knowledge arises (Hall 2010).

School placements on initial teacher education courses offer limited opportunities to develop a coherent knowledge base of SLCN or to form a deep understanding of how applied linguistics can help teachers to meet their legal obligations to pupils who struggle with language. A primary teaching student is very unlikely, for example, to undertake detailed diagnostic investigations of children with language, communication or literacy difficulties; most assessments will have been done prior to the student's arrival. Moreover, although students are encouraged to focus on the arrangements for co-professional working, they may not actually experience this personally. Anecdotal evidence from working on the largest initial teacher education course in Scotland is that a student on placement is more likely to be asked to teach the class whilst the teacher and SLT meet than to attend the meeting. Even when students do attend meetings, they are very unlikely to be asked to contribute evidence to the discussion.

Student teachers' attention is often focused on immediately pressing topics such as mastering basic content and pedagogical knowledge, understanding common patterns of development, forms of differentiation, techniques for classroom management and discipline, and on getting to know their pupils, the school systems, and the staff. In such an environment, it is highly unlikely that components focusing purely on applied linguistics would compete effectively for students' attention. Components of the type offered in this section by Apel and colleagues, Dombey and Briggs, and by Brooks, which support teachers in working with all children, are more likely to be found relevant and useful. Given the scarce opportunities to use the knowledge, university-based information on applied linguistics to support the additional needs of children with language difficulties would, we submit, be resented and forgotten by many.

A post-qualification system of continuing professional development for primary teachers may offer a better context for developing such knowledge. At this career point, primary teachers are likely to have one or two children in the class who need specific support and development and are more likely to see the applied linguistics knowledge as useful. We know that the most effective, professional learning is that provided at the 'point of need', so that skills and knowledge are used, reframed and integrated into existing knowledge sets (Datnow *et al.* 2002). We recognise the 'need to know now' imperative for primary school teachers, and suggest that supplying appropriate information at the point when teachers will need it to support a child in their class might be a welcome approach.

Co-working issues

It seems obvious that an SLT is in a good position to deliver linguistic knowledge to a class teacher, and there are various models of SLT/teacher co-working. McCartney (2009) provides an overview of the range of models and the implementation issues they pose, and Baxter *et al.* (2009) identify some further issues. It is likely that consultancy models, in which the SLT gives advice as an 'outside expert' and leaves the school staff to carry it out, do not always provide sufficient support for particular teachers or contexts. On the other hand, models that rely on staff collaboration (with all that implies in terms of trust, personal support, free and honest discussion and shared responsibility for planning) are time-consuming and are difficult to 'scale-up' in ways that work in mainstream contexts and with large numbers of staff and children.

Hargreaves (1998) notes that when 'collegiality' becomes an institutional principle rather than a personal preference it moves from a spontaneous, voluntary, development-orientated, pervasive and somewhat unpredictable culture, to one of 'contrived collegiality' that is administratively regulated, compulsory, instrumentation-orientated, fixed and predictable. It is this regulated approach that is mandated by current policies. The argument is that, if every child is to receive an equitable and appropriate service, it cannot be left up to individuals to choose to collaborate or not. To support equity a straightforward exchange of relevant information so that teachers can deal with the needs of individual children in their class is needed.

The importance of what primary teachers know and believe

Any model of co-professional working must be rooted in a clear understanding and respect for the different knowledge and the concerns that each profession brings. A number of research studies show that, despite their lack of training in applied linguistics, primary teachers do generally make accurate judgements about language and literacy attainment (Caball *et al.* 2009; Williams 2006). However, their diagnostic judgements of the underlying factors that contribute to poor attainment tend to be less accurate (Botting *et al.* 1997; Williams 2006) and this may hinder the primary teachers' capacity to consider how to adapt the curriculum, tuition and support so that it accurately meets children's needs. Moreover, primary teachers' judgements about language and literacy attainment may vary depending on the aspect of language in focus. Nation and Angell (2006) indicate that primary teachers generally notice high-visibility decoding problems in reading, but tend not to notice comprehension difficulties, which are less highly visible. Rickets and colleagues (this volume) similarly suggest that teachers are especially likely to overlook comprehension problems when a child's decoding skills are good. They suggest that some commonly used literacy tests may compound this by enabling children to obtain high reading scores despite poor comprehension.

We know that primary teachers in the UK have, in general, positive attitudes towards the integration of children with language difficulties. Jane Sadler's research (2005) showed that mainstream teachers in England saw the classroom as a good environment for language learning, but that they were concerned about their lack of content knowledge. Eighty-eight per cent of the teachers in her study described their own knowledge as 'limited' or 'very limited'. To put this in perspective, it is important to recognise that teachers are required to view language and language development through a range of different lenses. Frequently in their professional careers, primary teachers will be asked to think about pedagogical approaches to language and literacy learning arising from socio-linguistic, sociocultural, personal-identity, cognitive, literary and psycholinguistic theory perspectives. In the name of curriculum development, they regularly swap and combine approaches to get a classroom teaching mix that delivers particular policy outcomes or provides a more efficient and time-effective way to meet the curriculum requirements of the school. This model is premised on accepting that there can be many different paths to a common outcome. It results in a teaching profession that contains individuals with very diverse ideas about what matters most in language and literacy learning. Individual teachers are likely to have developed different views on the types of teaching content and language experiences that matter most, different views on the role of the teacher in promoting 'good' practice, and they are likely to have different views about what constitutes progression and evidence of progression.

Ethnographic studies provide firm evidence that primary teachers are not a homogonous group and that, even in a fairly well-defined field such as assessment, teachers have different understandings of what constitutes high-quality evidence and appropriate interpretation and use of that evidence. Whilst some teaching professionals concur with the view that assessment and diagnosis procedures are tools to examine a child's understanding and skills in order to plan the next course of action (which is likely to be close to an SLT's position), others may focus on an assessment outcome as evidence of the suitability of the educational experience offered, the impact of teaching, the level of engagement or the nature of the learning process itself. The lack of homogeneity about assessment is endemic, found amongst classroom teachers and educational policy makers at every level (Coburn and Talbert 2006).

Thus, when teachers say their knowledge is 'limited', it must be understood in terms of this crowded (and contested) context. We must also remember that this context forms the backdrop for conversations between SLTs and classroom teachers. The lack of homogeneity helps explain why effective staff development identifies the 'big ideas' of teaching but combines this with practical tutorial advice that clarifies the purpose of learning activities and prompts discussions about specific pupils' learning (Coburn 2001; 2003). Less effective approaches, which focus on organising activities or on management issues and throughput targets, fail to negotiate a common understanding of what matters most, and why.

Offering support to practising classroom teachers is often fraught with other, more practical, difficulties. There are heavy demands on the primary teacher's time in the classroom, and there is both limited time and a limited range of mechanisms that will prompt class teachers to draw on the SLT's advice and experience. Teachers differ in their enthusiasm and energy levels, in their ability to plan and organise their work, in their willingness to liaise with other professionals, and in their ability to organise the work of other adults such as classroom assistants. Some teachers may find it harder than others to recruit children successfully to learning tasks, to explain things clearly, to focus children's attention, and to adapt the pace and content of teaching in ways that keep children motivated. These points reinforce our assertion that how primary teachers and SLTs might work together to support children with language development problems in the classroom is highly complex. It is not enough to itemise the SLT's knowledge base or to give teachers vague direction about the sort of activities to try. We need to take account of the fact that primary teachers may hold different views on what matters. They may act upon advice differently because of differences in their knowledge framework, their models of teaching, their pedagogical and professional skills, the school and classroom context, and the wider policy frameworks, which shape how the teachers see constraints and possibilities for action. We will unpick some of these issues in relation to three studies relating to effective language learning for children with language problems in mainstream schools.

Study 1: An efficacious intervention for language disordered children

For some children, inclusion in a mainstream classroom is only a start in accessing an effective education; tailored learning activities are necessary and helpful. The first issue facing anyone wishing to help children with language and communication needs is to identify which interventions and delivery methods work. There is limited evidence on interventions in general, but some evidence relating to severe and persistent specific language disorders. The first study we will discuss shows that, with the right support, such children can make progress in expressive language. Boyle *et al.* (2007; 2009) undertook a randomised controlled trial comparing different methods of delivering language intervention, involving 161 children with diagnosed language disorders. Language intervention was delivered in four modes, either by an SLT or an SLT assistant, and to individual children or to children in groups. A fifth control group received their 'usual therapy' from community SLT services. The pupils were all in mainstream primary schools in two cities in Scotland. They had been diagnosed as language impaired with no known cause and had no need for specialist SLT skills concerning speech, stammering, hearing, swallowing or alternative communication needs. They had a non-verbal IQ measured as greater than seventy-five. The study involved language learning sessions, delivered three times per week in thirty- to forty-minute sessions, for fifteen weeks. The maximum number of sessions possible was, therefore, forty-five, and the average number of sessions attained was thirty-eight.

The content and focus of the sessions was determined by a research SLT and the language-leaning activities were taken from a therapy manual written for the project (McCartney 2007a). This provided a catalogue of activities, along with advice about their implementation for SLT assistants. Language learning was in the areas of comprehension monitoring, vocabulary development, later oral grammar and narrative. There was also advice to classroom teachers on how to create a communication-friendly classroom.

Standardised pre- and post-intervention tests (CELF-3 UK: Semmel *et al.* 2000) indicated that there were no significant differences in outcomes amongst the modes of research therapy, but that children completing the research intervention made significant progress in expressive language compared to the group receiving 'usual therapy'.

Study 2: Implementation in schools is problematic

Although intervention by a SLT or SLT assistant is not the most common model of SLT support in UK schools, the above study has implications for all schools. It indicates that a positive intervention is possible and that SLTs can apply their knowledge through other people (in this case SLT assistants) who do not have the deep knowledge of applied linguistics frameworks fostered by the SLT's professional training. This could provide a positive evidence-base for the delivery model that is most common in UK schools, consultancy. In the consultancy model, the SLT offers advice and guidance to the school staff, who engage in language-learning activities with the children.

A cohort study was therefore designed to test this approach. It used the same language-learning areas and therapy manual as the randomised controlled trial, and the intervention was undertaken by thirty-eight children in nineteen schools in one Scottish local authority. All the children met the same inclusion criteria as the randomised controlled trial. However, in this study education staff delivered the activities in the context of the classroom and school (McCartney *et al.* 2009; McCartney, Boyle *et al.* 2010). The research SLT discussed specific language targets for each child with their class teacher, and together they identified suitable language-learning activities and advice from the therapy manual constructed for the randomised controlled trial, with language-learning materials provided for school use by the research project. The teachers and head teachers agreed to provide activities on the same schedule as in the randomised controlled trial and to log each contact session. The children were assessed immediately pre- and post-intervention using the same standardised test used in the randomised controlled trial.

Many children worked with a learning support teacher and a class teacher, and/or a classroom assistant. At the end of the study, children's activity logs were analysed. Their classroom teachers and learning support teachers were asked to comment on the pattern of language-learning activities they had undertaken, and whether they thought this was enough, too much or too little. They were asked if their involvement with the project had developed their understanding of working with the research child, and with other children, and whether it had altered their more general communication in the classroom.

The views of classroom assistants and of learning support teachers (who in Scotland often have postgraduate-level qualifications in supporting children with additional learning needs) are important, but only responses from classroom teachers are reported here, in line with the focus of this volume. Responses were received from classroom teachers for twenty-four children. They reported that language activities were scheduled to be carried out two-to-three times per week, as recommended by the researchers, for fifteen children (62 per cent of those for whom responses were available), and four-to-five times a week for a further four (17 per cent). The remaining children were scheduled for one session per week, or less. For children whose teachers responded, therefore, around 80 per cent were meant to receive intervention as frequently as, or more frequently than, the randomised controlled trial. The teachers reported that the intervention as scheduled was not enough for only four children, three of whom were scheduled to receive intervention less than once a week, or erratically.

However, the amount of language-learning activity logged suggested that schedules were not always sustained. Logs maintained throughout the research intervention period were returned for twenty-seven (71 per cent) of the children in the cohort, with comments included for seventeen. Logs for other children were not returned or were incomplete. The mean number of language-learning contacts logged was twenty-six (range eight to seventy contacts), which would equal one or two per week over the four-month period. The length of a contact was not usually recorded, just whether a contact took place and what was done during that session. It is possible that more language work could have been carried out within other class activities.

Teachers of fourteen children (58 per cent of responses) reported that the project had made a positive impact on their classroom communication in areas such as understanding the importance of good listening, the need to keep instructions simple and clear, slowing their delivery, having children summarise, and checking throughout lessons that children remained focused. Teachers of thirteen children (54 per cent) noted that the project had helped them develop ideas for working with other children, such as adapting the therapy manual activities for other children's use, offering children more thinking time in class discussions generally, and giving more listening practice to groups of children or the class.

Despite such positive teacher views, analysis of child assessment scores post-intervention showed no significant changes on children's expressive or receptive language scores. This may have been related to a lower amount of language-learning activity logged than planned, and to the apparently lower amount of targeted language-learning activity achieved in this study, compared to the efficacious randomised controlled trial. The logs and teacher comments indicated that planned sessions were not delivered for a variety of reasons, including difficulties in planning, in managing time, and in accessing and managing the staff allocated to support the children.

This cohort study yields important information about the operational issues that any consultancy model of intervention faces in schools, even when it is well-supported in terms of materials and advice. The teachers knew that they were not delivering the intervention as frequently as they had intended, and the cohort study showed that one or two sessions a week had no significant impact. This type of knowledge is as important for teachers and SLTs as core knowledge about the intervention activities and the principles of intervention. The study also provides evidence that, across the group as a whole, the teachers' reported increased understandings of the needs of children with SLCN did not compensate for the lack of dedicated intervention sessions. Nor did their more general adaptations to classroom routines and pedagogies.

Study 3: What might work?

It is clear that relying purely on activities and advice, even when well supported by a written manual of possible activities and a written record of delivery in the form of teacher logs, did not ensure implementation of tailored activities. The question then becomes: what type of system or knowledge base will allow effective intervention to take place?

There are two possible responses to this: one is to insist on compliance with predetermined activities by designing strict planning, record-keeping and monitoring systems at various levels of policy implementation, so that successive management levels 'check' and ensure delivery. This risks positioning teaching staff as complicating factors who must be controlled or circumvented, and it focuses attention on record-keeping and instructional routes through programmed material. Although it remains an empirical question whether this would enhance teachers' knowledge or capacity for diagnostic teaching, studies by Coburn (2003) and Munn and Ellis (2005) indicate that it is unlikely to do so.

We did, however, take the issue to classroom teachers and SLTs and asked them to identify when and how head teachers, teachers and classroom assistants might be more effectively involved in the process of implementation (McCartney, Ellis *et al.* 2010).

This project first involved a small group of teachers and the research SLT who had been actively involved in the cohort study. We asked them about their experiences of the study, and where improvements could be made. We charted and summarised their comments, and then, secondly, took the resulting documents to a small number of teachers and community SLTs in three other education authorities for evaluation. These participants had not been involved in previous research projects, although the teachers had experience of working with SLTs, and of working with children with language difficulties. We challenged both groups to design a model that would deepen teachers' knowledge, and empower them to become more involved in teaching and learning discussions. They devised the model summarised in Table 19.1.

This model, the *Language Support Model for Teachers* (McCartney 2007b), details the discussions and agreements – about both the content and the operational parameters and requirements of the language learning – that must take place amongst a range of participants, including SLTs and school managers. It also details when language-learning activities should be undertaken. It includes a system of nudges and prompts between the SLT and teachers to ensure that SLTs are involved in assisting delivery of the intervention, that delivery develops as needs change, and that any problems of delivery are identified and addressed quickly. It also supplies advice for teachers, based on applied linguistics principles, for creating a communication friendly classroom, encouraging

Table 19.1 Support Model summary chart (from www.strath.ac.uk/humanities/speechlanguagetherapy/resources/)

This chart relates to the process of implementing the Support Model for an individual child. Before language teaching begins, assessment will have been undertaken, the SLT will have decided the Support Model is appropriate, the head teacher will have agreed that it is feasible to deliver it within the child's classroom, and parents will have given consent. The Support Model chart starts with Meeting 1. 'Assistant' includes learning support assistant and classroom assistant. 'X 'is the number of weeks a child is expected to remain on the targets set, and will be decided for an individual child when targets are set. It is typically 6–9 weeks, but this is flexible and can be reviewed.

Meetings and monitoring	People involved	Purpose and decisions	Documentation
Support Model Week 1 Meeting 1 – Setting up the Support Model	Head/deputy-head teacher; classroom teacher; SLT; learning support teacher (if relevant).	1 Understand the model. 2 Exchange contact information, determine main school contact. 3 Decide upon weekly time-table for delivering support. 4 Discuss how to obtain language materials – via library service?	1 LSM Document 1. Introduction to the Language Support Model. 2 Contact information. 3 LSM Document 2. Principles of the 'Communication Friendly' Classroom. LSM Document 3. Principles of Comprehension Monitoring. 4 Any relevant schools libraries or IT service leaflets.
Support Model Week 3 Meeting 2 – Setting First Targets	Classroom teacher; SLT; learning support teacher; assistant (if relevant).	1 Plan language targets. 2 Discuss activities. 3 Confirm timetable for delivery of activities. Discuss language work record sheets. 4 'Pencil in' target review meeting date in X weeks. 5 Inform parents of targets and timetable.	1 LSM Document 4: Principles of Vocabulary Development; LSM Document 5: Principles of Grammar Development; LSM Document 6: Principles of Oral Narrative Development, as relevant. LSM Document 7: Development of the Language Support Model, for information. Detailed intervention plans re. child-specific target(s) from Therapy Manual. 2 Published materials for activities. 3 Language work record log sheets. 4 Note of Meeting 3 in SLT and school diaries. 5 SLT – Template letter to parents.

Table 19.1 (*cont.*)

Meetings and monitoring	People involved	Purpose and decisions	Documentation
Support Model Weeks 4, 5 Starting activities and 'troubleshooting'	Classroom teacher contacts SLT.	1 Call SLT if any difficulties arise, such as: materials not suitable/not liked by the child, activities too easy/hard, need for reassurance that something is 'OK', activities missed for two weeks for any reason, child not doing well, materials have run out, any other concerns.	1 Email correspondence or telephone: meeting if necessary.
Support Model Week 6 Ongoing work and routine email	SLT to classroom teacher; learning support teacher and assistant if relevant.	1 If no correspondence has arisen about difficulties, routine email sent checking all is progressing as planned.	1 Routine email to those carrying out activities: 'Since we have not heard otherwise, we assume all is going to plan. Please email back a brief comment on how things are progressing. Do be honest – improvements can often be made.'
Support Model Week X - 1, (i.e. 1 week before targets are due to be completed.) Confirm or re-schedule Meeting 3	Classroom teacher to SLT.	Either: 1 Agree to continue with targets for a stated number of weeks, then review. Or: 2 Confirm arrangements for SLT to see child to consider new targets, and for target-setting Meeting 3.	1 Note of review in SLT and school diaries. 2 Note of Meeting 3 in SLT and school diaries.
Support Model Week X Meeting 3 – Setting next targets	Classroom teacher; SLT, learning support teacher and assistant if relevant.	1 SLT sees child to carry out probes for attainment of targets, and to plan next/ongoing targets. Meeting 3 with Classroom teacher; SLT; learning support teacher and assistant if relevant. 2 SLT informs parents of next/ongoing targets.	1 Classroom teacher – completed Language activity record log sheets with comments. SLT – probes and assessment results. 2 SLT – Template letter to parents.

Starting, 'troubleshooting', routine monitoring and alerting cycle is repeated for new targets. Alternatively, a decision can be made to change the model. It could be agreed for example to stop language activities and to review after some months, or to discharge the child from SLT service, or to develop another aspect of communication, such as speech, or to move the child to direct SLT intervention.

comprehension monitoring and for teaching vocabulary, oral grammar and oral narrative, with suggested activities to be taken from the therapy manual. Relevant information, tailored to a child's individual language learning, is offered in written form to teachers 'just in time', at the point when they need the information to work with an individual child. There is provision to update language-learning targets and activities, and to monitor progress.

There are as yet no empirical studies of the implementation of the model, and participant numbers were small. However, it reflects the views of teachers and SLTs about what might be possible, and deals with a difficult area, where school staff are individually and personally responsible for delivering additional learning activities.

Conclusion

The three studies reported in this chapter concern a group of vulnerable children in mainstream school who are not all having their language needs met, but who do have legal and moral rights to effective support. These children form a largish group, and the numbers of SLTs employed in the UK means that SLTs cannot meet the demand for their skills by working directly with all individuals in schools, and many would not in any case consider this to be best practice (and see Gascoigne 2006). We also know that adults without a background in applied linguistics (SLT assistants) can deliver a language intervention that makes a significant difference to this vulnerable group of pupils.

Teachers have a powerful role to play in offering differentiated language-learning activities.

It would be relatively easy to list the types of applied linguistics knowledge that it would be nice for primary teachers to have. However, applied research seeks to make a significant difference given the landscape that actually exists rather than the one that purists might like to see. It requires practitioners to consider what is realistic, what is reasonable and what is practical in the real world as well as what is desirable in the best of all possible worlds. The fact that the professions of SLT and teaching are positioned differently in relation to children, that they speak with different 'voices' and that they lack a common applied linguistics framework for talking about language and communication is not necessarily an insurmountable barrier to working together.

The value of any approach to co-professional working will lie in how powerfully it strengthens teachers' content knowledge in ways that impact on pupils. To do this, the mode of working needs to ensure that the SLT provides support at the point of need, and it needs to ensure that primary teachers are fully engaged and actually provide the support to which pupils are entitled. It may be that primary teachers need first to use linguistics applied in a relevant way to the children in their classroom, rather than to fully understand linguistic principles. We are suggesting that perhaps there is value in a model that provides support at the level of implementation, but is framed in a way that affords opportunities to promote the growth of teachers' knowledge over time, as they work with different SLTs and use the approach to support their work with different children.

Clearly, collegiality and a genuinely collaborative working relationship thrive when there are repeated opportunities for SLTs and teachers to meet over time. However, both SLTs and teachers are busy and have limited time and availability for this. We therefore need a 'good enough' model; one that is able to provide a fast response with the minimum amount of set-up time and which does not require full collaboration, but does entail more accountability and information exchange than is offered by many consultancy models. Given that we know that intervention for children with language problems in mainstream schools can produce positive benefits, and that school-based delivery is likely to remain the main vehicle for intervention, researchers, professionals and policy makers have a duty to recognise and deal pragmatically with the very real issues that arise. Non-delivery, along with the equity and rights issues to which this gives rise, is a key area of concern.

It is not a given that increasing teachers' content knowledge of applied linguistics would tackle the problems of non-delivery. However, it might be possible to tackle the problem of non-delivery in productive and robust ways that could increase teachers' understanding of applied linguistics. The challenge is to harness pressures from within the system to promote delivery of an effective intervention in a way that is thoughtful, informed and avoids overly bureaucratic systems that distract teachers from delivery. If such a 'rough and ready' model enables teachers to use some applied linguistics perspectives to see and accommodate some of the less visible language and literacy problems in their classrooms, it will be a positive move forward.

20 Communication impairment in a multilingual context

Carolyn Letts

Introduction

According to a recent government review in England carried out by John Bercow (DCSF 2008b) around 7 per cent of children entering primary school are thought to have speech, language and communication needs (SLC needs: also referred to here with the covering term communication impairment). This figure includes children who have SLC difficulties that are secondary to diagnosed conditions such as hearing impairment, autistic spectrum disorder or neurological impairments, and also the significant number of children who have primary communication impairments for which there is no immediate or obvious cause. There is some evidence to suggest that children living in conditions of social deprivation are particularly vulnerable to delays in language impairment (see, e.g., Locke *et al.* 2002; Clegg and Ginsborg 2006), but communication impairment is by no means restricted to this group. A fundamental assumption when considering communication impairment is that vulnerability is not affected by the child's first language or languages. This means it is not the case that English-speaking children are more or less vulnerable than, say, Japanese-speaking children. So we would expect similar proportions of children to experience SLC needs in communities where English is not spoken as a first language, or where the community is bi- or multilingual. Features of the child's environment will have an influence, but not the specific language(s) spoken.

Where a child is identified as having a communication impairment, investigation and intervention by a speech and language therapist (SLT) and other professional experts as appropriate is required. However, identification of any such child, regardless of language background, can be problematic. Referral is made by parents or by a range of other professionals in the children's workforce, such as teachers, health visitors, educational psychologists, nursery workers, classroom assistants and so forth. Referrers will base their concerns on comparisons with the child's peers, their knowledge of 'norms' for speech and language acquisition and/or the child's own behaviour (for example, reluctance to talk, aggression, frustration). Parents contributing to the Bercow review reported immense variability in the process of obtaining adequate assessment and intervention for their children, and this is referred to directly in the report as a 'postcode lottery' (DCSF 2008b: 11). This situation is magnified for children who come from a background where English is not the first or only language spoken. Teachers and other school personnel will often be working in a context which for the child involves their second or non-dominant language (i.e. in the UK, English), and difficulties may be put down to weakness in that language that will be resolved with increased exposure. Parents may be unaware of services that exist for children with communication difficulties, or may not know how to access them. Winter (2001) reports both under- and over-referral for children from multilingual backgrounds, while Stow and Dodd (2003) report under-referral.

In addition to these difficulties, a variety of misconceptions regarding the impact of bilingualism on children and their language development has led to further confusion. Grosjean (2008) lists a number of 'myths' surrounding bilingualism, most of them negative. These include the suggestions that bilingual individuals somehow have split personalities, that being bilingual will cause a delay in language acquisition and that bilingual children are at constant risk of 'mixing' or confusing their two languages. Some of these misconceptions have probably reinforced unsatisfactory patterns of referral. However, eagerness to avoid this sort of pitfall may also have led to a tendency to avoid referral of children with real SLC needs, working on the above-mentioned assumption that any apparent problems are the result of the child not yet having had enough exposure to English. It has been found that two years of exposure may be needed before the child has conversational fluency in a new language. For a deeper academic style of language, five years or more may be required (Cummins and Swain 1986). Given these issues, it is difficult for a teacher to identify an underlying language problem when the evidence is limited to the child's attempts to use their second or weaker language.

The multilingual context in the UK

Calculations of the numbers of different languages spoken by children attending a particular school, or within one local authority area, abound, and numbers in the UK have been swelled recently by the recruitment of workers from the wider European Union. It is difficult to find a term to encompass all of these speakers. English as an additional language (EAL) is a useful term, but does not include the child who lives in a bilingual home where one of the languages spoken is English. Many children grow up in homes where a language (or languages) other than English is spoken, and gain early exposure to English through television, English-speaking friends and neighbours, older siblings who are in school and through English-speaking playgroups and nurseries.

Some of these children will be part of a large linguistic community that has settled in the UK, but many are more isolated. Some will live in areas of social deprivation, while others will be so-called 'elite' bilinguals, whose parents are involved in professions such as diplomacy, translating/interpreting, medicine or education. Depending on exposure patterns, some of these children will arrive at primary school with good English, while others will have had very limited exposure through nursery school and will need more time to develop English. Some will have parents who speak different languages and will be bilingual 'from birth', and some of these will have parents who use a further third language (usually English) to communicate with each other because neither is competent enough in their partner's language. It is important to consider each child individually: when such an extreme variety of cases are all lumped together as 'EAL' or 'bilingual', it becomes impossible to know what to expect in terms of the children's competence in their languages, the speed with which they will learn English, and their capacity to learn in an English-speaking classroom.

Professional responsibilities

The teacher in the multilingual classroom is faced with two challenges. First of all, there is the requirement to promote optimal learning for the children, taking into account and adjusting for their linguistic and cultural backgrounds. This will mean being able to gauge the child's English-language skills and respond accordingly, as well as promoting opportunities for home language use. Secondly, the teacher is part of the professional team which should be able to identify special educational needs, including SLC needs, and respond appropriately. This requirement is supported and exemplified in England by the Department for Children, Schools and Families' Inclusion Development Programme (DCSF 2007d) for dyslexia and speech, language and communication needs. Both of the above challenges require an ability to observe and describe the child's linguistic abilities, and knowledge about typical language acquisition. Professionals working in the primary school are potentially hampered by lack of knowledge/training in identifying children with communication impairments (Sadler 2005) and by the relative paucity of research on language acquisition in languages other than English and on bilingual language acquisition. This is further complicated by the large number of different languages spoken by bilingual communities, at least within the UK context. Teachers are encouraged to respect home languages and use them in the classroom; the DCSF Standards site, Home Languages in the Literacy Hour (DfE 2002), gives examples of how this can be done, providing home language support is available within the classroom. However, at the time of writing, there is little advice regarding how to tap into these activities when identifying children who may have difficulties, and no formal assessment of written work is carried out in the child's home language. It is also not clear how facilitative are English-based literacy hour activities in enabling a child with English as an additional language to further their English language skills by using the opportunity to ask questions and gain clarification (Scott 2003).

Identifying children at risk of communication impairment

In the case of a child from a bilingual background, accurate identification of children who have SLC needs is dependent on being able to build a picture of the child's 'total' language abilities including each and all the languages to which they are exposed and in a range of contexts. Differing abilities in different languages and contexts will suggest that the child lacks appropriate exposure and opportunities to practice in these particular situations. So the child who has only limited exposure to English on school entry is likely to be limited in terms of communication and participation in their first English-speaking classroom. This limitation does not constitute evidence for 'impairment', but reflects issues around second language learning that can be addressed with EAL support. There is an abundance of materials and advice available around providing this support (see, e.g., *Supporting pupils learning English as an additional language*, DCSF 2007d).

More pervasive difficulty across languages and contexts will suggest some sort of communication impairment. Building a comprehensive picture across languages and situations can be extremely problematic however. SLTs have traditionally used a combination of standardised assessments, spontaneous language samples and general observations in making judgements about monolingual children. These opportunities are curtailed when it comes to assessing through the medium of other languages. For example, it is not good practice to use direct translations of standardised tests for this purpose, since the demographic characteristics of the standardisation sample are likely to differ considerably from the child's own; in test development, bilingual or second language speakers are routinely excluded from standardisation samples as they are likely to skew results. Furthermore, translations do not take into account differences between languages that may influence order of acquisition (put crudely, a basic concept that is 'easy' to express in one language may be far more difficult to express in another, and hence be acquired later by children). Assessment based around spontaneous language samples will be difficult unless the professional either speaks the child's non-English language or can rely on good interpreters, preferably with some linguistic training, to help. This leaves observation of the child's communicative behaviour which may still yield very useful information.

Finding out about the child's language

For professionals working with children in education or health environments, it may be difficult to get even basic information about the home language(s) of the child. The name of the language reported to be the home language by parents or referring agencies may not be accurate. For example Pakistani heritage speakers in Rochdale, England, speak any of the languages Mirpuri, Urdu and Punjabi, either singly or in combination. In a study reported by Pert and Letts (2003), ten out of thirteen reported Urdu speakers and two out of three reported Punjabi speakers were actually found to speak Mirpuri. Reasons behind misreporting vary and the intention is seldom to mislead. Parents may want to use the name of a language that the professional will recognise, or there may be issues around the perceived status of the language variety used. It may be considered by scholars in the home country as a substandard dialect, rather as regional varieties of English in the UK were viewed some decades ago. For Mirpuri, it is unclear whether it is a distinct language or a dialect of Urdu or Punjabi; however it is clear that for children these languages are not mutually intelligible (Pert and Letts 2006). Some languages, typically those of low status, may be pre-literate (i.e. have no written form), which will also make any analysis of the child's speech difficult. Whatever the status of the language, norms for its acquisition as a first language are likely to be unavailable as will comparison norms for other languages learned as one of a bilingual pair or as a second language. (For an example of comparison norms of this kind, see the Welsh vocabulary assessment, *Prawf Geirfa Cymraeg*, developed by Gathercole and Thomas 2008.)

At the age of school entry, any child with normal language development should be able to construct simple and complex sentences, be able to hold a conversation with peers and adults that they know well and should have speech that is reasonably clear with perhaps one or two immaturities. For the child from a bilingual background this should also apply for at least one of their languages, or for a code-switched form (see below). The problem for the professional is identifying whether this is in fact the case, given that the child's English may be limited in all these respects. One of Grosjean's myths is that 'bilinguals have equal and perfect knowledge of their languages' (Grosjean 2008: 4), something that is not true for adult or child bilinguals. What should be the case, however, is that the children will eventually have a level of overall linguistic competence that permits them to deal competently with a range of social situations, whether this be talking respectfully in the home language with older members of their wider family, or producing a piece of academic written work in English. The child's linguistic behaviour needs to be judged in the light of this goal, and an assessment made as to whether he or she is making satisfactory progress towards it. Furthermore there is now evidence that aspects of bilingual children's vocabulary and grammatical development in each language may lag behind that of the typical monolingual child for a temporary period during the pre- and early school years, but catch up during the early school years (Pearson *et al.* 1993; Gathercole and Thomas 2007). This cannot be viewed as a delay as such, since overall the child is dealing with the complexity of two or more language systems. For grammatical development, it is hypothesised that a 'critical mass' of exposure to different structures is needed before the child becomes aware of the correct patterns. More complex and less transparent structures will take the longest to reach this point (Gathercole and Thomas 2007).

Code-switching

Another myth discussed by Grosjean is that 'mixing languages is a sign of laziness in bilinguals' (2008: 4). Code-switching, where speakers use items from two or more languages in close juxtaposition, has long been recognised as appropriate language behaviour in situations where both interlocutors understand and can express themselves in both languages (Myers-Scotton 2002). Code-switching may be inter-sentential, where a sentence in one language may be immediately followed by a sentence in another, or it may be intra-sentential, where the switch takes place as the sentence progresses. In the latter case, ways in which words can be combined in the sentence have been found to conform to grammatically based rules, often with a high degree of sophistication (Myers-Scotton, 2002). To date there have been only a few studies on code-switching behaviour in children (e.g. Paradis, Nicoladis and Genesee 2000); language mixing has been addressed, but this is usually taken as an indication of lack of capacity, for example with regard to specific vocabulary in one language, leading the child to fall back on their other language. The child is then expected to grow out of this behaviour as his or her competence in each language improves (Lanza 1997). Where the adults in a child's community routinely code-switch, however, the ability to do this in an increasingly sophisticated way will also form part of the child's linguistic repertoire. Pert and Letts (2006) report on code-switching by Mirpuri-English nursery children aged 3;06–4;05 years, when describing pictures to an adult known to speak both their languages. The study was carried out in the child's nursery, so the default language would be expected to be English. However, out of a group of twenty-five children, all code-switched at some point and around 40 per cent of their utterances contained intra-sentential switches. Far from being symptomatic of immature or deficient language ability, these utterances displayed a degree of grammatical sophistication such that, for example, gender agreement between subject and verb (required in Mirpuri) was maintained even when an English rather than Mirpuri main verb was used. Gender in this instance was indicated through operator (support) and auxiliary verbs, placed at the appropriate place in the sentence structure. If required to speak in either language alone, however, the child may well be unable to display their true levels of language ability.

Distinguishing second language learning from language impairment

Where monolingual school-age children have problems with language acquisition, their language will display features (sometimes called markers) that will distinguish them from other speakers of the same age. Children with specific language impairment (SLI), for example, have language skills that are differentially affected while other developmental skills, especially non-verbal cognitive skills, are developing normally. A feature that marks out many English-speaking SLI children is the lack of consistent use of grammatical inflections, especially those on verbs that indicate 3rd person singular present tense agreement (*jump* versus *jumps*) and past tense (*jumped*), along with omission of auxiliary verbs (e.g. the verb *to be* in 'he *is* going') (Rice, Wexler and Cleave 1995; Leonard 1998). Unfortunately, features associated with second language acquisition may be very similar: children acquiring English as an additional language may show these characteristics in their expressive language. Research to disentangle the two is beginning to develop, with one example being work in Amsterdam on Turkish-Dutch bilinguals with and without a diagnosed specific language impairment (de Jong, Orgassa, Baker and Weerman 2008). Until differentiation becomes clearer, identification of a bilingual child with this sort of communication impairment must involve assessment and observation in all the languages available to the child.

What can the teacher do?

The classroom teacher is not only instrumental in the initial identification of a child with SLC needs, but also has an obligation to ensure that the classroom environment will optimally support the child once they are identified. To take the issue of identification first, the teacher is in a uniquely advantageous position to make observations around both the child's social interactive skills and his or her learning in the classroom situation. This may include observation of interaction with peers who have the same home language and cultural background. Any child who does not interact well with these peers or join in the same activities and games, may have some sort of communication difficulty. Such a child may also use the home language in a more immature way, for example with much shorter utterances than those used by peers. Similarly, if a child is much slower than peers to acquire English as an additional language, this may indicate a difficulty. Slower learning in general may be associated with either a specific language learning difficulty leading to the child being unable to access the language of education, or more generalised learning difficulties. It should be remembered, however, that each child will bring a unique set of language learning skills to the situation, as well as a unique background in terms of environmental factors and experiences that may impinge on their learning, so that group comparisons should be treated with caution. Observation may, however, provide a useful starting point.

Where there are no same-language peers in the class, identification will be more difficult. Talking to parents or to other adult members of the child's community may be helpful. In either case it will be important to get the opinion of other professionals at an early stage (e.g. SLT, educational psychologist); these will be able to extend observation to other situations such as the home. It will be useful to think about the following questions:

1. Where same language-peers are in the same school, does the child talk freely with them, or is the child isolated?
2. In acquiring English, is the child going through the same sorts of stages at a similar rate, or is the progression much slower or does it feel qualitatively different (e.g., the mistakes made are different from those you have observed in other children acquiring English)?
3. Is the child lagging behind peers in school subjects, especially those such as maths where accurate English language skills are not so important in terms of making progress?
4. How do parents and/or other adults from the same language background describe the child's communication in their home language? Do they feel it is slower than expected, or different in some way?

In terms of the ongoing education of the bilingual child with SCL needs, it is important that the child gets good stimulation in and exposure to all the languages that are present in the immediate social environment. There are several reasons for this. First, the child needs every opportunity to acquire a firm basis of language and to hear good models from those around them. Where input is restricted to the majority language (English, in the UK), this will usually mean that at least some significant people around the child will be forced to use what is for them a second language, one therefore used less spontaneously and containing second language learner errors. Furthermore, unlike their peers, children with communication difficulties are very unlikely to be able to go back to the home language and pick it up later. This will mean increasing disadvantage (not to mention distress) when communicating with older members of the child's cultural community or on visits to a home country. In fact there is plenty of evidence of home language attrition and loss for children with typically developing language, in the face of the cultural dominance of a majority language like English; see, for example, Seliger and Vago (1991). Finally, the child needs to feel that the language that he or she is likely to be most competent in is respected and valued by family, community and school.

In day-to-day education, ways of working with bilingual teaching assistants/ co-workers need to be developed, in conjunction with other professionals, to formulate appropriate educational plans and strategies to work with an individual child. This is really an extension of 'business as normal' when working with monolingual children with SLC needs, combined with ways of working with children acquiring English as an additional language. Care needs to be taken that language tasks are geared to the child's level, that the child is exposed to activities in both languages and that the adults around the child adapt and simplify their language appropriately when interacting with the child and promoting learning in all topic areas. An advisory role is also important with respect to other adults in the school environment who may work with the child, and in respect of parents.

Conclusions

To conclude, for the primary school child who comes from a bilingual background and who has communication difficulties, it is important that adults in school have relevant knowledge and can employ appropriate strategies to help them access the curriculum and learn. Teachers need to have an awareness of language development, including different levels of language and some idea of sequences and stages of language development. They also need to be able to apply this knowledge when observing a child interacting with others in his or her home language, even though the language itself may be unknown to the teacher. They need to develop and use observation skills around communication in the playground and classroom.

As regards strategies, it is necessary to develop ways of working with bilingual co-workers and parents in order to promote optimal experience with language per se rather than just one specific language. Home language and code-switched varieties need to be respected and built on.

21 Teacher education and applied linguistics: what needs to be understood about what, how and where beginning teachers learn

Viv Ellis and Jane Briggs

Introduction

What teachers know and how this knowledge figures in classroom practices has been of enduring interest to governments, professional bodies and educational researchers for a very long time. The predominant way of conceptualising teachers' knowledge in relation to their practice in education policy and in much of the research has been essentially objectivist, underpinned by an acquisition view of learning (where 'bits' of knowledge accumulate brick-by-brick inside a teacher's head) and an input–output interpretation of learning (where what is in our heads simply migrates into yours) (cf. Edwards 2009; Ellis 2010). More than twenty-five years of empirical research into learning has questioned objectivist and input–output views of knowledge and transfer, research informed *inter alia*, by cognitive anthropology (e.g. Hutchins 1996; Lave 1988; Lave and Wenger 1991; Scribner and Cole 1988), ecological psychology (e.g. Bronfenbrenner 1979; Gibson 1979; Greeno 1994) and sociocultural or cultural-historical theory (e.g. Vygotsky 1978, Wertsch 1991). Yet insights into human learning and development from these perspectives have been slow to inform teacher education research and perhaps even slower to inform the design of teacher education programmes. Thus, even apparently radical shifts to school-based pre-service teacher education in countries like England – shifts that might appear to address questions of knowledge and transfer by proposing, for example, a participatory view of knowledge construction in the workplace and a sociocultural interpretation of learning transfer – instead leave these central questions to one side. Rather, new categories of teachers' 'craft knowledge' or 'professional knowledge' are advanced by teacher educators (e.g. Tom 1984; Hagger 1997) in order to value the 'tacit' forms of expertise held by teachers in their practices. Yet what Edwards (2009) has called the 'conceptual muddle' (p. 37) at the heart of teacher education remains unaddressed: teacher education does not consistently – nor readily, perhaps – address the 'knowledge' problem when knowledge is defined as the concepts, values and modes of interaction associated with school subjects or disciplines. Instead, historically, teacher education has constructed a rather different knowledge problem, concerned with tacit, un-codifiable forms of professional action. Moreover, teacher education's 'conceptual muddle' in countries like England coincides with a withering away of research and development in the field, such as the decline in activity noted by the 2008 UK Research Assessment Exercise (HEFC 2009).

The problem and its implications extend beyond the present moment and England, however. They are historical and international. So, in the USA, several states' attempts to specify what all teachers should know has led to de-contextualised online testing of teacher candidates using standardised items in testing regimes controlled by major publishing houses, under contract to test an entire state's population of prospective teachers' 'subject matter' knowledge. Teachers' professional organisations such as the National Council for the Teaching of English (NCTE) frequently point out the problems with such a standardised approach to teacher knowledge in relation to highly diverse student populations *and* with its commercial exploitation (e.g. McCracken and Gibbs 2001) but such policies continue to proliferate, especially when high test scores can be held up as proxies for highly knowledgeable (and what are assumed to be highly effective) teachers by politicians. And in England, a nineteenth-century interest in specifying what prospective elementary school teachers should know (Ellis 2007a) has persisted through the twentieth-century Teacher Training Agency's (TTA) requirements to 'audit' subject knowledge (DfEE 1998e) to its current interest in identifying the 'fundamental concepts' required to teach different subjects (TDA 2009a).

We are sure our editors are not aiming to generate an essential list of applied linguistics items that teacher educators input and their students output with a tick on an 'audit' or a click on a standardised online test. We are sure that teachers *do* need to know quite a bit about language, about how it works in the world, how it develops and, vitally for teachers, how it might be extended within the very specific interactional setting of a school classroom. But we thought that it might be useful to indicate that the questions posed by this book should be read within continuing policy and research traditions focused on teacher knowledge and teacher (and school) effectiveness. In this chapter, we wish to focus on teachers' learning, which we argue needs to be taken just as seriously as young people's learning. Fundamentally, that means regarding teacher education as an intellectual field in its own right, that has important relationships with other fields of inquiry such as linguistics and psychology, but need not succumb to a phenomenon the cultural critic Marjorie Garber calls 'discipline envy' (Garber 2001). In other words, teacher education should not privilege, submit to or otherwise aspire to be another discipline. Understanding how language works in the world, how it develops and how it might be taught is something that should be part of teacher education – but on terms appropriate to the development of the discipline. We shall return to this point at the end.

With reference to the *what* in our title ('*what* teachers learn'), we follow Myhill (2008) and others in a focus on learning to teach writing in schools, and in particular, the concept of genre. We wish to emphasise that our intention is to try to move the argument much closer to an examination of how concepts (in this case, concepts that might be claimed by applied linguistics) can be accessed and developed in the contexts in which they might have value (specifically, school classrooms) and what teacher education's role might be in such school processes.

What teachers learn: more than an accumulation of fragments

Myhill (Myhill *et al.* 2008) provided a fascinating review of the literature about 'effective ways of teaching complex expression in writing'. The underlying purpose of the review was to establish the best way of developing 'quality of expression in pupils' written work' (Myhill *et al.* 2008: 4), but specifically from a predominantly syntactic perspective with a predetermined focus on complex sentences and subordinate clauses, variation in complex sentences, and sentence-combining (Myhill *et al.* 2008: 4). The review therefore follows many others that have sought to identify and provide evidence of the importance of explicit linguistic knowledge in the composing process and, consequently, in the education of teachers (for a recent example, see Andrews *et al.* 2006).

The Hillocks meta-analysis and the failure of the 'presentational mode'

Notable omissions from the Myhill review, however, are two important researches by George Hillocks. The first study – from 1984 (and technically outside of the review cut-off date) – was a meta-analysis of the 'experimental treatment studies' in the field of composition (Hillocks 1984; 1986). Hillocks and his team identified 500 items published between 1963 and 1982 that reported studies of ways to improve the quality of writing in elementary and high schools and the first year at university. Hillocks made himself unpopular with some of the leading writing researchers of the time by only including studies that met the standard of a randomised control trial (RCT). Even in the context of RCTs as an experimental method, however, Hillocks' procedures were rigorous. The treatment applied to the experimental group had to be very clearly defined and replicable across settings and the teaching given to the control group was also examined for bias. He excluded from his sample any studies that only coded for errors or for various syntactic features; he also excluded any studies that made pre- and post-test measures using poor quality

Table 21.1 *Modes of instruction from Hillocks' meta-analysis (Hillocks 1984)*

Mode of Instruction	Characteristics
Presentational	1. Objectives focused on particular rhetorical techniques 2. Teacher-led discussion of concepts to be applied 3. Study of models that illustrate concepts 4. Tasks that involve imitating a pattern or model 5. Feedback primarily from teachers
Natural process	1. Generalised objectives such as to increase fluency 2. Free-writing and regular journal-writing to explore a subject 3. Writing for an audience of peers 4. Generally positive feedback from peers 5. Opportunities to redraft and revise 6. High levels of interaction among students
Environmental	1. Clear objectives (e.g. to increase the use of figurative language) 2. Materials and problems selected to engage students with each other 3. Small group, problem-centred discussion conducive to high levels of peer interaction 4. Tasks that engage individual students with a concrete problem within a social view of language
Individualised	1. Tutorials and programmed (scheme) materials 2. Assistance for students on an individualised basis

standardised tests. If a study was to be included in his review, it had to make use of a scale of writing quality that was applied holistically to actual samples of pupils' writing pre- and post-treatment. He also checked that studies met minimum criteria for duration in the knowledge that development in writing takes time and needs to be sustainable.

Sixty-one published items corresponding to twenty-nine research studies met his sample criteria. Across the various treatments, Hillocks identified four 'modes of instruction' and six 'focuses of instruction'. Table 21.1 shows the four modes of instruction.

Hillocks sought to identify effective practices. But whereas Myhill was confined to examining the role of syntactic knowledge in teaching and learning writing, Hillocks' review went much wider in terms of examining modes of instruction and the focuses of teaching within those modes. To identify the mode that led to the greatest gains in students' writing quality, Hillocks relied on a sophisticated set of statistical procedures and concluded: 'The environmental mode is responsible for higher gains than other instructional mode ... On pre-test to post-test measures, the environmental mode is over four times more effective than the presentational mode and three times more effective than the natural process mode' (Hillocks 1984: 160).

One might raise some justifiable concerns about the extent to which the principles of the environmental mode were elaborated in Hillocks' early analysis. However, our point is that it seems to be premised on a complex and embodied understanding of pedagogy and classroom interaction on the part of the teacher rather than the presentation of linguistic knowledge. The presentational mode – the mode that dominated US writing instruction at the time (Applebee 1986) and we believe also describes the current situation in England – persists in its appeal, however, as it prioritises making knowledge visible and explicit in classrooms, albeit in fragments. Researchers such as Applebee (1996), Ellis (2010), Fones (2001), Johannessen and McCann (2008) and Smagorinsky (see Johnson *et al.* 2003) all provide evidence of the persistence of the presentational mode in the USA and in England.

The importance of dispositions towards knowledge, learners and learning

Within modes, Hillocks identified six focuses of instruction, which had to appear in the experimental treatment but not the control group. By focus of instruction, Hillocks meant areas that came in for significant attention during the experimental group's lessons. For example, one focus of instruction was 'grammar and mechanics' and the treatments that involved a focus on grammar and mechanics might have used interactive games or reading a textbook. The six focuses of instruction identified in the treatments were as follows:

1. Grammar and mechanics
2. Models
3. Sentence-combining
4. Scales (assessment scales, criteria, peer assessment)
5. Inquiry
6. Free-writing

Hillocks found that a focus of instruction on grammar and mechanics had a negative effect on the students' writing (.29 of one standard deviation less than their peers in no grammar or mechanics treatments) and he concluded:

'Taught in certain ways, grammar and mechanics instruction has a deleterious effect on student writing ... Every other focus of instruction examined in this review is stronger' (Hillocks 1984: 248).

Our purpose in dwelling on Hillocks' work is not to make a contestable point about grammar instruction from Hillocks' meta-analysis, nor is it to equate grammar with applied linguistics. Rather, we wish to foreground his finding that the focus of instruction that enabled the most significant gains was *inquiry*, a stance or disposition towards knowledge and learning promoted and exemplified by the teacher that came to be shared by the students in the experimental groups. Inquiry as a focus of instruction involved the teacher planning for the students to investigate, explore and play with ideas and texts. Inquiry meant emphasising genuine questions and developing strategies in learners that enabled them to engage with such questions. Inquiry promotes a view of knowledge as something that we can participate in and contribute to. The important message of Hillocks' meta-analysis is that a disposition towards knowledge and learning is the most significant factor in the effective teaching of writing, which is one dimension of a particular sort of pedagogic relationship between learners and teachers. It seems reasonable to conclude on the basis of Hillocks' meta-analysis and other work (e.g. Andrews *et al.* 2006; Johannessen and McCann 2008; Johnson *et al.* 2003) that teachers' knowledge about how language works must be considered in relation to other, perhaps more significant (for *teachers*) concepts, such as pedagogy.

Ways of thinking, ways of teaching

Hillocks later developed longitudinal case studies of nineteen English teachers in secondary schools and community colleges (Hillocks 1999). He studied these teachers' practices in the teaching of writing and, again, was interested in identifying those teachers who were the most effective. By this time, Hillocks was speculating that the differences among teachers and the effectiveness of their practices could not be tied simply to their subject knowledge or their 'pedagogical content knowledge' (Shulman 1987), but could be associated with their 'epistemological stance' and their attitude towards learners (Hillocks 1999: 6).

Within his sample, Hillocks distinguished between two epistemological stances – *objectivist* (knowledge is a thing that can be transmitted from head to head) and *constructivist* (knowledge is built by engaging in social processes). He also distinguished between two sets of beliefs about the likelihood of learners being successful: *optimistic* ('by golly, they are going to do it') and *pessimistic* ('they're just not smart enough') (Hillocks 1999: viii). His conclusion was that the small minority of effective teachers could be categorised as the *constructivist optimists* and the least effective the *objectivist pessimists*. For Hillocks, it was epistemological stance and values and beliefs about learners and learning that were the defining characteristics of these effective teachers of writing. Together, this view of knowledge and set of beliefs about learners came together in these teachers' classroom practices. We accept that this study by Hillocks was of secondary and community college-level teachers but we also believe that it is reasonable to suggest that how teachers view knowledge in relation to their students is just as likely to be true of primary school teachers, especially given the widespread acceptance of the beginnings of early learning in play.

Hillocks has not been alone in suggesting that values and beliefs about literacy, learning *and* learners are highly significant in the development of effective teaching. His insights also align with the significant body of research into teachers' learning, research that has consistently demonstrated the limitations of the input–output model. Gudmunsdottir's study (1991) of expert and experienced high school teachers showed how these teachers' values and beliefs about their subject orient their pedagogies and suggested that the difference between expert and novice teachers was that novices' 'values do not seem to have achieved the influence' that experienced and expert teachers' have in the reorganisation of their knowledge as it plays out in the classroom. Leach and Moon (2000) placed 'personal subject construct' as the key dynamic at the heart of their research-informed model of British teachers' professional knowledge. And Medwell and her colleagues demonstrated that the most effective teachers of literacy in primary schools were characterised by highly coherent sets of belief about literacy that focused on 'purpose, communication and composition' (Medwell *et al.* 1998: 25) rather than high scores on a test of linguistic knowledge. McIntyre and the 'Learning without Limits' team (Hart *et al.* 2004) more recently showed that optimism as a value underpinning teachers' work is more than sentimental but is a generative disposition that enables teachers to think and act in effective ways. In other words, there is a body of high-quality research over at least two decades that strongly suggests that what makes a positive difference in teaching and learning are certain stances or dispositions on the part of the teacher, their capacity to form certain kinds of pedagogic relationships with their students, and a view of knowledge and of learning (and of, in the Hillocks' examples, writing) as sociocultural phenomena. Knowledge about how language works in the world is important but it is not the determining factor and is not something that can necessarily be fragmented and 'inputted'. And perhaps we should not be surprised by this understanding if we retain our focus in teacher education as contriving opportunities for our own students *to learn* to teach.

How *and* where *beginning teachers learn: questioning 'subject knowledge' in relation to 'transfer'*

Behind much of the research on teacher learning and development are the complex and highly contested concepts of subject knowledge and transfer. Subject knowledge was raised to an almost pre-eminent position in the minds of teacher educators in England by the 4/98 reforms of teacher education and the National Curriculum for Initial Teacher Training (DfEE 1998e). But, as Poulson demonstrated, it would be a mistake to regard the increased importance attached to subject knowledge as an effect of policy (Poulson 2001; Ellis 2007a, 2007b). Teacher educators themselves in the USA and to an extent in the UK had become increasingly concerned about subjects (literacy, English, science, etc.) as the 'missing conversation' in learning to teach (Feiman-Nemser and Parker 1990) in the 1980s. Yet over time, research has questioned the assertion of a direct association (never mind a causal link) between a teacher's subject knowledge and the effectiveness of their teaching. Wilson's systematic review of the research is compelling (Wilson *et al.* 2002), as is the work of Darling-Hammond and Youngs (2002); both draw our attention to flaws in the studies that aim to measure subject knowledge and 'prove' its influence on effective teaching. As one example, such studies often have to settle for some sort of proxy for a teacher's subject knowledge – like prior educational qualifications, a score on a standardised test or a tick on a 'subject audit' sheet – rather than answering the more difficult question which is what does subject knowledge look like *in practice*, how might it be conceptualised, and what is its relationship to classroom teaching.

So, just as some educational researchers who are interested in how children develop mathematical knowledge, for example, have stopped trying to answer the question 'what does this child know that allows her to do this sum' – and ask instead how does this child *think* and what can she *do* in this mathematical situation? (cf. Ball 2000) – teacher education as a field, we believe, needs to take teachers' knowledge about language *and* their learning much more seriously. So, rather than beginning with the conclusion of the argument (what should teachers know), we also suggest that it is probably more productive to ask how should primary teachers be able to think and what should they be able to do in certain situations? Posing the question in this way allows for the necessary, wider consideration of other factors rather than a sole focus on linguistic concepts.

Crossing boundaries

A key dimension of the problem of what happens to what teachers know as they cross the boundaries between the multiple settings of teacher education – various school classrooms and potentially fragmented university programmes – is that of the 'wash-out' effects (Zeichner and Tabachnik 1981) of field experiences or school placements. A good deal of American research puts the problem of learning within school–university partnerships into stark relief (e.g. Borko and Eisenhart 1989; Cook *et al.* 2002; Dickson and Smagorinsky 2006; Ritchie and Wilson 1993; Smagorinsky *et al.* (see Johnson *et al.* 2003; Wideen *et al.* 1998). Smagorinsky (2007) summarises the problem as the 'tendency of pre-service teachers to gravitate to the norms of their schools' (Smagorinsky 2007: xii). Ellis' research (2007a) noted that a set of socially and historically formed dispositions about the subject taught and about learning were dynamic factors in the cognitive development of the pre-service English teachers he studied over their pre-service and induction years. As they moved between settings, the development of these teachers' subject knowledge was one dimension of a sociocultural process, a move towards full participation in a community of practice (Lave and Wenger 1991) or, with a slightly different (and more historical) emphasis, knowledge that is accessed and developed in joint work on the object of activity – English teaching in England (Engeström 2007). Under this analysis, teachers' subject knowledge exists as much *among* participants in the field as it does *inside their heads*. The extent to which teacher educators can judge whether subject knowledge is adequate is related both to the pre-existing intellectual resources that, in Jean Lave's formulation, are 'stretched over' the school placement as a learning environment (Lave 1988) but also the freedom of movement in that environment for student teachers to exercise agency in their learning. It is a complex process and not a simple input–output one.

All of which also raises the question of *transfer*. Rather than naively assume that what is learned or acquired in one setting (the university) can simply be applied in another (the classroom), teacher education research is moving beyond the notion of transfer. Beach's (1999) elaboration of 'consequential transitions' is now advanced as a more apt interpretative metaphor of learning across multiple social settings than transfer. Beach distinguished between four types of consequential transition, which all had in common the understanding that learning how to think and act in societally significant ways across the boundaries of different settings (such as university departments of education and multiple school classrooms):

potentially involves the construction of knowledge, identities and skills, or transformation, rather than the application of something that has been acquired elsewhere. Consequential transitions therefore involve a notion of progress for the learner and are best understood as a developmental process. Each is consequential and often involves changes in identity as well as knowledge and skill. Therefore, individuals and institutions are often highly conscious of the development that is taking place, and they have particular, sometimes publicly debated, agendas for how and why it should or should not happen. (Beach 1999: 119)

Perhaps the most significant implication for teacher education of understanding teachers' learning as a horizontal movement across the 'consequential' boundaries of multiple settings is the need to help beginning teachers mediate these transitions. Teacher education can often tell a good story about close relationships with schools but teacher educators' roles need to be more than quality-assuring the beginning teacher's right to practise in terms defined by their placement school. These 'consequential transitions' can be powerful development opportunities, spaces between boundaries where both individuals and social systems can learn.

A consequential transition: mediating beginning teachers' learning about genre in the boundaries between school and the university

The following scenario may strike a chord with many teacher educators: the university tutor observes a lesson taught by a student teacher during which the class is taught – using a school lesson plan and resources – that 'all broadsheet newspapers are written in complex sentences and all tabloids in simple sentences'. To say that a three-way conversation (university tutor, school mentor-teacher, student) about practice is difficult following this sort of lesson would be an understatement. Given that the resources have been prepared by the school, that the lesson is part of a school scheme of work, and the mentor herself is usually confident of their quality, a conversation in the spirit of 'partnership' is often impossible. This is not a reflection of personal cowardice or poor-quality teacher education programmes. Oxford University, in England, runs an influential 'internship scheme' for teaching students which involves a close partnership between the university department and local comprehensive schools. Prospective teachers (known as interns) are attached to the same school for much of the year, making it possible for them to get to know teachers and pupils in the school really well and to understand the school's policies and practices. Yet Burn's doctoral study of the Oxford University Internship Scheme at work, noted that it was increasingly difficult if not impossible to have the kinds of open dialogue the architects of the partnership teacher education had proposed (Burn 2004).

So although the student teacher who taught the lesson might have known that 'broadsheet' papers are not composed entirely of complex sentences and 'tabloids' of simple; and although she may also have known that the distinction between 'tabloid' and 'broadsheet' had blurred considerably and that newspapers could no longer be assigned to categories based on paper size; and although her university tutors might have organised investigations of newspaper sentence type and length, this student teacher teaches the lesson anyway. And, initially at least, she feels confident in doing so as her host school's rationale for reifying such a (false) tabloid/broadsheet distinction is often appealing: young people, especially those from less affluent backgrounds assumed to be 'less literate', need explicit teaching about the conventions of texts in order to do as well in exams as their affluent peers. The effect of such a rationale in making a call on young teachers' ideals of social justice is powerful. So the conversation between student teacher and university tutor often has to take place back at the university with, at times, something of a conspiratorial feel.

To begin to address this fundamental problem of school-based teacher education, co-author Ellis spent three years working on a research and development project. The goal was to work in the key settings for student teachers' learning – the school – to improve the potential of these settings for beginning teachers' learning, not by naively aspiring somehow to make them all excellent and exemplary departments, but by opening out practice as a problem that can be worked on collaboratively (cf. Ellis *et al.* 2010; Ellis 2010; 2008; 2007c). From a research perspective, the goal was to develop, through an intervention, a theoretical account of how a school's English teaching practices have been shaped culturally and historically. Although the following example is from work in a secondary school context, we believe the principles are just as relevant and valid in the context of primary education.

Four secondary school English departments worked with Ellis as teacher educator and researcher and a group of sixteen student teachers on problems of practice identified by each of the departments. In and of itself, the initial questioning process proved difficult and the teachers explained it was unusual for them to be asked to come up with genuine questions about their practice and how it might be developed, rather than responding to an agenda set by the English government inspectorate, Ofsted. Once areas of interest were identified, the student teachers worked with Ellis and a research assistant to generate data about current 'problematic' teaching and learning in those departments. This data was then analysed in a participatory way within the framework of Developmental Work Research (Engeström 2007), an interventionist methodology that works with the conceptual tools of neo-Vygotskian activity theory.

As an example, one of the four schools involved in the research identified the teaching of writing as their 'problem of practice'. The teachers were concerned that their students were not achieving the highest levels and grades in England's statutory Key Stage 3 (KS3) tests and in General Certificate of Education (GCSE) English exams. Although they had worked on the problem at KS3 with local authority consultants and, through them, the Secondary National Strategy materials (DfEE 2001a), there had been no improvement. The department felt the situation was deteriorating at GCSE. So, the ground for that department's Post-Graduate Certificate in Education (PGCE) students' first assignment was an investigation of the English department's practices of teaching writing at GCSE, an investigation coordinated by the school-based teacher mentor and supported by Ellis. His visits to the department became largely focused around this investigation (referred to as the collaborative 'professional inquiry'), and the implementation of new ways of working with pupils on writing that had been developed by the department in collaboration with the student teachers and with Ellis as university tutor. An evaluation of the implementation of the new forms of practice became the ground for the students' second PGCE assignment. This way of working represented a shift in traditional patterns of teacher education work within Ellis's programme but was nonetheless supported from within existing resources (i.e. this new way of working was not made possible by additional funds from the research grant).

By engaging in this inquiry the PGCE student teachers and the school department learned that there was an approach to the teaching of writing, informed by a social semiotic theory of communication and systemic functional (SF) linguistics, which was sometimes known as (Australian) genre theory (e.g. Kress 1989; Cope and Kalantzis 1993). The student teachers also distinguished between Australian versions of genre theory, associated with SF linguistics and a critical literacy stance, and North American genre theory, informed by a rhetorical perspective on communication drawn from US and Canadian traditions of Speech and Composition research (e.g. Miller 1984; Freedman 1995). So, for each assessed writing task, the school's English department had prepared what they referred to as a 'writing frame'. This was not a writing frame in the sense that, for example, Lewis and Wray (1995) proposed. Rather, it was a highly specified plan (at the level of content and stages) with explicit references to the marks available for each section. In other words, 'writing frames' like this were the focus of instruction in their English department within what Hillocks had referred to as a 'presentational mode' of instruction. The 'writing frame' was presented to students for completion; the concept of genre, insofar as it emerged in the classroom interactions at all, was fossilised.

The student teachers also learned from interviews and observations that the young people in these classes were disengaged from the writing task; that they saw the tasks as unchallenging; and that pupils complied with the tasks because their teachers told them that they would get good grades that way. Ironically, by scrutinising exam papers and Chief Examiners' reports, the student teachers found out that far from scaffolding these young writers' work towards the higher grades, this 'scaffolding' was actually known to be a barrier to achieving those grades. So they learned that scaffolding as a metaphor should refer to a social relationship rather than a template for completion. Moreover, they learned that a genre-based approach to the teaching of writing was not intrinsically flawed but that it needed to be understood more fully within a social practice view of reading and writing in which there are certain recognisable patterns of communication. They also learned that, fundamentally, the rhetorical relationship between a writer and an intended reader needed closer examination. In other words, the problem as they saw it was in the department's appropriation of certain surface level features of the practical tools of genre: the department had made the 'writing frame' a rule without fully understanding its conceptual inheritance.

In this case, what the PGCE students, the department and the teacher educator needed to understand was that the professional practices of the teaching of writing in this department had become sedimented – normalised in unproductive ways. For whatever reasons, at this point, the department did not have the resources to appropriate genre-based writing pedagogies meaningfully. Far from being an argument for more teaching about social theories of language in the university setting, however, what Ellis as teacher educator needed to understand was that this activation of knowledge about language and learning became an outcome of collaborative inquiry in the school setting. The device of the collaborative inquiry was an important tool in helping the student teachers mediate the consequential transitions between the settings for their learning – reconstructing knowledge of genre in a new setting – as well as re-activating the learning of the host department and the teacher educator (see Max 2010 and Jóhannsdóttir 2010 for other examples in teacher education in Luxembourg and Iceland). The student teachers were still required to cross the boundaries of different settings in order to learn to teach – the university department and two schools – but by opening out practice in a boundary zone as a problem that can be worked on rather than as a set of routines to imitate, the intended outcome was that the PGCE students would feel safe enough to learn about the concept.

Developing a language curriculum for teacher education

In supporting this book's ultimate aim of contributing to the improvement of the teaching of literacy and English in our schools, we have deliberately focused our attention on taking teachers' knowledge and learning seriously. We have drawn attention to some seminal studies from the teacher education literature that question input–output models of teacher learning in relation to effective classroom teaching. In other words, what happens to what teachers know as they enter complex classroom ecologies is much less predictable than policy makers, researchers and the profession would sometimes wish. In particular, we have referred to research that demonstrates the ways in which teachers construct and reconstruct what they know in the course of learning to teach in specific school settings. In dwelling on research that rejects simplistic notions of transfer, we have also argued that much research on teacher learning and teacher effectiveness demonstrates the importance of teachers' values and beliefs about what they are teaching and who they are teaching, as well as their epistemological stance or their understanding of or orientation towards knowledge and learning.

We hope it is also clear that we believe that beginning teachers do need to learn about language, about how language works and how it might be extended in school classrooms. Whether it is by understanding how the professional practices of teaching writing have come to be shaped in their placement schools and departments, or by other means of creating spaces for teacher learning, we believe that what teacher education can and should help beginning teachers to develop is a deep understanding of the social practices of reading, viewing, writing, speaking and listening, and of language as a tool in the development of mind. For beginning teachers to develop these understandings, we have argued, they need to engage in the cultural practices we wish them to learn (*teaching* literacy and English) and construct a conscious awareness of those practices. So an important implication for teacher educators and researchers is that it is time to rethink what we as teacher educators can do to re-activate, support and research teacher development in schools as the key settings for their learning. Knowledge, in other words, is obviously a good thing, including concepts drawn from applied linguistics that might help teachers and students gain some measure of control over what they do in classrooms and that provide opportunities for creativity and agency in learning. So how can teacher education as a field move beyond the relatively safe environs of professional 'craft' knowledge and engage with the concepts of the subjects and disciplines being learned and taught? And how can both teacher education and other fields such as applied linguistics resist the temptation of making lists of itemised bits of 'knowledge' to tick, test or 'input'?

Finally, as an opening move in a possible answer to these questions, we would like to pick up on our earlier comment about teacher education not succumbing to 'discipline envy'. Teacher education can benefit from interdisciplinary dialogues with linguistics, psychology, sociology, sports science, philosophy, nutrition and a host of other fields of intellectual inquiry. Those disciplines can also benefit from dialogues with teacher education (a suggestion that is perhaps less frequently asserted). Key figures in the history of teacher education as a field have made highly significant contributions to the study of language in education. For example, it was Harold Rosen (1981) in teacher education in England and William Labov (1978) in linguistics in the USA who offered us complementary insights into 'non-standard' language usage. And although there was sometimes criticism of the ways in which those in teacher education treated language, their response at the time still stands true: the terms of their analysis of language were fit for purpose, the purpose being the education of teachers and the improvement of schools as places for young people to learn. This statement is not meant to be a rejection of applied linguistics or any other discipline, but a suggestion that teacher education itself needs to value teachers' learning about language more highly if it is to continue to be judged an intellectual field in its own right.

References

Achugar, M., Schleppegrell, M. J. and Oteiza, T. 2007. 'Engaging teachers in language analysis: a functional linguistics approach to reflective literacy', *English Teaching: Practice and Critique* **6**: 8–24.

Adamson, S. 1999. 'Literary language' in Lass, R. (ed.) *The Cambridge History of the English Language*, vol. III (Cambridge University Press). Chapter 7.

Addison, J. [ed. Donald Bond] 1965. *The Spectator*, 5 vols., Oxford: Clarendon Press.

Addison, J. [ed. Erin Skye Mackie] 1998. *The Commerce of Everyday Life: Selections from The Tatler and The Spectator*. Basingstoke: Palgrave Macmillan.

Addison, J. N.d. 'Extract from drafts of *The Spectator*', MS Don d.112, Bodleian Library.

Afasic Scotland and Edinburgh City Council 2007. *Including Young People with Speech and Language Impairments in Secondary School*. Edinburgh: Edinburgh City Council.

Agosto, D. 1999. 'One and inseparable: interdependent storytelling in picture storybooks', *Children's Literature in Education* **30**: 267–280.

Ahlberg, A. 1976. *Each Peach Pear Plum*. London: Kestrel.

Ahlberg, A. and Ahlberg, J. 1986. *The Jolly Postman*. London: Heinemann.

Ainscow, M. and Sandill, A. 2010. 'Developing inclusive education systems: the role of organisational cultures and leadership', *International Journal of Inclusive Education*, **14**: 401–416.

Al-Azami, S., Kenner, C., Ruby, M. and Gregory, E. 2010. *Transliteration as a bridge to learning for bilingual children*.

Alexander, R. J. 1995. *Versions of Primary Education*. London: Routledge.

  2001. *Culture and Pedagogy: International Comparisons in Primary Education*. Oxford: Blackwell.

  2004. 'Talking to learn', *Times Education Supplement* 30 January: 12–13.

  2005. *Towards Dialogic Teaching: Rethinking Classroom Talk*, 2nd edn. Cambridge: Dialogos.

  2009. *Children, Their World, Their Education: Final Report and Recommendations of the Cambridge Primary Review*. London: Routledge.

Allison, P., Beard, R. and Willcocks, J. 2002. 'Subordination in children's writing', *Language in Education* **16**: 97–111.

Anderson, J. 2008. 'Towards integrated second language teaching pedagogy for foreign and community/heritage languages in multilingual Britain', *Language Learning Journal* **36**: 79–89.

Andrews, R., Torgerson, C., Beverton, S., Locke, T., Lowe, G., Robinson, A. and Zhu, D. 2006. *The Effect of Grammar Teaching (Syntax) in English on 5 to 16 year olds'*

Accuracy and Quality in Written Composition. York: Department of Educational Studies, University of York.

Anon. 1688. *The Advice of a father, or, Counsel to a child directing him to demean himself in the most important passages of this life.* Reproduction of original in the British Library. University Microfilms International, 1983. 1 microfilm reel; 35 mm. Early English books (1641–1700; 1413: 4): London.

Apel, K. and Masterson, J. J. 2001. 'Theory-guided spelling assessment and intervention: a case study', *Language, Speech, and Hearing Services in Schools* **32**: 182–195.

Apel, K., Masterson, J. J. and Hart, P. 2004. 'Integration of language components in spelling: Instruction that maximizes students' learning' in E. R. Silliman and L. C. Wilkinson (eds.) *Language and Literacy Learning in Schools* (New York: Guilford Press), pp. 292–315.

Apel, K., Masterson, J. J. and Niessen, N. L. 2004. 'Spelling assessment frameworks' in A. Stone, E. R. Silliman, B. Ehren and K. Apel (eds.) *Handbook of Language and Literacy: Development and Disorders* (New York: Guilford Press), pp. 644–660.

Apel, K., Wilson-Fowler, E., Goldstein, H. and Masterson, J. J. 2008, November. 'Measuring developmental changes in spelling skills: determining the appropriate analysis.' Paper presented at the annual convention of the American Speech-Language-Hearing Association, Chicago, IL.

Applebee, A. 1986. 'Problems in process approaches: Towards a reconceptualization of process instruction' in A. Petrosky and D. Bartholomae (eds.) *The Teaching of Writing; 85th Yearbook of the National Society of the Study of Education* (University of Chicago Press).

1996. *Curriculum as Conversation: Transforming Traditions of Teaching and Learning.* University of Chicago Press.

Arizpe, E. 2009. 'Sharing visual experiences of a new culture: immigrant children's responses to picturebooks and other visual texts' in J. Evans (ed.) *Talking Beyond the Page: Reading and Responding to Picturebook* (London: Routledge), pp. 134–151.

Arizpe, E. and Styles, S. 2003. *Children Reading Pictures Interpreting Visual Texts.* London: RoutledgeFalmer.

Arnbak, E. and Elbro, C. 2000. 'The effects of morphological awareness training on the reading and spelling skills of young dyslexics', *Scandinavian Journal of Educational Research* **44**: 229–251.

Arthur, J. and Martin, P. 2006. 'Accomplishing lessons in postcolonial classrooms: comparative perspectives from Botswana and Brunei Darussalam', *Comparative Education* **42**: 177–202.

Aston, G. (ed.) 2001. *Learning with Corpora.* Houston, TX: Athelstan.

Aston, G., Bernardini, S. and Stewart, D. (eds.) 2004. *Corpora and Language Learners.* Amsterdam: John Benjamins.

Au, K. H. 1980. 'Participation structures in a reading lesson with Hawaiian children: analysis of a culturally appropriate instructional event.' *Anthropology and Education Quarterly* **11**, 2: 91–115.

2002. 'Multicultural factors and the effective instruction of students of diverse backgrounds' in A. Farstrup and S. J. Samuels *What Research Says About Reading Instruction* (Newark, DE: International Reading Association), pp. 392–413.

Au, K. H. and Jordan, C. 1981. 'Teaching reading to Hawaiian children: finding a culturally appropriate solution' in H. T. Trueba, G. P. Guthrie and K. H. Au (eds.) *Culture and the Bilingual Classroom: Studies in Classroom Ethnography* (Rowley, MA: Newbury House), pp. 130–152.

Baker, C. and Luke, A. (eds.) 1991. *Towards a Critical Sociology of Reading: Papers of the XII World Congress on Reading.* Amsterdam: John Benjamins.

Baker, P. and Eversley, J. (eds.) 2000. *Multilingual Capital: the Languages of London's Schoolchildren and their Relevance to Economic, Social and Educational Policies.* London: Battlebridge.

Ball, D. L. 2000 'Bridging practices: Intertwining content and pedagogy in teaching and learning to teach', *Journal of Teacher Education* **51**: 241–247.

Ball, S. 1997. 'Policy sociology and critical social research: a personal review of recent education policy and policy research', *British Educational Research Journal* **23**: 257–274.

2008. *The Education Debate.* London: Policy Press.

Barlex, D. and Givens, N. 1995. 'The Nuffield approach to the teaching of mechanisms at key stage 3' in Smith, J. S. (ed.) *International Conference on Design and Technology Educational Research and Curriculum Development IDATER 95* (Loughborough: Loughborough University Department of Design and Technology), pp. 48–51.

Baumann, J. F., Edwards, E. C., Boland, E. M., Olejnik, S. and Kame'enui, E. J. 2003. 'Vocabulary tricks: effects of instruction in morphology and context on fifth-grade students' ability to derive and infer word meanings', *American Educational Research Journal* **40**: 447–494.

Baumann, J. F., Edwards, E. C., Font, G., Tereshinski, C. A., Kame'enui, E. J. and Olejnik, S. 2002. 'Teaching morphemic and contextual analysis to fifth-grade students', *Reading Research Quarterly* **37**: 150–176.

Baxter, S., Brookes, C., Bianchi, K., Rashid, K. and Hay, F. 2009. 'Speech and language therapists and teachers working together: exploring the issues', *Child Language Teaching and Therapy* **25**: 215–234.

Baynham, M. 1995. *Literacy Practice: Investigating Literacy in Social Contexts.* London: Longman.

Beach, K. 1999. 'Consequential transitions: a sociocultural expedition beyond transfer in education', *Review of Research in Education* **24**: 101–139.

Bearne, E. 1998. *Making Progress in English.* London: Routledge.

Beck, I., Perfetti, C. and McKeown, M. 1982. 'Effects of long-term vocabulary instruction on lexical access and reading-comprehension', *Journal of Educational Psychology* **74**: 506–521.

Beers, J. and Henderson, E. 1977. 'A study of developing orthographic concepts among first and second grade children', *Research in the Teaching of English* **11**: 133–148.

Bereiter, C. and Scardamalia, M. 1987. *The Psychology of Written Composition.* Hillsdale, NJ: Erlbaum.

Berman, R. A. and Verhoeven, L. 2002. 'Cross-linguistic perspectives on the development of text production abilities: speech and writing', *Written Language and Literacy* **5**: 1–43.

Besser, S., Brooks, G., Burton, M., Parisella, M., Spare, Y., Stratford, S. and Wainwright, J. 2004. *Adult Learners' Difficulties with Reading: an Exploratory*

Study. London: National Research and Development Centre for Adult Literacy and Numeracy.

Beykont, Z. F. (ed.) 2002. *The Power of Culture: Teaching Across Language Difference*. Boston, MA: Harvard Education Publishing Group.

Bhatt, A., Bhojani, N., Creese, A. and Martin, P. 2004. *Complementary and Mainstream Schooling: a Case for Reciprocity?* York: Naldic Publications.

Bishop, D.V.M. and Adams, C. 1989. 'Conversational characteristics of children with semantic-pragmatic disorder II: What features lead to a judgement of inappropriacy?', *British Journal of Disorders of Communication* **24**: 241–263.

Bishop, D. V. M. and Snowling, M. J. 2004. 'Developmental dyslexia and specific language impairment: Same or different?', *Psychological Bulletin* **130**: 858–886.

Blachowicz, C. L. Z. and Fisher, P. J. L. 2000. 'Vocabulary instruction' in R. Barr, M. L. Kamil, P. B. Mosenthal and P. D. Pearson (eds.) *Handbook of Reading Research*, vol. III (Mahwah, NJ: Erlbaum), pp. 503–523.

Blachowicz, C. L. Z., Fisher, P. J. L., Ogle, D. and Watts-Taffe, S. 2006. 'Theory and research into practice: vocabulary: questions from the classroom', *Reading Research Quarterly* **41**: 524–539.

Blackledge, A. and Creese, A. 2010. *Multilingualism: a Critical Perspective*. London: Continuum.

Blondin, C., Candelier, M., Edenbelos, P., Johnstone, R., Kubanek-German, A. and Taeschner, T. 1997. *Foreign Languages in Primary and Pre-School Education: Context and Outcomes. A Review of Recent Research within the European Union*. Brussels: European Commission.

Borko, H. 2004. 'Professional development and teacher learning: mapping the terrain', *Educational Researcher* **33**: 3–15.

Borko, H. and Eisenhart, M. 1992. 'Learning to teach hard mathematics: do novice teachers and their instructors give up too easily?', *Journal for Research in Mathematics Education* **23**: 194–222.

Botting, N. and Conti-Ramsden, G. 2000. 'Social and behavioural difficulties in children with language impairment', *Child Language Teaching and Therapy* **16**: 105–120.

Botting, N., Conti-Ramsden, G. and Crutchley, A. 1997. 'Concordance between teacher/ therapist opinion and formal language assessment scores in children with language impairment', *European Journal of Disorders of Communication* **32**: 517–527.

Bourne, J. 2001. 'Doing 'What comes naturally': how the discourses and routines of teachers' practices constrain opportunities for bilingual support in UK primary schools', *Language and Education* **15**: 250–268.

Bowler, T. 2002. 'Write off your plans and go with the flow', *Times Educational Supplement* 16 August. www.tes.co.uk/article.aspx?storycode=367418

Boyle, J., McCartney, E., Forbes, J. and O'Hare, A. 2007. 'A randomised controlled trial and economic evaluation of direct versus indirect and individual versus group modes of speech and language therapy for children with primary language impairment', *Health Technology Assessment* **11**, 25: 1–158.

Boyle, J., McCartney, E., O'Hare, A. and Forbes, J. 2009. 'Direct versus indirect and individual versus group modes of language therapy for children with primary language impairment: principal outcomes from a randomised controlled trial and economic evaluation', *International Journal of Language and Communication Disorders* **44**: 826–846.

Bradley, L. and Bryant, P. 1983. 'Categorising sounds and learning to read – a causal connection', *Nature* 301: 419–421.

Braun, S., Mukherjee, J. and Kohn, K. (eds.) 2006. *Corpus Technology and Language Pedagogy: New Resources, New Tools, New Methods.* Frankfurt am Main: Peter Lang.

Bronfenbrenner, U. 1979. *Ecology of Human Development. Experiments by Nature and Design.* Cambridge, MA: Harvard University Press.

Browne, A. 1981. *Hansel and Gretel.* London: Julia MacRae.

1983. *Gorilla.* London: Julia MacRae.

1990. *Changes.* London: Julia MacRae.

1992. *Piggybook.* London: Walker.

Bryan, A. 1997. 'Colourful semantics: thematic role therapy' in S. Chiat, J. Law and J. Marshall (eds.) *Language Disorders in Children and Adults* (London: Whurr), pp. 143–161.

Bubb, S. and Earley, P. 2007. *Leading and Managing Continuing Professional Development*, 2nd edn. London: Sage.

2008. *The journey from self-evaluation to school improvement: the significance of effective professional development.* Paper presented at the American Education Research Association Conference, New York, 24 March 2008.

Buckingham, D. 1993. *Children Talking Television: the Making of Television Literacy.* London: Falmer Press.

Bulwer, J. 1644. *Chirologia*, 2 vols. London.

Burbules, N. C. 1993. *Dialogue in Teaching: Theory and Practice.* New York: Teachers College Press.

Burn, K. 2004. 'Learning to teach history as a continual process of hypothesis-testing: a critical examination of key principles of the internship scheme.' DPhil thesis, University of Oxford.

Burnard, L. and McEnery, T. (eds.) 2000. *Rethinking Language Pedagogy from a Corpus Perspective.* Frankfurt am Main: Peter Lang.

Burningham, J. 1971. *Mr Gumpy's Outing.* London: Puffin.

1984. *Granpa.* London: Cape.

Burton, M. and Brooks, G. 2005. *The Case for Using the International Phonetic Alphabet (IPA) in Teaching Teachers about Phonics: a Submission to the Rose Review of Best Practice in the Teaching of Reading.* Sheffield: The Authors.

Butler, K. G. and Stillman, E. R. 2002. *Speaking, Reading, and Writing in Children with Language Learning Disabilities: New Paradigms in Research and Practice.* Hove: Erlbaum.

Butyniec-Thomas, J. and Woloshyn, V. E. 1997. 'The effects of explicit strategy and whole-language instruction on students' spelling ability', *Journal of Experimental Education* **65**: 293–302.

Caball, S. Q., Justice, L. M., Zucker, T. A. and Kilday, C. R. 2009. 'Validity of teacher report for assessing the emergent literacy skills of at-risk preschoolers', *Language, Speech and Hearing Services in Schools* **40**: 161–173.

Cain, K. 2003. 'Text comprehension and its relation to coherence and cohesion in children's fictional narratives', *British Journal of Developmental Psychology* **21**: 335–351.

2006. 'Children's reading comprehension: the role of working memory in normal and impaired development' in S. J. Pickering and G. D. Phye (eds.) *Working Memory and Education* (Oxford: Academic Press).

Cain, K. and Oakhill, J. 1999. 'Inference making ability and its relation to comprehension failure in young children', *Reading and Writing* **11**: 489–503.

2006. 'Profiles of children with specific reading comprehension difficulties', *British Journal of Educational Psychology* **76**: 683–696.

2007. *Children's Comprehension Problems in Oral and Written Language: a Cognitive Perspective.* New York: Guildford Press.

Cain, K., Oakhill, J. and Elbro, C. 2003. 'The ability to learn new word meanings from context by school-age children with and without language comprehension difficulties', *Journal of Child Language* **30**: 681–694.

Cain, K., Oakhill, J. and Lemmon, K. 2004. 'Individual differences in the inference of word meanings from context: the influence of reading comprehension, vocabulary knowledge, and memory capacity', *Journal of Educational Psychology* **96**: 671–681.

Caramazza, A., Laudana, A. and Romani, C. 1988. 'Lexical access and inflectional morphology', *Cognition* **28**: 297–332.

Carlisle, J. F. 1995. 'Morphological awareness and early reading achievement' in L. Feldman (ed.) *Morphological Aspects of Language Processing.* Hillsdale, NJ: Erlbaum, pp. 189–209.

Carlo, M. S., August, D., Mclaughlin, B., Snow, C. E., Dressler, C. and Lippman, D. N. 2004. 'Closing the gap: addressing the vocabulary needs of English-language learners in bilingual and mainstream classrooms', *Reading Research Quarterly* **39**: 188–215.

Carretti, B., Cornoldi, C., De Beni, R. and Romanò, M. 2005. 'Updating in working memory: a comparison of good and poor comprehenders', *Journal of Experimental Child Psychology* **91**: 45–66.

Carter, R. (ed.) 1990. *Knowledge about Language.* London: Hodder and Stoughton.

Carter, R. and McCarthy, M. 2006. *Cambridge Grammar of English.* Cambridge University Press.

Catone, W. V. and Brady, S. A. 2005. 'The inadequacy of individual educational program (IEP) goals for high school students with word-level reading difficulties', *Annals of Dyslexia* **55**: 53–78.

Catts, H. W., Adlof, S. M. and Weismer, S. E. 2006. 'Language deficits in poor comprehenders: a case for the simple view of reading', *Journal of Speech, Language, and Hearing Research* **49**: 278–293.

Catts, H. W., Fey, M. E., Zhang, X. and Tomblin, J. B. 2001. 'Estimating the risk of future reading difficulties in kindergarten children: a research-based model and its clinical implications', *Language, Speech, and Hearing Services in the Schools* **32**: 38–50.

Cazden, C. B. 2001. *Classroom Discourse: the Language of Teaching and Learning,* 2nd edn. Portsmouth, NH: Heinemann.

Chiat, S. 2000. *Understanding Children with Language Problems.* Cambridge University Press.

Christie, F. and Martin, J. R. 1997. *Genres and Institutions: Social Processes in the Workplace and School.* London: Pinter.

Christie, F. and Martin, J. R. (eds.) 2007. *Language, Knowledge and Pedagogy: Functional Linguistics and Sociological Perspectives.* London: Continuum.

CILT 2009. *Primary Languages website.* www.primarylanguages.org.uk/home.aspx

Clay, M. 1979. *The Early Detection of Reading Difficulties* (3rd edn). Auckland: Heinemann Education.

Clarke, P. J., Snowling, M. J., Truelove, E., and Hulme, C. (2010). 'Ameliorating children's reading comprehension difficulties: a randomised controlled trial'. *Psychological Science,* **21**(8), 1106–1116.

Clegg, J. and Ginsborg, J. (eds.) 2006. *Language and Social Disadvantage: Theory into Practice.* Chichester: Wiley.

Clegg, J., Hollis, C., Mawhood, L. and Rutter, M. 2005. 'Developmental language disorders – a follow-up in later adult life. Cognitive, language and psychosocial outcomes', *Journal of Child Psychology and Psychiatry* **46**: 128–149.

Coburn, C. 2001. 'Collective sense-making about reading: how teachers mediate reading policy in their professional communities', *Educational Evaluation and Policy Analysis* **23**: 145–170.

   2003. 'Rethinking scale: moving beyond numbers to deep and lasting change', *Educational Researcher* **32**, 6: 3–12.

Coburn, C. E. and Talbert, J. E. 2006. 'Conceptions of evidence-based practice in school districts: mapping the terrain', *American Journal of Education* **112**: 469–495.

Coffield, F., Steer, R., Allen, R., Vignoles, A., Moss, G. and Vincent, C. 2007. *Public Sector Reform: Principles for Improving the Education System.* London: Institute of Education.

Coffin, C. 2005. 'Constructing and giving value to the past: an investigation into secondary school history' in F. Christie and J. R. Martin (eds.) *Genres and Institution: Social Processes in the Workplace and Schools.* London: Continuum.

Coleridge, S. T. 1834. *Biographia Literaria.* Boston: Crocker and Brewster.

Connor, C. M., Morrison, F. J., Fishman, B. J., Schatschneider, C. and Underwood, P. 2007. 'The early years: algorithm-guided individualized reading instruction', *Science* **315**, 5811: 464–465.

Connor, C. M., Morrison, F. J. and Katch, E. L. 2004. 'Beyond the reading wars: the effect of classroom instruction by child interactions on early reading', *Scientific Studies of Reading* **8**: 305–336.

Connor, U. and Upton, T. A. (eds.) 2004. *Applied Corpus Linguistics: a Multidimensional Perspective.* Amsterdam and Atlanta: Rodopi.

Conteh, J. 2007a. 'Opening doors to success in multilingual classrooms: bilingualism, codeswitching and the professional identities of ethnic minority primary teachers', *Language and Education* **21**: 457–472.

   2007b. 'Bilingualism in mainstream primary classrooms in England' in Z. Hua, P. Seedhouse, L. Wei and V. Cook (eds.) *Language Learning and Teaching as Social Interaction* (London: Palgrave Macmillan), pp. 185–198.

Conti-Ramsden, G., Durkin, K., Simkin, Z. and Knox, E. 2009. 'Specific language impairment and school outcomes. I: Identifying and explaining variability at the end of compulsory education', *International Journal of Language and Communication Disorders* **44**: 15–35.

Cook, L. S., Smagorinsky, P., Fry, P. G., Konopak, B. and Moore, C. 2002. 'Problems in developing a constructivist approach to teaching: one teacher's transition from teacher preparation to teaching', *Elementary School Journal* **102**: 389–413.

Cope, B. and Kalantzis, M. 1993. *The Powers of Literacy: a Genre Approach to Teaching Writing.* Pittsburgh, PA: University of Pittsburgh Press.

   2000. *Multiliteracies: Literacy Learning and the Design of Social Futures.* London: Routledge.

Cordingley, P., Bell, M., Rundell, B. and Evans, D. 2003. *The Impact of Collaborative CPD on Classroom Teaching and Learning.* London: EPPI-Centre, Social Science Research Unit, Institute of Education, University of London.

Cornoldi, C. and Oakhill, J. (eds.) 1996. *Reading Comprehension Difficulties: Processes and Intervention.* Mahwah, NJ: Erlbaum.

Council of Europe 2007. *Common European Framework of Reference for Languages.* Cambridge University Press.

Cragg, L. and Nation, K. 2006. 'Exploring written narrative in children with poor reading comprehension', *Educational Psychology* **26**: 55–72.

Creese, A., Baraç, T., Bhatt, A., Blackledge, A., Hamid, S., Li Wei, Lytra, V., Martin, P., Wu, C. J. and Yağcıoğlu-Ali, D. 2008. *Investigating Multilingualism in Complementary Schools in Four Communities.* www.esrcsocietytoday.ac.uk/esrcinfocentre/viewawardpage.aspx?awardnumber=RES-000–23–1180

Creese, A. and Blackledge A. 2010. 'Translanguaging in the bilingual classroom: a pedagogy for learning and teaching', *Modern Language Journal* **94**, 1: 103–115.

Crossley-Holland, K. 2004. *How Many Miles to Bethlehem?* London: Orion.

Crystal, D. 1987. 'Teaching vocabulary: the case for a semantic curriculum', *Child Language Teaching and Therapy* 3: 40–56.

1992. *Dictionary of Linguistics and Phonetics.* Oxford: Blackwell.

1996. *Discover Grammar.* London: Longman.

2004. *The Stories of English.* London: Penguin/Allen Lane.

Cummings, L. 2008. *Clinical Linguistics.* Edinburgh University Press.

Cummins, J. 2000. *Language, Power and Pedagogy: Bilingual Children in the Crossfire.* Clevedon: Multilingual Matters.

2001. *Negotiating Identities: Education for Empowerment in a Diverse Society*, 2nd edn. Los Angeles: California Association for Bilingual Education.

2005. 'A proposal for action: strategies for recognizing heritage language competence as a learning resource within the mainstream classroom', *Modern Language Journal* **89**: 585–592.

Cummins, J. and Swain, M. 1986. *Bilingualism in Education.* London: Longmans.

Cutting, L. E. and Scarborough, H. S. 2006. 'Prediction of reading comprehension: relative contributions of word recognition, language proficiency, and other cognitive skills can depend on how comprehension is measured', *Scientific Studies of Reading* **10**: 277–299.

D'Agostino, J. and Murphy, J. 2004. 'A meta-analysis of reading recovery in United States schools', *Educational Evaluation and Policy Analysis* **26**: 23–38.

Darling-Hammond, L. 2000. 'Teacher quality and student achievement: a review of state policy evidence', *Education and Policy Analysis Archives* **8**: 1–35.

Darling-Hammond, L. and Brandford, J. 2005. *Preparing Teachers for a Changing World: What Teachers Should Learn and Be Able to Do.* San Francisco: Jossey-Bass.

Darling-Hammond, L. and Youngs, P. 2002. 'Defining "highly qualified teachers": what does "scientifically-based research" actually tell us?', *Educational Researcher* (December): 13–25.

Datnow, A., Hubbard, L. and Mehan, H. 2002. *Extending Educational Reform: From One School to Many.* New York: RoutledgeFalmer.

Davies, N. 2009. 'View from the chair', *Naldic Quarterly* **6**, 2: 3.

DCSF 2005. *Key Stage 2 Framework, Parts 1 and 2.* London: DCSF Publications.

2007a. *Inclusion Development Programme, ref: 00070–2008DVD-EN.* London: DCSF. www.standards.dcsf.gov.uk

2007b. *Letters and Sounds: Principles and Practice of High Quality Phonics.* http://nationalstrategies.standards.dcsf.gov.uk/node/84969

2007c. *Speech, Language and Communications Review Launched by Ed Balls and Alan Johnson* www.dcsf.gov.uk/pns/DisplayPN.cgi?pn_id=2007_0162

2007d. *Supporting Pupils Learning English as an Additional Language.* http://nationalstrategies.standards.dcsf.gov.uk/node/85117

2008a. *Better Communication: an Action Plan to Improve Services for Children and Young People with Speech, Language and Communication Needs.* London: DCSF Publications.

2008b. *Bercow Review of Services for Children and Young People (0–19) with Speech, Language and Communication Needs.* London: DCSF Publications.

2008c. *Building Brighter Futures: Next Steps for the Children's Workforce.* London: DCSF.

2008d. *Annual Schools Census.* (Department for Business, Innovation and Skills) London: DCSF.

2009a. *Developing Language in the Primary School: Literacy and Primary Languages: the National Strategies Primary.* 00482–2009DWO-EN-01. London: DCSF.

2009b. *The Independent Review of the Primary Curriculum: Final Report.* 00499–2009DOM-EN. London: DCSF.

2009c. *The Independent Review of the Primary Curriculum: Interim Report.* London: DCSF.

2009d. *Primary Framework for Literacy: Learning Objectives.* http://nationalstrategies.standards.dcsf.gov.uk/strands/34758/34266/110198

De Jong, E. J. and Freeman Field, R. 2010. 'Bilingual approaches' in C. Leung and A. Creese (eds.) *English as an Additional Language: Approaches for Teaching Linguistic Minority Students* (London: Sage).

De Jong, J., Orgassa, A., Baker, A. and F. Weerman 2008. 'Bilingual SLI: a cumulative effect of bilingualism and language impairment?' Abstract of paper given at: *Models of Interaction in Bilinguals.* ESRC Conference: Centre for Research on Bilingualism, Bangor. October 2008.

Deacon, S. H. and Kirby, J. R. 2004. 'Morphological awareness: just "more phonological"? The roles of morphological and phonological awareness in reading development', *Applied Psycholinguistics* **25**: 223–238.

Dearing, R. and King, L. 2007. *Languages Review.* London: DfES.

Defoe, D. 1719. *The Life and Adventures of Robinson Crusoe.* London.

Denham, K. and Lobeck, A. (eds.) *Linguistics at School: Language Awareness in Primary and Secondary Education.* Cambridge University Press.

DES 1998. *The National Literacy Strategy.* The Standards Site: Department for Education and Skills www.standards.dfes.gov.uk/primary/publications/literacy/nls_framework/

DfE 2002. *Home Languages in the Literacy Hour.* http://nationalstrategies.standards.dcsf.gov.uk/node/85340?uc=force_uj

DfEE 1997. *Teaching: High Status, High Standards: Circular 10/97.* London: HMSO.

1998a. *The National Literacy Strategy: Literacy Training Pack.* London: DfEE.

1998b. *Meeting Special Educational Needs: a Programme of Action.* London: DFEE.

1998c. *The National Literacy Strategy.* London: DfEE.

1998d. *The National Literacy Strategy: Framework for Teaching.* London: DfEE.

1998e. *Teaching: High Status, High Standards: Requirements for Courses of Initial Teacher Training: Circular 4/98.* London: DfEE.

2000. *The National Literacy Strategy: Grammar for Writing.* London: DfEE.

2001a. *Framework for Teaching English in Years 7, 8 and 9 (Key Stage 3) National Strategy.* London: DfEE.

2002. *Provision for Children's Speech and Language Needs in England and Wales: Facilitating Communication between Education and Health Services.* Nottingham: DfEE.

DfES 2001. *Special Educational Needs Code of Practice.* London: DfES Publications.

2002a. *Languages for All: Languages for Life. A Strategy for England.* Nottingham: DfES Publications.

2003. *Speaking, Listening, Learning: Working with Children in Key Stages 1 and 2: Handbook.* http://nationalstrategies.standards.dcsf.gov.uk/node/84856

2004. *Every Child Matters: Change for Children.* www.dcsf.gov.uk/everychildmatters/

2006. *National Statistics First Release: Special Educational Needs in England.* London: DfES.

Diaz-Rico, L. T. and Weed, K. Z. 2002. *The Crosscultural, Language, and Academic Development Handbook: a Complete K-12 Reference Guide.* Boston: Allyn and Bacon.

Dickson, R. and Smagorinsky, P. 2006. 'Are methods enough? Situating teacher education programs within the multiple settings of learning to teach', *English Education* **38**: 312–328.

Dockrell, J. 2008. 'Strategic models for supporting language competence. Where, what and how?' in *Meeting Children's Needs in Times of Change: Papers from the National Association for Professionals Concerned with Language Impaired Children Residential Conference 2006.* www.naplic.org.uk/?q=node/123

Dockrell, J. and Lindsay, G. 2001. 'Children with specific speech and language difficulties: the teachers' perspective', *Oxford Review of Education* **27**: 369–394.

Dombey, H. 1992 'Lessons learnt at bedtime' in K. Kimberley, M. Meek and J. Miller (eds.) *New Readings* (London: A. and C. Black).

Doonan, J. 1992. *Looking at Pictures in Picture Books.* Stroud: Thimble Press.

Doyé, P. and Hurrell, A. (eds.) 1997. *Foreign Language Learning in Primary Schools.* Strasbourg: Council of Europe.

Dr. Seuss 1979. *I Can Read with My Eyes Shut!* London: Collins.

Driscoll, P. 1999. 'Modern foreign languages in English primary schools: an investigation of two contrasting approaches.' PhD thesis, University of Kent.

Dufficy, P. 2005. *Designing Learning for Diverse Classrooms.* Sydney: Primary English Teaching Association.

Duke, N. K. 2000. '3.6 minutes per day: the scarcity of informational texts in first grade', *Reading Research Quarterly* **35**: 202–224.

Earl, L., Watson, N., Levin, B., Leithwood, K., Fullan, M. and Torrance, N. 2003. *Watching and Learning: OISE/UT Evaluation of the Implementation of the National Literacy and Numeracy Strategies.* Nottingham: DfES Publications.

Education Queensland. *Productive Pedagogies Classroom Observation Manual 2002.* Brisbane: Curriculum Innovation Branch, Education Queensland.

Edwards, A. 2009. 'Becoming a teacher' in H. Daniels, J. Porter and H. Lauder (eds.) *Critical Perspectives on Education* (London: Routledge).

Edwards, A. D. and Westgate, D. P. G. 1994. *Investigating Classroom Talk*, 2nd edn. London: Falmer.

Ehri, L. C., Nunes, S. R., Willows, D. M., Schuster, B. V., Yaghoub-Zadeh, Z. and Shanahan, T. 2001. 'Phonemic awareness instruction helps children learn to read: Evidence from the National Reading Panel's meta-analysis', *Reading Research Quarterly* **36**: 250–287.

Elklan 2009. *Aiming High with Communication*. www.elklan.co.uk

Ellis, S. 2007. 'Policy and research: lessons from the Clackmannanshire synthetic phonics initiative', *Journal of Early Childhood Literacy* **7**: 281–298.

Ellis, S. and Barrs, M. 1996. *The Core Book*. London: CLPE.

Ellis, V. 2007a. *Subject Knowledge and Teacher Education: the Development of Beginning Teachers' Thinking*. London: Continuum.

    2007b. 'Taking subject knowledge seriously: from professional knowledge recipes to complex conceptualisations of teacher development', *Curriculum Journal* **18**: 447–462.

    2007c. 'More than "soldiering on": realising the potential of teacher education to rethink English in schools' in V. Ellis, C. Fox and B. Street (eds.) *Rethinking English in Schools: Towards a New and Constructive Stage* (London: Continuum).

    2008. 'Exploring the contradictions in learning to teach: the potential of developmental work research', *Changing English – Studies in Reading and Culture* **15**: 53–63.

    2010. 'Impoverishing experience: the problem of teacher education in England', *Journal of Education for Teaching* **36**: 105–120.

Ellis, V., Edwards, A. and Smagorinsky, P. (eds.) 2010. *Cultural-Historical Perspectives on Teacher Education and Development: Learning Teaching*. London: Routledge.

Emmorey, K. 1996. 'The confluence of space and langauge in signed languages' in P. Bloom, M. Patterson, L. Nadel and M. Garrett (eds.) *Language and Space* (Cambridge, MA: MIT Press).

Emmott, C. 1999. *Narrative Comprehension: a Discourse Perspective*. Oxford University Press.

Engeström, Y. 2007. 'Putting Vygotsky to work: the change laboratory as an application of double stimulation' in H. Daniels, M. Cole and J. Wertsch (eds.) *Cambridge Companion to Vygotsky* (Cambridge University Press).

Escamilla, K. 2000. 'Bilingual means two' in *A Research Symposium on High Standards in Reading for Students from Diverse Language Groups: Research, Practice and Policy* (Washington, DC: Office of Bilingual Education and Minority Languages Affairs), pp. 100–128.

Evans. J. (ed.) 2009. *Talking Beyond the Page: Reading and Responding to Picturebooks*. London: Routledge.

Fairclough, N. 1989. *Language and Power*. London: Longman.

Feiman-Nemser, S. and Parker, M. B. 1990. 'Making subject matter part of the conversation in learning to teach', *Journal of Teacher Education* **41**, 3: 32–43.

Fillmore, L. W. and Snow, C. E. 2002. 'What teachers need to know about language' in C. T. Adger, C. Snow and D. Christian (eds.) *What Teachers Need to Know about Language* (McHenry, IL: Delta Systems), pp. 7–54.

Fones, D. 2001. 'Blocking them in to free them to act: using writing frames to shape boys' personal responses to literature in the secondary school', *English in Education* **35**, 3: 21–31.

Forbes, J. 2008. 'Knowledge transformations: examining the knowledge needed in teacher and speech and language therapist co-work', *Educational Review* **60**: 141–154.

Foster, H. 2007. *Single Word Reading Test 6–16.* London: NFER-Nelson.

Freebody, P. and Luke, A. 2003. 'Literacy as engaging with new forms of life: the 'four resources' model' in G. Bull and M. Anstey (eds.) *The Literacy Lexicon,* 2nd edn. (Sydney: Pearson Education Australia).

Freedman, A. 1995. 'The what, where, when, why, and how of classroom genres' in J. Petraglia (ed.) *Reconceiving Writing, Rethinking Writing Instruction* (Mahwah, NJ: Erlbaum).

Frey, N. and Fisher, D. 2006. *Language Arts Workshop: Purposeful Reading and Writing Instruction.* Upper Saddle River, NJ: Merrill/Prentice Hall.

Galton, M. J., Croll, P. and Simon, B. 1980. *Inside the Primary Classroom.* London: Routledge.

Galton, M., Hargreaves, L., Comber, C., Wall, D. and Pell, A. 1999. *Inside the Primary Classroom: 20 Years On.* London: Routledge.

Gandra, P. 2002. 'A study of High School Puente: what we have learned about preparing Latino youths for postsecondary education', *Educational Policy* **16**: 474–495.

Garber, M. 2001. *Academic Instincts.* Princeton, NJ: Princeton University Press.

García, O. 2007. 'Foreword' in S. Makoni and A. Pennycook (eds.) *Disinventing and Reconstituting Languages* (Clevedon: Multilingual Matters), p. v.
2009. *Bilingual Education in the 21st Century: a Global Perspective.* Oxford: Wiley-Blackwell.

García, O., Skutnabb-Kangas, T. and Torres-Guzman, M. E. 2006. 'Weaving spaces and (de)constructing ways for multilingual schools: the actual and the imagined' in O. Garcia, T. Skutnabb-Kangas and M. Torres-Guzman (eds.) *Imagining Multilingual School:. Languages in Education and Globalization* (Clevedon: Multilingual Matters), pp. 3–50.

Garmon, M. A. 2004. 'Changing preservice teachers' attitudes/beliefs about diversity', *Journal of Teacher Education* **55**: 201–213.

Gascoigne, M. 2006. *Supporting Children with Speech, Language and Communication Needs within Integrated Children's Services: Royal College of Speech and Language Therapists Position Paper.* London: RCSLT.

Gathercole, S. E. 1995. 'Is nonword repetition a test of phonological memory or long-term knowledge? It all depends on the nonwords', *Memory and Cognition* **23**: 83–94.

Gathercole, S. E. and Baddeley, A. D. 1989. 'Evaluation of the role of phonological STM in the development of vocabulary in children: a longitudinal study', *Journal of Memory and Language* **28**: 200–213.

Gathercole, S. E., Hitch, G. J., Service, E. and Martin, A. J. 1997. 'Short-term memory and new word learning in children', *Developmental Psychology* **33**: 966–979.

Gathercole, V. and Thomas, E. 2007. 'Miami and North Wales, so far and so near: constructivist account of morpho-syntactic development in biligual children.', *International Journal of Bilingual Education and Bilingualism* **10**: 224–247.

2008. *Prawf Geirfa Cymraeg*. Bangor: Bangor University.

Gathercole, S. E., Willis, C., Emslie, H. and Baddeley, A. D. 1992. 'Phonological memory and vocabulary development during the early school years: a longitudinal study', *Developmental Psychology* **28**: 887–898.

Gebhard, M., Demers, J. and Castillo-Rosenthal, Z. 2008. 'Teachers as critical text analysts: L2 literacies and teachers' work in the context of high-stakes school reform', *Journal of Second Language Writing* **17**: 274–291.

Gee, G. 2002. 'Preparing for culturally responsive teaching', *Journal of Teacher Education* **36**: 1–16.

Gerald, D. E. and Hussar, W. J. 2003. *Projections of education statistics to 2013*. Washington, DC: National Center for Education Statistics.

Gibbons, P. 2002. *Scaffolding Language, Scaffolding Learning: Teaching Second Language Learners in the Mainstream Classroom*. Portsmouth, NH: Heinemann.

2003. 'Mediating language learning: teacher interactions with ESL students in a content-based classroom', *TESOL Quarterly* **37**: 247–273.

2008. ' "It was taught good and I learned a lot": intellectual practices and ESL learners in the middle years', *Australian Journal of Language and Literacy* **31**: 155–173.

2009. *Challenging Expectations: Literacy, Intellectual Quality and English Language Learners in the Middle Years*. Portsmouth, NH: Heinemann.

Gibson, J. J. 1979. *The Ecological Approach to Visual Perception*. Boston, MA: Houghton Mifflin.

Gillon, G. T. 2005. 'Facilitating phoneme awareness development in 3- and 4-year-old children with speech impairment', *Language, Speech and Hearing Services in Schools* **36**: 308–324.

2003. *Phonological Awareness: From Research to Practice*. New York: Guilford Press.

Giroux, H. and McLaren, P. 1986. 'Teacher education and the politics of engagement: the case for democratic schooling', *Harvard Educational Review* **56**: 213–238.

Golombek, P. 1998. 'A study of language teachers' personal practical knowledge', *TESOL Quarterly* **32**: 447–464.

Gonzalez, N., Moll, L. C. and Amanti, C. 2005. *Funds of Knowledge: Theorizing Practices in Households, Communities, and Classrooms*. Mahwah, NJ: Erlbaum.

Goswami, U. and Bryant, P. 2007. *Children's Cognitive Development and Learning* (Primary Review Research study 2/1a). Cambridge: University of Cambridge Faculty of Education.

Gouch, K. and Lambirth, A. 2008. *Understanding Phonics and the Teaching of Reading: Critical Perspectives*. Maidenhead: McGraw-Hill/Open University Press.

Gough, P. and Tunmer, W. 1986. 'Decoding, reading, and reading disability', *Remedial and Special Education* **7**: 6–10.

Gourevitch, P. (ed.) 2007. *The Paris Review Interviews*, vol. II. Edinburgh: Canongate.

Graham, S., Morphy, P., Harris, K., Fink-Chorzempa, B., Saddler, B., Moran, S. and Mason, L. 2008. 'Teaching spelling in the primary grades: a national survey of instructional practices and adaptations', *American Educational Research Journal* **45**: 796–825.

Granger, S., Hung, J. and Petch-Tyson, S. (eds.) 2002. *Computer Learner Corpora: Second Language Acquisition and Foreign Language Teaching*. Amsterdam: John Benjamins.

Grant, R. A. and Wong, S. D. 2003. 'Barriers to literacy for language minority learners: an argument for change in the literacy education profession.' *Journal of Adolescent and Adult Literacy* **46**: 386–394.

Greaves, M. 1990. *Tattercoats.* London: Frances Lincoln.

Green, L., McCutchen, D., Schwiebert, C., Quinlan, T., Eva-Wood, A. and Juelis, J. 2003. 'Morphological development in children's writing', *Journal of Educational Psychology* **95**: 752–761.

Greeno, J. 1994. 'Gibson's affordances', *Psychological Review* **101**: 336–342.

Gregory, A. 1996. 'Primary foreign language teaching – influences, attitudes and effects.' MEd thesis, University of Leeds.

Grosjean, F. 2008. 'My favourite myths around bilingualism', *Bilingual Family Newsletter* **25**: 4–5.

Guardian 2008. 'Teacher shortage in key subjects feared'. www.guardian.co.uk/uk/2008/feb/07/teachershortage.teachertraining

Gubb, J. 1982. '"A dog I wons new" – the logic of non-standard spelling', *Remedial Education* **17**, 2: 70–74.

Guberina, P. (1991). 'Rôle de la perception auditive dans l'apprentissage précoce des enfants', in M. Garabédian (ed.) *Enseignements/Apprentissage précoces des langues* (Paris: Hachette), pp. 67–70.

Gudmunsdottir, S. 1991. 'Values in pedagogical content knowledge', *Journal of Teacher Education* **41**, 3: 44–52.

Hagger, H. 1997. 'Enabling student teachers to gain access to the professional craft knowledge of experienced teachers' in P. Benton (ed.) *The Oxford Internship Scheme* (London: Paul Chapman).

Hagley, F. 1987. *The Suffolk Reading Scale.* Windsor: NFER-Nelson.

Hall, C. 2008. 'Imagination and multi-modality: reading picture books and anxieties about childhood' in L. Sipe and S. Pantaleo (eds.) *Postmodern Picture Books: Play, Parody and Self-referentiality* (London: Routledge), pp. 130–147.

Hall, K. 2002. *Listening to Stephen Read: Multiple Perspectives on Literacy.* London: Open University Press.

2010. 'Significant lines of research in reading pedagogy' in K. Hall, U. Goswami, C. Harrison, S. Ellis and J. Soler (eds.) *Interdisciplinary Perspectives on Learning to Read* (London: Routledge).

Hall, K., Goswami, U., Harrison, C., Ellis, S. and Soler, J. (eds.) 2010. *Interdisciplinary Perspectives on Learning to Read: Culture, Cognition and Pedagogy.* London: Routledge.

Hall, K. M. and Sabey, B. L. 2007. 'Focus on the facts: Using informational texts effectively in early elementary classrooms', *Early Childhood Education Journal* **35**: 261–268.

Halliday, M. A. K. 1978. *Language as Social Semiotic: the Social Interpretation of Language and Meaning.* London: Edward Arnold.

1994. *An Introduction to Functional Grammar*, 2nd edn. London: Edward Arnold.

Hammond, J. (ed.) 2001. *Scaffolding: Teaching and Learning in Language and Literacy Education.* Sydney: Primary English Teaching Association.

Hammond, J. 2008. 'Intellectual challenge and ESL students: implications of quality teaching initiatives', *Australian Journal of Language and Literacy* **31**, 2: 128–154.

Hammond, J. and Derewianka, B. 1999. 'ESL and literacy education: revisiting the relationship', *Prospect: a Journal of Australian TESOL* **14**, 2: 24–39.

Hammond, J. and Gibbons, P. 2005. 'Putting scaffolding to work: the contribution of scaffolding in articulating ESL education', *Prospect* **20**, 1: 6–30.

Hancock, T. 2009. 'How linguistics can inform the teaching of writing' in R. Beard, D. Myhill, J. Riley and M. Nystrand (eds.) *International Handbook of Writing Development* (London: SAGE).

Hargreaves, A. (1998). 'Contrived collegiality: the micropolitics of teacher collaboration' in N. Bennett, M. Crawford and C. Riches (eds.) *Managing Change in Education* (London: Paul Chapman).

Harmon, J. M., Hedrick, W. B., Strecker, S.K. and Martinez, M. G. 2001. 'Field experiences in reading: contextualizing and tailoring a reading specialization program', *Reading Professor* **23**: 49–77.

Harpaz, Y. and Lefstein, A. 2000. 'Communities of thinking', *Educational Leadership* **58**, 3: 54–57.

Harper, C., Cook, K. and James, C. 2010. 'Content-language integrated approaches for teachers of EAL learners: examples of reciprocal teaching' in C. Leung and A. Creese (eds.) *English as an Additional Language: Approaches for Teaching Linguistic Minority Students* (London: Sage).

Harpin, W. 1976. *The Second R: Writing Development in the Junior School.* London: Unwin.

Harris, J. and Conway, M. 2002. *Modern Languages in Irish Primary Schools.* Dublin: Institúid Teangeolaíochta Éireann.

Harris, R. 1986. *The Origin of Writing.* London: Duckworth.

Hart, S., Dixon, A., Drummond, M. J. and McIntyre, D. 2004. *Learning Without Limits.* Buckingham: Open University Press.

Hartas, D. 2004. 'Teacher and speech-language therapist collaboration: being equal and achieving a common goal?', *Child Language Teaching and Therapy* **20**: 33–54.

Hartshorne, M. 2006. *The Cost to the Nation of Children's Poor Communication.* I CAN Talk Papers Series 2. London: I CAN.

Hartshorne, M., Bush, M. and Daly, S. 2002. *Explaining Speech, Language and Communication Needs.* London: Communications Trust.

Haviland, J. 1988. *Take care, Mr Baker!* London: Fourth Estate.

Hayes, J. R. 2006. 'New directions in writing theory' in C. MacArthur, S. Graham and J. Fitzgerald (eds.) *Handbook of Writing Research* (New York: Guilford Press), pp. 28–40.

Heald, R. 2008. 'Musicality in the language of picture books', *Children's Literature in Education* **39**: 227–235.

Heap, J. 1991. 'A situated perspective on what counts as reading' in A. Luke and C. Baker (eds.) *Towards a Critical Sociology of Reading* (Amsterdam: John Benjamins).

Heath, S. B. 1982. 'What no bedtime story means: narrative skills at home and school', *Language and Society* **11**: 49–76.

1983. *Ways with Words: Language, Life, and Work in Communities and Classrooms.* Cambridge University Press.

2000. 'Seeing our way into learning', *Cambridge Journal of Education* **30**: 121–132.

2004. 'Learning language and strategic thinking through the arts', *Reading Research Quarterly* **39**, 3: 8–12.

Heath, S. B. and Wolf, S. 2005. 'Focus in creative learning: drawing on art for language development', *Literacy* **39**: 38–45.

Higher Education Funding Council 2009. *Research Assessment Exercise 2008: Education Unit of Assessment Panel Report*. London: HEFC.

Heller, M. 1999. *Linguistic Minorities and Modernity: a Sociolinguistic Ethnography*. London/New York: Longman.

Henderson, E. H. and Templeton, S. 1986. 'A developmental perspective of formal spelling instruction through alphabet, pattern, and meaning', *Elementary School Journal* **86**: 304–316.

Hill, E. 1980. *Where's Spot?* London: Picture Puffin.

Hill, H. C., Rowan, B. and Ball, D. L. 2005. 'Effects of teachers' mathematical knowledge for teaching on student achievement', *American Educational Research Journal* **42**: 371–406.

Hill, H. C., Schilling, S. G. and Ball, D. L. 2004. 'Developing measures of teachers' mathematics knowledge for teaching', *Elementary School Journal* **105**: 11–30.

Hillocks, G. 1984. 'What works in teaching composition: a meta-analysis of experimental treatment studies', *American Journal of Education* **93**: 133–170.

1986. *Research on Written Composition: New Directions for Teaching*. www.ncrll.org/Hillocks_ResearchOnWrittenComposition.pdf

1999. *Ways of Thinking, Ways of Teaching*. New York: Teachers College Press.

HM Government 2004. *Every Child Matters: Change for Children*. London: Department for Education and Skills.

HMSO 1988. *Education Reform Act 1988*. London: HMSO.

Hoffman, J. V. and Pearson, P. D. 2000. 'Reading teacher education in the net millennium: what your grandmother's teacher didn't know that your granddaughter's teacher should', *Reading Research Quarterly* **35**: 28–44.

Hoffman, L. and Sable, J. 2006. *Public Elementary and Secondary Students, Staff, Schools and School Districts: School Year 2003–04*. www.nces.ed.gov/pubs2006/2006307.pdf

Homza, A., Ngo, S. F. and Mitchell, K. 2008. 'Fieldwork with bilingual learners.' Paper presented at American Education Researchers Association Annual Conference, New York, 25 March.

Hooper, S. J., Roberts, J. E., Zeisel, S. A. and Poe, M. 2003. 'Core language predictors of behavioural functioning in early elementary school children: concurrent and longitudinal findings', *Behavioral Disorders* **29**: 10–21.

Hornberger, N. 2005. 'Opening and filling up implementational and ideological spaces in heritage language education', *Modern Language Journal* **89**: 605–609.

2009. 'Multilingual education policy and practice: ten certainties (grounded in Indigenous experience)', *Language Teaching* **42**: 197–211.

Hornberger, N. and Skilton-Sylvester, E. 2000. 'Revisiting the continua of biliteracy: international and critical perspective', *Language and Education* **14**: 96–122.

House of Commons Children Schools and Families Committee 2009. *National Curriculum*. Fourth report of session 2008–09. Vol. I. London: House of Commons.

House of Commons Education and Skills Committee 2006. *Special Educational Needs*. Third report of session. Vol. I. London: The Stationery Office.

Howe, C. and Mercer, N. 2007. *Children's Social Development, Peer Interaction and Classroom Learning (Primary Review Interim report 2/1b)*. www.theprimaryreview. org.uk

Hudson, R. and Walmsley, J. 2005. 'The English patient: English grammar and teaching in the twentieth century', *Journal of Linguistics* **41**: 593–622.

Hughes, T. 1987. 'To parse or not to parse: the poet's answer'. *The Sunday Times* 22 November.

Hunston, S. 1995. 'Grammar in teacher education: the role of a corpus', *Language Awareness* **4**: 15–31.

2002. *Corpora in Applied Linguistics*. Cambridge University Press.

Hunt, K. W. 1965. *Grammatical Structures Written at Three Grade Levels*. Champaign, IL: NCTE.

Hurrell, A. and Satchwell, P. (eds.) 1996. *Reflections on Modern Languages in Primary Education*. London: The Centre for Information on Language Teaching.

Hutchins, E. 1996. *Cognition in the Wild* (new edn). Cambridge, MA: MIT Press.

Hutchins, P. 1969. *Rosie's Walk*. London: Bodley Head.

I CAN 2001. *Joint Professional Development Framework*. London: I CAN.

2008. *Primary Talk*. London: I CAN.

2009. *Make Chatter Matter Campaign*. London: I CAN.

Inkpen, M. 2000. *In Wibbly's Garden*. London: Hodder.

Institute of Education 2009. *English as an Additional Language (EAL) Provision in Schools – 10 Case Studies*. Report produced by the Institute of Education under contract from the Training and Development Agency for Schools. www.nrdc.org. uk/uploads/documents/doc_4429.pdf

International Technology Association (ITEA) 2009. *Condensed Glossary*. www. iteaconnect.org/TAA/Resources/TAA_Glossary.html

Jacobson, R. and Faltis, C. (eds.) 1990. *Language Distribution Issues in Bilingual Schooling*. Clevedon: Multilingual Matters.

Jaffré, J. P. 1997. 'From writing to orthography: the functions and limits of the notion of system' in C. A. Perfetti, L. Rieben and M. Fayol (eds.) *Learning to Spell: Research, Theory, and Practice across Languages* (Mahwah, NJ: Erlbaum), pp. 3–20.

Jajdelska, E. 2007. *Silent Reading and the Birth of the Narrator*. Toronto: University of Toronto Press.

Janks, H. 2009. 'Writing: a critical literacy perspective' in R. Beard, D. Myhill, J. Riley and M. Nystrand (eds.) *International Handbook of Writing Development* (London: Sage).

Jaworski, A. 1993. *The Power of Silence: Social and Pragmatic Perspectives*. London: Sage.

Johannessen, L. and McCann, T. 2008. 'Adolescents who struggle with literacy' in L. Christenbury, R. Bomer and P. Smagorinsky (eds.) *Handbook of Adolescent Literacy Research* (New York: Guilford Press).

Jóhannsdóttir, T. 2010. 'Deviations from the conventional: contradictions as sources of change in teacher education' in V. Ellis, A. Edwards and P. Smagorinsky (eds.) *Cultural-Historical Perspectives on Teacher Education and Development: Learning Teaching* (London: Routledge).

Johnson, S., Dunn, K. and Coldron, J. 2005. *Mapping Qualifications and Training for the Children and Young People's Workforce*. Sheffield: Sheffield Hallam University.

Johnson, T. S., Smagorinsky, P., Thompson, L. and Fry, P. G. 2003. 'Learning to teach the five-paragraph theme', *Research in the Teaching of English* **38**: 136–176.

Johnson-Glenberg, M. C. 2005. 'Web-based training of metacognitive strategies for text comprehension: focus on poor comprehenders', *Reading and Writing* **18**: 755–786.

Johnston, K. and Hayes, D. 2008. ' "This is as good as it gets": classroom lessons and learning in challenging circumstances', *Australian Journal of Language and Literacy* **31**, 2: 109–127.

Johnstone, R. 1994. *Teaching Modern Languages at Primary School*. Edinburgh: Scottish Council for Research in Education.

Juel, C. and Minden-Cupp, C. 2000. 'Learning to read words: linguistic units and instructional strategies', *Reading Research Quarterly* **35**: 458–492.

Kahan, J. A., Cooper, D. A. and Betha, K. A. 2003. 'The role of mathematics teachers' content knowledge in their teaching: a framework for research applied to a study of student teachers', *Journal of Mathematics Teacher Education* **6**: 223–252.

Keenan, J. M. and Betjemann, R. S. 2006. 'Comprehending the gray oral reading test without reading it: why comprehension tests should not include passage-independent items', *Scientific Studies of Reading* **10**: 363–380.

Keenan, J. M., Betjemann, R. S. and Olson, R. K. 2008. 'Reading comprehension tests vary in the skills they assess: differential dependence on decoding and oral comprehension', *Scientific Studies of Reading* **12**: 281–300.

Keith, G. 1997. 'Teach yourself English grammar', *English and Media Magazine* 36.

Kellogg, R. T. 2008. 'Training writing skills: a cognitive developmental perspective', *Journal of Writing Research* **1**: 1–26.

Kelman, M. and Apel, K. 2004. 'The effects of a multiple linguistic, prescriptive approach to spelling instruction: a case study', *Communication Disorders Quarterly* **25**, 2: 56–66.

Kenner, C. 2004. 'Living in simultaneous worlds: difference and integration in bilingual script learning', *International Journal of Bilingual Education and Bilingualism* **7**: 43–61.

Kenner, C., Ruby, M., Gregory, E. and Al-Azami, S. 2007. 'How research can link policy and practice: bilingualism as a learning resource for second and third generation children', *NALDIC Quarterly* **5**: 10–13.

Kershner, R. and Howard, J. 2006. *Psychology of Education Review* [Themed issue – Open Dialogue on Phonics Teaching in Teaching of Reading] **30**, 2: 1–60.

Kintsch, W. and Rawson, K. A. 2007. 'Comprehension' in M. J. Snowling and C. Hulme (eds.) *The Science of Reading: a Handbook* (Oxford: Blackwell), pp. 209–226.

Kirk, C. and Gillon, G.T. 2008. 'Integrated morphological awareness intervention as a tool for improving literacy', *Language, Speech, and Hearing Services in Schools* **40**: 341–351.

Kirsch, I., *et al.* de Jong, J., Lafontaine, D., McQueen, J., Mendelovits, J. and Monseur, C. 2002. *Reading for Change: Performance and Engagement across Countries: Results from PISA 2000*. Paris: OECD.

Kolb, D. 1984. *Experiential Learning as the Science of Learning and Development*. Englewood Cliffs, NJ: Prentice Hall.

Krauss, S., Brunner, M., Kunter, M., Baumert, J., Blum, W., Neubrand, M. and Jordan, A. *et al.* 2008. 'Pedagogical content knowledge and content knowledge of secondary mathematics teachers', *Journal of Educational Psychology* **100**: 716–725.

Kress, G. 1989. *Linguistic Processes in Sociocultural Practice*, 2nd edn. Oxford University Press.

1994. *Learning to Write*. London: Routledge.

1997. *Before Writing: Rethinking the Paths to Literacy*. London: Routledge.

1999. 'Genre and the changing contexts for English language arts', *Language Arts* **76**: 461–458.

Kress, G. and van Leeuwen, T. 2001. *Reading Images: the Grammar of Visual Design*. London: Routledge.

Kucer, S. B. 2001. *Dimesions of literacy: a conceptual base for teaching reading and writing in school settings*. Mahwah, NJ: Lawrence Erlbaum.

Labov, W. 1972. 'The logic of non-standard English' in A. Cashdan and E. Grugeon (eds.) *Language in Education: a Source Book* (London: Routledge and Kegan Paul).

1978. *Language in the Inner City: Studies in the Black English Vernacular*. Philadelphia, PA: University of Philadelphia Press.

Lanza, E. 1997. *Language Mixing in Infant Bilingualism*. Oxford University Press.

Lave, J. 1988. *Cognition in Practice*. Cambridge University Press.

Lave, J. and Wenger, E. 1991. *Situated Learning: Legitimate Peripheral Participation*. Cambridge University Press.

Law, J. (ed.) 1992. *The Early Identification of Language Impairment in Children*. London: Chapman and Hall.

Law, J., Boyle, J., Harris, F., Harkness, A. and Nye, C. 1998. 'Screening for speech and language delay: a systematic review of the literature', *Health Technology Assessment* **2,** 9: 1–184.

Law, J., Lindsay, G., Peacey, N., Gascoigne, M., Soloff, N., Radford, J. and Band, S. 2002. 'Consultation as a model for providing speech and language therapy in schools: a panacea or one step too far?', *Child Language Teaching and Therapy* **18**: 145–163.

Leach, J. and Moon, B. 2000. 'Pedagogy, information and communications technology and teachers' professional knowledge', *Curriculum Journal* **11**: 385–404.

Learning and Teaching Scotland 2009. *Curriculum for Excellence*. www.ltscotland.org.uk/curriculumforexcellence/index.asp

Lee, C. D. 2007. *The Role of Culture in Academic Literacies: Conducting our Blooming in the Midst of the Whirlwind*. New York: Teachers College Press.

Lee, W. 2008. *Speech, Language and Communication Needs and Primary School-aged Children*. London: I CAN.

Lefstein, A. 2005. 'Teacher enactments of the English National Literacy Strategy: an extended case study.' Doctoral dissertation, King's College London.

2008. 'Changing classroom practice through the English National Literacy Strategy: a micro-interactional perspective', *American Educational Research Journal* **45**: 701–737.

2010 'More helpful as problem than solution: some implications of situating dialogue in classrooms' in K. Littleton and C. Howe (eds.) *Educational Dialogues: Understanding and Promoting Productive Interaction* (London: Routledge).

Lemke, J. 1990. *Talking Science: Language, Learning and Values*. Norwood, NJ: Ablex.

Leonard, L. B. 1998. *Children with Specific Language Impairment*. Cambridge, MA: MIT Press.

Leonard, L., Wong, A. M-Y., Deevy, P., Stokes, S. F. and Fletcher, P. 2006. 'The production of passives by children with specific language impairment: acquiring English or Cantonese', *Applied Psycholinguistics* **27**: 267–299.

Leong, C. K. 1989. 'The effects of morphological structure on reading proficiency – a developmental study', *Reading and Writing: an Interdisciplinary Journal* **1**: 357–379.

Levinson, S. C. 1979. 'Activity types and language', *Linguistics* **17**: 356–399.

Levy, R. 2009. 'Children's perceptions of reading and the use of reading scheme texts', *Cambridge Journal of Education* **39**: 361–377.

Lewis, D. 2001. *Reading Contemporary Picture books: Picturing the Texts*. London: RoutledgeFalmer.

Lewis, M. and Ellis, S. (eds.) 2006. *Phonics: Practice Research and Policy*. London: Paul Chapman.

Lewis, M. and Wray, D. 1995. *Developing Children's Non-fiction Writing*. Leamington Spa: Scholastic.

Lewis, S. and Speake, J. 1997. 'When is a rolling pin a "roll the pen": a clinical insight into lexical problems' in S. Chiat, J. Law and J. Marshall (eds.) *Language Disorders in Children and Adults* (London: Whurr), pp. 77–101.

Leyden, J., Stackhouse, J. and Szczerbinski, M. 2007. 'Language and Social Disadvantage', Presentation at Afasic Fourth International Symposium, University of Warwick, UK, April 2007.

Lin, A. M. Y. 1999. 'Doing-English-lessons in the reproduction or transformation of social worlds?', *TESOL Quarterly* **33**: 393–412.

Lin, A. M. Y. and Martin, P. (eds.) 2005. *Decolonisation, Globalisation. Language-in-Education Policy and Practice*. Clevedon: Multilingual Matters.

Lindsay, G. 2003. 'Inclusive education: a critical perspective', *British Journal of Special Education* **30**: 3–12.

    2007. 'Educational psychology and the effectiveness of inclusive education/mainstreaming', *British Journal of Educational Psychology* **77**: 1–24.

Lindsay, G. and Dockrell, J. 2002. 'Meeting the needs of children with speech, language and communication needs: a critical perspective on inclusion and collaboration', *Child Language Teaching and Therapy* **18**: 91–101.

Lindsay, G., Dockrell, J. and Palikara, O. 2010. 'Self-esteem of adolescents with specific language impairment as they move from compulsory education', *International Journal of Language and Communication Disorders*, **45**: 561–571.

Lindsay, G., Soloff, N., Law, J., Band, S., Peacey, N., Gascoigne, M. and Radford, J. 2002. 'Speech and language therapy services to education in England and Wales', *International Journal of Language and Communication Disorders* **37**: 273–288.

Littleton, K. and Howe, C. 2010. *Educational Dialogues: Understanding and Promoting Productive Interaction*. London: Routledge.

Lo Bianco, J. and Freebody, P. 1997. *Australian Literacies: Informing National Policy on Literacy Education*. Canberra: Commonwealth of Australia.

Loban, W. 1976. *Language Development: Kindergarten through Grade Twelve (Research Report 18)*. Urbana, IL: National Council of Teachers of English.

Locke, A., Ginsborg J. and Peers, I. 2002. 'Development and disadvantage: implications for the early years and beyond', *International Journal of Language and Communication Disorders* **37**: 3–15.

Locke, J. 1693. *Some Thoughts Concerning Education*. Menston: Scolar Press facsimile reprint, 1970.

Locke, T. 2009. 'Grammar and writing: the international debate' in R. Beard, D. Myhill, J. Riley and M. Nystrand (eds.) *International Handbook of Writing Development* (London: SAGE).

Lokan, J., Greenwood, L. and Cresswell, J. 2000. *15-Up and Counting, Reading, Writing and Reasoning ... How Literate are Australia's Students?* Report of Results from Programme for International Students Assessment (PISA). Melbourne: Australian Council for Educational Research.

Lortie, D. C. 1975. *Schoolteacher: a Sociological Study*. Chicago: University of Chicago Press.

Low, L. (ed.) 1996. *MLPS in Scotland. Practice and Prospects. Proceedings of a Conference, Stirling, 1996.* Stirling: Scottish Centre for Information on Language Teaching.

Low, L. 1999. 'Modern languages' in T. Bryce and W. Humes (eds.) *Scottish Education*. Edinburg: Edinburgh University Press.

Lucas, T., Villegas, A. M. and Freedson-Gonzalez, M. 2008. 'Linguistically responsive teacher education: preparing classroom teachers to teach English language learners', *Journal of Teacher Education* **59**: 361–373.

Luke, A. 1993. 'The social construction of literacy in the primary school' in L. Unsworth (ed.) *Literacy Learning and Teaching: Language as Social Practice in the Primary School*. Melbourne: Macmillan Education.

Lyon, G. R. 1998, April 28. 'Overview of reading and literacy initiatives: Statement of G. Reid Lyon. Testimony before the Senate Committee on Labor and Human Resources'. www.eric.ed.gov/ERICDocs/data/ericdocs2sql/content_storage_01/0000019b/80/16/61/c9.pdf

MacDonald, M. 1995. *The Old Woman Who Lived in a Vinegar Bottle: a British Fairy Tale*. Little Rock, AR: August House.

Macken-Horarik, M. 1996. 'Literacy and learning across the curriculum: towards a model of register for secondary school teachers' in R. Hasan and G. Williams (eds.) *Literacy in Society* (New York: Addison Wesley Longman), pp. 232–278.

Macquitty, M. 1994. *Eyewitness Guides: Desert*. London: Dorling Kindersley.

Marshall, J., Ralph, S. and Palmer, S. 2002. 'I wasn't trained to work with them: Mainstream teachers' attitudes to children with speech and language difficulties', *International Journal of Inclusive Education* **6**: 199–215.

Marshall, J., Stojanovik, V. and Ralph, S. 2002. 'I never gave it a second thought: PGCE students,' attitudes towards the inclusion of children with speech and language impairments', *International Journal of Language and Communication Disorders* **37**: 475–489.

Martin, J. 1985. *Factual Writing*. Geelong, Victoria: Deakin University Press.

Martin, P. 2005. ' "Safe" Language practices in two rural schools in Malaysia: tensions between policy and practice' in A. M. Lin and P. W. Martin (eds.) *Decolonisation, Globalisation: Language-in-Education Policy and Practice* (Clevedon: Multilingual Matters), pp. 74–98.

Martin, P., Bhatt, A., Bhojani, N. and Creese, A. 2006. 'Managing bilingual interaction in a Gujarati complementary school in Leicester', *Language and Education* **20**: 5–22.

Martin-Jones, M. and Saxena, M. 2003. 'Bilingual resources and "Funds of Knowledge" for teaching and learning in multi-ethnic classrooms in Britain', *International Journal of Bilingual Education and Bilingualism* **6**: 267–282.

Marton, K., Abramoff, B. and Rosenzweig, S. 2005. 'Social cognition and language in children with specific language impairment (SLI)', *Journal of Communication Disorders* **38**: 143–162.

Masterson, J. J. and Apel, K. 2000. 'Spelling assessment: charting a path to optimal intervention', *Topics in Language Disorders* **20**, 3: 50–65.

——— 2007. 'Spelling and word-level reading: a multilinguistic approach' in A. G. Kamhi, J. J. Masterson and K. Apel (eds.) *Clinical Decision Making in Developmental Language Disorders* (Baltimore, MD: Brookes Publishing), pp. 249–266.

Masterson, J. and Crede, L. 1999. 'Learning to spell: Implications for assessment and intervention', *Language, Speech, and Hearing Services in Schools* **30**: 243–254.

Masterson, J., Lee, S. and Apel, K. 2008. 'The spelling sensitivity score: a measure of children's developing linguistic knowledge', Poster presented at the *XI International Congress for the Study of Child Language*, July 2008, Edinburgh.

Masterson, J., Apel, K. and Wasowicz, J. 2006. *SPELL-2: Spelling Performance Evaluation for Language and Literacy*. Evanston, IL: Learning By Design.

Maun, I. and Myhill, D. A. 2005. 'Text as design, writers as designers', *English in Education* **39**, 2: 5–21.

Max, C. 2010. 'Learning-for-teaching across educational boundaries: an activity theoretical analysis' in V. Ellis, A. Edwards and P. Smagorinsky (eds.) *Cultural-Historical Perspectives on Teacher Education and Development: Learning Teaching* (London: Routledge).

Maybin, J. 2006. *Children's Voices: Talk, Knowledge and Identity*. Basingstoke: Palgrave Macmillan.

Maybin, J. and Moss, G. 1993. 'Talk about text: reading as a social event', *Journal of Research in Reading* **16**: 138–147.

McCartney, E. (ed.) 2007a. *The Language Therapy Manual*. www.strath.ac.uk/humanities/speechlanguagetherapy/resources

——— (ed.) 2007b. *The Language Support Model for Teachers*. www.strath.ac.uk/humanities/speechlanguagetherapy/resources

——— 2009. 'Joining up working: terms, types and tensions' in J. Forbes and C. Watson (eds.) *Service Integration in Schools: Research and Policy Discourses, Practices and Future Prospects* (Rotterdam: Sense), pp. 23–36.

McCartney, E., Boyle, J., Ellis, S., Bannatyne, S. and Turnbull, M. 2010. 'Indirect language therapy for children with persistent language impairment in mainstream primary schools: outcomes from a cohort intervention', *International Journal of Language and Communication Disorders*. Online 26 Mar 2010.

McCartney, E., Ellis, S. and Boyle, J. 2009. 'The mainstream primary classroom as a language-learning environment for children with severe and persistent language impairment: implications of recent language intervention research', *Journal of Research in Special Educational Needs* **9**, 2: 80–90.

McCartney, E., Ellis, S., Boyle, J., Turnbull, M. and Kerr, J. 2010. 'Developing a language support model for mainstream primary school teachers', *Child Language Teaching and Therapy* **26**, 3: 359–374.

McCracken, T. and Gibbs, S. 2001. *NCTE/NCATE Research Project on the Preparation of Teachers of English Language Arts: Final Report*. Urbana, IL: NCTE.

McCutchen, D., Abbott, R. D., Green, L. B., Beretvas, S. N., Cox, S., Potter, N. S., Quiroga, T. and Gray, A. L. 2002. 'Beginning literacy: links among teacher knowledge, teacher practice, and student learning', *Journal of Learning Disabilities* **35**: 69–86.

McDermott, R. and Raley, J. 2008. 'The tell-tale body: the constitution of disability in schools' in W. Ayers, T. Quinn and D. Stoval (eds.) *Handbook of Social Justice in Education* (Mahwah, NJ: Erlbaum), pp. 431–445.

McDermott, R. and Tylbor, H. 1983. 'On the necessity of collusion in conversation', *Text* **3**: 277–297.

McDonald, T. 2008. *Positively Plurilingual*. London: Centre for Information on Language Teaching.

McEnery, T., Wilson, A. and Barker, P. 1997. 'Teaching grammar again after twenty years: corpus-based help for teaching grammar', *ReCALL* **9**, 2: 8–16.

McGregor, K. K., Newman, R. M., Reilly, R. M. and Capone, N. C. 2002. 'Semantic representation and naming in children with specific language impairment', *Journal of Speech, Language, and Hearing Research* **45**: 998–1014.

McGuinness, D. 1997. 'Decoding strategies as predictors of reading skill: a follow-on study', *Annals of Dyslexia* **47**: 117–150.

McKee, D. 2004. *The Conquerors*. London: Andersen Press.

Medwell, J., Wray, D., Poulson, L. and Fox, R. 1998. *Effective Teachers of Literacy*. Exeter: School of Education and Teacher Training Agency.

Meek, M. 1988. *How Texts Teach What Readers Learn*. Stroud: Thimble Press.

Mehan, H. 1979. *Learning Lessons: Social Organization in the Classroom*. Cambridge, MA: Harvard University Press.

  1992. 'Understanding inequality in school: the contribution of interpretive studies', *Sociology of Education* **65**: 1–20.

Mehta, P., Foorman, B. R., Branum-Martin, L. and Taylor, P. W. 2005. 'Literacy is a unidimensional construct: validation, sources of influence, and implications in a longitudinal study in grades 1 to 4', *Scientific Studies of Reading* **9**, 2: 85–116.

Menyuk, P. and Brisk, M. E. 2005. *Language Development and Education: Children with Varying Language Experience*. New York: Palgrave Macmillan.

Mercer, N. 1994. 'Neo-Vygotskian theory and classroom education' in B. Steirer and J. Maybin (eds.) *Language Literacy and Learning in Educational Practice* (Clevedon: Multilingual Matters), pp. 92–110.

  2000. *Words and Minds: How We Use Language to Think Together*. London: Routledge.

  2008. 'Talk and the development of reasoning and understanding', *Human Development* **51**: 90–100.

Michaels, S., O'Connor, C. and Resnick, L. B. 2008. 'Deliberative discourse idealized and realized: accountable talk in the classroom and in civic life', *Studies in Philosophy and Education* **27**: 283–297.

Miller, C. 1991. 'The needs of teachers of children with speech and language disorders', *Child Language Teaching and Therapy* **7**: 179–191.

Miller, C. J. 1984. 'Genre as social action', *Quarterly Journal of Speech* **70**: 151–167.

Mitchell, R., Martin, C. and Grenfell, M. 1992. *Evaluation of the Basingstoke Primary Schools Language Awareness Project for Language Education*. Southampton: University of Southampton Centre for Language in Education.

Mittins, W. 1988. *English: Not the Naming of Parts*. London: National Association for the Teaching of English.

Moats, L. C. and Foorman, B. R. 2003. 'Measuring teachers' content knowledge of language and reading', *Annals of Dyslexia* **53**: 23–45.

Moll, L. C., Amanti, C., Neff, D. and Gonzalez, N. 1992. 'Funds of knowledge for teaching: Using a qualitative approach to connect homes and classrooms', *Theory into Practice* **31**, 2: 132–141.

Moll, L. C. and Arnot-Hopffer, E. 2005. 'Sociocultural competence in teacher education', *Journal of Teacher Education* **56**, 3: 25–36.

Moll, L. C. and Gonzalez, N. 2004. 'Engaging life: a funds of knowledge approach to multicultural education' in J. A. Banks and C. A. Banks (eds.) *Handbook of Research on Multicultural Education*, 2nd edn. (San Francisco: Jossey-Bass), pp. 699–715.

Moon, J. 2004. *Reflection in Learning and Professional Development: Theory and Practice*. London: RoutledgeFalmer.

Morgan, L. 2008. *Speech, Language and Communication and the Children's Workforce*. London: I CAN.

Moss, G. 2007. *Literacy and Gender: Researching Texts, Contexts and Readers*. London: Routledge.

——— 1993. 'Children talk horror videos: reading as a social performance', *Australian Journal of Education* **37**: 169–181.

Moss, G. and McDonald, J. W. 2004. 'The borrowers: library records as unobtrusive measures of children's reading preferences', *Journal of Research in Reading* **27**: 401–413.

Mroz, M. 2006. 'Providing training in speech and language for education professionals: challenges, support and the view from the ground', *Child Language Teaching and Therapy* **22**: 155–176.

Muir, C., Morales, Y., Falchi, L. and García, O. 2009. 'Appendix: myths and realities' in O. García (ed.) *Bilingual Education in the 21st Century: a Global Perspective* (Oxford: Wiley–Blackwell).

Munn, P. and Ellis, S. 2005. 'Interactions between school systems and reading recovery programmes: Evidence From Northern Ireland', *Curriculum Journal* **16**: 341–362.

Muter, V., Hulme, C., Snowling, M. J. and Stevenson, J. 2004. 'Phonemes, rimes, vocabulary, and grammatical skills as foundations of early reading development: evidence from a longitudinal study', *Developmental Psychology* **40**: 665–681.

Myers-Scotton, C. 2002. *Contact Linguistics: Bilingual Encounters and Grammatical Outcomes*. Oxford University Press.

Myhill, D. 2000. 'Misconceptions and difficulties in the acquisition of metalinguistic knowledge', *Language and Education* **14**, 3: 151–163.

Myhill, D., Fisher, R., Jones, S., Lines, H. and Hicks, A. 2008. *Effective Ways of Teaching Complex Expression in Writing: a Literature Review of Evidence from the Secondary School Phase*. Nottingham: DCDF.

Myhill, D. A. 2009. 'Becoming a designer: Trajectories of linguistic development' in R. Beard, D. Myhill, J. Riley and M. Nystrand (eds.) *International Handbook of Writing Development* (London: SAGE).

Myhill, D. A. and Jones, S. M. 2007. 'More than just error correction: children's reflections on their revision processes', *Written Communication* **24**: 323–343.

NAEP 2005. (US Department of Education, National Center for Education Statistics) http://nces.ed.gov/nationsreportcard/ Retrieved on 15 April 2009.

Nagy, W., Berninger, V. W. and Abbott, R. D. 2006. 'Contributions of morphology beyond phonology to literacy outcomes of upper elementary and middle-school students', *Journal of Educational Psychology* **98**: 135–147.

Nagy, W. E. and Anderson, R. C. 1984. 'How many words are there in printed school English?', *Reading Research Quarterly* **19**: 304–330.

Nagy, W. E. and Scott, J. A. 2000. 'Vocabulary processes' in M. Kamil, P. B. Mosenthal, P. D. Pearson and R. Barr (eds.) *Handbook of Reading Research* (Mahwah, NJ: Erlbaum), pp. 269–284.

Naldic 2009. 'Developing a bilingual pedagogy for UK schools' *Naldic Working Papers 9*. Naldic Publications.

NATE 1997. *Position Paper 1: Grammar*. Sheffield: NATE.

Nathan, L. and Simpson, S. 2002. 'Designing a literacy programme for a child with a history of speech difficulties' in J. Stackhouse and B. Wells (eds.) *Children's Speech and Literacy Difficulties: Identification and Intervention – Book 2* (London: Whurr), pp. 249–298.

Nation, K. 2005. 'Children's reading comprehension difficulties' in M. J. Snowling, C. Hulme and M. Seidenberg (eds.) *The Science of Reading: a Handbook* (Oxford: Blackwell), pp. 248–265.

2009. 'Reading comprehension and vocabulary: What's the connection?' in R. K. Wagner, C. Schatschneider and C. Phythian-Sence (eds.) *Beyond Decoding: the Behavioral and Biological Foundations of Reading Comprehension* (New York: Guilford Press).

Nation, K., Adams, J. W., Bowyer-Crane, C. A. and Snowling, M. J. 1999. 'Working memory deficits in poor comprehenders reflect underlying language impairments', *Journal of Experimental Child Psychology* **73**: 139–158.

Nation, K. and Angell, P. 2006. 'Learning to read and learning to comprehend', *London Review of Education* **4**: 77–87.

Nation, K. and Norbury, C. F. 2005. 'When reading comprehension fails: insights from developmental disorders', *Topics in Language Disorders* **25**: 21–32.

Nation, K. and Snowling, M. J. 1997. 'Assessing reading difficulties: the validity and utility of current measures of reading skill', *British Journal of Educational Psychology* **67**: 359–370.

1998. 'Semantic processing and the development of word recognition skills: evidence from children with reading comprehension difficulties', *Journal of Memory and Language* **39**: 85–101.

2000. 'Factors influencing syntactic awareness skills in normal readers and poor comprehenders', *Applied Psycholinguistics* **21**: 229–241.

2004. 'Beyond phonological skills: Broader language skills contribute to the development of reading', *Journal of Research in Reading* **27**: 342–356.

Nation, K., Clarke, P., Marshall, C. M. and Durand, M. 2004. 'Hidden language impairments in children: parallels between poor reading comprehension and specific language impairment', *Journal of Speech, Language, and Hearing Research* **47**: 199–211.

Nation, K., Cocksey, J., Taylor, J. S., and Bishop, D. V. M. (2010). 'A longitudinal investigation of early reading and language skills in children with poor reading comprehension'. *Journal of Child Psychology and Psychiatry*, **51**(9), 1031–1039.

Nation, K., Snowling, M. J. and Clarke, P. 2005. 'Production of the English past tense by children with language comprehension impairments', *Journal of Child Language* **32**: 117–137.

2007. 'Dissecting the relationship between language skills and learning to read: semantic and phonological contributions to new vocabulary learning in children with poor reading comprehension', *Advances in Speech-Language Pathology* **9**: 131–139.

National Curriculum Board 2009. *Shape of the Australian Curriculum: English*. www. acara.edu.au/verve/_resources/Australian_Curriculum_-_English.pdf

National Reading Panel Report 1997. www.nichd.nih.gov/health/topics/national_ reading_panel.cfm

Neale, M. 1997. *Neale Analysis of Reading Ability*, 2nd rev. British edn. Windsor: NFER.

Nelson, N. 1994. 'Curriculum-based language assessment and intervention across the grades' in G. P. Wallach and K. G. Butler (eds.) *Language Learning Disabilities in School-age Children and Adolescents* (New York: Macmillan), pp. 104–131.

New South Wales Department of Education 2003. *Quality Teaching in NSW Public schools: Discussion Paper*. Ryde, NSW: Professional Support and Curriculum Directorate, NSW Department of Education and Training.

(2004). *Quality Teaching in NSW Public Schools: an Assessment Practice Guide*. Ryde, NSW: Professional Learning Directorate, NSW Department of Education and Training.

Newman, F. M. and Associates 1996. *Authentic Achievement: Restructuring Schools for Intellectual Quality*. San Francisco: Jossey-Bass.

Nichols, M. 2006. *Comprehension through Conversation: the Power of Purposeful Talk in the Reading Workshop*. Portsmouth, NH: Heinemann.

Nikolajeva, M. 2003. 'Picturebook characterisation: word/image interaction' in M. Styles and E. Bearne (eds.) *Art, Narrative and Childhood* (Stoke on Trent: Trentham), pp. 37–49.

Nikolajeva, M. and Scott, C. 2000. 'Dynamics of picturebook communication', *Children's Literature in Education* **31**: 225–239.

NLT 2006. *Talk to Your Baby Campaign* www.literacytrust.org.uk

2010. *Literacy and Education Levels by Ethnic Group and Populations* www.literacytrust.org.uk/Database/STATS/EALstats.html

Nodelman, P. 1988. *Words about Pictures: the Narrative Art of Children's Picture Books*. Atlanta, GA: University of Georgia Press.

Nuffield Foundation. 2000. *Languages: the Next Generation: Final Report and Recommendations*. London: Nuffield Foundation.

Nunes, T. and Bryant, P. 2006. *Improving Literacy through Teaching Morphemes*. London: Routledge.

2009. *Children's Reading and Spelling: Beyond the First Steps*. Chichester: Wiley/ Blackwell.

Nunes, T., Bryant, P. and Bindman, M. 1997. 'Morphological spelling strategies: developmental stages and processes', *Developmental Psychology* **33**: 637–649.

Nystrand, M., Gamoran, A., Kachur, R. and Prendergast, C. 1997. *Opening Dialogue: Understanding the Dynamics of Language and Learning in the English Classroom*. New York: Teachers College Press.

Oakhill, J. 1994. 'Individual differences in children's text comprehension' in M. Gernsbacher (ed.) *Handbook of Psycholinguistics* (San Diego, CA: Academic Press).

Oakhill, J., Cain, K. and Bryant, P. 2003. 'The dissociation of word reading and text comprehension: evidence from component skills', *Language and Cognitive Processes* **18**: 443–468.

Ofsted 2005. *Primary Initial Teacher Training Partnership based on University of Brighton Higher Education Institute: Report of the Short Inspection 2004/5.* www.ofsted.gov.uk/oxedu_reports/display/(id)/33198

2006. *The Logical Chain: Continuing Professional Development in Effective Schools.* London: Ofsted.

2008. *A Primary Initial Teacher Training Short Inspection Report 2007/08.* www.ofsted.gov.uk/oxedu_reports/download/(id)/96981/(as)/70005_330269.pdf

Okawa, G. Y. 2000. 'From "bad attitude" to(ward) linguistic pluralism: Developing reflective language policy among preservice teachers' in R. D. Gonzalez (ed.) *Language Ideologies: Critical Perspectives on the Official English Movement* (Mahwah, NJ: Erlbaum), pp. 276–296.

Online Etymology Dictionary 2009 www.etymonline.com/index.php?term=design

Özyürek, A. 2002. 'Do speakers design their cospeech gestures for their addressees? The effects of addressee location on representational gestures', *Journal of Memory and Language* **46**: 688–704.

Palmer, B. C., El-Ashry, F., Leclere, J. T. and Chang, S. 2007. 'Learning from Abdallah: a case study of an Arabic-speaking child in a U.S. school', *Reading Teacher* **61**: 8–17.

Pappas, C. C. 2006. 'The information genre: its role in integrated science literacy research and practice', *Reading Research Quarterly* **41**: 226–250.

Paradis, J., Nicoladis, E. and F. Genesee *et al.* 2000. 'Early emergence of structural constraints on code mixing', *Language and Cognition* **3**: 245–261.

Parsons, S., Law, J. and Gascoigne, M. 2005. 'Teaching receptive vocabulary to children with specific language impairment: a curriculum-based approach', *Child Language Teaching and Therapy* **21**: 39–59.

Pea, R. and Kurland, D. 1987. 'Cognitive technologies for writing', *Review of Research in Education* **14**: 277–326.

Pearson, B., Fernandez, S. and Oller, D. K. 1993. 'Lexical development in bilingual toddlers: comparison to monolingual norms', *Language Learning* **43**: 93–120.

Pearson, P. D., Hiebert, E. H. and Kamil, M. L. 2007. 'Theory and research into practice: vocabulary assessment: what we know and what we need to learn', *Reading Research Quarterly* **42**: 282–296.

Pellegrini, A. D. 2002. 'Some theoretical and methodological considerations in studying literacy in social contexts' in S. B. Neuman and D. K. Dickinson (eds.) *Handbook of Early Literacy Research* (New York: Guilford Press), pp. 54–65.

Perera, K. 1984. *Children's Writing and Reading: Analysing Classroom Language.* Oxford: Blackwell.

1993 'The good book: linguistic features' in R. Beard (ed.) *Teaching Literacy: Balancing Perspectives* (London: Hodder and Stoughton), pp. 95–113.

Perfetti, C. A. 2003. 'The universal grammar of reading', *Scientific Studies of Reading* **7**: 3–24.

Perfetti, C. A. and Liu, Y. 2005. 'Orthography to phonology and meaning: comparisons across and within writing systems', *Reading and Writing* **18**: 193–210.

Perkins, M. R. 2007. *Pragmatic Impairment*. Cambridge University Press.

Pert, S. and Letts, C. 2003. 'Developing an expressive language assessment for children in Rochdale with a Pakistani heritage background', *Child Language Teaching and Therapy* **19**: 267–290.

2006. 'Codeswitching in Mirpuri speaking Pakistani heritage preschool children: bilingual language acquisition', *International Journal of Bilingualism* **10**: 349–374.

Planty, M., Hussar, W., Snyder, T., Kena, G., KewalRamani, A., Kemp, J., Bianco, K. and Dinkes, R. (2009). *The Condition of Education 2009*. http://nces.ed.gov/pubsearch/pubsinfo.asp?pubid=2009081

Plaza, M., Cohen, H. and Chevrie-Muller, C. 2002. 'Oral language deficits in dyslexic children: weaknesses in working memory and verbal planning', *Brain and Cognition* **48**: 505–512.

Poole, B. 1999. ' "Is younger better?" A critical examination of the beliefs about learning a foreign language at primary school.' Ph.D. thesis, Institute of Education, University of London.

Portes, A. and Rumbaut Rubén, G. 2001. *Legacies: the story of the immigrant second generation*. Berkeley and Los Angeles: University of California Press.

Poulson, L. 2001 'Paradigm lost? Subject knowledge, primary teachers and education policy', *British Journal of Educational Studies* **49**: 40–55.

Primary National Strategy 2007. *Letters and Sounds: Principles and Practice of High Quality Phonics*. London: Department for Education and Skills.

Pullen, P., Lane, H. Lloyd, J., Nowak, R. and Ryals, J. 2005. 'Effects of explicit instruction on decoding of struggling first grade students: a data-based case study', *Education and Treatment of Children* **28**: 63–76.

Purcell-Gates, V., Duke, N. K. and Martineau, J. A. 2007. 'Learning to read and write genre-specific text: roles of authentic experience and explicit teaching', *Reading Research Quarterly* **42**: 8–45.

Qualifications and Curriculum Authority/UKLA 2004. *More than Words*. London: QCA.

Qualifications and Curriculum Authority 2005. *Opening up talk* [DVD]. London: QCA.

Raban, B. 1988. 'Speaking and writing: young children's use of connectives', *Child Language, Teaching and Therapy* **4**: 13–25.

Ragnarsdóttir, H., Aparici, M., Cahana-Amitay, D., van Hell, J. and Viguié, A. 2002. 'Verbal structure and content in written discourse: expository and narrative texts', *Written Language and Literacy* **5**: 95–126.

Rall, J. and Harris, P. 2000. 'In Cinderella's slippers? Story comprehension from the protagonist's point of view', *Developmental Psychology* **36**; 202–208.

Rampton, B. 1995. *Crossing: Language and Ethnicity among Adolescents*. New York: Longman.

2006. *Language in Late Modernity: Interaction in an Urban School*. Cambridge University Press.

Rampton, B., Tusting, K., Maybin, J., Barwell, R., Creese, A. and Lytra, V. 2004. *UK Linguistic Ethnography: a Discussion Paper*. www.ling-ethnog.org.uk/documents/papers/ramptonetal2004.pdf

Ravid, D., van Hell, J., Rosado, E. and Zamora, A. 2002. 'Subject NP patterning in the development of text production: speech and writing', *Written Language and Literacy* **5**: 69–93.

Reddy, M. J. 1979. 'The conduit metaphor: a case of conflict in our language about language' in A. Ortony (ed.) *Metaphor and Thought* (Cambridge University Press).

Rice, M. 2000. 'Grammatical symptoms of specific language impairment' in D. Bishop and L. Leonard (eds.) *Speech and Language Impairments in Children: Causes, Characteristics, Intervention and Outcome* (Hove: Psychology Press), pp. 17–34.

Rice, M., Wexler, K. and Cleave, P. *et al.* 1995. 'Specific language impairment as a period of extended optional infinitive', *Journal of Speech and Hearing Research* **38**: 850–863.

Richards, T., Aylward, E., Berninger, V., Field, K., Grimme, A., Richards, A. and Nagy, W. 2006. 'Individual fMRI activation in orthographic mapping and morpheme mapping after orthographic or morphological spelling treatment in child dyslexics', *Journal of Neurolinguistics* **19**: 56–86.

Richards, T. and Berninger, V. W. 2007. 'Abnormal fMRI connectivity in children with dyslexia during a phoneme task: before but not after treatment', *Journal of Neuropsychology* **21**: 732–741.

Richardson, S. 1741. *The Life of Pamela*, 2 vols. London: Anonymous pirated adaptation of Samuel Richardson's original.

Ricketts, J., Bishop, D. V. M. and Nation, K. 2008. 'Investigating orthographic and semantic aspects of word learning in poor comprehenders', *Journal of Research in Reading* **31**: 117–135.

Ricketts, J., Nation, K. and Bishop, D. V. M. 2007. 'Vocabulary is important for some, but not all reading skills', *Scientific Studies of Reading* **11**: 235–257.

Risko, V., Roller, C., Cummins, C., Bean, R., Collins Block, C., Anders, P. and Flood, J. 2008. 'A critical analysis of research on reading teacher education', *Reading Research Quarterly* **43**: 252–288.

Ritchie, J. and Wilson, D. 1993. 'Dual apprenticeships: Subverting and supporting critical teaching', *English Education* **25**: 67–83.

Rivers, W. 1964. *The Psychologist and the Foreign-Language Teacher*. Chicago: University of Chicago Press.

Roach, J. 1985. *The Player's Passion: Studies in the Science of Acting*. London and Toronto: Associated University Presses.

Roberts, T. and Meiring, A. 2006. 'Teaching phonics in the context of children's literature or spelling: influences on first-grade reading, spelling, and writing and fifth-grade comprehension', *Journal of Educational Psychology* **98**: 690–713.

Robertson, L. 2006. 'Learning to read properly by moving between parallel literacy classes', *Language and Education* **20**: 44–61.

Rogers, T., Marshall, E. and Tyson, C. 2006. 'Dialogic narratives of literacy, teaching, and schooling: preparing literacy teachers for diverse settings', *Reading Research Quarterly* **41**: 202–225.

Rose, D. 2009. 'Writing as linguistic mastery: the development of genre-based literacy pedagogy' in R. Beard, D. Myhill, J. Riley and M. Nystrand (eds.) *International Handbook of Writing Development* (London: SAGE).

Rose, J. 2006. *Independent Review of the Teaching of Early Reading*. Nottingham: DfES Publications.

Rosen, H. 1981. 'Language in the education of the working class', *English in Education* **16**, 2: 17–25.

Royal College of Speech and Language Therapists 2010. *Guidelines for Pre-registration Speech and Language Therapy Courses in the UK, Incorporating Curriculum Guidelines*. London: RCSLT.

Rubin, R. and Carlan, V. 2005. 'Using writing to understand bilingual children's literacy development', *Reading Teacher* **58**: 728–739.

Sadler, J. 2005. 'Knowledge, attitudes and beliefs of mainstream teachers of children with a preschool diagnosis of speech/language impairment', *Child Language Teaching and Therapy* **21**: 147–163.

Saenger, P. 1997. *Space Between Words: the Origins of Silent Reading*. Stanford, CA: Stanford University Press.

Saint Augustine, trans. Chadwick, H. 1992. *Confessions*. Oxford University Press.

Schleppegrell, M. and Go, A. 2007. 'Analyzing the writing of English learners: a functional approach', *Language Arts* **84**: 529–538.

Scott, C. 2003. 'Interaction in the literacy hour: a case study of learners with English as an additional language', *British Studies in Applied Linguistics* **18**: 184–202.

Scott, M. 2004. *WordSmith Tools Version 4*. Oxford University Press.

Scott, P., Mortimer, E. and Aguiar, O. 2006. 'The tension between authoritative and dialogic discourse: a fundamental characteristic of meaning making interactions in high school science lessons', *Science Education* **90**: 605–631.

Scottish Education Department 1969. *French in the Primary School*. Edinburgh: HMSO.

Scottish Executive 2002. *Standards in Scotland's Schools etc. Act 2000: Guidance on Presumption of Mainstream Education*. www.scotland.gov.uk/Publications/2002/05/14630/3866

Scottish Government 2006. *Getting it Right for Every Child: Implementation Plan* www.scotland.gov.uk/Resource/Doc/131460/0031397.pdf

Scottish Office Education and Industry Department 1999. *Standards and Quality: Primary and Secondary Schools 1994–98: in Modern Languages*. www.hmie.gov.uk/documents/publication/sqml.htm

Scribner, S. and Cole, M. 1988. *The Psychology of Literacy*. Cambridge, MA: Harvard University Press.

Sealey, A. 2009. 'Exploring vocabulary with young L1 learners: the contribution of a corpus' in H. Daller, D. D. Malvern, P. Meara, J. Milton, B. Richards and J. Treffers-Daller (eds.) *Vocabulary Studies in First and Second Language Acquisition: the Interface Between Theory and Application* (London: Palgrave Macmillan).

Sealey, A. and Thompson, P. 2004. ' "What do you call the dull words?" Primary school children using corpus-based approaches to learn about language', *English in Education* **38**: 80–91.

2006. ' "Nice things get said": corpus evidence and the National Literacy Strategy', *Literacy* **40**: 22–28.

2007. 'Corpus, concordance, classification: young learners in the L1 classroom', *Language Awareness* **16**: 208–223.

Seliger, H. W. and R. M. Vago (eds.) 1991. *First Language Attrition*. Cambridge University Press.

Semel, E., Wiig, E. and Secord, W. 2000. *Clinical Evaluation of Language Fundamentals* (CELF-3 UK). 3rd edn UK, Adjusted Norms, 2003. London: Harcourt Assessment/The Psychological Corporation.

Sendak, M. 1963. *Where the Wild Things Are*. New York: Harper and Row.

Setati, M., Adler, J., Reed, Y. and Bapoo, A. 2002. 'Incomplete journeys: code-switching and other language practices in mathematics, science and English language classrooms in South Africa', *Language and Education* **16**: 128–149.

Sfard, A. 2008. *Thinking as Communicating: Human Development, the Growth of Discourses, and Mathematizing*. New York: Cambridge University Press.

Sharpe, K. 2001. *Modern Foreign Languages in the Primary School*. London: Kogan Page.

Sharples, M. 1999. *How We Write: Writing as Creative Design*. London: Routledge.

Shin, S. J. 2005. *Developing in Two Languages: Korean Children in America*. Clevedon: Multilingual Matters.

Shulman, L. 1986. 'Those who understand: knowledge growth in teaching', *Educational Researcher* **15**: 4–14.

  1987. 'Knowledge and teaching: foundations of the new reform', *Harvard Educational Review* **57**: 1–22.

Sinclair, J. M. 1992. 'Trust the text' in M. Davies and L. Ravelli (eds.) *Advances in Systemic Linguistics* (London: Pinter).

  (ed.) 2004. *How to Use Corpora in Language Teaching*. Amsterdam: John Benjamins.

Sinclair, J. M., and Coulthard, M. 1975. *Towards an Analysis of Discourse: the English used by Teachers and Pupils*. London: Oxford University Press.

Singleton, D. 1989. *Language Acquisition: the Age Factor*. Clevedon: Multilingual Matters.

Singson, M., Mahony, M. and Mann, V. 2000. 'Reading ability and sensitivity to morphological relations', *Reading and Writing* **12**: 191–218.

Sipe, L. 1998 'How picture books work: a semiotically framed theory of text-picture relationships', *Children's Literature in Education* **29**: 97–108.

Smagorinsky, P. 2007. 'Foreword' in V. Ellis, *Subject Knowledge and Teacher Education: the Development of Beginning Teachers' Thinking* (London: Continuum).

Smith, F., Hardman, F., Wall, K. and Mroz, M. 2004. 'Interactive whole class teaching in the National Literacy and Numeracy Strategies', *British Educational Research Journal* **30**: 395–411.

Smith, V. 2001. 'All in a flap about reading: Catherine Morland, Spot and Mister Wolf', *Children's Literature in Education* **32**: 225–236.

Sneddon, R. 2000. 'Language and literacy: children's experience in multilingual environments', *International Journal of Bilingual Education and Bilingualism* **3**: 265–282.

Snell, J. 2008. 'Pronouns, dialect and discourse: a socio-pragmatic account of children's language in Teesside.' Ph.D. thesis, University of Leeds.

Snow P. C. and Powell, M. B. 2004. 'Developmental language disorders and adolescent risk: a public health advocacy role for speech pathologists?', *Advances in Speech Language Pathology* **6**, 4: 221–229.

Snowling, M. J. 2000. *Dyslexia*, 2nd edn. Oxford: Blackwell.

Snowling, M. J., Adams, J. W., Bishop, D. V. M. and Stothard, S. E. 2001. 'Educational attainments of school leavers with a pre-school history of speech-language impairments', *International Journal of Language and Communication Disorders* **36**: 173–183.

Snowling, M. J., Stothard, S. E., Clarke, P., Bowyer-Crane, C., Harrington, A. and Truelove, E. 2009. *York Assessment of Reading for Comprehension*. London: GL Assessment.

Spear-Swerling, L. and Brucker, P. O. 2004. 'Preparing novice teachers to develop basic reading and spelling skills in children', *Annals of Dyslexia* **54**: 332–364.

SPELL Links to Reading and Writing Word List Maker 2008. Version 1.0 [computer program]. Evanston, IL: Learning By Design.

Spooner, A. L., Baddeley, A. D. and Gathercole, S. E. 2004. 'Can reading accuracy and comprehension be separated in the Neale Analysis of Reading Ability?', *British Journal of Educational Psychology* **74**: 187–204.

Stackhouse, J. 2006. 'Speech and spelling difficulties: what to look for' in M. Snowling and J. Stackhouse (eds.) *Dyslexia, Speech and Language: a Practitioner's Handbook.* Chichester: Whurr.

Stern, T. 2000. *Rehearsal from Shakespeare to Sheridan.* Oxford University Press.

Stothard, S. E. and Hulme, C. 1992. 'Reading comprehension difficulties in children: the role of language comprehension and working memory skills', *Reading and Writing* **4**: 245–256.

Stothard, S. E., Hulme, C., Clarke, P., Barmby, P., and Snowling, M. J. 2010. *York Assessment of Reading for Comprehension: Passage Reading Secondary.* London: GL Assessment.

Stow, C. and Dodd, B. 2003. 'Providing an equitable service to bilingual children in the UK: a review', *International Journal of Language and Communication Disorders* **38**: 351–378.

Strauss, S., Ravid, D., Zelcer, H. and Berliner, D. C. 1999. 'Relations between teachers' subject matter knowledge about written language and their mental models about children's learning' in T. Nunes (ed.) *Learning to Read: an Integrated View from Research and Practice* (Dordrecht: Kluwer), pp. 259–282.

Street, B. 1984. *Literacy in Theory and Practice.* Cambridge University Press.

Street, B. V., Lefstein, A. and Pahl, K. 2007. 'The National Literacy Strategy in England: contradictions of control and creativity' in J. Larson (ed.) *Literacy as Snake Oil: Beyond the Quick Fix*, 2nd edn. New York: Peter Lang.

Stringer, H. and Clegg, J. 2006. 'Language, behaviour and social disadvantage' in J. Clegg and J. Ginsborg (eds.) *Language and Social Disadvantage: Theory into Practice* (Oxford: Wiley).

Stuart, M., Stainthorp, R. and Snowling, M. 2008. 'Literacy as a complex activity: deconstructing the simple view of reading', *Literacy* **42**, 2: 59–66.

Stubbs, M. 1996. *Text and Corpus Analysis.* Oxford: Blackwell.

2001. *Words and Phrases: Corpus Studies of Lexical Semantics.* Oxford: Blackwell.

2009. 'The search for units of meaning: Sinclair on empirical semantics', *Applied Linguistics* **30**: 115–137.

Suárez-Orozco, C. 2004 'Formulating Identity in a Globalized World' in M. Suárez-Orozco and D. B. Qin-Hilliard (eds.) *Globalization: Culture and Education in the New Millennium* (Berkeley: University of California Press).

Suárez-Orozco, C. and Suarez-Orozco, M. 2001. 'Remaking identities' in *Children of Immigration* (Cambridge, MA: Harvard University Press), pp. 87–123.

Taft, M. 1988. 'A morphological-decomposition model of lexical representation', *Linguistics* **26**: 657–668.

2003. 'Morphological representation as a correlation between form and meaning' in E. G. H. Assink and D. Sandra (eds.) *Reading Complex Words: Cross Language Studies* (New York: Kluwer Academic), pp. 113–137.

Tahta, S., Wood, M. and Loewehnthal, K. 1981 'Foreign accents: Factors relating to transfer of accent from the first language to a second language', *Language and Speech* **24**: 265–272.

Tan, S. 2007. *The Arrival*. London: Hodder Children's Books.

Tatto, M. T. 2007. *Reforming Teaching Globally*. Oxford: Symposium Books.

TDA (Training and Development Agency for Schools) 2007. *Continuing Professional Development: National Priorities for Teachers*. www.tda.gov.uk/teachers/sen.aspx

— 2008a. *Speech Language and Communication Session 9: Special Educational Needs and/or Disabilities: Undergraduate Primary Materials for Initial Teacher Education*. www.behaviour4learning.ac.uk/viewarticle2.aspx?contentId=15002

— 2008b. *Professional Standards for Qualified Teacher Status and Requirements for Initial Teacher Training* (revised 2008). London: TDA.

— 2009a. *Letter to Providers Regarding the Development of Guidance: Curriculum Knowledge for Teaching Project*. London: TDA.

— 2009b. *QTS Standards and ITT Requirements*. www.tda.gov.uk/partners/ittstandards.aspx

— 2009c. *Turn your Talent to Teaching: Bachelor of Education (BEd)*. www.tda.gov.uk/Recruit/thetrainingprocess/typesofcourse/undergraduate/bed.aspx

Thompson, P. and Sealey, A. 2007. 'Through children's eyes?: Corpus evidence of the features of children's literature', *International Journal of Corpus Linguistics* **12**: 1–23.

Thompson, S. and de Bortoli, L. 2006. *Exploring Scientific Literacy: How Australia Measures Up*. The PISA survey of students' scientific, reading and mathematical literacy skills. Melbourne: Australian Council for Educational Research.

Thordardottir, E. T. and Weismer, S. E. 2002. 'Verb argument structure weakness in specific language impairment in relation to age and utterance length', *Clinical Linguistics and Phonetics* **16**: 233–250.

Thoresby, R. 1715, *Ducatus Leodiensis*. London.

N.d. 'Letter to Hans Sloane', MS 4039, f.136, British Library.

Tierney, D. 2009. 'The pedagogy and implementation of modern languages in the primary school: pupil attitudes and teachers' views.' PhD thesis, University of Strathclyde.

Tikly, L. 2004. 'Education and the new imperialism', *Comparative Education* **40**: 173–198.

Tom, A. 1984. *Teaching as a Moral Craft*. New York: Longman.

Tomblin, B., Records, N. L., Buckwalter, P., Zhang, X., Smith, E. and O'Brien, M. 1997. 'Prevalence of specific language impairment in kindergarten children', *Journal of Speech, Language, and Hearing Research* **40**: 1245–1260.

Torgerson, C. J., Brooks, G. and Hall, J. 2006. *A Systematic Review of the Research Literature on the Use of Phonics in the Teaching of Reading and Spelling*. www.dcsf.gov.uk/research/data/uploadfiles/RR711_.pdf

Unsworth, L. 2001. *Teaching Multiliteracies across the Curriculum: Changing Contexts of Text and Image in Classroom Practice*. Buckingham: Open University Press.

van Lier, L. 2004. *The Ecology and Semiotics of Language Learning: a Scoiocultural Perspective*. Dordrecht: Kluwer.

Venezky, R. L. 1995. 'How English is read: Grapheme-phoneme regularity and ortho-graphic structure in word recognition' in I. Taylor and D. R. Olson (eds.) *Scripts and Literacy* (Dordrecht: Kluwer), pp. 111–130.

   1999. *The American Way of Spelling: the Structure and Origins of American English Orthography*. New York: Guilford Press.

Verhoeven, L., Aparici, M., Cahana-Amitay, M., van Hell, J. V., Kriz, S. and Viguie-Simon, A. 2002. 'Clause packaging in writing and speech: a cross-linguistic devel-opmental analysis', *Written Language and Literacy* **5**, 2: 135–161.

Vilke, M. 1998. 'Some psychological aspects of early second language acquisition', *Journal of Multilingual and Multicultural Development* **9**: 115–128.

Vivet, A. 1995. *Sens et Rôle des Langues dans le Développement des Enfants: Report on Workshop 17*. Strasbourg: Council of Europe.

Vygotsky, L. S. 1978. *Mind in Society: the Development of Higher Psychological Processes*. Cambridge, MA: Harvard University Press.

   1986. *Thought and Language*. Cambridge, MA: MIT Press.

Waddell, M. 1992. *Owl Babies*. London: Walker Books.

Walker, D., Greenwood, C. R., Hart, B. and Carta, J. 1994. 'Prediction of school out-comes based on early language production and socioeconomic factors', *Child Development* **65**: 606–621.

Wallach, G. P. 2004. 'Over the brink of the millennium: have we said all we can say about language-based learning disabilities?', *Communication Disorders Quarterly* **25**: 44–55.

Walsh, M. 2009. 'Journeying through "flotsam": refugee students' reading of a post-modern picture book'. Paper presented at Second International Symposium on New Impulses in Picturebook Research: Beyond Borders: Art, Narrative and Culture in Picture Books, Glasgow University, September 18–20.

Wardhaugh, R. 1999. *Proper English: Myths and Misunderstandings about Language*. Oxford: Blackwell.

Wasowicz, J., Apel, K., Masterson, J. J. and Whitney, A. 2004. *SPELL-Links to Reading and Writing*. Evanston, IL: Learning By Design.

Waterland, L. 1985. *Read with Me: an Apprenticeship Approach to Reading*. Stroud: Thimble Press.

Weatherill, L. 1996. *Consumer Behaviour and Material Culture in Britain 1660–1760*. London: Routledge.

Wellington, W. and Wellington, J. 2002. 'Children with communication difficulties in mainstream science classrooms', *School Science Review* **83**: 81–92.

Wells, G. 1999. *Dialogic Inquiry: Towards a Sociocultural Practice and Theory of Education*. Cambridge University Press.

   1993. 'Reevaluating the IRF sequence: a proposal for the articulation of theories of activity and discourse for the analysis of teaching and learning in the classroom', *Linguistics and Education* **5**: 1–38.

Welsh Assembly Government 2005. *National Service Framework for Children, Young People and Maternity Services in Wales* http://wales.gov.uk/docs/caecd/publicatio ns/090414nsfchildrenyoungpeoplematernityen.pdf

Wertsch, J. V. 1991. *Voices of the Mind: a Sociocultural Approach to Mediated Action*. Cambridge, MA: Harvard University Press.

Wichmann, A., Fligelstone, S., McEnery, T. and Knowles, G. (eds.) 1997. *Teaching and Language Corpora*. Harlow: Addison Wesley Longman.

Wideen, M., Mayer-Smith, J. and Moon, B. 1998. 'A critical analysis of the research on learning to teach: making the case for an ecological perspective on inquiry', *Review of Educational Research* **68**: 130–178.

Wiesner, D. 2006. *Flotsam.* New York: Clarion Books.

Williams, C. 2006. 'Teacher judgements of the language skills of children in the early years of schooling', *Child Language Teaching and Therapy* **22**: 135–154.

Wilson, A. C. 2007. 'Finding a voice? Do literary forms work creatively in teaching poetry writing?', *Cambridge Journal of Education* **37**: 441–457.

Wilson, S. M., Floden, R. E. and Ferrini-Mundy, J. 2002. 'Teacher preparation research: an insider's view from the outside', *Journal of Teacher Education* **53**, 3: 190–204.

Windfuhr, K., Faragher, B. and Conti-Ramsden, G. 2002. 'Lexical learning skills in young children with specific language impairment (SLI)', *International Journal of Language and Communication Disorders* **37**: 415–432.

Winter, K. 2001. 'Numbers of bilingual children in speech and language therapy: theory and practice of measuring their representation', *International Journal of Bilingualism* **5**: 465–495.

Wortham, S. E. F. 2006. *Learning Identity: the Joint, Local Emergence of Social Identification and Academic Learning.* New York: Cambridge University Press.

Wray, D. and Medwell, J. 1997. *English for Primary Teachers.* London: Letts.

Wright J. A. 1992. 'Collaboration between teachers and speech therapists with language impaired children' in P. Fletcher and D. Hall (eds.) *Specific Speech and Language Disorders in Children* (London: Whurr).

Wright, L. 1935. *Middle-Class Culture in Elizabethan England.* Chapel Hill: University of North Carolina Press.

Wyse, D. 2001. 'Grammar for writing? A critical review of empirical evidence', *British Journal of Educational Studies* **49**: 411–427.

    2010. 'Contextualised phonics teaching' in K. Hall (ed.) *Interdisciplinary Perspectives on Learning to Read: Culture, Cognition and Pedagogy* (London: Routledge).

Wyse, D., Andrews, R. and Hoffman, J. (eds.). 2010. *The International Handbook of English, Language, and Literacy Teaching.* London: Routledge.

Wyse, D. and Goswami, U. 2008. 'Synthetic phonics and the teaching of reading', *British Educational Research Journal* **34**: 691–710.

Wyse, D. and Jones, R. 2008. *Teaching English, Language and Literacy*, 2nd edn. London: Routledge.

Wyse, D. and Opfer, D. 2010. 'Globalisation and the international context for literacy policy reform in England' in D. Wyse, R. Andrews and J. Hoffman (eds.) *The International Handbook of English, Language and Literacy Teaching* (London: Routledge).

Wyse, D. and Styles, M. 2007. 'Synthetic phonics and the teaching of reading: the debate surrounding England's "Rose report" ', *Literacy* **47**: 35–42.

Yuill, N. and Oakhill, J. 1988. 'Effects of inference awareness training on poor reading comprehension', *Applied Cognitive Psychology* **2**: 33–45.

    1991. *Children's Problems in Text Comprehension: an Experimental Investigation.* Cambridge University Press.

Yuill, N., Oakhill, J. and Parkin, A. J. 1989. 'Working memory, comprehension ability and the resolution of text anomaly', *British Journal of Psychology* **80**: 351–361.

Zeichner, K. M. and Tabachnik, B. R. 1981. 'Are the effects of teacher education "washed out" by school experience?', *Journal of Teacher Education* **32**, 3: 7–11.

Zentella, A. C. 1981. 'Tá bien, you could answer me en cualquier idioma: Puerto Rican codeswitching in bilingual classrooms' in R. P. Duran (ed.) *Latino Language and Communicative Behavior* (Norwood, NJ: Ablex), pp. 109–131.

Ziegler, J. and Goswami, U. 2005. 'Reading acquisition, developmental dyslexia, and skilled reading across languages: a psycholinguistic grain size theory', *Psychological Bulletin* **131**: 3–29.

Index

Printed in Great Britain
by Amazon